CATCH A WAVE

THE RISE, FALL & REDEMPTION OF THE

BEACH BOYS' BRIAN WILSON

PETER AMES CARLIN

RODALE®

To Anna Carlin,
Teddy Carlin,
and Max Carlin

Book design by Drew Frantzen

Song credits are listed on page 323.

Library of Congress Cataloging-in-Publication Data

Carlin, Peter Ames.
    Catch a wave : the rise, fall, and redemption of the Beach Boys' Brian
Wilson / Peter Ames Carlin.
        p.   cm.
    Includes bibliographical references and index.
    ISBN-13 978–1–59486–320–2   hardcover
    ISBN-10 1–59486–320–2   hardcover
    1. Wilson, Brian, date   2. Rock musicians—United States
Biography.   3. Beach Boys.   I. Title.
ML420.W5525C37   2006
782.42166092—dc22   2006004928

Distributed to the trade by Holtzbrinck Publishers

2   4   6   8   10   9   7   5   3   1   hardcover

LIVE YOUR WHOLE LIFE™

ACKNOWLEDGMENTS

I owe my first thanks to my brother, Greg, who came home with a copy of *Endless Summer* in the summer of 1974 and made me listen to it. My wife, Sarah Carlin Ames, makes everything else possible.

Many other friends and colleagues have provided invaluable support, advice, and scoldings through the years. I am particularly indebted to Tad and Trudy Ames, Greg Narver, Mike Thompson, Geoff Kloske, Tom Fields-Meyer, and Dan Conaway. Thanks also to Lanny Jones, Cutler Durkee, Jamie Katz, Peter Castro, Bill Plummer, and Carey Winfrey from my days at *People*. My bosses at the *Oregonian*—Fred Stickel, Sandy Rowe, and Peter Bhatia—gave me the time to do the bulk of this work. I also owe various debts to Barry Johnson, Karen G. Brooks, and JoLene Krawczak.

My editor, Pete Fornatale Jr., did a terrific job honing the manuscript and making it smarter and better. My agent, Simon Lipskar, is as smart, dedicated, and stubborn an advocate as any writer could hope to meet. I owe him—and his colleagues Daniel Lazar and Nikki Furrer—loads of gratitude. I also appreciate the editorial guidance of Fred Allen at *American Heritage* and Fletcher Roberts at the *New York Times*. Thanks also to Dave Walker, Geoff Edgers, Tad Ames, Barry Johnson, Jamie Katz, and Peter Reum for reading and responding to early drafts of these chapters.

I owe a massive debt to David Leaf, first for writing *The Beach Boys and the California Myth* and helping me understand the depth and wonder of Brian's work when I was still in high school. More recently he has been an invaluable friend, advisor, and cautionary voice. Jean Sievers kicked open doors and smoothed the road throughout this process. Van Dyke and Sally Parks have been more than generous with their time, friendship, and hospitality. Thanks also to Van Dyke for allowing me to quote the lyrics from "High Coin" (Van Dyke Parks/admin. by Bug Music). Peter Reum shared his experiences with and insights into Brian Wilson for hours on end and transformed my understanding along the way. Alan Boyd was tremendously helpful and patient, no matter how often I called him at odd hours. The Reverend Bob Hanes proved his coaching mettle yet again, making all the right connections at all the right times. Thanks to Neal Skok for his thoughts and generosity. A big thanks to Probyn Gregory for all of his insights—musical, cultural, and otherwise. Thanks also to the Beach Boys' manager, Elliott Lott. And big, big thanks also to Ross W. Hamilton for all of his help with the photos.

I also need to thank everyone who entertained my questions and shared the contents of their memories. They include Rich Sloan, Robin Hood, Mary Lou Van Antwerp, Ted Sprague, Irene Fernandez, Bruce Griffin, Keith Lent, Carol Mountain, Paula Springer, Stanley Love, Stephen Love, Maureen Love, Milton Love, Fred Vail, Lorren Daro (formerly Loren Schwartz), Tony Asher, Danny Hutton, Michael Vosse, Mark Linett, Stephen W. Desper, Hal Blaine, Carol Kaye, Jules Siegel, Frank Holmes, Stephen Kalinich, Stanley Shapiro, Gregg Jakobson, Annie Wilson, Barbara Wilson, Carnie Wilson, Trish Campo, Rick Henn, Pete Fornatale Sr., David Sandler, Earle Mankey, Billy Hinsche, Andy Paley, Joe Thomas, Jeffrey Foskett, Darian Sahanaja, and Probyn Gregory. I am particularly grateful to Melinda Wilson for all of her help, and to the surviving Beach Boys—Mike Love, Alan Jardine, and David Marks—for their time and recollections. Bruce Johnston wouldn't quite sit for a formal interview, but he did chat for a while and sent along a few revealing e-mails. I feel very fortunate that happenstance allowed me to meet and speak, albeit briefly, to both Carl Wilson and Dennis Wilson.

Finally, I want to thank Brian Wilson for his time and patience over the last few years—but mostly for his music. Ultimately, that's all that matters.

PROLOGUE

The people in flight from the terror behind—strange
things happen to them, some bitterly cruel and some
so beautiful that the faith is refired forever.

John Steinbeck, The Grapes of Wrath

B rian Wilson is sitting in a little room somewhere deep
in the recesses of the Austin Convention Center, staring
intently at the green linoleum floor. His face is blank;
his mouth, a thin, unmoving line. His biographer-turned-
friend-turned-advisor-and-documentarian, David Leaf, sits
nearby, next to Van Dyke Parks, the musician/arranger/song-
writer whose career has been inextricably bound to Brian's for
nearly four decades, though they've rarely seen each other most
of that time. David and Van Dyke are chatting mildly—about
restaurants, friends in common, their plans for the weekend.
But the man who brought them together is silent, examining
the universe beneath the toes of his black suede Merrell shoes.

Soon the three of them, along with a couple of music journalists, will sit on a stage in front of a jammed conference
room to discuss *Smile*, the album Brian and Van Dyke wrote
and recorded most of in 1966 and 1967. At the time—just
when the Beach Boys' early stream of surf/car/girl-focused
songs had given way to Brian's ambitious song cycle *Pet Sounds*
and the smash pop-art single "Good Vibrations"—*Smile* was

envisioned as a panoramic commentary on America's tangled past, ambivalent cultural inheritance, and spiritual future. Simultaneously nostalgic, sad, dreamy, and psychedelic, the songs struck those who heard them as a whole new kind of American pop music. Some observers called it the harbinger of a new era in pop culture.

Then something happened. Exactly what that something was—static from the other Beach Boys, interference from Capitol Records, the corrosive effect of drugs, Brian's own neurological problems, or some combination of the above—has never been resolved. But the aftermath was all too clear. Brian gave up on his musical ambitions and spent most of the next four decades adrift. The Beach Boys faded from the scene, only to return as a kind of perpetual motion nostalgia machine. And *Smile* became a folk legend: a metaphor for everything that had gone wrong with Brian, the Beach Boys, and the nation whose dreams and ideals they had once transformed into shimmering waves of harmony. End of story.

Except the story wouldn't end. Even as the years turned the Beach Boys small and dispirited, the passage of time seemed only to enhance *Smile*. Hundreds of thousands of words came to be written about its creation and demise, including a science fiction novel whose hero goes back in time and helps Brian finish his masterpiece. Televised biopics and theatrical documentaries told the group's story in various shades of personal, creative, and cultural melodrama. But all came to focus on Brian's dramatic rise and crushing fall, and this story always pivoted off the lost glories of *Smile*, what it was, what it could have been, why it never came to be. Eventually *Smile*, in all of its glorious absence, became something else altogether. And that is why we're here today.

David Leaf wants to get something going. "So Van Dyke," he says, his eyes gazing past the short, stocky man in the foreground to the taller one sitting just past him, "did you ever think you'd be here at South-by-Southwest talking about how you finally finished *Smile*?"

Van Dyke smiles broadly. "It has been a wild ride," he declaims in his storybook Mississippi drawl. "And I do need to thank Brian for the opportunity to take it with him."

Both men look over at Brian, wondering if he's going to toss in his own observation, perhaps priming the pump for the onstage discussion they're about to have. But Brian is still gazing down at his toes, his face stony and empty. The two magazine writers on the panel—Alan Light from *Tracks* and Jason Fine from *Rolling Stone*—come in, but this only makes Brian seem more disconsolate. He shakes hands. He says hi. But he doesn't even try to smile, and when the festival organizers come to shepherd the gang upstairs to the stage, Brian moves with the dark resignation of a man headed for the gallows.

Upstairs the room is crowded, buzzing with excitement. The ovation begins the moment Alan Light steps onto the stage, then grows more intense when Van Dyke steps into the light. The crowd jumps to its feet when Brian emerges, but he either doesn't see this or doesn't care to acknowledge it. Instead he moves robotically to his seat, sits, and stares stone-faced into the darkness beyond the footlights. The applause continues, now mixed with cheers, and finally the taut cast of his face loosens. He mouths a silent thank-you, and then, finally, his lips slip into a small, shy smile.

Light, serving as the event's moderator, leads off with some background on *Smile*'s history. Then he throws the session open to questions, and the first one comes instantly, from a man whose eyes glisten as he addresses the stage. "Brian, I just want to thank you," he says. "Your music has saved my life so many times . . ."

Brian nods. "You're welcome."

"I just want to ask, why did you decide to finish *Smile* now, after all this time?"

This is the key question, of course. You could write a book about it.

The room is silent, waiting to hear what combination of internal and external phenomena has led this man—so often described as a genius, just as often dismissed as a burnout or pitied as the victim of untold spiritual and physical torment—to make this unexpected leap back into the creative fires.

"Well, I knew people liked watching TV," he begins. Brian is talking out of the side of his mouth, both because he's nearly deaf in one ear and because this is what he does when he's extremely nervous. "And, uh, *Smile* moves really quickly, right? So I figured people could hear it now."

This is puzzling. But another hand shoots up, and another man stands to ask Brian about his decision to perform "Heroes and Villains" at a tribute concert in 2001. "Heroes" is one of *Smile*'s key songs, and Brian had refused to play it in public for more than 35 years. Was he frightened to take it on again—particularly on a show that would be broadcast on national TV?

"Oh, it took me about half an hour to prepare for it," Brian says, shrugging. "But then it was great."

"Oh. Well." The man sounds a bit deflated. "It meant a lot to me. Thanks for doing it. And for bringing *Smile* back to life."

"Oh, sure. Thank *you*," Brian says.

Someone asks Van Dyke about how it felt the day Brian called to ask him to help him finish their long-lost masterwork.

"You must be talking about November 16, 2003," he says. "Obviously, the day means nothing to me."

This gets a laugh, and the glimmer of feeling behind his words prompts Light to ask Brian about the recording of "Fire," the cacophonous instrumental piece that represented both the heights of his creative daring and the start of his emotional devolution. How did he get such a vivid, scary sound out of the drums, cello, violins, fuzz bass, guitars, and theremin? Did he really think the music had sparked a rash of fires in downtown Los Angeles? And did this inspire his decision to not finish *Smile* at all? Brian listens and nods—and once again refuses to provide an answer. Instead, he retells the story of how he had an assistant build a fire in a bucket so the studio musicians could smell smoke while they played. They all wore plastic fire hats, too. And the song came out great, he adds. "But then we junked it." He shrugs. Light seems pained. But he smiles at Brian and nods. "Great. Thanks."

This goes on for 45 awkward minutes. Throughout, two things are obvious: the depth of the audience's feeling for Brian and his music; and Brian's near-total unwillingness to acknowledge, let alone engage, that feeling. What it comes down to is this: The people who love him the most need Brian to be something that he is no longer able or willing to be. The journey was too difficult, the price too steep. He shed that skin a long time ago, and he has no intention of looking back. Which may be one reason he engenders the passion he can no longer abide.

Brian Wilson's music became a part of the American cultural fiber not just because it was innovative and instantly memorable or even because it was so often set in a dreamland of open space and windswept horizons. It's the desperation that inspired those visions—the darkness that ignited the flight to freedom—that tugs at people's hearts. Like all of Brian's best work, *Smile* tells the American story in those same visceral terms: innocence, pain, flight, joy, corruption, desolation, redemption. It's in the music. It's in the story behind the music. It's in the sorrow that haunts Brian's eyes even when he's smiling.

This feels important, like something that should be talked about and understood, particularly while Brian is still alive, still able to put his thoughts into words. Only that's not where he likes to put his thoughts. It's the sound that matters to him. The feelings, the emotions, the vibrations, are all in the sound.

Eating lunch in Los Angeles a few weeks later, he addresses the same questions. Only now Brian is in a good mood, feeling the sun warming his back and sharing a piece of cheesecake with a friend and a writer he has come to know a little bit. He speaks easily and illustrates his thoughts with occasional bursts of song—a line of melody; a rhythm pounded out on the tabletop.

"Sometimes I think I sing too sarcastically. Like I get worried I can't sing sweet anymore, so I sing it rough." He's talking about *Smile* again, contemplating the dozens of times he'll perform the once-lost work for audiences during his summer tour. "I worry about that all the time, like I'm losing the sweetness in my soul or something. But then I hear myself singing sweetly and I think, *Hey! Listen to me! A sweet sound, all full of love!*"

He laughs and shakes his head.

"Listen to me! Just listen!"

CHAPTER 1

It's eighty degrees and sunny in Hawthorne this afternoon, with a gentle breeze brushing against the trees and a sky so perfectly and deeply blue that it seems like a dream. And it would be just another spring day in the Southland, were it not also the day the Beach Boys will be elevated into the official annals of California state history. The ceremony is taking place right here, at the out-of-the-way intersection of West 119th and Kornblum streets, where Murry and Audree Wilson once raised their sons Brian, Dennis, and Carl. Now the spot is marked by California Historical Landmark #1041, a ten-foot structure that is at this moment draped by a large white cloth.

"When the wintry winds start blowing, and the snow is starting to fall . . ."

That's Al Jolson singing, his voice echoing from the speakers on the stage that has been set up near the hidden monument. Several rows of chairs line the front of the stage, many of them filled with the wives, ex-wives, widows, children, friends, and compatriots of the Wilsons and their bandmates. A row of journalists—cameras, microphones, notebooks, dangling credentials—comes next, and behind them stands a thick crowd of onlookers. Fans, mostly, some from as far away as Australia. Many wear souvenir T-shirts from long-ago concerts and albums, the faces on them young and sweet, redolent of another time. Their presence here today pays tribute both to the younger musicians pictured on their chests and the younger fans they were when they plunked down the five or ten or fifteen bucks at the merch stand and pulled the shirts over their heads. Perhaps this is why the atmosphere is so hushed, the mood such a strange mix of ebullience and melancholy.

"California, here I come! . . ."

Then, from off in the corner closest to the VIP section, the crowd starts to cheer. Brian Wilson has appeared, steered gently by his wife and a few friends to his seat near the front of the stage. He is a large man with broad shoulders, a prominent belly, and a weathered face that is neither friendly nor hostile, but almost entirely impassive. Voices from the crowd call his name, but Brian doesn't look up. He seems detached from the world around him. Or maybe just lost in his own memories of a life touched by so much fortune—good, bad, and horrendous—that he seems less like a living, breathing person than a personification of every dream and nightmare borne upon the westward tide.

"Right back where I started from . . ."

Jolson's song comes to an end, and soon you can hear Brian's own teenaged voice coming out of the speakers, captured on a summer evening that passed on this very street nearly forty-five years ago. He's singing and chattering with Dennis and Carl and cousin Mike Love, the four of them smoothing out the rough spots in their vocals to "Surfin'," their first song. "If you laugh, I'm gonna pop you in the mouth! And if I laugh, you can pop *me* in the mouth!" someone says, but this only inspires a gale of giggles. The voices start to sing, accompanied by a slightly out-of-tune guitar. "*Surfin' is the life, the only way for me/So surf! Surf! Surf!*"

There are speeches memorializing Dennis and Carl, then the unveiling of the monument, for which Brian rises to be joined by original Beach Boy Alan Jardine and also David Marks, a Hawthorne neighbor and not-quite-original group member who served for a couple of key years in the early '60s. The three men perform their task in silence, yanking on the sheet to reveal a massive brick-and-brass monolith. They take a moment to examine it up close, pointing to its ornamental records and the brass fresco that shows them as they were, sort of, on the cover of their first album, *Surfin' Safari*. They pose for a few pictures, then they walk away in three separate directions.

Something is going on here that no one is acknowledging. And it's not just the lingering sorrows of death or the obvious discomfort felt by the three survivors who have come here. It's larger than that. A feeling that underscores every note they ever sang and every song that drew so many people here. When the current mayor presents Brian with a ceremonial plaque, he speaks emotionally about the vision of Hawthorne the songwriter presented to the world. "I just want to thank you for playing positive music," he declares. "No drugs, no sex, no violence."

Eventually Jardine gets his turn to speak. He grew up just a few blocks away, and now he's brought his mother and his own kids back to witness this moment. And yet he struggles to be upbeat, plugging his new kids' book and a cable show called *Rock Stars and Muscle Cars* he says he'll soon be hosting. Then he reflects on old times. "Dennis always gave you the truth. That means more than ever. Especially now." He laughs bitterly.

Al is referring to Mike Love, the other surviving original Beach Boy. He can't be here today because he's 3,000 miles away playing a show with a group called the Beach Boys that doesn't include any of the other people being celebrated today. Mike sent his official regrets, noting the schedule conflict. But just a few days later, his story will change markedly. "See, my memories of those days are very sweet and great, before I got cheated by my uncle Murry and by my cousin Brian, too. It was a more innocent time." So, why not pay tribute to those times? Mike hemmed and hawed for a while, then shrugged. "I didn't want to go. So how's that? A lot of the people there don't get along with me . . . how about Al Jardine? He's suing all of us now, including Brian Wilson and the estate of Carl Wilson. So I didn't particularly want to see *him*."

When Al finishes, Brian takes the stage with four of his current bandmates to sing stripped-down versions of two early songs, "Surfer Girl" ("The first song I ever wrote," he notes) and "In My Room." This last one is particularly poignant, performed so close to the actual spot where he had dreamed it up, lying in his childhood bed fending off the darkness that hovered just outside. *"In this world I lock out all my worries and my fears . . ."*

Brian stands stiffly onstage, singing with his eyes closed, losing himself in the familiar melody, the weave of voices that is now as familiar as the walls, doors, and windows of the house that once stood at his back. But the actual house has been gone for twenty years, bulldozed into dust by eight lanes of the I-105 free-way. So what we're really looking at here, gleaming beneath that brilliant afternoon sun, is a line of cars rocketing westward, all of them hurtling away from wherever they came from into the very horizon the Beach Boys spent their lives singing about.

"California, here I come/Right back where I started from . . ."

―――――

Brian Wilson, the Beach Boys' original songwriter, producer, and visionary, is in his sixties now, a man of age and wealth and almost no discernible interest in the world as it existed before him, particularly with regard to his family and their own journey across the continent to the golden coast where he was born. "We never talked about that stuff," Brian says. It is the spring of 2004, and he's in one of his favorite restaurants, a bustling hillside deli in a mall down the street from his home on the crest of Beverly Hills. "That's the one thing they never did, never talked about our ancestors at all." Now, it's hard to know if Brian is saying this because it's true or because he just doesn't remember any such conversations. Or, more likely, he just doesn't want to address the issue. He's an intimidating man, both for all he's achieved in his life and for all he's suffered along the way. And given the remove of his celebrity and his psychic torment, it's hard to separate the humor from the horror in his eyes when he does recall something his father did like to say.

"Kick some ass!" Brian is smiling now, in his silly, sad way. "Exactly, that's what my dad said. *Kick ass! Kick ass!*"

Murry Wilson was a big guy with a big personality and even bigger dreams of glory. That he would attain them through the work of his sons was a source of great pride and outrage from the old man. "My relationship with my dad was very unique," Brian says. "In some ways I was very afraid of him. In other ways I loved him because he knew where it was at. He had that competitive spirit which really blew my mind."

"Don't be afraid to try the greatest sport around." That's the story of Brian's life. But also the story of his brothers, his cousin and friends, and all of the ancestors whose ambitions, fears, hopes, and determination delivered them to this land beneath the unyielding sun. California, here we come. Right back where they started from. *"Catch a wave and you're sitting on top of the world."*

As described by Timothy White in his intricately researched *The Nearest Far-away Place,* the story of the Wilsons in America begins in the late eighteenth century, when the first Wilson to venture to the New World settled in New York. The first American-born family member, named Henry Wilson, was born in 1804 and eventually moved west to Meigs County, Ohio, where he worked as a stonemason. His son, named George Washington Wilson in the spirit of the times, was born in 1820, and he and his family farmed a plot of rich, river-fed land in Meigs County for more than six decades until his own son, William Henry Wilson, decided to pursue fortune west to the wide-open plains of Hutchinson, Kansas. So west they went, with patriarch George in tow, settling onto a large, if relatively arid, farm that William Henry soon abandoned in order to go into the industrial plumbing business. Contracts to work on the state's new reformatory system, along with the many opportunities afforded by the modernizing world around them, provided a decent working-class living and a solidly built clapboard bungalow on one of Hutchinson's nice residential streets. As the nineteenth century gave way to the twentieth, William Henry began to think again of chasing fortune into the western horizon.

California! At the dawn of the new century, this was the setting of every ambitious man's dreams. The real estate flyers papering the town painted in the details, describing the valley soil as every bit as rich and fertile as the sun was warm and the breezes gentle. Thus inspired, William Henry scraped together the cash to buy, sight unseen, ten acres of prime farmland in the southern California village of Escondido. William Henry loaded up his wife, kids, and even his eighty-five-year-old father into the family jalopy; they arrived in 1904 and spent the year laboring on their new vineyard. And though the sun did indeed shine, and the water flowed as promised, and the vines did erupt with fat, juicy fruit, the farming was every bit as hard as it had been back in Kansas, and the money not nearly as vast as previously anticipated. By 1905, William and family were back in the plumbing business in Kansas. Still, memories of the California sun and the dreams of ease and fortune that had once stirred William Henry's soul came to rest in the imagination of his teenaged son, William Coral "Buddy" Wilson. As the boy grew, so too did his visions of the golden future that awaited him in the Golden State.

Dark-eyed, heavy-browed, and thick-featured, Buddy Wilson took off for California in 1914. Then in his early twenties, the young man—already married to Edith Shtole and the father of a child or two—fairly seethed with ambition. Surely, he imagined, a man with his drive and appetite could find an untapped stream of gold somewhere in that rich, open economic frontier. Leaving his family back in Hutchinson, Buddy would spend months at a time searching for his place in the sun, looking increasingly in the oil fields of the southern coast. Guys could make a fortune if they latched onto the right rig, and so Buddy used his plumbing skills as his entrée, working as a steamfitter on the pipes that channeled the gushers out of the ground and into the pockets of the rich men whose example he was desperate to follow.

But Buddy would never join them in the gilded halls of the powerful. Moody and scattered, plagued by searing headaches and a self-destructive thirst for whiskey, Buddy wandered from job to job to long stretches of unemployment, which he passed grumbling into a glass in a dim barroom. When Edith and the kids finally joined him in 1921, taking the train to the elegant-sounding village of Cardiff-by-the-Sea, he couldn't afford to lease an apartment in town. Instead, the family spent their first two months living in a snug eight-by-eight-foot tent with all the other squatters on the beach.

Edith took a job pressing clothes for a garment manufacturer, and eventually the family moved to a small home on an unpaved road in Inglewood where the eight Wilson kids attended school, worked weekend jobs, and marched the thin line dictated by their sour father and stern, demanding mother. Escape, such as it was, came in the occasional afternoon bike rides to the open, breezy expanse of Hermosa Beach.

Escape was a necessity for Buddy Wilson's kids. Buddy, now in middle age and resigned to his life of small prospects and severely limited horizons, had long felt his ambition curdle into resentment. Often awash in alcohol and self-pity, Buddy's bile regularly boiled over into violence, directed most often at Edith. But he could also turn his fists on his children, once beating the school-aged Charles so savagely (for mistakenly shattering his glasses) that Murry, then a teenager, had to come to his brother's rescue, shoving the old man out of the house until he sobered up. And this wasn't the only time Murry had come to blows with his father. Increasingly, the family's second-oldest boy found himself thrust into the role of his mother's protector, raising his own fists against the father he loved but who seemed unable to love him or anyone else in the family.

As in most abusive families, the physical and psychic violence that ruled their home became an unacknowledged presence, a force that both dominated their lives and forced them into silence. But if they couldn't talk about their problems, the Wilsons could always sing their way to a kind of amity. Indeed, group sings had been a Wilson family tradition dating back to Kansas and beyond, as an eighty-seven-year-old Charles Wilson (an uncle to Brian, Dennis, and Carl) would tell Timothy White, describing nights on the Kansas plains when "we'd have shows on Saturday nights, with three of the oldest brothers on guitars and mandolins. This was at home, with the windows open to the street, and people would stop and listen."

Even Buddy, a man with no discernible instincts toward paternal tenderness, loved to sing with his kids. He'd long since come to admire the sound of his own tenor voice anchoring the family blend. But even more important, weaving his voice together with those of his wife and kids was as close as Buddy could get to actual emotional intimacy with his family. And perhaps this was why Murry, the son who had come to be the family's last line of defense against their drunk, vicious father, came to love music so very much. He taught himself to play guitar, too, and he picked up piano from his big sister. And when the living room radio picked up broadcasts from the elegant nightclubs of Hollywood or downtown Los Angeles, Murry sat in front of the speaker and soaked it in, his face glowing happily. What he was hearing was an entirely new vision of the world. Here, life was filled with luxury and ease; a place where careers could be made and fortunes earned, all by the grace of a clever new song. Sitting in front of the radio, aloft on the arc of a pretty melody, Murry Wilson had come to realize something: More than anything else in the world, he wanted to be a songwriter.

But if Murry could be just as dreamy as the next aspiring pop star, he was also a realist who had grown up knowing exactly how important—and difficult—it could be to buy the bare essentials of day-to-day life. He was a mediocre student at George Washington High School, but the rock-jawed youngster left school in 1935 armed with a steely resolve to find work. And though the rest of the nation was still mired in the teeth of the Depression, Murry landed a job as a clerk with the Southern California Gas Company. He was still employed there when he met and, in 1938, married Audree Korthof, the sweet-natured daughter of a stern, hard-working baker who had moved his family west from Minnesota when Audree was a schoolgirl. Murry and his new wife settled in southern Los Angeles, reveling for a time in Murry's ascendance from the gas company office trenches to a junior administrative post. When Audree became pregnant in the fall of 1941, Murry's determination to succeed and to outdo the sad, bitter legacy of his father only grew more intense. The couple's first son, Brian Douglas Wilson, was born on June 20, 1942, bearing the same blue eyes, dark hair, and prominent brow that had followed the family across the generations.

Murry and Audree welcomed two more boys into their family in the next four years—the fair-haired Dennis Carl Wilson coming in late 1944 and Carl Dean Wilson, another dark-featured boy, at the end of 1946. Moving his family to a modern, if cozy, two-bedroom ranch house on West 119th Street in the blue-collar suburb of Hawthorne, Murry rolled his sleeves up over his bulky forearms and set to scratching out his own slice of the postwar economic boom. He'd already made some progress, jumping to a junior administration job at the Goodyear Tire and Rubber Company just after Brian's birth and then, just as the war ended, to a foreman's position in the manufacturing plant of AiResearch, an aeronautics company that made parts for Seattle-based Boeing Aircraft's growing line of civilian and military airplanes.

By the end of World War II, the South Bay revolved around the thriving aerospace industry. Borne up by the dual demands of a rapidly expanding civilian airline market and the just-as-rapidly-growing tension with the Soviet Union, aeronautics presented opportunities for hardworking men that were seemingly as limitless as their own aspirations. But while Murry's timing was spot-on, and he was a tireless worker with a penchant for big ideas, nothing came easily for him. A gruesome accident at Goodyear cost him his left eye, and that twist of fate only emphasized an aggressive-to-bellicose personality that tended to alienate him from co-workers and superiors alike. Stalled on the lower rungs of management and increasingly frustrated with his flat career arc, Murry descended into dark moods all too reminiscent of his own father's. Still, unwilling to resign himself entirely to the old man's fate, he scraped together as much cash as he could and opened his own business, an industrial equipment rental outfit he called A.B.L.E. (Always Better Lasting Equipment) Machinery. From that point on, Murry Wilson would be his own boss. The arrangement suited him just fine.

So in the mornings Murry would dress in his pressed white shirts and skinny tie knotted just so, his horn-rimmed glasses perched on his thick, bulldog's face, his suit jacket straining against the prominent belly and muscular shoulders that testified both to his appetite for work and for the rewards awaiting a man at the end of his day. Steering his Ford down the quiet, sun-washed streets of mid-1950s Hawthorne, he'd see a hundred houses just like the one he shared with Audree and his three boys: small but neat, with a lush lawn and a wide driveway for the late-model Ford, Buick, or Chevy, its tail fins gleaming in the cool morning light.

These were the cars of men who were determined to get somewhere in their lives. Like Murry, many of Hawthorne's men were either born in the Midwest or

CATCH A WAVE

were the children of men and women who had made the westward trek sometime in the first few decades of the twentieth century. "It was like a little Midwestern town that just got moved right there to eighty acres of land," recalls Robin Hood, who grew up a few blocks from the Wilsons. "There were a lot of farmers from Kansas and Missouri, a lot of Dust Bowl–era folks who settled in with their big, extended families. Nobody was rich, but we didn't know it."

But their parents certainly did. And if one belief held the community together, it was the one about the transformative potential of hard work. No matter where you came from, no matter what your people used to be or what anyone expected you to become, in a working-class West Coast town like Hawthorne—which had been a stretch of empty coastal flats and swamp a generation ago—you could work your way into being anything or anyone you felt like being. This belief is liberating, of course, but it's also evidence of internal currents that can give the pursuit an undertone of desperation. As Joan Didion would write, the California of this era was a place "in which a boom mentality and a sense of Chekhovian loss meet in uneasy suspension; in which the mind is troubled by some buried but ineradicable suspicion that things had better work here, because here, beneath that immense bleached sky, is where we run out of continent."

Eventually the Baby Boom generation would turn the very edge of the continent into its own proving ground. But the impulse that propelled them there, that restless need for deliverance and the intuitive belief that it could be divined by your own hands somewhere out past the wild fringe of the western horizon, was the same one that had dragged their families across the American frontier and into the dreamy, bustling, sun-glazed cities they had built for themselves. And this was where Murry's sons, Brian, Dennis, and Carl, came to understand their father's need for them to kick the world in the ass. He wanted so much for them. He wanted so much for himself. In the worst possible way, you might say.

CHAPTER 2

I
n Brian's memory he's still a toddler, maybe two years old,
sitting on the floor and staring up into the empty air
above him. Only the air isn't really empty because it is
full of music. He and his mother are at his grandmother's
house, and the record player is pumping George Gershwin's
"Rhapsody in Blue" across the room and into the open, ecstatic
ears of the child sitting open-mouthed on the floor.

"Oh, I *loved* it," he says in the spring of 2005. "Looking
back now, I can see what I heard, even if I couldn't express it
in words back then. Listening to it now brings back some bad
memories, because I had such a bad childhood. But good
memories too, because I loved that song."

In his heavily ghostwritten (and deeply controversial) 1991
memoir, Brian wrote that "Rhapsody" contained "every emotion I've ever experienced." Indeed, almost nothing in his life
is without musical accompaniment. And to him, music is present and tangible, with all the dimension and significance of a
lover.

From the start, he seemed to feel things more intensely
than other children. Tall and skinny, with dark blue eyes, the
Wilson family's prominent brow, and a shy, crooked smile,
Brian's emotions played vibrantly across his freckled face. And
though Murry didn't like to see his oldest boy cling to his

mother quite so much, he did nothing to discourage Brian's fascination with music. Murry first noticed his son's skill just before Brian's first birthday, when he was walking down the street on a warm summer day with the boy on his shoulders. To pass the time and keep the boy entertained, Murry started singing "When the Caissons Go Rolling Along," only getting through a verse or two before the preverbal Brian was humming along, mimicking his father's voice in a note-perfect rendition of the song's melody. "He was very clever and quick," Murry said in an interview much later. "I just fell in love with him."

But love was a complicated thing in the Wilson family, particularly between fathers and sons. And though middle brother Dennis had the tough exterior Brian lacked ("He just kissed it all off," one friend recalls), and baby brother Carl followed his mother's example by watching the hysteria from as far away as possible, the boys all came to understand that the whims, moods, and expectations of their pugnacious father would define the texture of their lives until they left his home. Indeed, Murry was determined to be as present in their lives as his father had been absent in his. He also needed them to conform to certain ideals he had formed and to follow his orders with rigid precision. First and foremost, he expected them to be tough. "You think the world owes you a living?" he'd demand. "You think the world is going to be fair? You've got to get in there and kick ass!" To emphasize the point, he'd give his boys a shove or maybe a slap. And if Murry's motivational talks could be jarring, they were far less brutal than his punishments. Confronted by a son who had neglected one of his chores or, worse yet, had violated a direct paternal order, Murry's temper could erupt in the worst possible ways. He screamed and roared. "I'm the boss, goddammit!" He slapped their blushing cheeks and whipped them with a leather belt. He taunted them in front of their friends, making loud points about their Little League errors, the grass cuttings they failed to rake, even the slovenly way they sat in the shade while eating Popsicles with their friends. And if none of that seemed to achieve the desired effect, Murry had more quiet, if vicious, ways of getting the job done.

Later, when the boys were young adults, as famous for their gothic personal lives as they were for their music, they told murky, often contradictory tales of their past that raised as many questions as answers. Did Murry once force a grade school–aged Brian to defecate on a plate in order to punish some small misdeed? Did he force tomato-hating Dennis to eat them nonstop until he vomited? Did he beat Brian with a two-by-four when he found the grade-schooler had unleashed a neighbor's puppy while playing with him? Did he attempt some twisted form of character building by plucking out his artificial eye and forcing his sons to sit nose to nose with him, peering into the jagged maw of his blood-red socket? Carl, perpetually quiet and nonconfrontational, never confirmed or denied anything. Dennis, on the other hand, was abrupt: "We had a shitty childhood," he declared in 1976, three years after Murry's death. "Our dad used to whale on us."

Brian, always the most vulnerable of the brothers, never seemed to come to terms with what had happened. "He was like our coach," Brian said of his father in 1998. "He scared me so much I actually got scared into making good records."

But that raises one of the most disturbing aspects of Brian's relationship with Murry: He blames his father for delivering the blow to his head that destroyed almost all of the hearing in his right ear. It's not something he always acknowledges in public. In fact, Brian has denied the story in recent years, echoing his mother, who could never decide if the real culprit was another boy in the neighborhood or a congenital nerve defect. Still, mid-1960s collaborator Tony Asher recalls Brian telling him about losing his hearing after Murry hit him. Brian's recollection of his dad's role in his deafness faded to uncertainty for his 1991 autobiography, then hardened into doubt by the start of the twenty-first century. "I remember my dad whacking me in the ear when I was six," he said recently, letting the memory stand only for a few seconds before adding another thought: "But I was born deaf."

But he nonetheless seems to have spent years convinced that his partial deafness—a crushing blow to a man who would spend his life manipulating sound textures but could never hear music in stereo—was a direct result of the beatings he got from his father, the same man who nurtured his love of music, who bought him an organ and a stereo whose sonic complexity he would never truly comprehend.

And yet, he knew that music was the best, most reliable way to win his father's love, or at least a respite from his rage. So when the brothers were lying in their beds at night, Brian would lead Dennis and Carl in a three-part rendition of the old hymn "Come Down from Your Ivory Tower," or perhaps "Good News," knowing that the sound of their voices could draw their father to their doorway, where he'd listen silently, eyes glistening with the love that the emotionally scarred man could never quite express.

"In some ways I haven't gotten beyond my dad," Brian said with a tired shrug. He was in his midfifties then, almost exactly the age Murry was when he died in

1973. "I was so afraid of my dad and the way he talked to me that something got inside of me and I just started making great records. My relationship with him was very unique." But as a sensitive schoolboy whose world began and ended with his family's home, the street where they lived, and the school around the corner, Brian (and his brothers) just wanted to seem like all the other kids in the neighborhood—and that's precisely how the Wilson boys appeared. Like all the other grade-schoolers on West 119th Street, they spent their early years tossing balls from yard to yard, racing their bikes up the smooth, clean street, and running in and out of one another's houses. "We all just hung out together, all the kids on the block," recalls Mary Lou Manrikus (now Van Antwerp), who grew up down the street. "None of our mothers worked, so they all watched over us kids."

Brian—who had matured into a lithe and muscular adolescent—was a baseball nut who loved the New York Yankees, worshipped Mickey Mantle, and could throw a ball farther than anyone else on the block. Baby brother Carl was pudgy and quiet, but he was also one of those kids who always seemed older than his years, even in kindergarten. Dennis, on the other hand, was a freckle-faced terror, skipping school to look for frogs in the nearby swamps, climbing the Manrikuses' fragile apricot tree even after Mr. Manrikus had repeatedly ordered him to stop, and greeting a new kid on their block by taunting and throwing garbage at him from across the street. "He wasn't too menacing," says David Marks, the new neighbor who would become a family friend and eventually join forces with the Wilsons. "We actually hit it off pretty quickly."

The neighbor kids got on just as easily with Audree, whose motherly nature was emphasized by the fluffy white apron she usually wore. Like most neighborhood moms, Audree focused entirely on domestic affairs: wiping the boys' noses, mopping the kitchen floor, dusting the shelves, and getting dinner on the table by 6:00 p.m. A short, plump woman with a twinkle in her eye, she presented a striking contrast to her husband, whose gruff demeanor made him a fearsome presence on West 119th Street. "Everyone thought he was mean," says Mary Lou Manrikus, maybe the only neighborhood kid who wasn't afraid of him. "The other kids would send me down to get Brian because Murry was always so grumpy." And as David Marks remembers, even Murry's more playful moments with the neighborhood kids tended to be oddly aggressive. "He liked to give all of us the Vulcan nerve pinch and bring us to our knees. And he'd be making this sinister laugh while he did it." At this, Marks laughs ruefully. "Good, clean fun, right?"

Hardly anyone knew what to make of Murry. As a businessman, he prided himself on his strict code of ethics, believing that every handshake and verbal agreement should be just as binding as a signed contract. When the Manrikus family moved onto the block, Murry was the first neighbor to knock on their door and offer his help. He referred to his wife as Mrs. Wilson, and even when money was tight, he made sure she and their kids wore nice clothes, ate good food, and lived in a comfortable home. When business was good, Murry brought home lavish gifts: the best new go-karts and BB guns for the boys and a professional-quality organ so he and Audree could play duets in the music room. But as the boys got older and their friends became mature enough to understand the signs of emotional turmoil, Murry developed an even darker reputation in their circle. "He was bad news," says Ted Sprague, a friend of Brian's who spent countless hours in the Wilson home. "Never a word of encouragement. He taunted the boys mercilessly, and it never ended. It was just a relentless barrage when Murry was around." By the time Brian got to Hawthorne High School in the fall of 1956, he'd built a reputation on the Little League ballpark with his cannon arm and extraordinary speed. Tall, handsome, witty, and sweet-natured, he moved easily with the other athletes, the pretty girls, and the other class leaders who recognized and respected his understated charisma. Unlike the athletes who strutted around campus using their muscles and varsity jackets to woo girls and intimidate weaker boys, Brian impressed friends and parents alike with his warmth and easygoing inclusiveness. "He's always been a group person, always loved having a lot of people around," says Bruce Griffin, a friend of Brian's despite being a year behind him in school. "And he was the quarterback in any group, always telling people what to do."

Rich Sloan, a classmate who played sports and hung out with Brian throughout high school, both enjoyed and took advantage of his friend's appetite for practical jokes. Although Brian loved nothing more than to spoof friends and strangers alike—staging fake fistfights at school, leaning out of his car and dumping a milk carton of oatmeal on Hawthorne Boulevard while pretending to vomit, organizing his pals to affect limps onstage at their high school graduation—he didn't seem to mind being the butt of the jokes, either. It's a good thing too, because Sloan can recall half a dozen gags that ended with Brian being drenched with ice water, splashed with invisible ink, and even peed on (!), the latter stunt taking place in the Hawthorne High locker-room showers while Brian was feigning grievous injury on the shower-room floor. "Brian was fun-loving," Sloan says. "He didn't care if he was the butt of a joke or part of it. People laughed and had a good time when he was around."

And yet some of Brian's friends could sense something unsettled, and a bit unsettling, behind his crooked smile and high-pitched guffaws. Bruce Griffin, who became a singing partner and regular confidant, recalls Brian "always snorting and laughing at jokes other people just didn't get." Keith Lent, who joined in on a lot of the same harmony sessions, remembers his friend's nervous habit of hitching up his pants—a habit Sloan believes he picked up on the football field thanks to his skinny hips and perpetually oversize hip pads—when something made him anxious. And though music was deeply (and increasingly) important to Brian, news that he would spend his senior year of high school riding the bench with the fifth-stringers sent the young quarterback into an emotional tailspin, prompting him to quit the team on the spot. "He could throw the ball a long ways, probably farther than anyone else, but Brian was flaky on the field and couldn't hit the guy he was throwing at," Griffin says. A large group of teammates tried to talk the struggling quarterback out of quitting football, but he had already made up his mind to join the cross-country team instead. "That was the first time I'd ever seen him get so emotional about something," Griffin says. "I really didn't know what was going on."

Griffin also wondered about Brian's impromptu visits: He'd routinely pop over unannounced, sometimes after ten o'clock in the evening, eager to sing a new song or talk about the latest twist in the school social scene. In search of privacy, they'd end up sitting in the front seat of Brian's '57 Ford, singing rock 'n' roll songs or talking about friends, girls, and sports until past midnight. Brian was always fascinated with the romantic and social entanglements of his peers, Griffin recalls, and loved nothing more than to come knocking with some scrap of back-channel information about his friend's latest flame: whose car she was seen riding in, whom she danced with at another party. Sometimes Griffin would get annoyed at Brian's eagerness to trash his girlfriends. "I asked him, what kind of friend likes to deliver bad news all of the time? He was shocked because friends were very important to him, and he couldn't see himself being disloyal." A decade later, Brian would recall those evenings in the title track of the Beach Boys album *Friends*. *"You told me when my girl was untrue/I loaned you money when the funds weren't too cool . . ."*

Robin Hood, a close friend since seventh grade, had also grown used to

Brian's late-night visits. Brian also made a point of dropping by his friend's house on holidays, including Christmas, Thanksgiving, and the Fourth of July—in other words, the major holidays families tend to spend together. Hood's father was particularly patient with Brian because he heard so many stories about Murry from a friend who worked for the senior Wilson at A.B.L.E. Machinery. Robin can't remember if his father ever told him exactly what he'd heard, "but when Brian would leave, my dad would shake his head and say, 'That poor kid,'" Hood recalls. Eventually, Bruce Griffin reached the same conclusion: "I realized he just needed to get away from home and whatever was happening there," he says.

Most of Brian's quirks seemed harmless enough. Unlike most Hawthorne kids, he rarely enjoyed going to the beach to swim or sit in the sun. When he did join the gang at the shore, he was likely to show up in his jeans and T-shirt, mostly because his fair skin burned so easily in the strong California sun. He was an absentminded driver, usually far too fixated on the radio dial to have a reliable sense of the traffic around him or the lines on the highway. (Brian once told an old classmate that it took him five tries to get his driver's license. "Big surprise!" she remembers thinking.) Whimsical and absentminded off the road as well, Brian would forget all about earlier commitments—say, meeting a friend for miniature golf—if some other opportunity caught his fancy in the interim. Not that he was consciously abandoning one friend for another, Sloan says. "His attention span was limited. And when he got excited about something, that was it." Similarly, when he got embroiled in a project—particularly if it involved music—Brian would work obsessively for hours, so thoroughly losing track of time that he'd call for his friends well after midnight.

And though Brian was a varsity athlete, a decent student, and popular, his friends sensed his vulnerability. He was desperately insecure around girls, particularly the ones he knew other people found attractive and charismatic. Chief among these was Carol Mountain, a witty, dark-haired cheerleader Brian adored. "That was a big-time crush," Sprague recalls. And though they never kissed or even went out on a casual date, Hood remembers Carol as Brian's "first true love." He would speak about her obsessively, praising her lovely skin and long, dark hair and fantasizing about the series of events that would lead to her accepting his invitation to go out. The only person who didn't seem to know about Brian's crush, it seems, was Carol herself. "I really had no idea until twenty-five years later," she says. And yet she does remember how easily Brian spoke to her in

Spanish class, how quick he was to help her remember homework assignments, and how eager he was to play boogie-woogie piano at her house when the gang came over for a party. "He was just a really nice guy," she says. "Someone you kind of wanted to protect."

Brian continued to mythologize his unattainable crush into adulthood, eventually projecting her into the role of surfer girl, a sweet girl he'd want to marry so "we wouldn't have to wait so long," and, as his perspective darkened, into a mature woman so hardened by life she had traded her silky locks for a shorter, more severe look. "Where did your long hair go?" he imagined asking, concluding, "Carol, I know." ("Pet Sounds" lyricist Tony Asher rewrote Brian's reverie, leading to the lyric "Caroline, No.") Indeed, the feelings that led to the creation of Brian's 1966 album seemed to reawaken Brian's affection for Carol. They were both married by then, but she began to receive phone calls from her old classmate, sometimes at odd hours. "He didn't sound drugged or anything, but it was very strange," she says. "He'd call at 3:00 a.m. and want to talk about music. I was such a nerd I'd say, 'What? Who?' and have him talk to my husband. But it was nothing inappropriate. It was just a strange thing he was going through, calling and connecting. We treated him with respect. We didn't get angry. And he didn't talk long."

Ten years after that, Brian called Robin Hood out of the blue. They hadn't spoken in years, but suddenly the thirty-five-year-old Brian was talking like it was 1959. "He wanted to come and pick me up, and we'd call Carol Mountain and Carol Hess and a few others and get together. He was serious." When Robin told him that several of his friends had long since scattered across the country, Brian was unperturbed. "He wanted to fly them in and have a party next week." Brian forgot all about his party idea soon enough, but Robin never forgot his boyish excitement or, for that matter, his Sam Spade–like ability to track down his old pal's number, no matter how often he moved. "I had other friends who could never find me. But Brian always could. It just blew me away."

Despite his lack of confidence with girls, Brian did date regularly, if casually, during his high school years. Irene Callahan (now Fernandez) recalls her junior prom date as being funny and sweet, meeting her after class to walk her to the lunchroom, cracking jokes and making silly observations about the other kids the whole way. Still, he could be shy and a trifle awkward. "I'd say he was more intense than the other kids," she recalls. "He always seemed serious, even though we also had a lot of laughs." He didn't talk to Irene about music very much, which made it all the more surprising when they had left the prom to dance to Tony Bennett's band at the Ambassador Hotel, and Brian, in a romantic mood, started singing along. "I'm sure other people could hear—it wasn't soft! I was embarrassed at the time."

But like so many of his friends, Irene couldn't imagine making sport of Brian for any reason. He was too nice, for one thing. "He was a sensitive person," she says. Carol Mountain felt the same way. "He was such a gentle soul, and you could sense something wasn't quite right," she says. Perhaps it's unsurprising that Brian gravitated toward other kids whose internal lives were more complicated than they let on in public. Hood, for example, was an epileptic whose neurological condition not only kept him from driving but also prompted occasional small fits of muttering that made other kids giggle uncomfortably. Brian moved immediately to protect his friend, coolly telling the other kids to back off and leave his pal alone. "He's fine," he'd snap. Ted Sprague, another jock who lettered in several sports, also used his letterman's jacket as a shield, given a past that included an unmarried mother and years spent bouncing from city to city and house to house. "I never knew my father, so maybe I was accustomed to being hurt," Sprague says now. Sensing that injury, Brian would invite Sprague to come to Sunday services at the Inglewood Covenant Church along with Audree and his brothers on Sunday, a weekly ritual he valued both for the emotional succor the sermons offered and the weekly respite from Murry, who had no interest in religion. Sprague, then a determined atheist, would have none of it. But the gesture made an impression on him, particularly in the years that Christianity became a central focus of his life.

Church may have given Brian some sense of ease, but as with most teenagers hoping to find their own way, he found more reliable transcendence in the physical world and the simple joys of friendship. So when Ted Sprague would propose a late-afternoon workout by the water, Brian would go happily. He always loved to escape, particularly in the company of a friend who shared so many of the same frustrations and felt the same instinctive need to find a life that was larger and more meaningful than the one they knew.

So they would drive west together to Hermosa Beach, leaving the car in the lot and walking down to the water's edge. It was usually close to dusk, the sun already sinking beneath the horizon, and in the fading light the boys would blast off on what they called a training run but was actually a full-bore sprint down the hard, wet sand toward Hermosa Pier. Their tennis shoes slapping the sand, the water spraying up behind them, their thoughts were momentarily lost in the thunder of the waves, the rush of the wind, and the pounding of their hearts. "It was a spiritual thing," Brian remembers. "Down there right on the water, with the sun going down, and we'd run so fast, it was amazing."

And yet, the real spiritual frontier for Brian—his most reliable place to escape, to discover himself and express his feelings—was the one he'd first glimpsed in the notes of "Rhapsody in Blue" when he was two years old. Brian had soon displayed glimmers of talent, particularly as a result of his high-pitched, powerful singing voice that made him an instant standout in the church choir. This ability didn't always make him popular with his peers. Dennis long ago recalled seeing his big brother run home in tears after some schoolmates laughed about his girl-ish falsetto. Still, Brian learned volumes about the visceral power of music by watching his father throw all of his bearish weight into his own music. Even as he earned his living in the machinery business and reveled in his authoritative role as master of his wife and family, Murry Wilson still harbored his childhood dream of writing hit songs.

He'd sit at the piano in the evenings—sometimes alone, sometimes with a friend to bounce ideas off of—his thick fingers groping for new melodies, string-ing them through the pretty, jazzy chords and danceable rhythms he heard com-ing from the radio. When Murry found something that tickled his ear, he would jump up and down with excitement, delighting in what he was sure would be a smash hit. Summoning Audree to the keyboard, he would painstakingly teach her to sing a harmony part, making sure she had the inflection just so, in order to emphasize the tune's devil-may-care bounciness, the essential charm he knew would make it leap up the charts.

Combining his musical talent with his business acumen, Murry would draw up some sheet music and take his latest tune to the small music publishers in Hollywood, hoping to get it out into the world where someone, somewhere, might hear its potential and record it. And he wasn't entirely unsuccessful— Murry published several songs during the '50s, all with eyebrow-raising titles like "Hide My Tears," "His Little Darling," and "Fiesta Day Polka." But his big-gest success by far was a novelty dance number called "Two-Step, Side-Step," which was recorded by a group called the Bachelors in 1952 and became popular enough that Lawrence Welk performed it on his weekly radio show. The tri-umph of that moment—Murry was a *huge* Lawrence Welk fan—put a spring in his step for months.

Along with all the other gratification it gave him, Murry's success in music gave him some welcome bragging rights over his siblings and in-laws. "The Wilson brothers were always bickering," recalls Maureen Love, whose mother, Emily (whom everyone called Glee), was Murry's sister. "Some of them had wars over business deals or other money things." But Glee, like her sister Mary, had also seen Murry protecting their mother against the upraised hand of Buddy. These memories endeared Murry to them for the rest of their lives. "She would never let anyone say shit about Murry," remembers Stan Love, Maureen's youngest brother. "She and Aunt Mary would throw your ass out of the room if you did that." Indeed, if Glee Love had anything, it was an indelible memory, particularly when she felt wronged. Her father learned this the hard way, and so too would her oldest son.

Married in 1938 to high school sweetheart Milton Love, who worked in his father's thriving sheet metal business, Glee had her first child, Michael, in 1941. Maureen came two years later, followed by Stephen in 1947, Stanley in 1949, Stephanie in 1951, and Margie in 1960. The war years were particularly lucrative for the sheet metal business, and by the early '50s Milton had done well enough to move his family into a spacious, Mediterranean-style home he'd had built in the elegant View Park neighborhood. "We always did nice, creative things, loading up the car with easels and paints and going out to Palos Verdes to paint barns," Maureen says. "That was my mother's influence; she was the creative one. We all had music lessons. And both of our parents were athletes, so we had plenty of sports, too."

Glee's life in View Park granted her physical distance from the crowded, unhappy circumstances of her own childhood. But she remained a high-strung woman whose fears often prompted her to forbid her children from participating in even the most normal childhood activities. "My mom came from a chaotic background, and I guess she overcompensated," Maureen says. "We could barely walk down the sidewalk by ourselves. In fact, we used to have a joke that we'd have to be fifteen before we could cross the street alone." Mike rolls his eyes when he remembers his mother's rules. "She was more than protective," he says. "She didn't want me to join the Boy Scouts because she didn't want me to fall off a cliff. And yeah, of course it bothered me."

As the oldest of six children, it was predictable that Mike bore the brunt of his parents' rigid discipline. The fact that he was such an energetic and outgoing kid only made it more difficult for him. "He chose to sneak around a little and lie a little just to do the things he wanted to do," Maureen recalls. "He rebelled and got into trouble, and so he had the reputation of being a liar and a sneak around our house. And my mother had a dark, kind of unforgiving side. And she and Mike just clashed." As he got older, Mike learned to pursue feminine approval from girls his own age. "I remember him being so girl-crazy," Maureen says. "Whenever my friends came over, he was always there, wanting to be around the girls. And he was charming and handsome, so he had fun."

Mike's pursuit of fun didn't end at the schoolhouse door. As a grade-schooler, he often got in trouble for reading his own books at his desk while the teacher was holding a lesson at the front of the room. Mike made a habit of ignoring homework assignments, and by the time he got to high school, he was far more interested in the track team than anything that was going on in the classrooms. One of his fondest memories, in fact, is the day he used a high-jump move to escape a boring social studies lecture. "The teacher's back was turned, and I did a western roll out of the window," Mike says with a laugh. "I had a good time in high school. And we always loved singing, too. Singing those Everly Brothers songs with Brian and other guys. We always loved it."

As it had been for the earlier generations of Wilsons, music had become a bonding agent for Glee, Murry, and their families. It helped Murry get beyond his resentment of Milton Love's financial success—which Milton was rarely too shy to put on display. And when Glee threw the family's annual Christmas party, which always climaxed with the guests going out on a long caroling expedition around the View Park streets, the Wilsons were always there. In fact, the Loves' Christmas parties were peak moments in the year for Brian and his brothers, rare occasions when their family seemed connected to something larger, happier, and more prosperous than the lives they knew. When the group divided into generations, Brian, Dennis, and Carl would join the Love kids to sing the latest tunes by Chuck Berry or Elvis Presley. Brian came naturally to the fore, sitting at the piano and showing his cousins and brothers exactly how to combine their voices and instruments in order to capture the sound they heard on the radio. "He was so kindhearted, talented, and cute," Maureen remembers. "When Brian came over, he'd barely say hi, just go right to the piano. He'd start banging out songs, give Mike his bass part, give my mom an alto part, and we'd all sing together, harmonizing. Those are some of my favorite memories."

Brian was always most comfortable when he was in the middle of a song. When he wasn't playing music himself, Brian loved to listen to the radio, just then turning electric with the sounds of Bill Haley, Chuck Berry, and Elvis Presley. Mike turned him on to rhythm and blues, particularly the street corner harmonies of the Drifters and the other doo-wop singing groups. But as catalytic as the propulsive beat of "Rock Around the Clock" and stinging guitar of "Johnny B. Goode" might have been, it was the sound of four dorky guys in sweaters that changed the course of Brian's life.

The group was the Four Freshmen, a clean-cut vocal quartet that sang old-fashioned jazz-pop tunes with intricately arranged four-part vocal harmonies. Hearing those lithe voices swell and slide through the sambalike "Day by Day" on the car radio one afternoon in the mid-1950s, Brian was awestruck. He cajoled Audree into taking him to a record store, where he took one of their albums—*The Four Freshmen and the Five Trombones*—and listened to the whole thing. The record mesmerized Brian, and talking about it later, he speaks in near-religious terms, describing his soul opening up, the music entering him and carrying him to another sphere of consciousness. "It brings a feeling of love inside of me," he says. "It does. It really does. That feeling of harmony." Soon he had all the group's records, listening to them over and over again as he sat hunched over the piano, his fingers searching for the combination of notes and countermelodies that would unlock the secret harmonies in each song. When he could play the chords on the piano, Brian would call in Audree and Carl and arrange their voices to echo the Freshmen. Eventually Murry and Audree bought Brian a portable Wollensak tape recorder, which he could use to record and analyze his work.

Falling deeper under the music's spell, Brian became increasingly intrigued by the possibilities of recorded sound. Tapes that survive from the era reveal his earliest vocal arrangements and also his first attempts to use recording technology as a way to double or triple the power of two or three voices. He also captured a tantalizing array of ordinary moments in the Wilson home, including Dennis as a rusty-voiced fourteen-year-old, begging his big brother for a chance to recite a pretend commercial for Ipana toothpaste. "Just a little bit!" he pleads, only to be rebuffed by a taunting Brian. "Ladies and gentlemen, I know you can't hear me. I hope you can't hear me. But I just wanna say that Dennis is a prick!" Dennis yowls in protest—"Come on, Brian!"—but Brian is on a tear, turning his attention to chubby baby brother Carl. "Tell me, Carl, how'd you get all that flab?" he says, answering himself in a whiny version of his brother's feathery preadolescent voice: "Well, it's fun to lay on your ass all day!"

Brian recorded himself and Keith Lent practicing a Spanish dialogue that focuses largely on ordering food and arguing about the price of a used car, then recorded himself complaining bitterly about the Wollensak's occasional break-downs. "I think we are recording. I now think the goddamn fuckin' recorder is fixed," he says in a voice taut with anger. This outburst ends the moment he sees his temper pushing the needles into the red zone. "I'm not too pissed off or any-thing," he adds hastily. "It's just that I'm sorta wimped."

Mostly, Brian was impatient to get back to his music, where he could always attract a crowd, and they would always expect him to be the quarterback. As the Wollensak tapes reveal, Brian liked nothing more than to gather his friends around the piano. He leads spirited, if ragged, sing-alongs of "Sloop John B." and the hymn "Good News," the music often breaking down into self-conscious giggles, flirtatious asides, or both, between the girls and guys gathered around the piano. Later, with just the boys, Brian sings lead on endless takes of the jokey "Bermuda Shorts," taking it seriously enough to snort angrily when the final take falls apart: "What the hell!" Given the authority music gave him among his high school friends, Brian made singing an increasingly public part of his persona. At lunch he'd grab a few friends and sit in the corner of the cafeteria, leading them in schoolboy ditties such as the aforementioned "Bermuda Shorts," "Larry, Larry, Dingleberry," or the latest Kingston Trio tune. Most often he'd harmonize with Keith Lent, Robin Hood, and a few other friends from the senior class. But if Brian tended to find his singing partners among the set of popular jocks he socialized with, friendship and status mattered less to him than singing on key. So when a short, stocky underclassman named Bruce Griffin stepped up out of the crowd and added his voice to the mix, Brian smiled, nodded, and beckoned him into the inner circle. "That was the democratizing aspect of music," Griffin says now. "You could just walk up and sing, and they'd accept you if you could harmonize. Then Brian kind of adopted me."

By the start of his senior year, Brian was ready to make his music even more public. When Carol Hess, a popular girl in his social set, ran for commissioner of the student government, Brian worked with Keith Lent to adapt "Hully Gully" into a campaign song, which they performed with Robin Hood and Bruce Griffin at an all-school assembly: *We need a new commissioner, and what is her name?/Carol, Carol Hess/Ask the student body and they'll tell you the same/ Carol, Carol Hess/She's ready and she's willing and she's able, too/Seniors vote for*

Carol, Juniors vote for Carol/Sophomores and freshmen, too . . ."

The tune earned an ovation from their fellow students, encouraging Brian to sign up to sing for the multigenerational crowd that would flock to the fall arts program held in the evening in the Hawthorne High auditorium. Signing up Hood, Griffin, and his cousin Mike as partners, Brian worked up renditions of Dion and the Belmonts' "To Spend One Night with You" and, far more ambitiously, the Four Freshmen's "It's a Blue World," a jazz song with long stretches of unaccompanied harmonies, the voices sliding from one augmented minor chord to the next. Figuring "Blue World" would allow him to show off his arranging skills, Brian pushed his friends to master the hairpin turns of the convoluted song. The challenge proved too steep for Hood, who abandoned the group at the last minute ("I can't sing!" he wailed, piteously), thus impelling Brian to rename his group Carl and the Passions in order to convince less-than-eager younger brother Carl to step in. Unfortunately, Hood's anxiety was well placed. The group stumbled so badly in those first bars of "Blue World" that the audience actually laughed.

As focused as Brian was on the performance, the laughter coming from the auditorium didn't seem to register in his mind. But when he and Lent took a moment to help another student's mom change a flat in the school parking lot and the best she could say about his performance was, "Well, at least you tried," Brian's face reddened and his jaw fell open. "He took it so seriously, he was really crushed," Lent recalls. And no matter how much acclaim his music would gain in the next few decades, the echo of those laughs continued to haunt him.

Still, the performance made a lasting impact on Al Jardine, another Hawthorne High senior and aspiring musician who was watching from the audience. Al already knew Brian from the Cougar football team—he was a halfback whose career ended, as legend has it, thanks to a broken leg suffered on a broken play following a sloppy pitch-out from QB Brian Wilson. But this was the first time Al had glimpsed Brian's prowess as a singer and arranger. "That was also the first time I ever saw Carl Wilson," Al recalls. "This short, pudgy kid with a guitar who didn't even look like a high school student. Later I found out he was Brian's baby brother." Another scion of a musical family from the Midwest (he was born in Lima, Ohio), Al played guitar and had already teamed up with his pals Gary Winfrey and Bob Barrow in a folk-inspired group he called the Tikis, then the Islanders. But Jardine remembered Brian's group and figured that if he ever ran into him again, they should make a point of singing together.

Brian continued to focus on his music, too. At school he took classes in position and harmony, soaking up the basics of notation and orchestration even as he ignored his teachers' admonitions to avoid the guttural sounds of rock 'n' roll. Outside the classroom Brian took every opportunity to perform, harmonizing with his friends in the lunchroom, banging out boogie-woogie tunes for his friends at parties (though, as Bruce Griffin discovered, Brian took immediate and vocal exception if someone's piano was out of tune), and turning casual after-school get-togethers into recitals of pop and gospel favorites. Now old enough to explore the local music scene, Brian led friends on expeditions to see local surf guitar phenom Dick Dale, and he made solitary pilgrimages to the resort hotels of Catalina Island to see the Four Freshmen.

Eager to show off his ever-developing skills, Brian worked with his core group of singers—some combination of Hood, Griffin, Keith Lent, and Mike Love, with occasional assists from Carl—to polish a small repertoire of popular Kingston Trio and R & B tunes, with the now-mastered vocal gymnastics of the Freshmen's "It's a Blue World" serving as a romantic showstopper. As the summer shifted the focus of South Bay teen life away from the local schools and toward the beach, the group plied their tunes at the bigger beach parties and the regular talent shows held at the Hermosa Biltmore Hotel, whose airy, weather-worn ballroom catered to the younger set. "This was just fun for us; we never talked about doing it for a living," Hood remembers. But that didn't mean Brian and particularly his ambitious older cousin weren't thinking more enterprising thoughts.

In fact, Mike was even more desperate than Brian to turn their pop music avocation into a career. Years of indifferent effort in school had left him, after graduating from Dorsey High in the spring of 1959, with no prospects beyond the menial job he had at his father's sheet metal company and a nighttime gig pumping gas at a nearby service station. Barely able to support himself, Mike's resources were stretched beyond the breaking point when his girlfriend became pregnant in the fall of 1960. Word of the mishap—and Mike's plan to sneak off to Tijuana for a quick abortion—leaked to her parents, who stormed up to the Loves' house to demand Mike do right by their eighteen-year-old daughter. Milton and Glee agreed that Mike should do the honorable thing and marry her. But that didn't mean Glee was going to abide anything about his behavior.

Once the placated parents had driven away, Glee stormed up to her eldest son's bedroom and set methodically to throwing his things out of the window. "I came home from school, and all his clothes were on the porch," Maureen says. "She had thrown them out in a rage. It had always been tense with them, with his sneaking and lying and cheating. And pregnancy was just so shameful back then. I remember thinking, 'Oh my God, if we cross Mother, this is what happens?' Stephen and I came in at the same time and saw what had happened, and I think it affected Stephen permanently. I can't imagine how horrible it was for Mike." These days, Mike just shrugs it off. "Yeah, she threw my stuff out of the window. It didn't help the typewriter." His girlfriend was a lovely girl, he says. They enjoyed each other's company, and nature took its course. "There was a little trauma at first, but I understood why Mom was upset, so I wasn't mad at her. I moved to a small apartment and it was fine. I kept working."

Yet the episode still seems to trouble Milton Love. "It seemed harsh to me. But what the hell are you gonna do?" he says. "She was in charge; I wasn't. That's why I married her. I'm a wuss. And fortunately some wusses marry very domineering, active women. It worked out great for us. But I don't think Michael has ever had the measure of love for his mother after that that all the other kids had." But the familial rejection didn't just come from his mother. Mike had taken some measure of security in his job at Love Sheet Metal, particularly after his child was born. But when his outside interests and particularly a suddenly burgeoning music career disrupted Mike's attendance, Milton Love responded the only way he knew how. "I fired him, hell yeah. And he didn't take it very well," he says. "It'll hurt anyone's feelings, if you're human at all, when you get fired. But he still speaks to me."

As it turned out, Milton's anxiety about Mike's absences stemmed from the overwhelming financial problems the company was having. Within months, Love Sheet Metal would collapse from a crushing debt, an event that swept the Loves from their custom-built Spanish home in an elegant neighborhood to a moribund house in a rough section of Inglewood bordering the Los Angeles airport. "It was a two-bedroom house with an enclosed patio area where Stanley and Steve slept, which was pretty cold in the wintertime," Maureen remembers. "But we already had three of us in my bedroom, in this tiny little room. I remember Dad borrowed some money from my puny bank account. I can only imagine how horrible it must have been for him to come to the kids to see if they had any money."

Doubly humiliated and determined to reclaim the affirmation and love he'd enjoyed during his varsity track days at Dorsey High, Mike lobbied his cousin to follow the example of local up-and-comers Jan and Dean—a couple of college kids who recorded in their garage—and turn themselves into a pop act. Meanwhile, as Brian started first-year classes in music and psychology at El Camino Junior College, he finally ran into Al Jardine, who was still eager to sing with him and just as determined to chase a career in music. Meeting Hood and a few other friends in the school nurse's office (where the echo was particularly sweet), the gang would sing their songs, debate the merits of the tunes already on the charts, and gab wistfully about how they might get there themselves. When Brian and Mike got together in the evenings, they'd continue the conversation. Guys all over L.A. were getting into rock 'n' roll and making a fortune—what did those guys have that they didn't? All they needed was something to sing about.

If eighteen-year-old Brian wasn't quite sure about what to do with his life, at least he had it in his mind to do something. Dennis, on the other hand, seemed determined to do as little as possible. The years of Murry's unrelenting authority had turned him knotty and emotionally stilted—a restless, unfocused adolescent as prone to misbehavior as he was to a puppylike craving for affection. Always eager to ditch school, Dennis wandered frequently to the nearby beaches, where he had fallen in with the surfers who wandered from break to break in search of the day's best waves. Drawn to the formless, bohemian life they led—and delighted to indulge in the booze, marijuana, and easygoing women they always seemed to have at hand—Dennis convinced Murry to spot him the money for a board, and soon he became a regular fixture among the itinerant beach bums of the South Bay beaches that stretched beneath central Los Angeles. Soon he'd come home bearing the scars and salt-blond hair of a habitual surfer, talking easily in their slang about how this new sport would quickly sweep across the entire West Coast. Dennis was so completely in the thrall of the surfing life in the summer of 1961 that when he heard his big brother musing about the challenge of finding something new to write a pop song about, he quickly blurted out a piece of advice: "You oughta write about surfing!" Why, he'd even write down a few of the coolest words and make a list of the best surfing spots, if that would help . . .

It wasn't the first time the idea had come up. Robin Hood recalls a parody version of "The Stroll" Brian wrote well before the summer of 1961 that traded out the Diamonds' dance lyrics with surfer's slang. But that was just a schoolboy gag composed for a laugh. This time around, Brian took the idea far more seriously. He called his cousin to set up a writing session, during which Brian pounded out an original Chuck Berry–style three-chord tune. Meanwhile,

Mike—who also knew a thing or two about surfing—scratched out some words about life on the beach, starting with the morning surf report heard on the radio and ending with the late-night parties at which the surfers and their honeys cranked up the radio and kicked up clouds of sand doing the surfer stomp, because, as it turns out, *It's the latest dance craze!* The chorus boiled everything down to a simple assertion that in two sharply composed lines elevated surfing from a mere sport into something closer to a belief system: *"Surfin' is the only life, the only way for me/So surf! Surf! With me!"*

Just about the same time Brian and Mike were pounding out their tune, aspiring folkie Al Jardine was following Murry's advice and looking in on Hite and Dorinda Morgan at their offices on Melrose Avenue in Los Angeles. The mom-and-pop song publishers had bought a few of the elder Wilson's tunes, and they always had an eye out for interesting new acts. Jardine's folk trio hadn't impressed them very much—they were so much like every other folk group already out there, for one thing. But they liked his sharp voice and assertive spirit, so when he returned in late August in the company of Brian, Carl, Dennis, and Mike, they agreed to listen to the new group's arrangements of popular rock and pop tunes. Once again, the Morgans liked the singing, but, as before, they were looking for something a bit more original. Didn't these kids have anything new to offer? Some new fad all their friends were talking about that had yet to end up in a pop song? "How about surfing?" Dennis chimed in. Before long he was on a tear, going on about how huge the sport was becoming and how everyone listened to the surf report in the morning and planned their days according to the size and location of the best waves. Sensing the Morgans' piqued interest, he ended with the capper: "Brian already has a song called 'Surfin'"! We could practice it for you and come back!"

The Morgans took them up on the offer, and eager to get going, the boys returned to Hawthorne. Happily, Murry and Audree had already planned to spend Labor Day weekend in Mexico City with some friends, leaving their sons with a refrigerator stocked with food and a pile of cash to use in case of emergency. When that didn't prove to be enough to rent the microphone, amp, and stand-up bass they needed, Al took Brian, Carl, Dennis, and Mike over to his parents' house to appeal directly to his mother, Virginia. "We had to sing the song for her," Al recalls. "We had to show her what we were all about. So we were sitting on the living room floor in a little circle—we didn't have enough chairs, I think, which is kinda quaint. But she liked 'Surfin',' and she really liked 'Our

Hearts Were Full of Spring.' That was the one we always pulled out when we needed to knock someone out." Virginia Jardine dug into her purse and found $300 ("Probably a month's salary," he says), and then Al took Brian to the music store on Hawthorne Boulevard, where he knew they could rent a stand-up bass, and they were in business.

The five boys spent the next two days in the Wilsons' music room working out the kinks in the lyrics, structure, and harmonies of "Surfin'" and were in fact still hard at it when the elder Wilsons returned from Mexico, surprising the five boys in midrehearsal.

Murry was furious, flying into a rage the moment he figured out how his sons had used his emergency money. "Just listen, Dad! Listen!" Brian cried, peeling himself from the living room wall Murry had hurled him against. The boys picked up the instruments, Brian gave a quick count-in, and they started singing: *"Surfin' is the only life, the only way for me . . ."* The old man's beefy red face went slack. He listened. He nodded. When it was over, his mood had shifted considerably. "I remember him being excited," Al says. "He was impressed with our performance, and he saw a lot of potential there." The tune, Murry decreed, was rude and crude, not nearly as sophisticated as the sort of stuff he did . . . but maybe that's what sells now. "You could record that," he concluded.

At this point the rehearsals turned serious. And now that Murry had declared himself the group's manager, his first point of order was to declare the group a family business. "Everyone else will screw you over," he reasoned. Which meant Brian's bandmates would include Carl, obviously, and Mike. Dennis could be in too, despite his previous disinterest in singing (or doing anything) seriously, because he was family and because—as Audree pointed out—the song *had* been his idea. Brian's regular singing partners from high school need not apply. Same deal for neighborhood pal David Marks, even though he played a decent guitar and had been a regular in the Wilson music room for years. So strict was Murry's family-only edict, in fact, that even Alan Jardine was dealt out of the band just after the seminal Labor Day weekend get-together. The break was so short-lived that Al didn't know about it until the spring of 2005. "I got kicked out of the band, and I didn't even know it!" he marveled. "Thanks, Uncle Murry!" But Brian (who confirmed the whole story) soon convinced his father that Al was too strong a singer and musician to live without. "He lost that battle," Brian says ruefully. But it's intriguing to note how the roots of the group's decades-long struggles for power and control predate all but its first semiofficial rehearsal.

The seeds for much of what was to come can be heard in a rehearsal taped on Brian's Wollensak sometime in early September 1961, between the Labor Day weekend get-together and the group's first recording session with the Morgans on the fifteenth. The session begins with a few random noises—Brian checking the levels, dropping something ("awww shit"), and then doing a brief count-in to the song. Then Mike leans into his bass part—"bom, bom, dip-duh-dip-duh-dip"— soon to be joined by the others in a shaky, off-kilter major seventh triad chant of "surfin', surfin'." They're raw at first, their voices still seeking their place in the blend. But all those nights of singing in bed gave the brothers an easy vocal rapport, and it doesn't take long for their voices to fall in line. After a few minutes Audree walks in the door with a friend and her junior high–aged son, who gapes at what he sees unfolding before him.

"You guys wrote that song by yourself?" he asks in a voice thick with adolescent incredulity. "You think it'll make good?"

At that point they could only hope—and bicker about who really wrote the lyrics to the song they had already credited to just Brian and Mike, because as Dennis bitterly pointed out, "We all wrote a tremendous amount of words!" Mike didn't deny it ("yeah, we did"), but he didn't entertain the subject either. "We shouldn't even sweat it, 'cause it's gonna be a big flop the way we're goin' now!" (Indeed, songwriting credits were a lawsuit for another day.) Brian cut off the debate, asking, "Look, who's boss? Me! Now, sing out naturally. Don't hold back! Step back if you come in too strong."

The singing gets tighter on the tape, the background chorus snapping together into a sharply defined chord. Brian cut off the next attempt, offended by the absence of *excitement* in the backing oohs and aahs. "Sing out regularly; stand with your hands on your hips and you'll get a lot more breathing," he instructs. All these intricacies bored hyperactive Dennis, who not only made a point of burping into the microphone but also decided to make some mysterious off-mike display that prompted Brian to howl angrily—"Aw, DON'T! Dennis! Please don't!"—before losing his patience and threatening to dump his middle brother from the group altogether. "I'm not kidding! I'll get Alan Jardine!"

"I get the hiccups and you kick me out?" Dennis protests, his feelings wounded.

"You get the hiccups, and you don't sing the words, *and* you geek us out!" Mike says in a voice less aggrieved than that of the still-seething Brian, who obviously has had enough of his brother's antics.

"As soon as you start screwin' up or laughing, we'll pull the goddamn mike out and we'll quit. You got it? As soon as you start laughing, we'll pull the mike out!"

Brian then signals Carl, who starts strumming his guitar, and Mike gets back into the *Bop-bop-dip-duh-dips*. The four of them huddle up to the microphone again, and their voices together spin their tale about life on the beach and the challenge of the waves.

Not long after that, they performed the song in the recording studio, along with "Luau," a vaguely "Tequila"-like Hawaiian-themed party song composed by the Morgans' son Bruce, as a B-side. The song was released on December 8 on the local Candix label, credited not to the Pendletones (the band name they'd chosen as a tip of the hat to the Pendleton wool shirts favored by surfers) but to the Beach Boys (a more commercial name for a surfing band, according to the label). But whatever disappointment this last-second change caused gave way instantly to the thrill of hearing their voices echoing from cars and beach parties all over Los Angeles. This in turn was dwarfed by the even larger thrill of seeing "Surfin'" rise to the number two slot on the local charts and, thanks to sales of 50,000 units in the southlands, the number seventy-five spot on *Billboard*'s national charts.

Now it was happening for real. Brian dropped out of El Camino and begged Murry to help the group strengthen their foothold in the local music business. They played a few tentative shows that winter and girded to climb even higher. They didn't know where they were going, exactly. But they were moving, and that was the important thing.

CHAPTER 3

They were away from Hawthorne. Away from school, away from work, away from their parents and the expectations of the past. Freed from the failures and resentments of their parents, beyond their punishments, insults, and abuses.

Is that what they felt in the summer of 1962? We can only imagine now, looking at a picture of five young men perched on an old yellow pickup truck on a California beach. But what we know, looking at the cover of *Surfin' Safari*, is that they are Beach Boys now, dressed up in matching blue Pendleton button-ups, white T-shirts, and worn khakis. They're all barefoot as well, fingers pointing to the horizon as the two sitting on top of the truck grasp a single yellow-and-blue-striped surfboard.

> *Let's go surfin' now*
> *Everybody's learning how*
> *Come on and safari with me . . .*

The first song on the first side of their first album didn't tell a literal truth about the lives of the young men singing it—no one save the drummer was ever likely to go surfing with anyone at any time under any circumstances—but there's truth in the voices. It crackled through the guitars and drums, and in 1962 it spoke not just to kids in Los Angeles, but also in hundreds of far-flung, landlocked cities. None of those kids would ever know how it feels to be anglin' at Laguna and Cerro Azul or kickin' out in Doheny too. But when they listened to the Beach Boys and saw their faces on the album cover, they could feel the cool light of the morning and sense the thrill of paddling across black water into a mysterious horizon.

In the first months of 1962, Brian Wilson and the Beach Boys lugged their guitars and drums to school assemblies and Saturday night hops, played for free at Saturday afternoon beach parties put on by radio stations, and sang again and again that *surfin' is the only life, the only way for me,* trying to sing on key without screwing up the words, and all the while hoping that no one would laugh at their matching suits and schoolboy harmonies. Sometimes they'd be so scared that Dennis would thrash wildly on his drums, while Carl's fingers found all the wrong notes on the neck of his guitar. Brian's voice squeaked and shrilled, while Mike stood stiffly at his microphone, hands hanging dead at his side. Eventually, though, they relaxed and were able to stand in a spotlight and still feel like themselves. Still, by the end of the winter, "Surfin'" had faded from the charts; nothing else seemed to be happening; and it was far too easy to imagine that their ride was over. They'd captured their one moment, and it seemed like it had come and gone.

But they weren't about to give up. Brian was too absorbed in his music to think of anything else, and Mike didn't have anything better to do, so they sat down to write another tune, figuring they might as well take another shot at the surf music crowd. They came up with "Surfin' Safari" and were still working out the arrangement with the other guys in the Wilsons' music room when another aspiring twenty-year-old musician named Gary Usher, in Hawthorne to visit his grandparents, happened down the street and heard the music. Attracted by the sounds, Usher knocked on the door to say hello. Brian sat at the organ while they talked, and twenty minutes later he and Usher had written "Lonely Sea," a pensive ballad that gave the group's standard maritime imagery a darker, even existential, cast. Usher was a car nut too, and his lectures about the superiority of Chevrolet's 409 engine inspired another song. They got so excited by that one that they dragged Brian's Wollensak out to the street (a couple of extension cords did the trick) to capture the sound of Usher roaring up and down 119th Street in his car. Unfortunately, it was well past midnight at the time, and the neighbors weren't pleased.

Murry, for once, wasn't upset. The local success of "Surfin'" proved that Brian was onto something, and so even if he didn't approve of the rock scene or understand the appeal of silly surfin' tunes, he took out a mortgage on A.B.L.E. Machinery and pushed his boys onward, paying for studio time to record demos of Brian's new songs. When Candix fell into bankruptcy—due partially to the steep capital demands that came along with having an unexpected hit single—Murry found an escape clause in the group's contract and prepared to leverage his boys into a better deal. From there he got on the phone and talked his way into the Capitol Tower in Hollywood, ending up in the office of a junior A and R guy at Capitol Records named Nick Venet, who only had to get through the first verse and chorus of "Surfin' Safari" to understand that he was listening to a hit song. The rumbling, roaring hot rod tune "409" hit him even harder, and by the end of the day, Murry and Brian walked out with a major label contract and another, even better shot at success.

The Capitol execs tapped "409" as the A-side of a new Beach Boys single, figuring that "Surfin' Safari" would appeal only to the beachside crowd that had bought "Surfin'." But once the disc jockeys in Phoenix heard the B-side, they flipped the record over and put it in heavy rotation. The New York jocks did the same, and when their listeners caught on, the rest of the nation followed suit. By the end of the summer, "Surfin' Safari" had climbed all the way into the Top Fifteen of *Billboard*'s singles chart.

So maybe surfing music wasn't just a regional fad after all. Riding high on "Surfin' Safari's" coast-to-coast popularity, the group set to work on their first full-length album, compiling the A- and B-sides of the first two singles with a couple of covers (including Eddie Cochrane's hit "Summertime Blues"), an instrumental or two, and a handful of new Brian Wilson originals. As performed by the road-tested band, the songs on the album they called *Surfin' Safari* make for a fairly standard collection of mainstream rock 'n' roll, set against a distinctly suburban backdrop of county fairs, drive-ins, and California beaches. And yet there's something plaintive and weird about it, too: "County Fair," for instance, turns a standard evening on the local midway into a failed test of manhood that ends with our hero losing his girl to a muscle-bound jerk who can actually ring the Test-Your-Strength bell. *"I don't need you anymore, loser!"* the girl's voice calls out across the guitars as the song fades. "Cuckoo Clock" tells another tale of romantic frustration, set this time in a suburban living room decorated with a cuckoo clock that tends to erupt just when the teenaged swain is making his move. Brian's falsetto approximates the bird's cries of *Cuc-koo! Cuc-koo!* in the chorus, reputedly mimicking an actual mynah bird Murry kept in his family's living room during the Wilson boys' teenage years.

Surfin' Safari also included the band's third single, "Ten Little Indians," a rocked-up take on the nursery rhyme that owes more than a little to "Running Bear," Johnny Preston's chart-topping Native American novelty tune from 1960 (which Brian liked enough to cover during sessions in 1976). But that attempt to look backward at the Old West barely dented the top fifty at the end of 1962. Though that commercial backslide caused no small amount of consternation for Murry and the rest of the group, Brian had already hatched an idea for a new surfing song that excited him even more than "Surfin' Safari." It all began when he heard the first verse of Chuck Berry's "Sweet Little Sixteen" and started thinking about how the song's quick references to cities across the country—Boston, Pittsburgh, San Francisco—transformed the tale of an imaginary teenybopper into a national rallying cry. In one sense, the civic name-checks were almost entirely gratuitous. But then again, they made the story universal, as if the exploits of these characters could happen—*were* happening—everywhere at the same time. So if you could make one teenager represent teens all across the nation, why couldn't one sport become an emblem for fun everywhere? Equipped with a list of surfing terms and locations from a young surfer named Jimmy Bowles—the baby brother of his new girlfriend, Judy Bowles—Brian set to work in the family music room, pounding out the chords on Murry's upright piano as he coalesced the strands of surf, St. Louis R & B, and western utopianism into a call to arms that transformed surfing from a physical act with strict geographic limitations into a metaphorical one available to anyone, anywhere, at any time.

As every multiculti note of "Surfin' USA" implied, having a beach at your doorstep wasn't what mattered. Surfing itself was a veneer, a modern pastime laid across the same longing that had called all American adventurers out into the frontier. The song's chorus pushed the point home, riding Brian's rocketing falsetto toward the song's climax. Everybody, in their own hearts, can go surfing—"Surfin' USA."

By now even the Capitol Records execs were starting to believe it. Released at the start of spring 1963, "Surfin' USA" catapulted up the *Billboard* charts, claiming the number three slot. Disc jockey enthusiasm for "Shut Down," the drag race anthem on the flip side, sent that song into the top twenty-five, and by the time school let out for summer, the Beach Boys were the most popular band in the United States of America.

Even if they didn't really surf themselves, living in Hawthorne put Brian and company in close contact with the kind of surf rats who, like Dennis once did, projected their entire lives into the currents of beach life. So even if it wasn't their lives, exactly, it was happening all around them. Thus, "Surfin' Safari," like "Surfin'," captured the rhythms of Los Angeles beach life, from the early morning surf reports on KFWB-AM to the late-night dance parties on the sand. And the band's subsequent songs described the scene in even more detail, from the huarache sandals to the "bushy bushy" blond hairstyle the surfers preferred, the calluses (surfer's knots) they developed from the hours spent paddling through the waves, and the woody station wagons that were big enough to carry pals and their boards to whichever secret, locals-only cove had the best break that day.

Like the members of all-exclusive, self-selecting subcultures, the surfers developed a language that was distinctive to the point of being incomprehensible. In the course of ordinary affairs, surfers spoke of going on safaris. They flirted with honeys and turned their noses up at hodads. On the water, they angled and kicked out, walked the nose and shot the pier. To catch a big one—the true purpose of any surfer boy—was to be the Number One Man. To fail meant risking the pain and humiliation of body whop.

This was cutting edge to the vast majority of the world in 1962, and surf culture would only become more prevalent as the boards themselves became lighter, cheaper, and more widely available around the coastal towns of both the West and East Coasts. Still, the literal act of surfing was far less important to the (non-surfing) Beach Boys than the feelings evoked in the journey to the waves: the friendships, the sense of liberation, the [mere] pursuit of inspiration. *"It's a genuine fact that the surfers rule!"* they sang, but not because anyone's ability to ride the waves on a board mattered to them. On the contrary—it was the journey that mattered. *"Don't be afraid to try the greatest sport around!"* they chimed. *"Catch a wave and you're sittin' on top of the world."*

The idea seduced young Americans all over the country, which seems surprising until you realize how familiar a notion it was. This same kind of hardy American story had been written a thousand times before, set on whaling ships, on rafts floating down the Mississippi, or on the backs of horses galloping into the untamed frontier. "It was rough living in the house all the time, considering how dismal regular and decent the old widow was in all her ways; and so when I couldn't stand it no longer I lit out," Huckleberry Finn declared in *The Adventures of Huckleberry Finn,* Mark Twain's epochal 1885 novel. And no matter how much the world would change in the intervening years, young Americans kept yearning to light out for uncharted territory. The paths changed to suit the times—Herman Melville's whaling ship gave way in turn to Twain's river raft, Hemingway's grand adventures, Kerouac's highway, Elvis's southern-fried sexiness, and the lysergic meanderings of the Grateful Dead. But the impulse to break free from buttoned-down society remained precisely the same.

Granted, the Beach Boys of the early '60s, resplendent in their matching striped shirts, neat haircuts, rigorously structured harmonies, and consuming fascination for food, girls, and cars—the faster the better, on all accounts—may not seem like cultural revolutionaries. Indeed, while Mark Twain consciously used the journey down the Mississippi and Huck's relationship with the escaped slave Jim to work through America's seemingly intractable problems of racism and cultural divide, the Beach Boys' songs don't ask their characters to confront serious hardship or make any sort of moral choice. They are utopians, after all, determined to describe and celebrate the laid-back, sun-splashed, middle-class world of ease their fathers and grandfathers had envisioned on their slow journey west. Now the journey was over; paradise platted out, subdivided, and built; its clean, wide streets teeming with tall, blond, athletic guys and the blue-eyed cheerleaders who admired them.

Nevertheless, the group, and particularly Brian, confronted their own challenges on the road to the horizon. Al Jardine bailed from the group at the end of the school year in 1962, heading off to Michigan to pursue a pharmacy degree at Ferris University in Grand Rapids. The group tapped Carl's guitar-playing pal David Marks to take Al's place, but he was young and obnoxious and spent most of his time aggravating Murry. "I was kind of a cocky kid," David says. "But he was always turning my amp down, putting treble on it, telling me to smile. Just kind of cramping my style." The mood became even more tense in the recording studio. "There were constant arguments over what sound to put on the instruments," David continues. "Murry wanted to produce, and he didn't trust the fact that Brian was perfectly capable of doing it himself. But I have to admit that if Murry hadn't been so adamant about that twangy, tinny guitar sound, those early records would never have sounded like that. Our guitar sound was really his doing."

The group's first extended concert tour through the Midwest was an exhausting chain of state fairs and small-town VFW halls, with the entire group, plus Murry, riding together in one station wagon. And though Mike and Brian were in their twenties and the rest of the guys in their late teens, Murry rode herd over them like a Boy Scout leader, rigidly enforcing the rules he'd established to keep the boys polite, disciplined, and out of trouble. Already pushed to the brink by the responsibilities of writing and recording and never an eager public performer, Brian's hatred of touring with his father in tow was only too obvious. He'd kept in touch with Al Jardine through the year, and he called him back to take his place for the group's summer tour in 1963. "It must have been a pressure cooker for him," Al says. "One can only imagine what his relationship with his dad must have been like, what it's like to have a dad trying to mold your entire existence."

After Murry managed to convince the Capitol executives to give up full control over the producer's chair, Brian—already the Beach Boys' chief songwriter, arranger, and co–lead singer—took on unprecedented authority over his band's musical output. "He was obsessed with it," David Marks recalls. "Brian was writing songs with people off the street in front of his house, disc jockeys, anyone. He had so much stuff flowing through him at once he could hardly handle it." Most often Brian used his collaborators to detail his fantasies of the wide-open world beyond the borders of the life his father had delineated for him. But he also wrote songs that were far more personal, revealing hints about the real life that inspired him to write such dreamy portraits of the far horizon.

"In My Room," written with Gary Usher just after Brian's twenty-first birthday, described his emotional escape in terms of the bedroom he'd once shared with his brothers. There, with the door shut and their father off in his own corner of the house, Brian had been free to be himself: listening to the Four Freshmen, obsessing over his latest crush, taping himself and his brothers as they sang. *"Do my dreaming, and my scheming . . ."* It could be the story of any teenager's inner life. But more than anything, "In My Room" described Brian's emotional interaction with *music,* which had always been his most private place, sometimes the only thing he had that felt truly safe. The significance he attaches to both the memory of his childhood respite and the one he carries with him into adulthood could be heard in the hymnlike meter of "In My Room" and its spare, elegant vocal arrangement. Though Brian and the group would perform the song with typical fresh-faced ease, armed with their immaculately white Fender guitars and their matching striped shirts, the implications of what waited outside his bed-room door *("Now it's dark and I'm alone . . .")* rang just as clear as the angelic falsetto that wards it off in the song's last refrain, a repetition of the title: *"In my rooooooom!"*

The escape and release Brian found in music inspired him to work nearly nonstop. He wrote and recorded not just for the Beach Boys, but also for an array of other bands ranging from established hit-makers like Jan and Dean (who rode "Surf City" to the very top of the *Billboard* charts just before "Surfin' USA" broke through) to friends like Bob Norberg, his roommate, who recorded with a girlfriend under the name Bob and Sheri, and a group called Rachel and the Revolvers. But even if the tunes he wrote for other acts (such as "Number One," "The Beginning of the End," and "After the Game") were fairly standard early '60s pop fare, light on musical innovation and heavy on teenaged melodrama, Brian's outside interests struck Murry as a betrayal. Usher's obvious contempt for Murry's musical ideas only made things worse, and so the Wilson patriarch maneuvered his son's collaborator out of the picture, nitpicking him over song credits and haranguing him about the quality of his work until Usher had finally had enough. If Brian was frustrated by his father's intervention into his creative life, he didn't have the courage to defy his father to his face. And when Murry told Brian he might want him to write some tunes with Roger Christian, a popu-lar Los Angeles disc jockey whom Murry had met, Brian did precisely that. As it turned out, that wasn't a bad match, either.

Murry first became interested in Christian when he tuned into the dj's nine-to-midnight show on the popular rock station KFWB-AM and heard him analyz-ing the Beach Boys' latest single, "409." "I said it's a great song about a poor car!" Christian recalled in a 1976 interview with Martin Grove. "I was explaining the lyrics about four-speed, dual quad, positraction because somebody had called up and said he couldn't understand what they were singing." Murry put a call into the station, and when it turned out that Christian kept a journal of car-based writings and poems, he got the disc jockey's number and said his eldest son would be call-ing. A few nights later, Brian drove up to Hollywood to meet Christian after his show ended, and they went together to eat hot fudge sundaes and flip through the journal of car writings the disc jockey had been keeping. Brian's eyes kept coming back to a few lines Christian had written about a street race between a Corvette and a Dodge 413. *"It happened on the street where the road is wide/Two cool sharks standing side by side . . ."* Soon Brian had a tune running through his mind, and before long he had an entire song, titled "Shut Down," for the Beach Boys to record at their next session. Better yet, he had another collaborator to help him focus and harness his overwhelming musical energy.

Most often they met just after midnight, when Christian's radio show ended. Often they'd go back to the same café for sundaes, talking first about the latest songs Christian had been playing on the air and what directions they might open up for Brian to explore with the Beach Boys. Then they'd break out Christian's notebook and either flip around in search of a likely phrase or two or try to come up with a poetic way to express something they'd already been talking about. Other times, Christian would come in with a completed lyric. "I'd try to come up with a story lyric, and I'd also have a rough idea for a melody, which Brian would promptly dismiss," Christian told Grove. "Sometimes he would improve on a lyric . . . just phrasing them so they'd sing a little better." And though it was Christian's expertise with automotive jargon that endeared him to Murry and then Brian, he also proved to have an excellent sense of narrative, filling racing tales such as "Little Deuce Coupe" and "Spirit of America" with vivid feelings of confidence, doubt, and excitement.

Nearly two decades older than Brian, a family man with a far more adult perspective on the world, Christian also became a reliable friend and mentor for the young musician. He listened to Brian's rants about his father and confessions of his own stage fright and romantic insecurities, using both of those themes as the inspiration for "Don't Worry, Baby," in which talk of an impending drag race all but vanishes beneath the seething anxiety of its performance-phobic narrator, which seems to have very little to do with the drag race the narrator claims to be concerned about. The earlier verses contrasted the narrator's lust for his girl—*"She makes me come alive"*—with his fears regarding the power of his car: *"I guess I should have kept my mouth shut when I started to brag about my car . . ."* But while his lover keeps telling him not to worry, her reassurances lead to the sexual encounter in the final verse and the intriguing reversal in the transitive verb that describes it. *She's* making love to *him,* which implies a sexual assertiveness (if not quite aggressiveness) that the narrator won't, or can't, claim for himself.

Romantic love never came easily to Brian. His relationship with Judy Bowles waxed and waned throughout 1962 and 1963, ending when he presented her with an engagement ring, which she refused to accept. Heartbroken, he found himself increasingly drawn to Marilyn Rovell, a fourteen-year-old high school student and singer he had met a year earlier when she came with her big sister Diane—two-thirds of a Ronettes-like group they would come to call the Honeys, after the "honeys" described in the first verse of "Surfin' Safari"—to see the Beach Boys perform at Pandora's Box, a teen club on Sunset Boulevard. Brian had spilled a cup of cocoa on Marilyn earlier in the evening, but if that was intended as a seduction, it didn't work: Marilyn's first crush was on Carl, who was much closer to her own age. The Rovells returned to see several of the group's shows, and the whole gang soon became friends.

Invited to visit the girls at their parents' house in the largely Jewish neighborhood off Fairfax Avenue where they had grown up, Brian hit it off immediately with Irving Rovell, a sheet-metal worker whose nature was as gentle as Murry's was harsh. Irving's wife May was every bit as sweet, and when Brian started coming over regularly, she made a point of welcoming the young pop star with a homemade meal, no matter the time. Sometimes Brian would show up so late that May would just invite him to stay in a guest room rather than driving all the way back to his apartment. Those nights eventually came to outnumber the nights he actually did make it home, and then Brian seemed to be living at the Rovells', serving as a virtual big brother for Diane, Marilyn, and their thirteen-year-old sister, Barbara. Brian began to see the Rovell girls with different eyes. His first crush was on Diane, the more moody and independent of the sisters, but Marilyn had an uncomplicated sweetness that also appealed to him. They became lovers—seemingly with the knowledge and permission of Irving and May, who were sleeping under the same roof at the time. The Rovells' kindness, along with their daughter's loving infatuation, would become increasingly important to Brian as the months passed.

When it came to his music, Brian was always in control. Working on "Surfin' USA" on January 31, 1963, he figured out that double-tracking the vocals—recording them twice, the singers matching their previous performance as closely as possible, and then superimposing the tapes into one track—would give the harmonies a fullness and brightness that made them leap out of the speakers. He repeated the trick on the single's B-side, "Shut Down" (recorded on the same day), and vocal double-tracking would become a Beach Boys trademark. So too would his vocal arrangements, elaborate structures of melody and counterpoint that washed across the tracks.

One after another, the Beach Boys' singles scaled the upper reaches of the *Billboard* charts. "Surfer Girl" climbed to number seven; "Be True to Your School" went to number six; "Little Deuce Coupe" got to number fifteen. Each new hit increased the band's drawing power on the road. Then they met teenaged concert promoter Fred Vail in Sacramento in the spring of 1963. The ambitious youngster—who at one point hired the group to play a fundraiser for the senior class prom (tellingly, his percentage of the gate was more than what the group earned for headlining the show)—saw a rich opportunity. Obviously, the William Morris Agency didn't know what they had in the group, so Vail proposed that Murry bring him on as an in-house promoter, helping the group stage their own shows in cities their agent hadn't thought to open for them yet. Murry agreed, and soon Vail booked the group into dozens of markets. Most of the shows were triumphs for the increasingly confident band. "This was the greatest era. Before alcohol and drugs, before divorces and paternity suits," Vail recalls. "They were all healthy, all full of youthful optimism. Every show was an event, and they loved the way they went over with the kids."

Brian, just past his twenty-first birthday, reveled in his new authority as a hit-maker. He rented office space on a high floor of the Sunset-Vine tower in Hollywood and set up what amounted to a private workroom and clubhouse. Fred Vail, who visited often with various group-related contracts, schedules, and papers, recalls a utilitarian space with a little reception area with a couple of disused chairs. An interior door led into a tiny hallway, past a coffeemaker and supply closet to Brian's actual office. Small and mostly undecorated (in Vail's memory it doesn't even have a window, though Brian has described a sweeping view of Hollywood), the office had a leather armchair, a coffee table that held a telephone, and, against a far wall, an upright piano. "It was just a getaway for Brian," Vail says. "I came in once and he was working on this song—I'd done dozens of shows with him at this point—and Brian says, 'You know the parts; you do Carl's part.' He's making some notes, and I said, 'What's this song? It's great!' He said, 'Well, I'm gonna call it "Fun, Fun, Fun." ' "

Brian had taken over the production duties for the group's third album, *Surfer Girl* (released in September 1963), and the difference could be heard immediately. The title track, a delicate ballad that was actually the first song he had ever written (musing on Carol Mountain and the melody of "When You Wish upon a Star" while driving down Hawthorne Boulevard), simplified the Four Freshmen harmony, adding a striking emotional directness. "Little Deuce

Coupe," the group's first great car song, ran like a hand-built speedster, with its bluesy melody playing out across a loping honky-tonk rhythm. "Catch a Wave" added harp glissandos and the rinse cycle of chords on the chorus. The goofball surfin' travelogue "Hawaii" *("I've heard about all those purty girls/With the grass skirts down to their knees")* transcended its own sophomoric credulity with three tiers of interlocking harmony and a soaring falsetto line. Those advancements paled in comparison to "I Get Around" (a single from the spring of 1964, also released on *All Summer Long* in July), with its jarring rhythmic shifts, fuzz guitar, off-kilter organ riffs, and Brian's own wailing falsetto coming together to kick the tune into overdrive.

On his quieter, more lyrical songs, Brian crafted melodies that looped and soared, often visiting several keys on their journey from verse to chorus to bridge and back again. The melancholy ballad "The Warmth of the Sun," written in late 1963, had a midverse modulation from the key of C major to E-flat that would shock the ear had Brian not found a melody that stayed rooted in the song's initial key, even as the chords beneath it meander from one to the next.

Hal Blaine, for years the most prominent session drummer in all of Los Angeles, says it took a few months before anyone in his circuit of elite musicians began to notice the records the Beach Boys were making. "Brian was just a child, really, and we were seasoned studio musicians who played with everyone. Nobody was knocked out by surf music. Nobody imagined they were gonna be one of the biggest groups ever. But then we began to realize that the music—well, it was just incredible."

Brian was just as floored by the songs Phil Spector was making. He first noticed the young songwriter/producer (who graduated from University High School, the same West L.A. institution that produced Jan and Dean and future utility Beach Boy Bruce Johnston two years before Brian left Hawthorne High) when he hit the top of the *Billboard* charts with "To Know Him Is to Love Him" as part of the Teddy Bears in 1958. But Spector stepped back from the spotlight just after that, choosing instead to focus on writing and producing for a stable of singers he would cultivate and discard as needed. Brian's own attempts to build a stable of outside artists had, thus far, failed to generate any hits. But that disappointment did nothing to quell Brian's ambition. And if anything, it made his admiration of Spector even more intense, particularly in 1961 and 1962, when he noticed how the young producer was beginning to use the recording studio as an instrument unto itself.

It was the sound that did it for Brian: the thundering drums; the zooming bass; the rattling, jingling percussion; and the cavernous echo that both amplified and unified it all into a monolithic roar. Writers started calling it the "Wall of Sound," but to Brian that description barely did Spector justice. To him, it was a natural wonder. When the Ronettes' "Be My Baby" came out, the song became a kind of spiritual touchstone. Brian would put the single on his record player and turn it up until those echoing drums made the windows rattle in their frames. Then he'd stand facing the speakers, his eyes squeezed shut, feeling the notes beating against his face, pushing against his chest, and wrapping around him. The sound was so immense he felt he could climb inside it and vanish, just as he had fallen into the spiraling melody of "Rhapsody in Blue" as a toddler and the interlocking harmony of the Four Freshmen as a teenager. Even forty years later, Brian's eyes widen and his jaw drops open at the memory of Spector's classic sides. "That awesome sound," he says. "I loved those records. 'Zip a Dee Doo Dah,' 'The Boy I'm Going to Marry,' 'Wait 'til My Bobby Gets Home.' Loved them. *Loved them.*"

Loved them so much, in fact, that Brian made a point of working in the same Hollywood recording studios—Western Recorders, Gold Star, Columbia—where Spector preferred to work. Brian became a fixture at Spector's sessions, observing his idol construct his famous sonic wall brick by brick. "He'd just sit there quietly in the corner. We had no idea who he was," recalls Blaine, who coordinated the core group of session musicians Spector preferred to use, which eventually came to be known as the Wrecking Crew. Spector's vast sound required multiple drummers and percussionists, two bassists, two or three keyboard players, and up to a half dozen guitarists, plus entire sections of horns and strings. Brian would look on eagerly, watching how the maestro voiced the parts, how he arranged the players around the studio, where he set up the microphones, how he set the levels on the board.

Determined to incorporate Spector's sound into the Beach Boys' records, Brian started calling in more and more of Spector's crew to supplement his own sessions. At first he'd just bring in a couple of players to enhance his band's own workmanlike licks. Blaine, in particular, sat in regularly for Dennis on the drums, which didn't bother the middle Wilson brother in the least. ("Are you kidding?" Blaine says. "He'd rather be riding his motorbike or surfing.") On "Fun, Fun, Fun," Brian put a subtle but vital automotive roar into the tune by doubling the rhythm guitar chords with a line of baritone saxophones. A cover of "Why Do Fools Fall in Love?"—recorded a few days later—was even more explicitly Spector-esque, its sound thick with echoing vocals, multiple layers of percussion, and a full saxophone section. And though Spector rejected Brian's custom-written "Don't Worry, Baby" as a follow-up to "Be My Baby," Brian took the song back and recorded it for the *Shut Down, Volume 2* album as a virtual homage, complete with Spector's heavy drum intro and a fat echo on the vocals.

Spector, a neurotic control freak with well-documented problems regarding impulse control (he was charged with murder in 2003 after an actress was found shot to death inside his mansion), seemed less than delighted by his acolyte's affections. In fact, he took perverse pleasure in insulting Brian as often and as publicly as possible. For instance, when Brian submitted "Don't Hurt My Little Sister" to the Ronettes, Spector rewrote the tune from top to bottom, ultimately tossing Brian and Mike's lyrics in order to use them as a throwaway jingle called "Things Are Changing (for the Better)." Spector invited Brian to play piano on the session, but then he tossed the younger musician out of the studio for what he called his substandard playing.

The abuse did nothing to cool Brian's ardor. In later years, his awe for Spector would seem detached from the relative merits of their work. "I never considered us to be anything but just a messenger of his music," Brian said in 1998. He also spoke of Spector when the topic turned to potential collaborators. "I once thought I wanted to work with Phil Spector, but then I thought, 'No, I would be too scared to be around the guy.' Blows that all to hell." He thought for a moment, then shrugged. "I would like to be produced by Spector. That is something that I have as a fantasy of mine, although I'm not really sure what I'm saying or what I'm up to or what that means. But I think it would be a real adventure—a music adventure—to work with him."

That said, once he mastered Spector's technique in the first weeks of 1964, it was Brian Wilson who quickly went on to become the far more innovative and adventurous composer and producer. By mid-1964 (at which point the Beatles had only just moved past the simple guitar, bass, drums, and occasional piano they started out with in Liverpool), Brian had come up with "When I Grow Up (to Be a Man)," which featured a harpsichord as its lead instrument and a wheezing harmonica for rhythmic texture. A cover of Bobby Freeman's "Do You Wanna Dance?" had all of Spector's instrumental grandeur but added a spectacular vocal arrangement in the chorus that all but drowned out the stampeding timpani.

Other tracks from the era featured vibes, celestes, marimbas, and an array of wind instruments (clarinets, oboes, and the huffing bass harmonica were particular favorites).

Once they'd played on a few of Brian's sessions, Hal Blaine and the rest of the session pros were awestruck by the chief Beach Boy's abilities. "We all studied in conservatories; we were trained musicians," he says. "We thought it was a fluke at first, but then we realized Brian was writing these incredible songs. This was not just a young kid writing about high school and surfing." And word of Brian's achievements had spread far beyond L.A.'s recording studios. "Brian was way advanced of what anybody was doing at that point, and I think the Beatles recognized that," Graham Nash recalled to music producer/filmmaker Don Was in the mid-1990s, thinking back to his days as a member of the British pop band the Hollies. David Crosby, Nash's future bandmate in Crosby, Stills, Nash, and Young, remembers reaching the same conclusion during his days with the Byrds. "I thought, 'I give up; I'll never be able to do that,'" he told Was during the same interview. "Brian was the most highly regarded musician in America, hands down."

One night when "Fun, Fun, Fun" was near the top of its arc on *Billboard's* singles charts, Fred Vail joined Brian and Al as they capped a night on the road by catching the Kingston Trio's midnight performance at the Sands casino in Las Vegas. Nearing the end of their set, the Trio's Nick Reynolds took a moment to point out the pair of famous musicians sitting near the lip of the stage. "I'd like to introduce you to the band who owns the world now," he declared, pointing the spotlight toward Brian and Al. "This is the Beach Boys." The two Beach Boys nearly levitated off of their seats, Vail remembers, both for the excitement of being recognized by one of their heroes and also because they knew that what he'd just told the crowd, no matter how overstated it seemed, was very close to the truth.

———

When the spotlight went off and the crowds went home, they were still content to be kids. Carl was sixteen years old in the fall of 1963, Dennis was all of eighteen, Brian and Al were just past their twenty-first birthdays, and Mike was the grand old man at twenty-two. As a result, inspiration for new songs was as close as the neighborhood kids Brian would see in the parking lot of Foster's Freeze, the hot rods cruising Hawthorne Boulevard, and the lights and noise of the football field at Hawthorne High. So, with one foot still planted in his old neighborhood and the other in the Hollywood pop music scene, Brian's songs absorbed the textures of teen life in the South Bay and reflected them as a universal teenaged daydream. But given the anxiety that seemed to hover so perpetually over their own lives, even their fantasy version of Southern California teen life was something other than easygoing. "Be True to Your School," "In the Parkin' Lot," and "Pom Pom Play Girl" transformed the halls, playing fields, and parking lots of public schools into settings for conflict and romance that played out with operatic passion. "Drive-In" got right down to the most cinematic aspects of the automotive theater experience, complete with tips on how to sneak in without paying admission, a cornucopia of junk food, and a few knowing jokes about what really takes place out there in the dark, climaxing (as it were) with a cryptic reminder about the importance of birth control: *"If you say you watched the movie, you're a couple of liars/And remember, only you can prevent forest fires . . ."*

But even sex in the backseat took a backseat to the life-altering possibilities looming down the road. "409" had been first out of the gate, but a swarm of glossy, souped-up vehicles soon followed, from "Little Deuce Coupe" *("She's got a competition clutch with a four on the floor/and she purrs like a kitten 'til the lake pipes roar"),* to the fuel-injected Corvette Stingray that stars in "Shut Down" *("My pressure plate's burnin', that machine's too much!"),* to the hand-built super-car in "Custom Machine" *("Well, with Naugahyde bucket seats in front and back/ Everything is chrome man, even my jack").*

All that detailed automotive erotica—much like the surf slang on the beach— gave a ground-level perspective into the experiences of the characters who described their lives in these terms. But for the mass of listeners who didn't know jack about cars, it became a kind of poetry, the cars doubling as vehicles of tran-scendence. Again, the destination (or finish line, in this case) was far less impor-tant than the journey itself. And for listeners from every regional, cultural, and socioeconomic background, the little emotional dramas hidden within the words and harmonies gave Brian's songs an emotional impact that went far beyond the typical pop song of the era.

Bruce Springsteen would explore the same highways a decade later, albeit with a far more sophisticated sense of its metaphorical significance. Indeed, Springsteen's cars are never just cars. They're "suicide machines" steered by "broken heroes on a last-chance power drive." They're deliciously pink Cadillacs whose female owners left tire tracks in the Garden of Eden. The stark "Racing in the Streets" begins with its narrator's loving description of his car's 396, fuelie heads, and the Hurst on the floor, and the boast that all comers would be, inevitably, shut down. None of this would be out of place in, say, "Shut Down," but this journey doesn't end until Springsteen steps back to describe the existential emptiness of the "promised land," then sets out for a beach where he and his baby can cleanse themselves of their sins.

The Beach Boys, on the other hand, sang cheerily of starting a car club so they can all get matching jackets to wear when they cruise in other towns. It's easy to sneer at the Hawthorne boys' gleeful plans to *set a meet, get a sponsor and collect some dues/And you can bet we'll wear our jackets wherever we cruise!* Yet consider the depth of feeling those jackets represent. Ponder the sense of liberation that animates the triumphant boast of ownership in "Little Deuce Coupe" (*"There's one more thing: I got the pink slip, Daddy,"*) and marvel at "I Get Around" and its lightning journey from frustration (*"I'm gettin' bugged drivin' up and down the same old strip"*) to promise (*"My buddies and me are gettin' real well known"*) to deliverance (*"I'm a real cool head/I'm makin' real good bread"*). Listen closely: "I Get Around" is life, liberty, and the pursuit of happiness, tricked out in metal flake paint and mag wheels.

In a more immediate way, "I Get Around" also told the story of Brian's triumph with the Beach Boys. As usual with Brian's compositions, the feelings come out most evocatively in the music itself, which in this case involves a modular structure, interlocking harmonic lines that build toward Brian's own wordless falsetto swoops. All of which snapped together to express the astonishing excitement he felt at being able not only to build a career in Hollywood (which was, of course, a long way from his old strip in Hawthorne) but also to succeed so magnificently, becoming famous and relatively wealthy at the same unbelievable clip. Indeed, when the Beach Boys toured from town to town, the evenings would end with Murry and Fred Vail lugging paper shopping bags stuffed with cash back to their dressing room, where they would count the proceeds, lock it all down, and prepare to deposit it at the bank at the start of business hours the next morning. "They were kings of the world," Vail remembers. "Sold out houses everywhere they went. In '63 the only competition they had anywhere was the Four Seasons, and they were mostly on the East Coast. The Beach Boys had no rivals in the West."

Still, no matter how big they got, Murry was there to make sure they kept their shirts tucked in, their pants neatly pressed, their hair trimmed and combed, and their attitudes appropriately humble. To enforce the rules, Murry set up a system of fines, docking each member $100 for each stray "shit" or "fuck" and even more when they missed bed check or showed up late for rehearsal or a flight. Their dad-turned-manager's heavy-handed authority was fast growing wearisome for the guys, particularly now that they had become accustomed to the influence their growing fame and wealth gave them with everyone else they encountered. What they didn't understand, however, was how Murry's determination to keep their feet on the ground also kept them rooted in the lives they'd had before they'd become famous. This grounding came through loud and clear in their songs, which were set most often in the same public schools, libraries, hamburger stands, and city beaches where the vast majority of working-to-middle-class kids found love, heartbreak, and meaning.

As in our fantasies of America, what matters about a person in a Beach Boys song has nothing to do with who he or she is and everything to do with the strength of his or her ambition and the things he or she chooses to do with it. The essential activities are freely available to all comers. This same message plays out across all cultural and racial lines in "Surfin' USA," and it's just as vivid in "The Girls on the Beach," where, as they repeat in the chorus, the young lovelies are *"all within reach."* That promise—extended in the warm, jazzy harmonies Brian cribbed from the Four Freshmen, who found them in the big band arrangements of Stan Kenton and Duke Ellington—had as much to do with social opportunity as sex.

Certainly, there is eroticism in "The Girls on the Beach," both in the lyrics and in the voices themselves, which fall, climb, and tangle languidly through a series of augmented chords with a loving intimacy that communicates all the passion simmering beneath the words. But also consider the underlying needs and desires that compel such dreaminess. In John Steinbeck's Depression-era novel *The Grapes of Wrath,* it's economic desperation that compels Ma Joad to insist, despite all evidence to the contrary, that California would be a real-life Eden. "An' fruit ever'place, an' people just bein' in the nicest place," she tells her skeptical son on the eve of their journey west. Tom Joad is less convinced, however, and indeed, they soon find themselves living in the same sort of hobo camp that Edith Wilson and family spent their first weeks residing in on the beach at Cardiff-on-the-Sea. And for the Wilsons, at least, the memory of that descent into poverty would be powerful enough to motivate and torment for decades.

The first real cloud over the Beach Boys' success, Fred Vail recalls, scudded onto the horizon the day the Beatles' jet touched down in New York in February 1964. And if the onset of Beatlemania was jarring enough to every other American pop musician, it was doubly so for the Beach Boys. And not just because they had been the nation's most popular rock group through the end of 1963. What made it all even more ticklish was that the Beatles were also signed to Capitol Records. And the moment the Liverpudlians came to these shores, the same executives who had until recently been in love with the Beach Boys were swooning for the moptops. "The Beach Boys had been it for two years, but now people thought the Beatles were the future," Vail says. "And loyalties ran thin at Capitol. Now they didn't have to cater to Murry and the Beach Boys, and so they didn't."

At least they didn't intend to. But Murry was too stalwart an advocate to be ignored for long. He made a point of visiting the Capitol Tower in person, most often without calling in advance, in order to twist executive arms until they snapped forth with more and better support for the Beach Boys. And to make sure his boys fulfilled their end of the deal, Murry cracked the whip extra hard in the recording sessions, questioning Brian's arrangement, engineer Chuck Britz's mix, or the way the boys *oohed* behind the lead vocal. "You're not going '*ooh*,' Carl, you're going '*uuuuuuunh*,'" he snapped at one session. "Let's fight for success, okay?"

Certainly, Murry had fought for them. He'd mortgaged his company to finance their first records and tours, and when the band seemed to be taking off, he gave up his own career in order to devote himself to its success. Along the way he'd made a lot of good decisions: He helped Brian set up his own publishing company so he would always have control over his songs and then forced the Capitol Records executives to give Brian complete authority over the group's music. Murry also realized that no matter how good a record was, it still needed the enthusiasm of the nation's disc jockeys, record distributors, and shop owners to sell it. So he mounted a charm offensive aimed at all of the industry's local and regional power brokers, constantly paying personal visits to their offices, shaking their hands, and sending handpicked presents (bought in bulk, of course) to cement their friendship. And if the rack-jobbers and program directors did treat him like a friend, well, Murry craved that kind of attention, too. He even had his own promotional photos taken, handing them out—hand-signed "Murry 'Dad'

Wilson"—to whomever would accept one. He'd come a long way from that tent on the beach at Cardiff-by-the-Sea, and he wanted his kids to know it.

Murry meant to inspire his kids. He'd spent his entire life repeating the same lectures about the importance of having a dream, of working hard to make it real, of never giving up. But Murry's glorious words came with the gloomy subtext of his own life: from the dismal failure his father had been, to Murry's own sputtering career in industry, to his desperate attempts to maintain control over his growing sons. Taught to believe they could achieve anything they could imagine and raised to understand exactly how brutal the consequences of failure could be, the younger Wilsons grew up splayed between hope and fear. "Kick ass! Kick ass!" their father liked to roar at them. And they already knew whose ass would be kicked if he began to suspect they weren't getting the message.

So even if Brian never liked touring, he was out there leading the band from show to show, keeping them sharp and focused at night, even as he spent his days working on new songs for their next single, the next B-side, the next album, and the album after that. Once they got back to Los Angeles, he had to get back to the studio to arrange and produce the new material, finding new sounds to fill his increasingly intricate tracks while also teaching the complex vocal arrangements to an often preoccupied and sometimes downright uncooperative group. If they couldn't get it right after eight hours or so, Brian would stay late and sing all the parts himself. The competition posed by the Beatles—whose music thrilled Brian just as much as it had everyone else with ears—made the pressure on him even more intense. Now he just worked harder, beating back his fears with more complex songs, Phil Spector–sized productions and vocal arrangements that looped, climbed, and soared above the instruments. When it worked, the sound was enough to sweep everything else away. But that meant making it bigger and better. Always, he knew, bigger and better.

The last surf song Brian wrote in the '60s was recorded in April, the month that began with the Beatles claiming each of the top five songs on *Billboard's* Hot 100. Brian worked with Mike on the lyrics, calling it "Don't Back Down," set on a beach bracketed by killer waves that pop up *"like a ton of lead"* and heartless women who *"dig the way the guys get all wiped out."* *"You've gotta be a little nuts/But show 'em man, who's got guts,"* Brian wailed during the choruses. Did he realize he was echoing his father's lectures about fighting for success? Perhaps not, but what seems clear is that, at least in some respects, the California paradise he'd imagined was already fading before his eyes. But now that Brian's talents had proven powerful enough to allow him and his family to finally complete their journey across the continent, they had nowhere else to go. "Kick ass! Kick ass!" Murry kept commanding. So Brian paddled out into the darkness, alone, humming a song to himself.

Don't back down from that wave!

CHAPTER 4

As the session gets rolling, Murry Wilson radiates warmth toward his sons, his nephew, and their bandmate, all of whom are recording vocals for what they hope will be the next Beach Boys hit.

"You've got a wonderful tune here," he calls down through the control room's intercom microphone. "Al, loosen up a little more, say *'Rhonda'* a little more soft and sexy. Carl, *'ooh'* better, and we got it. Dennis, don't flat anymore, and we got it."

They start another take but get only a few bars into it before a stray note clatters in Brian's ear. "Stop it!" he calls up to engineer Chuck Britz, who cuts off the tape. The singers chat amiably for a few moments, working out the kinks in what is, after all, a complicated construction of interlocking vocal lines. After a minute or two, they prepare to start up again.

"Brian, have the guys loosen up," Murry punches in again, his rumbling baritone echoing off the studio walls. "You've got a beautiful tune here! Loosen up here. You're so tight, fellas, I can't believe it."

But the more Murry urges the boys to relax, the tenser the mood becomes. Not that anyone seems able to acknowledge what the problem is, beyond a cryptic complaint, delivered off-mike, about "ten cooks out there messin' things up." A moment later, Brian turns to Alan Jardine, manning the lead singer's mike, with a new edge to his voice. "Try to syncopate it, Al," he says. *"Try."*

Another take falls apart, and when the intercom crackles, Murry's voice is back again, even louder than before. "Bear with me," he rumbles. "Brian asked me to relax and come down, which is why I got drunk." Hearing this, Brian cuts in quickly. "You're not drunk," he says, gloomily.

Actually, Murry does sound a little tanked. He's too loud, for one thing, and his tongue can't quite wrap around all of his *S*'s. Even so, he manipulates his quarry expertly, using one hand to stroke their egos and the other to slap their faces. "Loosen up and sing from your heart!" he says. "You got any guts? Let's hear it."

This is the sound of the Beach Boys recording "Help Me, Rhonda" on February 24, 1965. The tracking tape, which documents nearly forty minutes of the evening session, including the takes, rehearsals, and studio chatter, is an astonishing document that reveals why the song they're singing—destined to be the group's second number one single and one of the most beloved songs of their entire career—is both an infectious sing-along and also a tale of heartbreak whose exuberant chorus pivots on a plaintive cry for help. *"Help me get her out of my heart!"* They sing in perfect harmony, again and again, as Murry scowls down from the control room. Brian doesn't need to have his father in the room to feel the tug of his expectations or the weight of his disapproval. No matter how many hit songs Brian had written, no matter how sophisticated his music had become or how respected his studio work, there was always more to do. More records to make, more albums to fill, more shows to play. Brian had married his sixteen-year-old sweetheart, Marilyn, and her steady warmth had provided some comfort in the twenty-two-year-old's life. But it also made things more complicated, as he had to provide not just for his young wife, but also for his brothers, his parents, and a growing number of employees, compatriots, and contracted entities.

Naturally, Murry made sure his eldest son knew how much he owed all of them, particularly when Brian's attention seemed to wander. "Don't go Hollywood phony on me, baby," he'd say scornfully. "You've gotta fight for success."

Two months earlier, the pressure had finally overwhelmed Brian, as the increasingly chunky musician suffered a vicious anxiety attack during a flight to a show in Houston. "I can't take it anymore," he had wailed, his shrieks muffled only by the pillow he'd pressed to his face. It was a terrible episode—a nervous breakdown, according to his bandmates, but at least it convinced them to allow Brian, at long last, to step back from his touring obligations. Now he was free to focus his complete attention on the one thing that really mattered to him—writing and recording music. Now that they had to compete with the Beatles, the Rolling Stones, and Bob Dylan, recording new music was terribly important to all of them. "I foresee a beautiful future for us as a group," Brian told the others, and they all believed it.

Perhaps Brian was able to enjoy the "Help Me, Rhonda" recording session, carried away on the propulsive bass and twanging lead guitar, followed by the explosive vocals on the chorus, Mike and Dennis harmonizing on the low end, while Carl and Al joined Brian's wailing falsetto on the top. Their pure, young voices ring out in the studio tapes, as the recorded track echoes faintly from their headphones. *Help me Rhonda, yeah! Get her out of my heart!*

But Murry, who pushed through the heavy studio door to address the boys face-to-face, still wasn't satisfied. "All we're asking for here is a little syncopation," he says. But what he was really after was far more complicated: Only a few months earlier, Brian and the Beach Boys had, after months of private grumbling about his heavy-handed ways, fired the Wilson family patriarch from his management duties. "Because of the situation between father and son, you go nowhere," Brian explained to a magazine writer at the time. "It was done more or less maturely. Finally, we decided he is better as a father than a manager."

Plainly, though, the managerial strategies Murry employed with his sole clients grew directly out of the relationship he'd always had with his sons. His love for the Beach Boys, in other words, was just as intense, the commitment just as strong. The need to dominate was just as overwhelming, the subconscious impulse to destroy just as inescapable. The boys' connection to their father was just as paradoxical, especially when it came to Brian—the eldest and most talented of the boys, who was everything Murry wished he could have been. No matter how often his dad criticized his writing, tried to overrule his production decisions in the studio, or humiliated him in public, Brian couldn't suppress his need for his father's approval.

Excited about his new arrangement for "Rhonda"—a song he first recorded in January with a simpler, less energetic arrangement—Brian invited his dad to watch him rerecord it. Maybe now that they had some distance from each other the old man would finally see that Brian did know what he was doing and learn to respect and love him for it. But Murry had his own internal needs and desires to tend.

Back in the studio, Murry looms over Al, demanding that he read him the lyrics to "Rhonda," then half-singing, half-scatting them back, emphasizing the syncopation he's after. Brian glances up through the glass to the control room, which is crowded with guests including friends, music industry figures, and assorted hangers-on—all of whom are watching him lose control of his own session. Finally, he cuts his dad off.

"He's got it now. Don't sing it with him; jeez, let him sing it once."

This show of authority only aggravates Murry, who seems instantly wounded.

"You want me to leave, Brian?"

"No!" Brian laughs uneasily. "I just want you to let him *sing* it!"

"Mother and I can leave now, if you want."

"No, *stay,*" Brian insists. But when he invites his father to put on a pair of headphones so he can compare Al's new vocal with the recorded version he's trying to double-track, Murry thinks he is being insulted. "I can hear you here," he says, gazing coolly at his half-deaf son. "My ears are good enough to hear." The barb stings, and Brian's cheeks go instantly red.

"No! Get the phones on so you can hear the *other* voice!"

Then Murry has his arm around Al, purring conspiratorially into his ear. "You're too tense! Look, they have so many (hangers-on) here, you shouldn't have it. But loosen up and just forget it. You're doing a great job." Al mutters his halfhearted assent, but Murry, who isn't paying attention anyway, keeps going. "Look, I'm proud of you! You've got the lead, buddy, on their next single! Loosen up and sing from your heart. Right down here; that's all you need. The rest is easy!"

The evening spirals further out of control. When Al sings the song's opening lines to Murry's liking, the older man calls him a "genius," mostly, it seems, to ridicule Brian, whose string of hits inspired some L.A. music industry figures to bestow the same weighty accolade upon him. A moment later Brian calls up through the glass to Loren Schwartz, a new friend who recently introduced him to marijuana. "Can you turn me on in there?" Brian asks, hiding his real query in what was then-unknown hipster slang. Schwartz shoots him a thumbs-up, and Brian sings happily to himself: *"Rhonda, you look so fiiiiiine!"* Then he calls for a break.

When the session resumes again, Brian is scolding Mike for shoving Schwartz out of the studio. Mike—who knows exactly what his cousin and his pal did during the break—shrugs it off, and Brian calls for a vocals-only rehearsal of the interlocking patterns that make up the chorus. During the rehearsal, their unadorned voices edge close to perfection, but the intercom crackles again and Murry cites various flaws that only his ears have absorbed.

"Fellas, I have 3,000 words to say," he sighs. "So you're big stars. Let's fight, huh? Let's fight for success, okay? Let's go."

Finally, Brian loses it: "Oh, SHIT!" he screams out at his father. "You're embarrassing me now! SHUT UP!"

Sensing his cousin's distress, Mike steps in to offer reassurance. "Don't, don't worry about it." But his soothing makes no impact, particularly when Murry, affecting a wounded tone, starts playing the martyr.

"I'll leave, Brian, if you're gonna give me a bad time."

Brian, still upset: "Don't talk so loud. That really gets me."

Murry, hostile again: "I don't care if it does. Let's go. You got any guts? Let's see it. I don't care how many people are here."

Brian shouts back at him resentfully: "I got one ear left, and your big, loud voice is killin' it!"

Murry returns to the studio, stalking up to confront Brian face-to-face. "When you guys get too much money, you start thinking you're gonna make everything a hit," he rants as his son—slightly stoned and struck by the lunacy of the moment—taunts him by tilting a microphone toward the older man's lips. "Don't insult me!" Murry snarls, swiping a paw at the microphone.

"I just wanna make sure this is on tape," Brian says.

"You're an ingrate when you do this. Come on, dear." Murry gestures toward Audree, then turns back to Brian. "I'll never help you guys mix another single."

But Murry can't bring himself to leave, and as the conversation devolves, he mixes insults ("You're going downhill!") with affirmations ("I love you; your mother loves you") in what amounts to a toxic cocktail of emotional manipulation. Still, Brian seems to shrug it all off, which enrages Murry even more. He turns again to his wife, who observes the entire scene in silence, as she always did whenever her husband lashed out at their children. "I'm sorry, dear," he says, his voice taking on a pious tone. "We'll never come to another recording session. The kid got a big success, and he thinks he owns the business. I'm sorry. I'm so sorry, dear. I'm sorry." Then he addresses Brian again. "I've protected you for twenty-two years now, but I can't go on if you're not going to listen to an intelligent man."

Brian whispers: "Okay."

Murry: "Chuck and I used to make one hit after another, in thirty minutes. You guys are taking five hours to do it."

"Times are changing," Brian says flatly.

"You guys think you have an image," Murry retorts.

"Times are changing," Brian again responds.

Murry: "Don't ever forget."

"Times are changing," Brian says, one last time.

With that, Murry leaves. But he'd be back. And though many things in Brian's life and career would change in the next few weeks and months, the tangled snarl of love, hate, need, and resentment he felt for his father would not. In fact, it would define him for a long time to come.

That Brian would be tormented for years to come by his conflicted relationship with his father stands to reason. Murry, for his part, never came to terms with his father. Sitting in another recording studio a thousand miles and more than three decades removed from that caustic night in Los Angeles, Brian still spoke of his father with the same mix of admiration, love, and fear.

"In some ways I haven't gotten beyond my dad," he said matter-of-factly. "In some ways I was very afraid of my dad. In other ways I loved him because he knew where it was at. As we talk now, that's the first time I've ever said it to myself. My dad blew my mind."

In a positive way?

"Yeah. Yeah. Very positive way. So positive that it scared me to death. In my life, being scared has been probably the most driving force that I have. Because I'm so afraid of life and the people in it. I got to go through that." And yet even this admission comes with a happy ending. "If you have a little bit of fear in you, you push harder, you know? You fight better and you get more successful. That's what I did, anyway." That sentiment may well be at the heart of every song Brian has ever written.

———

A few months earlier, Brian thought that getting his dad away from the group's management would make everything easier. But nothing got easier. The fact that Murry wasn't physically present did nothing to remove his expectations or the relentless schedule of writing, recording, and performing enforced by the group's various contracts. Finally, just before Christmas, Brian had had enough. Flying to Houston for a show on December 23—the start of a two-week mini-tour—he began to weep, then wail. "I told Al Jardine I was going to crack up at any minute," Brian said at the time. Soon he was lying in the aisle, screaming into a pillow he had pushed up against his face. "I let myself go emotionally," Brian told *Teen Beat* magazine a little later. At first Brian said he wouldn't get out of the airplane when they landed. But he did, and he cooled down enough that afternoon to play that night's show at Houston's Music Hall. But Brian woke up the next morning with a terrible knot in his stomach. He flew back to L.A., arranging first to have session guitarist Glen Campbell fly out to fill in for him at that night's show in the Sam Houston Coliseum.

Back in Los Angeles that night, Brian was met by Audree—he'd decreed that she, and not Murry, meet him at the airport—and had her drive him to his family's now-empty home on West 119th Street. They walked the rooms together for a while, talking about the life they'd had there and where it had led them. After a while they got back in Audree's car and drove back to Los Angeles and the future that waited for them there. Brian never set foot in the house again. When the other Beach Boys returned to Los Angeles in January, he called them together to announce that he would no longer be touring with the band. He'd already skipped several tours ("Brian absolutely hated the road from the very beginning," David Marks recalls), and so the news shouldn't have come as much of a surprise. Nevertheless, Brian's perhaps fanciful recollection of the meeting (during which, he said, Al Jardine broke out in stomach cramps, Dennis threatened to hit someone with an ashtray, and Mike burst into tears and said there was no reason for the group to go on) became an oft-told tale in the band's story.

Campbell toured with the band for a few months, but he had his own career to nurture, so he left in the spring. The group replaced him with Bruce Johnston, a graduate of University High School, the same West L.A. high school that produced Jan and Dean, among others. Already a figure in the local music scene as half of Bruce and Terry (with Doris Day's son Terry Melcher), Bruce was young, talented, and extremely ambitious. He could sing Brian's falsettos onstage and shared enough of his features—the thick brown hair and baby face—that some fans didn't realize he wasn't Brian, which Bruce didn't mind at all. He reveled in the screams and the acclaim—and set out immediately to make himself indispensable to the group.

After the boys fired Murry, he had taken to his bed. He could barely summon the will to get out of his pajamas at first, but it was only a few weeks before he was up and nearly back to his grumbly, cantankerous self. Still, Carl could see that his father needed something to keep himself busy. And when Murry's youngest son met a group of ambitious young musicians at the Hollywood Professional School (he had transferred once the Beach Boys really took off) who called themselves the Renegades, he gave them his dad's number down in Hawthorne and suggested they give him a call. "I think Carl saw it as an opportunity to get Murry off of their backs," says Rick Henn, the group's drummer and main composer. "He could see his dad was grieving, and he really needed something to do. So that's where we came in."

Murry called the group down to Hawthorne and had them set up in the same family room where the Beach Boys had gotten their start. The new group played for him for hours—twelve or fifteen, according to Henn's memory—and finally he took his pipe out of his mouth and nodded. "I think you boys are ready to have some success," he decreed, much to the group's delight. "We knew this cat was our shot. He'd had this huge success with the Beach Boys, and we'd had a couple of singles fail," Henn says. "We were malleable." Indeed, they let Murry arrange their vocals and produce their albums in Brian's early '60s style. They even let him change their name to the Sunrays and dress them in the same striped shirts the Beach Boys had made famous. "He'd say, 'I did it with my sons; now I'm gonna do it with these guys. I love my sons with all my heart, but these guys need my help. They're my new Suns!'" Henn remembers.

Murry got the group a contract with a small Capitol Records subsidiary (Tower Records), then wrote and produced the Sunrays' first two singles, "Car Party" and "Outta Gas," at the same studio where Brian worked, using the same engineer (Chuck Britz) and drummer (Hal Blaine) his son preferred. The tunes both turned out to be small hits, and the next single, "I Live for the Sun," did a little better, thanks in part to Murry being in his full-on sales mode, calling all of his old radio contacts, schmoozing all of the rack-jobbers, distributing his bulk-purchased perfume and jewelry to anyone who might be able to do the band some good.

Murry made sure the Sunrays got invited to open some shows for the Beach Boys that summer, but by then no one in the established group was happy to see another band, especially one managed by their father, following their musical and stylistic footsteps so closely. The fact that the Sunrays had actually made it onto the national charts only made things more tense, Henn notes. The guys ran hot and cold with them, Henn says, and even when they seemed friendly, well, you could never really be sure. "I was in Hollywood with my girlfriend one day, and Dennis pulled up in his car and yelled, 'Hey, Rick! How you doin', man?' I remember thinking, 'Whoa! He's not pissed off!'" On the contrary, Dennis invited Rick and his friend up to his house, where he gave the seventeen-year-old high schoolers some drinks and shot the breeze for a while. Henn left feeling delighted with the encounter, but that changed the next morning when he got a call from an enraged Murry. "Son, I think I'm gonna have to drop you," he growled. "You're up in Hollywood with the phonies, drinking and going around town. I think we're through." Now Henn laughs at the memory. "Dennis set me up so he could burn me with his dad. That was weird."

Murry ended up forgiving Henn. But even as the Sunrays settled in to make a new album and try to leverage their success into something bigger and better, Henn couldn't help suspecting that the old man's real motivations sprang from relationships that had nothing to do with his band. This became particularly clear when Murry insisted that the group follow their string of upbeat singles with a slow, romantic ballad called "Still." The song itself wasn't as much of a problem as the fact that their previous songs had been so upbeat and fun. "Still," on the other hand, was a two-hankie weeper, whose chorus sulked mistily about a long-lost love who had broken the singer's heart, leaving him to worship her from afar. Says Henn, "I really think Murry wanted to talk to his kids through the radio while they toured the country. We knew the flip side should be the single, but he really insisted we do that one. And it killed our career." True enough, the Sunrays would never have another hit.

———

Brian Wilson, on the other hand, was determined to move his group, or at least himself, toward a fresh musical vision. Actually, the music had already been changing—it had never stopped changing—which was a large part of the reason why Brian's musical peers held him in such high regard. But the Beach Boys' public image hadn't matured along with his music. So even as Bob Dylan infused rock with a seething political consciousness and literary sensibility, as the Beatles expanded their musical and intellectual horizons in every conceivable direction, and as the Rolling Stones reveled in their own subversive decadence—and all three blazed trails for the politically/socially/intellectually aware groups that would soon transform youth culture entirely—the Beach Boys kept their hair barbered and their striped shirts neatly pressed. Capitol continued to bill them as "America's Top Surfin' Group!" Their TV appearances still took place on sets dressed with surfboards, beach balls, and chicks doing the twist in candy-colored bikinis. And when the summer sales season neared, everyone still expected Brian to crank out another batch of ready-made tunes set on the beaches, highways, and backseats he'd long since lost interest in describing.

Still, it was extremely difficult for Brian to resist the pressure to build on his greatest hits by repeating them over and over again. Ever since he'd been a child, music had been his joy; but now it was an industry, and a wildly lucrative one at that. Indeed, the Beach Boys' march across the record charts had gone uninterrupted (almost) since "Surfin' Safari" hit the top fifteen in 1962. Apart from *Surfin' Safari,* which snuck into the top twenty-five, every Beach Boys album between 1963 and 1966 reached the top ten, and most camped out in the top five for weeks at a time. *Beach Boys Concert,* recorded over two nights in 1964 in Sacramento (and subsequently enhanced with studio overdubs), hit number one at the height of the Christmas shopping season that year. It was an astonishing run by anyone's estimation, all but unbelievable in an era dominated by stars whose hit-making days were measured in months and sometimes weeks.

Changing the group's image hardly seemed like a sensible option to the Capitol execs or, for that matter, to the four Beach Boys, the parents, the wives, and the employees who depended on Brian's mainstream pop sensibility for their livelihoods. Brian was welcome to harbor as many artistic pretensions as he liked, but the moment the commercial momentum began to lag, he would have to get back to business. "See, I'm into success," Mike says. "I'm talking about a three-minute pop single here. And if you're going to make a single, why not make it a hit?"

Clearly, the group's disconnect from the cultural avant-garde was not all Capitol's doing or even entirely a product of the group's own commercial motivations. Bear in mind that the Beach Boys themselves were still college-aged, only none of them had been to college, nor (with the possible exception of Brian) had they shown much discernible interest in what you might call the world of ideas. Listen to them reminiscing with Capitol publicist Earl Leaf, who accompanied them on a late 1964 European tour, in the "Bull Session with the Big Daddy" filler track tagged on the end of *The Beach Boys Today* (especially on the longer, uncut version found on bootlegs), and you hear tales of the world's cultural capitals told by kids whose primary interest was drinking beer and trying to pick up women without benefit of speaking their native tongues. (Mike Love ended up spending a night in a German jail on that tour, either because he tried to intervene in a violent domestic squabble or because he got into a fight with a pimp whose hooker he tried to bed. The former version comes from Mike, the latter from Leaf, who uncorked it for *Rolling Stone* in 1971.) The released version of "Big Daddy" includes Brian's assertion that despite everything the band experienced on their international tours, "the only thing that sticks in my mind is the bread." The one anecdote involving a work of art revolves around Brian's impulsive decision to plant a kiss on the lips of a statue of a naked woman on the streets of Paris, which once again brought the Beach Boys to the attention of local law officers. And here's Brian's analysis of an evening at the theater: "I can take good entertainment. But when it comes to that French burlesque? Let me out. I just can't take it."

This makes the humanities students among us slap our foreheads and moan with sorrow. But what were you expecting? All the Beach Boys were products of the blue-collar suburbs of Los Angeles's industrial South Bay. To grow up in Hawthorne was to view the world, and particularly the more elegant corners of L.A., where people were prone to wax on about higher culture but all too often looked down on working-class communities, as a collection of bad guys and loud braggarts more than happy to explain why their school is great and yours doesn't measure up. Being true to your school means something to teenagers; being true to your social and economic class means just as much to their parents.

Of course, that didn't mean the suddenly rich Beach Boys family wasn't going to enjoy their newfound fortune, sometimes in astonishingly unsubtle ways. Once Murry's take from Brian's publishing fortune started rolling in, the old man had the once-humble ranch house on West 119th Street rebuilt into a meandering, if ill-designed, testament to his own financial ascendance. Then he promptly moved out to a swank hillside address in Whittier, twenty miles away. All the band members bought their own houses and fleets of cars, motorcycles, and other expensive toys. Fred Vail still recalls one morning during a 1964 concert tour when he met Al Jardine for breakfast in the hotel lobby and found the young guitarist and pharmacy school dropout dressed inexplicably in a full suit and tie, scanning that morning's *Wall Street Journal.* "I still don't know what he was thinking," Vail says now.

Brian enjoyed his new money, too, buying himself a flashy green Cadillac, good clothes, and regular haircuts at Jay Sebring's Beverly Hills salon. But that didn't mean he wanted to think about it all that much. For example, one day in 1965, one of his accountants paid a visit to him in the recording studio to talk finances, investments, and the like. "Brian kept saying, 'Would you please leave me alone? I'm trying to listen to the playback!'" recalls Hal Blaine, who sounds as put out by the briefcase-wielding accountant as Brian was forty years before. "But the guy kept saying, 'Look, you've got all this money stacking up in Sea of Tunes (the name Brian and Murry had given their song publishing company), and if you don't do something with it, they're gonna take it away!' Finally, Brian said, 'I don't care! Do what you want!' The suit guy wrote out a check right there, and Brian didn't even look; he just signed it and handed it back. *I* looked, though, and I swear it was for something like $500,000."

Brian found other ways to revel in his achievements. By the end of 1964, he was one of the most successful, influential young musicians in Los Angeles, which not so coincidentally made him a highly sought-after companion for other rock stars, actors, and the hip, young industry types they liked to hang around with. Despite, or perhaps because of, the anti-intellectualism pervading his family and band, Brian became particularly entranced by the sharp young aesthetes just beginning to collect into a distinct Hollywood demimonde. These were rich kids. Most had gone to college, and all of them could talk for hours about poetry, music, politics, and religion. One of the most prominent, in his own back-channel way, was Loren Schwartz, a twenty-seven-year-old former child actor, UCLA theater grad, and current William Morris agent, who hosted regular get-togethers in the small but finely appointed apartment he shared with his wife in West Hollywood. "I had a Gertrude Stein–style salon," Schwartz says. "I had the best pot and the happening musicians. (Stephen) Stills was there. (David) Crosby was my best friend at the time. Jim McGuinn was just forming the Byrds. Tony Asher, my best pal in college, introduced me to Brian Wilson at Western studios one day, and he and I hooked up."

Affable and garrulous, full of stories about his many travels and his readings of philosophy and world religions, Schwartz served as a kind of Hollywood Henry Higgins to Brian's Eliza Doolittle, introducing him to all of his hippest friends and turning him on to the works of Kahlil Gibran and Hermann Hesse.

"Brian was a big, goofy kid," says Schwartz (now known, for complicated reasons involving Subud numerology and a desire to assimilate into non-Jewish culture, as Lorren Daro). "Supremely talented. And not an ounce of guile or malice in him. He was a beautiful spirit. What a dazzling guy." Brian became a regular at Schwartz's apartment, diving happily into the social whirl and substances Schwartz always kept at hand. "I gave him his first joint," Schwartz says with an unsettling cackle. "Murry Wilson wanted to have me killed."

Indeed, Brian's drug use would eventually be blamed for much of his subsequent emotional and psychiatric ills. As a result, some consider Schwartz to be a truly dark figure, but, unsurprisingly, he sees things differently. Despite Brian's contention in his (since-disowned) 1991 autobiography that Schwartz pressured him to try marijuana, Schwartz insists that he actually fended off Brian's drug curiosity for months on end. "I feared messing with that febrile mind of his. But . . . he said, 'If you don't smoke me up, believe me, it's being offered all the time.' So I gave him his first joint."

Schwartz's proposed timeline—he says it took a year for him to pass Brian a joint, then another year to be convinced that his friend was ready for LSD—doesn't quite pencil out, since Brian recalls writing "California Girls," which was recorded in April 1965, while tripping on acid. Nevertheless, Schwartz's recollections of Brian's early drug experiences remain astonishingly vivid. "He had Disney visions of music staffs flowing through the air. A real *Fantasia* thing, while we were driving to a concert in Sacramento." Unsurprisingly, Brian's first acid trip was even more powerful. "So one night Brian took it. One hundred and twenty-five mics of pure Owsley. He had the full-on ego death. It was a beautiful thing." But it was not without its painful moments. As Schwartz told David Leaf in his documentary, *Beautiful Dreamer,* Brian was so terrified by the hallucinations he experienced that he ran into the apartment's bedroom, slammed the door, and collapsed trembling in bed, tucking his head beneath the pillows. He remained there for an hour or two, then burst back into the living room, his mood restored. "He said, 'Well, that's enough of that!'" Schwartz told Leaf's camera.

It was all far, far too much for the new Mrs. Brian Wilson. Just sixteen and even less worldly than her twenty-two-year-old husband, Marilyn was terrified by his new appetite for drugs, which seemed to make him even more distant and spacey than usual. At one point she moved out of their new apartment, telling him to choose between her and Schwartz. "And he chose me," Schwartz says. "But she came back."

Despite Marilyn's best efforts, Brian's appetite for pot no longer began and ended at Schwartz's door. Bumping into his old Hawthorne pal Bruce Griffin at Pickwick Books on Hollywood Boulevard, where his former singing partner now worked, Brian swept him up into his new secret life. "We'd drive all around Hollywood looking for pot," Griffin recalls. Once they located their quarry, they'd get stoned in Brian's new green Cadillac and then drive around the city, looking at the lights, listening to the radio, and talking. Comforted by his old friend, Brian opened up and told Griffin about his visits with the psychiatrist he had just started seeing and about the guilt he felt for his ongoing crush on his wife's older sister, Diane. And as ever, Brian talked about music. "I was with him the first time he ever heard 'Ticket to Ride' on the radio," Griffin says. "And I asked him what he thought of John Lennon. He said, 'Well, he knows what he's doing.' Another time he told me music was going to get spiritual. I guess he saw 'Good Vibrations' as their spiritual piece. But a lot of stuff they did was kind of spiritual."

As Brian continued to write and record through the first months of 1965, his work took on the ecstatic feeling of the *Fantasia*-like staff of music he imagined floating in his druggy daydreams. For a time it seemed like anything was possible. "California Girls," intended to be a sunny anthem for the summer of '65, could begin with an orchestral prelude as spare and stirring as anything by Aaron Copland. "The Little Girl I Once Knew," a single recorded later that fall, would combine a calliope-like organ with spoken-word segments and, far more daringly, four-beat pauses that had no precedent in rock music. Taking Al Jardine's advice to dust off the old Kingston Trio high school sing-along favorite "Sloop John B.," Brian transformed the simple folk tune into an epic construction of guitars, percussion, bells, flutes, a wild bass line, and a vocal arrangement that erupts into full flower for a breathtaking a cappella break.

Recorded in the summer of 1965, the instrumental track for "Sloop John B." sat on Brian's shelf for a few months while he figured out his next big move. To buy time from Capitol—which still expected the Beach Boys to produce original albums to greet every new season—he cranked out *Beach Boys Party!* The album was a simulated house party/jam session that actually was the product of several highly scripted, studio musician–assisted sessions at Western Recorders. A collection of old favorites, Beatles songs, and takeoffs on their own hits, *Party* sold every bit as well as the group's last fully realized album, *Summer Days (and Summer Nights!)*. The Capitol execs released *Party's* giggly, acoustic rendition of

"Barbara Ann" as a single that winter, and it became a number two hit, much to Brian's chagrin. Such simple, kid-friendly stuff was light-years behind him now. As he'd told his father a few months earlier—and as Al Jardine would warble in the brief Bob Dylan tribute Brian put on the second side of *Party*—times were changing.

CHAPTER 5

The feelings of panic first gripped him the moment the airplane lifted off the runway at Los Angeles International Airport. Brian was thinking about Marilyn, pondering the way his fifteen-year-old girlfriend had been looking at Mike in the moments before the cousins, along with the rest of the Beach Boys, had set out for their latest tour of Australia. It was the fall of 1964, and Brian was only weeks from his first nervous breakdown. But as the airplane glided over the Pacific Ocean, all Brian could think about was his growing suspicion that he was about to lose Marilyn. Increasingly frantic, Brian had sent a frantic telegraph from the airplane's cockpit. PLEASE WAIT FOR MY CALL, it read. I LOVE YOU, BRIAN. He called her the moment they touched down and pleaded with her to marry him. The couple had a civil ceremony on December 7 and settled down together in his apartment on Hollywood Boulevard.

Finally, Brian could claim the independence—and the stable, loving partner—he had sought for so long. And yet very little in his music projects a sense of happily ever after. This comes into particularly sharp focus on "In the Back of My Mind" from mid-1965. Written and recorded just after the start of his marriage, the song's narrator speaks to us from the bosom of domesticity. He feels blessed, he begins expansively, describing a world comfortable enough for a man to "cling" to. And already, we're stumbling: *Cling? * That's an odd choice of words, isn't it? Indeed, and it is actually what this song is about, as the next lines make clear: *"So happy at times that I break down in tears/In the back of my mind I still have my fears."*

Sung solo by Dennis in a conversational croon, the song begins in a supper-club arrangement of strings, horns, and bells. The big band swells with the first verse's penultimate line but recedes instantly as the next line (*"I still have my fears"*) kicks the oboes and violins into a worried minor chord. The next two verses describe the same joy and fear in slightly different terms, but the real crux of the song comes in the bridge, a strangely rushed, unmelodic digression that tumbles toward a climactic verse that identifies the source of the darkness in this seemingly sunny relationship as the singer's own doubts that it can last: *"What'll I do if I lose her?/It'll always be in the back of my mind."* This feeling is only emphasized by the song's brief instrumental coda, which, like the overture to "California Girls," swells toward the symphonic. Only this time the strings, horns, and bells are played out of synch, each instrument meandering alone into the descending silence.

"In the Back of My Mind" is an unsettling love song, to say the least. But love was never a comfortable thing in the songs Brian wrote for the Beach Boys, even back in their sunniest days. *"Wendy, Wendy, what went wrong?/We went together for so long,"* they wail in one song. *"When I watched you walk with him tears filled my eyes,"* Brian cried in another. *"You didn't answer my letter so I figured it was all just a lie,"* Carl states matter-of-factly in still another. More and more: *"She let another guy come between us and it shattered our plans/I cried when she said, 'I don't feel the same way.'"* The deeper the lovers look into one another's eyes, the more distant they seem to become. *"Can't remember what we fought about . . . but I remember when we thought it out/We both had a broken heart."*

And yet from a distance the Beach Boys describe women with giddy, school-boy ardor. In the wispy light of dawn, a girl appears on the beach. *"I have seen you on the shore, standing near the ocean's roar/Do you love me, do you, surfer girl?"* On the highway, another zooms by, a smile lighting her face and the wind blowing her long hair like a golden banner. *"She walks looks and drives like an ace, now/And she'll have fun, fun, fun til her daddy takes her T-bird away . . ."* Stepping back even further, the women become cultural icons, personifying the finest attributes of every region, from the stylish East Coast to the cornpone

South, the unassuming Midwest, and the warmhearted North, where a girl's kiss warms the coldest day. *"I wish they all could be California girls!"* the Beach Boys cry, their exaltation heralded with symphonic grandeur, then carried forth in a parade of marching percussion, ballpark organ, and pirouetting rounds of harmony. *"Girls! Girls! Girls! Yeah, I dig the girls! Girls! Girls! Girls!"*

In their adulation for and anxiety about women, the Beach Boys are cut from the same cloth as Stephen Foster, the legendary nineteenth-century songwriter. In Foster's "Jeanie with the Light Brown Hair," Jeanie is a vision of loveliness *"borne like a vapor in the soft summer air . . . radiant in gladness, warm with winning guile."* In "Gentle Annie," Foster rhapsodizes, *"We have roamed and loved 'mid the bowers/When thy downy cheeks were in bloom."* "Nelly Was a Lady" describes a woman whose beauty is such that when she rose *"Seem'd like the light of day was dawning/Just 'fore the sun began to rise."* What these lovelies have in common and what they share with a dozen or more romantic ideals celebrated by Foster is one thing: They're dead. Jeanie is so vaporous, we learn, because *"Her smiles have vanished and her sweet songs flown,"* while Gentle Annie's *"spirit did depart."* The subject of "Nelly Was a Lady," notice, is described in the past tense, and Foster's lyrics include the line *"Last night when Nelly was a sleeping/Death came a-knockin' at the door."*

They are birds of a feather, these pop songwriters of the nineteenth and twentieth centuries. Brian himself mentioned it to David Leaf in 2004, smiling shyly over the piano keys as he played the first bars of "Beautiful Dreamer" and noted how the first letters in the first verse of the song, *"Beautiful dreamer, wake unto me,"* are also his own initials. "That's me!" he declared to Leaf's camera. "Beautiful dreamer, wake . . . Brian Douglas Wilson!" That revelation served as both the point of entry and title for *Beautiful Dreamer,* Leaf's two-hour documentary about *Smile.* And indeed, like the twentieth-century water-phobe who wrote indelible songs about surfing, the Pittsburgh-raised Foster was a stranger to the southern plantations that inspired his muse and built his reputation. But the nineteenth-century boy who grew up moving from house to house put all of his own childhood yearning into his idyllic portraits of the antebellum South, just as he would project his own mourning for his dead sister (and later his mother) into those vaporous dead women.

"The love of my life, she left me one day/I cried when she said 'I don't feel the same way,'" Brian sang in "The Warmth of the Sun," one of the saddest, most beautiful songs he ever wrote with Mike. They'd started writing the song a day or two

before the assassination of John F. Kennedy, but they were still working on it on November 22, and the devastation of the president's death seeped into the song's final verse, which reaches out of the gloom for a bittersweet sense of hope: *"Our love's like the warmth of the sun/It won't ever die."*

———————

If Brian craved emotional stability, the new Mrs. Wilson did her best to provide it. She gave him the time and space he needed to work and made his burgers, sandwiches, or steaks when he called for them. Although there was no evidence Marilyn was involved in drugs, she forgave him for his LSD trips and learned to turn a blind eye when he and his friends sparked up a joint in the house. The young couple settled into their first real home in 1965: a modern ranch house with panoramic views of Beverly Hills in one direction and Los Angeles in the other. The house had a formal entry with marble floors, a shag-carpeted L-shaped living room, a restaurant-caliber kitchen, and three spacious bedrooms arrayed around a small interior fountain. Like the house itself, the furnishings they chose reflected the couple's appetite for the comforts of suburban affluence. Prints of Walter Keane's sad-eyed children shared space with an inexpensive print of the Mona Lisa and a vaguely medieval tapestry with a dark bird embroidered on it. A heavy Spanish table with high-backed, velvet-covered chairs dominated the dining room, and the yard featured a new swimming pool, complete with a spiraling slide.

Other features hinted at the young owner's new interest in the counterculture. Lava lamps oozed in the living room, casting a dim glow across the wind chimes hanging in the corner. The wooden cigarette box on the glass coffee table didn't hold tobacco, and the brownies that emerged from the kitchen sometimes came with more punch than the ones Mom used to make.

In retrospect, Brian's deepening interest in drugs would foreshadow the psychological catastrophes that would eventually overtake him. But at the time, drugs seemed more like a welcome escape from the considerable pressure of his status. "He'd become the superstar of the family; he obviously had the gift," Mike Love's younger brother Stan Love recalls. Then a star high school basketball player being wooed by college recruiters, Stan knew how it felt to live in the shadow of another family member and what it meant to carry the weight of other people's expectations. But if athletes learn to thrive under such high-pressure circumstances, the always-sensitive Brian was unsettled by his family's defer-ence. Their expectations weighed on him too, nearly as much as Murry's ongo-ing criticism. Mike did what he could to protect his cousin from his uncle's abuse. "Murry was very obnoxious and abusive," he recalls. "He constantly rode Brian, told him he didn't know what he was doing, and then he'd come in with these corny ideas from another generation." But the group's most driven, mar-ket-conscious member came with his own expectations and requirements, and these would soon become as much a stumbling block for Brian as Murry could ever be.

And yet in 1965, with his songs massing at the top of the charts, his produc-tions wowing the most elite music insiders, and the Beach Boys industry raking in fistfuls of cash, Brian still had the power to shut people out. After the phone stopped ringing, after his friends had come and gone and the exuberance of the day had faded, Brian would sit at his piano and slip inside himself. Often it would be late, sometimes past midnight, and he'd be alone in the living room of his new hilltop house, peering down at the lights of Beverly Hills while his fingers searched the piano keys for the chords that seemed to describe his unsettled emotions. He'd lose himself in the music, playing little fragments ("feels," he called them), exper-imenting with variations and voicings until something bigger began to take shape. While composing, Brian appeared strangely absent, as if he were functioning less as a conscious artist than as a kind of antenna, channeling signals no one else could see or hear. It seemed like he was thinking about nothing at all, really. But when his fingers fell across the keys into a chord progression and the rhythm of the changes would suggest a melody, it's easy to imagine him hearing something else coming through the notes. Some shred of a memory from the past, say, a fantasy about a girl he had seen, or just the echo of a poisonous thought that had occurred to him that morning. *("Sometimes I have a weird way of showing my love . . .")*

The Beach Boys Today!—the mid-1965 album produced in the months lead-ing up to and following Brian's marriage—devoted an entire side to his more introspective ballads, but it can't help fretting on its more rocking side, either. "Good to My Baby," for instance, presents one oddly defensive man's arguments against unnamed critics. *"All they know is from what they've seen,"* he grumbles, adding quickly: *"But when I get her alone you know we're happy as a couple can be."* "Don't Hurt My Little Sister" recounts Diane Rovell's pointed advice from the early (and surreptitious) days of Brian and Marilyn's affair, only with an uncomfortable fraternal ardor: *"Why don't you love her like her big brother?"* The first iteration of "Help Me Ronda" follows quickly, minus the "h" in Rhonda and the more lively musical and vocal arrangement of the song's better-known incarnation. The song's emotional desperation remains, however, and is echoed on the album's flip side, which leads off with "Please Let Me Wonder" and its delicately rendered pleas that the narrator's girl not confess her romantic misdeeds: *"Please let me wonder if I've been the one you love . . ."* A cover of the teen love ballad "I'm So Young" eases the mood briefly, but then come the battling couple of "Kiss Me, Baby" *("Kiss a little bit/Fight a little bit . . ."),* the anguished self-indictment in "She Knows Me Too Well" *("I always expect her to know what I'm thinking of . . ."),* and then, finally, the happy-ending-as-hall-of-mirrors "In the Back of My Mind."

Though the next album—the cranked-out-for-the-season *Summer Days (and Summer Nights!)*—spends much of its time riding the roller-coaster *("Let's take our car and do amusement parks USA!")* or flirting happily with out-of-town girls *("The L.A. boys all heard the noise/about the girl from New York City!"),* and Brian sounds thrilled with love in "You're So Good to Me," he also seems thoroughly surprised to be feeling that way. *"I know your eyes are not on the guys when we're apart/You're so true to me/How come you are?"* The narrator of the "Ticket to Ride"–like "Girl Don't Tell Me" has no such luck: *"I bet you went out every night during ol' school time/But this time I'm not gonna count on you."*

And all of this pales compared to the high-pitched tension of "Let Him Run Wild," whose layers of chiming vibes, guitars, interlocking percussion, and grumbling saxophones support a taut falsetto from Brian. *"When I saw you walk with him tears filled my eyes/And when I heard you talk with him I couldn't stand his lies,"* he wails. Brian would subsequently disown the song (whose lyrics he wrote himself, rather than collaborating with Mike Love, who had come to be his most consistent lyricist), complaining that his vocal on the track was far too shrill. "I sounded like a little girl," he said. Others wondered if the song—allegedly inspired by his father's extramarital affairs—reminded him of a painful moment in his past that he didn't care to relive. But it's also intriguing to note that the narrator in the song, at long last, is actually taking aggressive action to win the girl: *"Before he makes you over/I'm gonna take you over . . ."*

Of course, Brian may have only been using the song as a subtle way to tell off his father. If so, "Let Him Run Wild" finds a companion piece in "I'm Bugged at My Old Man," a tossed-off piano blues number he sings with his brothers.

One of the weirdest pieces of humor to ever turn up on anyone's album, the song—with Brian on piano and singing lead in a purposefully overwrought high tenor—describes a grouchy father who responds to minor adolescent infractions with an escalating series of outrageous punishments. By the end of the tune, Dad has confiscated the lad's surfboard and radio, cut off his hair, and locked him in his room with only bread crumbs and a glass of water for nourishment. *"I'm bugged at my old man,"* Brian concludes, breaking into an Elvis-like sneer: *"An' he doesn't even know where it's at!"* The fact that Murry and Audree had separated—moving into separate, if close by, homes in Whittier, only heightened Brian's simmering fury toward his father. Just as Murry had once stood to protect his mother from his father, now Brian was following that same impulse in his own way: in song.

By now, of course, Brian had his own house, a wife to cook him whatever he wanted to eat, and more than enough radios, record players, and high-tech recording equipment to keep him entertained. And when he turned on the radio, the chances were good that he'd hear one of his own songs blaring out of its speakers. To his friends and followers, Brian seemed capable of anything. "He was absolutely on top of the world," says Danny Hutton, then an aspiring musician producing tunes for the sound tracks of *The Flintstones* and other Hanna-Barbera cartoons. "Compare it to the hottest acts now, only times ten. The Beatles had that dominance, and so did Dylan. But none of those guys could do everything—write, arrange, sing, and produce—on the level Brian could. Brian had it all, and he *knew* he was good. When Brian was around, he was the authority. He was in control."

Borne up by his success, fueled by a limitless supply of drugs, food, books, and new, powerful friends, and pushed forward by his ambition and insecurities, Brian ventured further into his own musical imagination. Murry had urged him to trim the grand orchestral prelude to "California Girls" ("Simplify, son! Simplify!" he'd pleaded), but Brian would have none of it. Instead, he only grew more adventurous.

If Stephen Foster projected his utopian fantasies onto southern plantations, and Brian transferred his earliest yearnings onto the beaches and highways of California, the real vehicle and destination of his journey for salvation was the music itself. The more time he spent in his room, the deeper he allowed himself to fall into his emotions, the more vibrant and unrestrained his music became.

The only band that even seemed to be close to matching Brian's groundbreaking style was the Beatles, who Brian had come to regard with a combination of respect, admiration, and good-natured competition. Hearing the American version of *Rubber Soul* and the sheer quality of songs such as "Girl," "Norwegian Wood," and "I'm Looking Through You," along with the shared sensibility that united them all (enhanced, ironically enough, by the Capitol Records executives who hoped to capitalize on the ongoing folk rock boom by trading out the electrified "Drive My Car," "If I Needed Someone," and "Nowhere Man" for the acoustic "I've Just Seen a Face" and "It's Only Love," both of which were left off of the American release of *Help*) knocked Brian back a step. Like the vast majority of pop albums, every Beach Boys record contained a few filler tracks—tossed-off instrumentals, random cover songs, even a few comedy bits stitched together from studio patter. But *Rubber Soul* raised the stakes. All the songs were originals (a feat the Beatles had achieved before) for one thing, but even more impressive, none of them sounded like the sort of make-work tracks that tended to fill in the middle slots of the sides. "A whole album with all good stuff!" Brian marveled. And now he knew what he had to do next. As David Leaf writes in his 1978 biography, Brian brought the news to his wife in an urgent rush of excitement. "Marilyn, I'm gonna make the greatest album!" he declared. "The greatest rock album ever made!"

He went back to his piano, where he could disappear into himself and transform his anxieties and inspiration into music that went beyond anything he'd ever done before. Beyond anything *anyone* had ever done before. Emotional music; religious music, even. "It all starts with religion," he said in one 1966 interview that went on to connect his sense of faith with the way he could transform his feelings into beautiful sounds. "A lot of the songs are the results of emotional experiences, sadness and pain. . . . I find it possible to spill melodies, beautiful melodies, in moments of great despair. This is one of the wonderful things about this art form."

But if Brian had one weakness as a songwriter, he felt, it was expressing his feelings verbally. And though his songs almost always revolved around his feelings and ideas, he most often depended upon collaborators to transform his simply stated notions into lyrics. Better yet, Brian's collaborators served as a sounding board, not just for his musical ideas, but for all the other whims and fancies that caromed through his mind. And the more he began to think about this new album, the more Brian understood that he would need a new partner to help write the new songs. Someone who was articulate and sensitive, who had nothing to do with his family or any previous Beach Boys record. Talking one day with Loren Schwartz, Brian was reminded of Tony Asher, a youngish advertising executive he'd seen at the evening parties in his friend's Hollywood apartment. Interestingly, Asher—who wrote jingles for the Carson-Scott advertising agency (including spots for Mattel and Gallo wine) and often recorded them at Western Recorders—had actually introduced Brian to Loren back in January 1963.

"He was my best friend at Santa Monica High School," Schwartz says. "His mother was Laura LaPlante, a famous silent film actress, and his dad, Irving Asher, was a big movie executive. They lived in a big mansion on Maple Drive, with a real English butler. He played good piano, was a student of modern jazz and arranging, and was very clever with words." Indeed, Asher was an urbane, well-to-do bachelor who was well read and preferred jazz to rock. But if Asher didn't buy rock records for his collection, he listened to it on the radio and had long since come to appreciate the complexity and power of the Beach Boys' singles. "When a new song of theirs came on the radio, I'd think, 'Goddammit, they did it again!'" Asher recalls. "I had great respect and admiration for them and for Brian, but I didn't own any of their albums. I was buying Bill Evans albums."

Perhaps that's why Brian—who often made his most important decisions based on gut reactions—knew that Asher was exactly the guy he was looking for. He called him at the office one day in December 1965, explaining that he had an album to make and needed a new sound for the lyrics. "He said, 'I want this to be completely different. . . . I don't want to write with anyone I've written with before,'" Asher remembers. Once Asher was confident the voice on the other end was indeed the head Beach Boy and not a friend prank-calling him from down the hall, he accepted the collaboration offer on the spot. "Aside from the prestige, aside from the fact that the guy is like one of my idols," Asher told David Leaf in 1978, "that was like someone saying, 'How would you like $25,000?'" Securing a three-week leave of absence from his bosses at Carson-Scott, Asher packed up some yellow legal pads and pencils and drove up to Brian's house in Beverly Hills to begin his unexpected, exciting task.

The first assignment was atypical, as it turns out. After showing Asher around his house, Brian took him into his small music room, where he played him an acetate of a finished track he'd recorded for an echoing, circular song titled "In

My Childhood." Brian already had a set of lyrics that fit with the tune's sweet, vaguely melancholy sound and quirky textural effects (a bicycle horn and bell). But he didn't like his lyrics anymore and wanted to adapt the tune to another concept. What he had in mind for the new album, Asher recalls, had nothing to do with the Beatles or any kind of rock 'n' roll. "Brian had defined it as wanting to write something closer to classical American love songs, like Cole Porter or Rodgers and Hammerstein," he says. Brian asked Asher what his favorite songs were, and when it turned out the Beach Boy hadn't even heard of the romantic jazz ballad "Stella by Starlight," Asher sat at the piano and played it for him. "He was totally blown away. He hadn't heard it before, and he loved it."

Brian, in turn, dubbed a tape copy of "In My Childhood" and sent Asher home to write new words. Asher came back the next day with the lyrics to "You Still Believe in Me" sketched out on his yellow legal pad. For reasons he can't quite remember, Asher felt no doubt that Brian would approve of what he had done. "Ordinarily I'm not that self-confident," he says. "But I guess I'd already learned that he was insecure, too, and he didn't know what he wanted, either." But Brian knew he liked the new words, and so from that moment, their collaboration began in earnest. Most days, Asher would get to Brian's house at about 10:00 a.m., only to wait for his partner to roust himself from bed and get something to eat. That could take anywhere from one to three hours, during which they'd start chatting about whatever was on their minds. "We'd have like a two- or three-hour conversation that set a mood," Asher explains. "We'd ramble on about whatever: girls we had dated, relationships we'd had, heartbreak, and so on. And then we'd write within that mood. He'd play the piano for a while, and I'd sit with my yellow legal pad sketching out lyrics, and we'd be ignoring each other. Then we'd get together, tinkering with each other's work."

The idea of young love—particularly the kind that resembled the intense crush he'd once had on Carol Mountain during high school—seemed to obsess Brian. "Those times when you're young and you'd jump off a bridge for a girl, but then ten days later you'd be thinking the same thing about someone else," Asher says. "We were thinking about back when you're just beginning to understand what love is, acknowledging that it's immature but still universal." Brian clearly fed off of the emotional intensity he recalled from those early relationships, which may be why he didn't seem to recognize their inherent immaturity or, for that matter, what his fascination for them said about the state of his grown-up relationship with Marilyn. As Asher recalls: "He was constantly looking at teenage girls. Which wasn't like a forty-seven-year-old looking at teenagers [Brian was twenty-three]. But he thought they were all the most beautiful girls in the world. And he was married at the time, so it was fairly obvious he was confused about love."

Indeed, when Brian wasn't rhapsodizing about the random young women he encountered in drive-in restaurants or on the street, he was fantasizing about his own sister-in-law. "He'd stop in the middle of writing a song or a conversation or whatever and start going on about Diane, about how innocent, sweet, and beautiful she was. I'd be thinking, 'Huh! Your wife's in the next room, and you're talking about her sister!'" Other times, he would flash back to Carol Mountain, to the point of tracking his classmate down to her new home, where he would telephone or even appear at odd hours, desperate to re-experience the thrill she gave him in high school. But Mountain, like Brian, was married, setting out on a life that had very little to do with the one she had lived in Hawthorne. This became the subject of another long conversation with Asher, and by the time they were done, they had written "Caroline, No," the desolate ballad that would conclude the album.

As Asher recalls, Brian's mood could swing in a moment from bright-eyed and happy to bitterly depressed. He would spend hours avoiding work, sometimes leaping up from the piano to watch an episode of *Flipper* and bursting into tears when Sandy, the young boy, learned a touching lesson about life from his finny friend. And the songwriter's childlike sensibilities extended to his sense of responsibility when it came to doing business. Once word got out that Asher was working with Brian, the lyricist was inundated with urgent calls from the Beach Boy's lawyers, agents, and record label, all of them beseeching him to bring their latest bit of business to the attention of their key—yet entirely disinterested—client. *"We're just trying to send him some money!"* Asher recalls one sad executive wailing.

But Brian couldn't have cared less, and his disinterest was, Asher suspects, encouraged by Murry, to whose office the lyricist was sent when it came time to negotiate a publishing deal for his work. "His father protected him in an odd way. He wanted Brian to be tough, but he also saw him as an annuity who should not get distracted. And I'll tell ya, he was tough as nails when I went down to sign those contracts. I had a question, and he immediately said, 'You don't like 'em? Well, get the hell outta here! We'll get someone else! My son'll do anything I tell him to!' Meanwhile he was waving this check for $7,500, which in 1966 seemed to me like a million dollars." Asher signed the contract, of course, agreeing to take just a 25 percent cut of the publishing royalties, based on the assumption that Asher would have nothing to do with the music, while Brian would inevitably contribute to the lyrics. "Which was a *screw*," Asher says. "Until you consider that I was a nothing who had never done shit, and I had a chance to write with a guy who had something like nine million-selling records in a row. Well, *then* it doesn't seem so bad."

The hours at the piano ran smoothly, with Brian moving confidently to incorporate an entirely new vocabulary of melodic and structural ideas into his songs. They worked quickly, sometimes moving from a general idea and a few stray melodic fragments to an all-but-completed song in less than half an hour. "God Only Knows," with its intricate pattern of melodic themes, harmonic counterpoint, and inverted bass patterns, emerged nearly complete in about twenty minutes. They hadn't set out to write songs that fit together into a larger narrative, but the natural drift of their conversations led the songwriters toward a series of autobiographical tunes that began in innocence ("Wouldn't It Be Nice") and then mused on facets of romance ranging from forgiveness ("You Still Believe in Me"), to the power of nonverbal communication ("Don't Talk [Put Your Head on My Shoulder]"), to love's restorative power ("I'm Waiting for the Day"), to its permanence in an unstable world ("God Only Knows"). The characters take their first steps away from home ("That's Not Me"), discuss philosophy ("Hang On to Your Ego," later rewritten, slightly, into "I Know There's an Answer"), and experience life's disappointments ("Here Today") and the sting of disillusionment ("I Just Wasn't Made for These Times"). The album's final ballad ("Caroline, No") leaves the narrator alone and heartbroken, pondering the end of his romance as a train rumbles off into the distance.

Asher didn't write the lyrics to all of the songs and was surprised when Brian announced that the record—called *Pet Sounds*—was done after they had written eight songs. What he didn't know was that Brian had dusted off one old song ("I'm Waiting . . . ," written with Mike Love in 1964), cowritten one ("Hang On to Your Ego") with his assistant Terry Sachen, and recorded two instrumentals ("Let's Go Away for a While" on the first side and "Pet Sounds" on the second). Also, Brian bowed to pressure from Capitol executives to include his stunning rearrangement of "Sloop John B.," the old sea shanty he'd first sung after hearing the Kingston Trio's hit in the '50s and recorded—at Al Jardine's suggestion— during the summer of 1965. To some critics, the inclusion of "Sloop" looms as the one serious error on *Pet Sounds:* While its striking combination of flutes, percussion, sparkling guitars, jangling bells, melodic bass line, and layered vocal harmonies (particularly the a cappella break that serves as the tune's climax) fits easily with the rest of the album's songs, the tale of nautical mishaps and drunken misdeeds diverges too wildly from each of the other, autobiographical tracks. But even if "Sloop" isn't an original tune, even if it was recorded several months before the other *Pet Sounds* tracks, even if its inclusion was dictated by Capitol bean counters, it plays a distinct—and crucial—role in the album's lyrical and musical arc.

Despite Jardine's claims that he introduced Brian to the song (which Brian has repeated, though there are tapes of him singing the song with friends while in high school), "Sloop" serves both as a biographical touchstone and as a metaphorical expression of his own feelings of displacement and isolation. The yearning for home in the chorus *("I want to go home/let me go home/why won't they let me go home?")* expands on "That's Not Me," while the final line (revised by Brian to the vaguely druggy exclamation *"this is the worst TRIP I've ever been on")* foreshadows the hipster vocabulary that informs "I Know There's an Answer." But even more significant than "Sloop's" lyrical message is its musical arrangement. If *Pet Sounds* reflects the content of its creator's heart, soul, and imagination, then his dramatic re-envisioning of "Sloop" serves as an object lesson about his artistic process.

"This is one of the wonderful things about this art form," Brian said in 1966, when he was working on *Pet Sounds.* "It can draw out so much emotion, and it can channel it into notes of music in cadence . . . Music is genuine and healthy, and the stimulation I get from molding it and from adding dynamics is like nothing on earth." In this context, Brian's euphoric arrangement of "Sloop" becomes just as intimate as "In My Room" and just as confessional as "Don't Worry, Baby." On one hand he's showing off, displaying how his singular talents have grown and matured—that adventurous bass line; that lovely, arcing harmony—but on a deeper level he's expressing his spirituality, revealing how the divine in him—his singular musical ability—refracts loneliness, fear, and sorrow into melody, harmony, and sparkling musicianship. "One day I'll write songs people pray to," he told Rolling Stones producer Andrew Loog Oldham in 1965—and he wasn't kidding.

At the same time that Brian told a reporter that all music starts with religion, he told his old friend Bruce Griffin that pop music would inevitably become more spiritual in the coming years. "I simply believe in the power of the spirit and in the manifestation of this in the goodness of people," he said. And to Brian, whose experiments with marijuana and LSD had given him a visceral sense of sacred experience, music was an expression of spirituality. It was his own new world, his city on a hill, his western frontier. "When I was making *Pet Sounds,* I did have a dream about a halo over my head, but people couldn't see it," he said in a 1996 interview. "God was right there with me. I could see—I could feel that feeling in my head, in my brain." To bring that same feeling into the studio, Brian would start recording sessions by praying for light and guidance in making the record.

Thus, his sparkling "Sloop" was an affirmation of hope, and as such, the tune is less a digression from the central theme of *Pet Sounds* than a pivot point. Because even while Brian and Tony Asher were writing a melancholy-to-desolate story about romantic disappointment and disillusionment, the music Brian created to accompany it was so rich in melody and thick with harmonies—so elegantly arranged and so inventively orchestrated—that the overall sound of this dispiriting song cycle was nothing less than ecstatic.

The recording sessions began in mid-January 1966, about a month after Asher started working with Brian and just as the rest of the Beach Boys were flying to Japan to start a tour of the Far East. Working exclusively with Hal Blaine and his gang of crack studio players, Brian ran the sessions with easygoing authority. Unlike Spector, who started each session by presenting each musician with detailed arrangements with meticulous, scripted touches, Brian preferred to start the musicians with rough chord charts. "He'd play the songs for us (on the piano), let us run it down once, and then he'd tell us what he wanted: a higher guitar, more guitar, give me some timpani there, or something! And we'd try it," Blaine recalls. Often, Brian would sing what he wanted, establishing both the melody he was after and the texture of how it should sound.

While Brian continued to emulate Spector's use of large ensembles (often with multiple percussionists and musicians doubling, tripling, or quadrupling one another's parts on drums, bass, keyboards, and guitars), he also expanded his use of exotic instruments, or traditional instruments played or recorded in unlikely ways. The chiming introduction to "Wouldn't It Be Nice," for instance, is a slack-tuned electric guitar patched directly into the studio's board, with heavy reverb creating the echoing, distant sound. The rhythm section on the verses is dominated by accordions, with reeds and strings swelling on the bridge. "You Still

Believe in Me" begins with the ghostly sound of Tony Asher leaning inside a piano to pluck the strings with paper clips, while Brian played the keyboard. The rest of the track (again, recorded as "In My Childhood") evokes the sounds of youth with harpsichords, a harp, finger cymbals, clarinets, and, to seal the nostalgic mood, a bicycle horn and bell. The relatively hard-rocking "I'm Waiting for the Day" features flutes, a viola that doubles the lead vocal line on the verses, and, in an even more off-kilter move, a string interlude that departs entirely from the song's established rhythm and melodic theme. The lyrical, elegantly constructed love song "God Only Knows" features a similarly unexpected interlude—a burst of horns, percussion, and strings playing staccato block chords whose downward motion contrasts the upward-floating chords in the rest of the piece.

Elsewhere, Brian leans heavily on the guttural huffing of a bass harmonica—used at times instead of a real bass—banjos, ukuleles, organs, guiros, slide guitars, vibraphones, harpsichords, tack pianos, and mandolins, often set against entire sections of string and horn players, and percussionists fitted out with everything from timpani to the empty Sparklett's water jug that echoes throughout "Caroline, No." But the most striking innovation comes on "I Just Wasn't Made for These Times," which incorporates the eerie wail of a theremin, an electronic instrument familiar from the futuristic horror movies of the '50s and early '60s. Brian had first seen the instrument at the home of one of his parents' friends when he was a boy, and the ghostly shriek it made (generated by using your hand to interrupt a flow of air that moves across the surface of the instrument) both intrigued and terrified him. "I was scared to death of that sound," Brian said. "It sounded like one of those horrible scary movies—weird trip, weird facial expressions—almost sexual."

The precise steps Brian takes from "horrible scary movies" to "weird facial expressions" to "almost sexual" may be best left to the imagination. But no matter what was playing across the inner recesses of his mind, Brian was thoroughly in control during his recording sessions, directing the musicians with easygoing authority, guiding everything from the notes they played to their proximity to the microphones to the feelings their playing seemed to express. The musicians called back their own ideas—one studio player suggesting the brilliant idea that the instrumental break in "God Only Knows" should be played staccato. ("Everyone helped arrange, as far as I'm concerned," Hal Blaine says.) As long as he was in the studio, the erratic, emotionally wrought Brian seemed like nothing more than a bad rumor. Instead, he was focused, smart, and remarkably good company. He quoted bits from Del Close and John Brent's beatnik comedy album, *How to Speak Hip,* captured for posterity when calling to start a take of "Hang On to Your Ego." "Here we go, zoo-be-wah!" he says excitedly. "Just relax, me and this other cat are gonna straighten you guys out, and then we'll get to know world peace!" There is a brief, puzzled silence, during which Brian learns that no one else in the room had even heard of Close and Brent's 1959 album, and you can almost feel his embarrassment as he tries to explain what the hell he's talking about. "Oh, it's *funny.* . . . It was cut in '59. It's a very funny album."

Later, in the midst of recording "Caroline, No," one of the most emotionally devastating songs in his entire catalogue, Brian sounds cheerful to the point of giddiness. "A little faster; I want it like this!" he calls at one point, going on to establish the rhythm by snapping his fingers and singing with maximum syncopation, "All the *way,* like *that,* we'll get a *record* and . . ."

Most of the basic tracks were finished by February 9, when the rest of the Beach Boys—now back from Asia and ready to record—began overdubbing their vocals, at which point the atmosphere took a definite turn. Tony Asher, for one, got the distinct feeling that his lyrics were not being greeted with open arms. "All those guys in the band, certainly Al, Dennis, and Mike, were constantly saying, 'What the fuck do these words mean?' or 'This isn't our kind of shit!'" he remembers. "Brian had comebacks, though. He'd say, 'Oh, you guys can't hack this,' or 'You can't remember your fucking parts.' But I remember thinking that those were tense sessions. And I remember thinking, 'Being here isn't good for my mental health.'"

Perhaps Mike Love's feelings had been hurt because Brian had ditched him, yet again, for another lyricist. Maybe he had grown so accustomed to seeing the audiences go wild for the songs about hot rods, surfboards, and beach bunnies that this new batch of more mature songs sounded like the musical equivalent of bankruptcy, which just a few years ago had all but sent his family to the poor house. What's clear is that the lyrics Brian's friend Terry Sachen had written for "Hang On to Your Ego," rich with pop psychology phrases and a kind of hipster finger-wagging, sent Mike over the edge. First he mocked the lyrics for what he perceived as their intellectual pretensions, using Al Jardine's flailing attempts to cut a lead vocal to air out his derision. "Oh, it's *hilarious,*" he sneered at an increasingly flustered Brian. Later, Mike said he had picked up on drug references in the song—acidheads, including Loren Schwartz, referred to "ego death" as a vital part of a successful LSD trip.

Asher's lyrics, with their candid expressions of vulnerability and sadness, struck Mike as "nauseating" and "offensive." Brian's intricately wrought instrumental tracks also inspired Mike's derision, so much so that he was still snorting about them five years later (according to a source in David Leaf's book), when he referred to the entire *Pet Sounds* album as "Brian's ego music." What really seemed to bother him, Asher observed, was that Brian's new music abandoned the standard Beach Boy vocabulary of fun to the third power. The lyricist still recalls hearing Brian complain about Mike instructing him, in no uncertain terms: "Don't fuck with the formula." But he was too late. Brian had already lost interest in the beach and the wonders of hot rods. But just to keep the peace in the Beach Boys, he did allow Mike to take a run at the lyrics of "Ego," ultimately changing the chorus (and title) to the more direct "I Know There's an Answer."

That wasn't the only interference Brian would encounter on the road to finishing *Pet Sounds*. While he chose to release "Caroline, No" as a single under his own name—a move that struck terror into the hearts of his bandmates, as it turned out—the final recording had been sped up a whole tone, at Murry Wilson's insistence, in order to make Brian's voice sound younger. Still, Brian continued to work on the album into the spring, alternating the relatively smooth instrumental sessions with more contentious vocal sessions with the other Beach Boys. Determined to achieve a vocal perfection to match the quality of the instrumental tracks, Brian drove them through take after tortuous take, his one good ear locked tight on the sound, tone, and feeling of each singer. When they couldn't meet Brian's rigid specifications, he'd dismiss the group, wipe their vocals from the tape, and rerecord all the parts himself, as on "I'm Waiting for the Day" and "I Just Wasn't Made for These Times."

The final vocal overdubbing session took place on April 13, and Brian did a final mix at the Capitol Records studio in the company's Hollywood tower three days later. That night he took an acetate of the finished recording home to Marilyn and brought her into their bedroom to listen to it. "He prepared a moment," she recalled to *Rolling Stone* in 1976. "And he goes, 'Okay, are you ready?' But he was really serious—that was his soul in there, you know? And we just lay there alone all night, you know, on the bed and just listened and cried and did a whole thing. It was really, really heavy. We both cried." Speaking to David Leaf twenty years later, she remembered another detail: "He said he was scared nobody would like it."

Brian's fear seemed to become reality a few days later when he and Mike took the acetate back to the Capitol tower to preview the new work for the label's executives. And though the company's leading British band—the Beatles—was selling mountains of vinyl with their experimental records, the Capitol brass received the new Beach Boys disc with something less than complete enthusiasm. Nick Venet, the man who had signed the group to the label nearly five years earlier, summed it up like this: "I thought Brian was screwing up. He was no longer looking to make records; he was looking for attention from the business. He was trying to torment his father with songs his father couldn't relate to and melody structures his father couldn't understand."

The Capitol sales team was even less enthusiastic, leading to at least one high-placed conversation about shelving *Pet Sounds* altogether and releasing a greatest hits album instead—usually an indication that a band's hit-making career was nearing its end. Fortunately for Brian, calmer heads prevailed, and *Pet Sounds* was scheduled for a mid-May release. Titled by Mike (or perhaps Carl, depending on whom you ask), the album came in a sleeve dominated by a large photo of the group—dressed for a California's winter day in coats and sweaters—feeding apple slices to goats, an odd illustration for any nonagrarian project but weirder still coming from a rock group who ordinarily posed around sunlit beaches or gleaming hot rods. ("There was a weird vibe on that record," Sonic Youth's Thurston Moore noted in Don Was's 1995 documentary. "I would look at the cover of *Pet Sounds* and think . . . these guys with these sheep. I mean, what's going on here?") A green band across the top announced the album, along with the names of all the album tracks, while a montage of black-and-white photos on the rear cover was divided between shots of the touring group onstage, posing for publicity shots in Japan while wearing samurai outfits (perhaps an even worse design idea than the goat shot), and a couple of sober shots of Brian, one at home and the other leaning out of the window of his car.

Early reviews in the United States ranged from sour to confused to tentatively positive, while sales, as predicted and perhaps influenced by the Capitol sales staff, were also relatively underwhelming. Ultimately, *Pet Sounds* spent thirty-nine weeks on the Billboard album chart, peaking at number eleven. And though it included three top ten singles (the number three hit "Sloop John B." and the double-A-side "God Only Knows"/"Wouldn't It Be Nice," which rose to number eight), the album's sales of 500,000 units didn't compare to the chain of million-sellers that had preceded it. Of course, the greatest hits album Capitol released less than two months after *Pet Sounds* came out went gold almost immediately, catapulting to Billboard's number eight slot and then staying on the charts for a full year and a half. "That really hurt him badly," Marilyn Wilson told *Rolling Stone.* "He couldn't understand it. It was like, why put your heart and soul into something?"

But Brian couldn't have been that surprised; he all but predicted the demise of *Pet Sounds* in "I Just Wasn't Made for These Times" when he sang, *"Every time I get the inspiration to go change things around/No one wants to help me look for places where new things might be found. . . ."* Indeed, it wouldn't be very long before the song's lyrics—particularly the plaintive question, *"What can I do when my fair-weather friends cop out?"*—would seem to describe everything that had gone wrong in his life and career.

Maybe that's what inspired him to write the song. Maybe that's why, when he played it at home just before taking it into the studio, he imagined the song as a climax of sorts. It was an intricate construction of layered percussion, a Fender bass pirouetting above a bass harmonica, a harpsichord sharing space with a banjo that adds texture to the smooth clarinets blowing above the tack piano that honky-tonks through a chorus made up of four contrasting vocal lines that eventually make way for the queer wail of the theremin, repeating the song's central melodic motif in each chorus, then takes an entire verse leading into the song's conclusion, a round of *"I guess I just wasn't made for these times"* sung over a thick bed of falsetto *"ooohs"* while the drums bang out the beat and the bass marches double-time into the fade.

"Sometimes I feel very sad/Sometimes I feel very sad . . ."

Whatever the case, the music that Brian's sorrow inspired is nothing short of triumphant. While he describes his confusion, owns up to his failures, and more or less acknowledges his coming defeat, he can't help transforming his concession into an exaltation. To hear Brian explore new heights of beauty and possibility in pop music while simultaneously declaring the all-but-inevitable end of his creative journey was to experience the defining contradiction at the source of his music. *Pet Sounds* was meant to be a tragedy about the end of youth and the inevitable fraying of beauty, and its tragic hero is the sad-eyed young man peering shyly over the piano keys on the album's back cover.

CHAPTER 6

Brian had sensed their presence for years. The demons had always been there, chattering softly just beyond the edge of his vision, poking at his dead ear, threatening him, making him dizzy. But he didn't have to listen. Being with friends, keeping his hands and mind busy, made everything better. As ever, music was the real key. It brought people to him, for one thing. More importantly, it could drown the demons out even when he was alone. No wonder he had made music the center of his world, riding those childhood ecstasies to "Rhapsody in Blue" into the countless hundreds of teenaged hours wandering the intricate, swirling harmonies of the Four Freshmen, which led him straight to the soul-cleansing power of Phil Spector's productions. And by then he'd already made that world his own, adapting everything he'd learned from his heroes to build a sanctuary he could hide in forever.

But now he could hear the whispers beginning to infiltrate that world. The Capitol Records brass had already signaled the limits of their corporate patience, and once *Pet Sounds* faltered on the *Billboard* charts, the rest of the Beach Boys had more or less put him on notice: Forget the bullshit and get back to making hits. Everyone had mortgages to pay, wives and ex-wives to support, investments to keep afloat, offices to rent, and employees who needed to be paid. He listened and nodded, but he knew he couldn't confront those obligations on their own terms. Instead Brian looked to make music that was even more adventurous, still trusting in its power, and became determined to build a new sanctuary even bigger, louder, and more grandiose than the last one. All he needed to do was to keep moving, keep working, to fill the studio with more musicians playing bigger, more elaborate songs.

When *Pet Sounds* got to England (about a month following its Stateside release), the leading lights of mid-1960s hipness greeted the record with nothing short of rapture. Bruce Johnston had taken an early pressing of the record to London, where once-and-future Beatles publicist Derek Taylor worked with L.A.-based record producer and gadfly Kim Fowley to organize the album's UK unveiling. Stationing Bruce in a suite at the swank Waldorf Hotel, they shepherded the country's most influential music journalists in for interviews. The climax of the trip came during an exclusive listening party at which England's most popular and powerful musicians—led by John Lennon and Paul McCartney—filled the suite and sat in complete silence while the album's thirteen tracks played. McCartney instantly proclaimed "God Only Knows" to be the greatest song ever written. John and Paul leaped back into their limo and made directly for the EMI studio on Abbey Road, where sessions for *Revolver* were already in progress. As legend has it, the duo set immediately to work on the lush "Here, There, and Everywhere," laying down their own multilayered backing harmonies with the sound of Brian's intricate *Pet Sounds* vocal arrangements still echoing in their ears.

The rest of the British media and pop galaxy followed suit, more or less. Eric Clapton, then with Cream, said his entire band considered *Pet Sounds* to be ". . . one of the greatest pop LPs ever released. . . . It encompasses everything that's ever knocked me out and rolled it into one." Andrew Loog Oldham, then the manager of the Rolling Stones, was so thrilled that he wrote and paid for a full-page ad in the *Melody Maker* music trade magazine proclaiming *Pet Sounds* the greatest album ever made, an extraordinary gesture when you consider he had no stake in the record's success.

Such unfettered enthusiasm pushed *Pet Sounds* all the way to the number two slot of the British sales charts, while the singles released from the album in the UK ("Sloop John B." and "God Only Knows") both peaked at number two. The foreign chart action might have affirmed Brian's faith in *Pet Sound*s, if not his bandmates', but by the time his most recent album lit up the charts abroad, the head Beach Boy was already focused on his next musical vision. It was a song called "Good Vibrations," and he'd been working on it on and off for months.

It began during the *Pet Sounds* era as a kind of rhythm and blues track, its verses built around a minor progression with a heavy bass, organ, and flute arrangement that would have sounded at home in one of the Four Tops' gut-wrenching Motown love songs. In fact, the Tops' next hit, "Reach Out, I'll Be There," used a very similar chord progression and Spector-influenced orchestration, and the two songs would race one another into the top ten during the fall of 1966. But while Brian's tune was also a love song, his was far trippier. The initial inspiration came from an exchange he'd had with his mother as a child, about how dogs can sense if a person is going to be friendly to them even before they approach. "They feel the vibrations," Audree told him, and the image struck him immediately. "It scared me, the word *vibrations*. To think that invisible feelings, invisible vibrations, existed scared me to death," Brian told *Rolling Stone*'s David Felton in 1976. And yet the idea also appealed to him, particularly when he thought of lovers communicating on that same nonverbal plane. Musing on that notion one night, Brian had written some music he called "Good, Good, Good Vibrations" and played it for Tony Asher, who sketched out some preliminary lyrics: *"It's weird how she comes in so strong/And I wonder what she's pickin' up from me/I hope it's good, good, good, good vibrations . . ."*

Thinking of placing the song on *Pet Sounds*, Brian took a stab at recording "Good, Good, Good Vibrations" during a series of sessions that began at the Gold Star studio on February 17. Already hip-deep into the instrument closet for the other cuts on the album, Brian pulled out a harpsichord, tack piano, flutes, clarinets, a cello, a Jew's harp, electric fuzz bass, stand-up bass, bass harmonica, chromatic harmonica, organ, and the usual complement of percussion instruments to give the backing track the right exotic-to-majestic sound. The real crowning touch, however, came from the electronic theremin, whose high, ghostly wail he'd first added to the "I Just Wasn't Made for These Times" session three days earlier. Charged this time with evoking the vibrations zooming around on the psychic plane, the theremin soared above the entire track, playing the central melodic hook that lashed the chorus to the verse.

But as the song began to take shape in the studio, Brian began to realize that "Good Vibrations" didn't fit with the moodier, introspective songs that formed the nucleus of *Pet Sounds*. He put the song aside, even pondering handing it off to a soul singer such as Wilson Pickett, or to Danny Hutton, a young musician Brian had befriended. Hutton was managed by another mutual friend, David Anderle, who had recently started working for the Beach Boys, helping them set up a record label they would own and control. Maybe, Anderle proposed, Hutton could inaugurate the new label with his own rendition of "Good Vibrations"?

Instead, Brian kept the tune for himself. And the more he came back to it that winter and spring, the more convinced he became that the song should be even bigger than the tracks he was orchestrating for *Pet Sounds*. After all, he was writing about the higher frequencies; why limit the song to any of the constructs that governed pop music? Wandering out past all the traditional pop boundaries, Brian began to think of "Good Vibrations" as a smaller, psychedelic version of "Rhapsody in Blue." A "little pocket symphony," as he put it, built from parts whose distinct rhythms, moods, and sounds would flow together to form a larger, cohesive piece. To enhance the song's modular feel, he recorded different sections in different studios, using one room for its intimacy, the other for the grandness of its echo, and so on. "I saw the record as a totality piece," Brian said in 1976. But creating that totality didn't have to end with the chords and melody he wrote, the instruments he chose to play it, the vocals he arranged, and the way he chose to record them. Now he could play the recordings too, taking the pieces apart and putting them back together however it suited him.

It was an intricate process in the pre-digital, pre-sixty-four-track age, stretching to twenty-two recording sessions that took place in four studios over the course of seven months. As more time passed and the expenses added up ("Good Vibrations" would eventually cost a then-unbelievable $50,000 to record), the song's avant-garde sound, structure, and length (more than 3:30, also unbelievable for a pop single in the mid-1960s) became increasingly controversial in and around the group. "There was a lot of 'Oh, you can't do this; that's too modern' or 'That's going to be too long a record,'" Brian recalled in 1976. "I said, 'No, it's not going to be too long a record; it's going to be just right.'"

Still, there were times when the song flummoxed him completely, so much so that Brian would walk into a session, consider the myriad possibilities and problems that lay ahead, and cancel the session on the spot, sending a dozen of Los Angeles's most expensive studio players home without getting a note out of them. But if the intricacies of "Good Vibrations" scared him, they also enticed him.

Even as Brian took a six-week break from the studio that summer, leaving "Good Vibrations" in pieces and his family, bandmates, and corporate chiefs hovering somewhere between puzzled and furious, he had already started envisioning an album that would be even more ambitious. He already knew the entire album would follow the modular approach he was trying to master for "Good Vibrations," with individual sections flowing into songs that flowed into other songs that drifted into individual movements that ultimately formed a symphony. It would be his "Rhapsody in Blue."

When he sat at his piano at night and gazed out at the lights spreading out beneath him, he could feel something taking shape. It would be the spiritual music he'd been talking about for so many months. "A teenage symphony to God," was how he began to describe it. Sometimes, when Brian would take a few Desbutols (a kind of amphetamine) and stay up late at night thinking and playing, slowly working his way into that inner space where the melodies would start to arrive, he would see small figures moving through the air above him. They seemed angelic to him, and he figured them for the heavenly beings that were delivering the music to him. Brian began to call the album *Dumb Angel,* perhaps in their honor, but like so many of his plans, this would eventually change.

What didn't change was his need for a collaborator. Tony Asher had provided just the right straightforward sensitivity for *Pet Sounds,* but now the music was becoming wilder, more free-form, and the lyrics would have to be just as adventurous. He mentioned all this to Terry Melcher—who had helmed sessions for the Byrds, Paul Revere and the Raiders, and Judy Collins, among others—and the young producer (and son of Doris Day) thought immediately of Van Dyke Parks. The twenty-three-year-old musician had just written a song called "High Coin" for Harpers Bizarre, and the tune's playful, punning lyrics (*"We're in the high times, baby/Where words are lost and tempest tossed in lemon-lime/When times and places effervesce/In words of wonder, from down under, I'm no less/I'm fine, it's my time")* seemed to be exactly what the head Beach Boy was yearning for. Actually, Brian and Parks had already met several times in passing during the previous year, first when David Crosby brought him up to Laurel Way to hear an early acetate of "Sloop John B." They'd also bumped into one another at their mutual hangouts in Western Recorders and Loren Schwartz's apartment. "I had suggested the cello triplets in 'Good Vibrations,' so he knew what I was doing," Parks recalls. But they'd never really had a chance to get to know one another, so Melcher invited them both to a party at his house on Cielo Drive in mid-July and pulled them together out on the lawn to talk things over.

They made, at first glance, an oddly matched pair. Brian, tall, pale, and a bit doughy in his striped surfer's shirt and blue jeans, was always a bit awkward around new people, particularly when it came to making small talk. The bespectacled Parks, on the other hand, was elfin and slight, decked out in a paisley shirt and old-fashioned trousers held up with red suspenders. And Parks, who spoke with a warm southern drawl, could talk a blue streak about his boyhood in Hattiesburg, Mississippi, the years he spent as a child actor in New York and Los Angeles (he'd shared the screen with Grace Kelly in *The Swan*), the years he'd spent studying music and literature at Carnegie Tech in Pittsburgh, and the burgeoning music career that had already taken him from the concert halls of the Northeast (as a part of the Greenwood County Singers) to the leading folk clubs of Los Angeles (where he and his older brother Carson performed as the Steeltown Two) to a studio career. But really, he was just as interested in discussing the poetry of Bukowski and Ferlinghetti or, better yet, the impenetrable beauty of James Joyce.

Parks can't remember what they talked about that night, but it's clear that Brian was impressed. "He seemed like a really articulate guy," he said many years later. "Like he could write some good lyrics." Brian first suggested that Parks finish off the still-incomplete lyrics to "Good Vibrations." But while Parks appreciated his new friend's egalitarianism ("I liked his inclusive attitude to get me involved with him. That took a lot of straight, normal good manners.") and was so broke he and his wife were living above a garage in an apartment that didn't even have a bathroom of its own, he was as conscious of his own unique abilities as he was of his new friend's commercial success. Thus, he concluded, if they were going to collaborate, it should be on something they both had a hand in creating. Brian saw the logic to that, and off they went. "He said, 'You write some words for me,' and we just started immediately," Parks says.

A few days later, Brian asked Parks to come up to his house on Laurel Way. He arrived on his motorcycle, trailed by a police officer who hadn't been convinced that this shaggy-haired little guy actually had any legitimate business roaring around Beverly Hills. Things got even tenser when it turned out that the shaggy little guy had neglected to bring his driver's license. But a little fast talk from Parks convinced Johnny Law to at least lead him to Wilson's house, where his host would not only welcome him with open arms but also vouch for his identity. Brian opened the door, as promised, and when it turned out that the cop's sister was a Beach Boys fan and would just *love* an autographed album, well, that was the end of that scrape with the law.

Brian and Van Dyke talked for a while, touching briefly on business matters. The sum of their collaboration agreement went, more or less, like this: Brian asked what Van Dyke needed, and Van Dyke told him he needed a car. Brian asked what kind, and Van Dyke mused that Volvos are supposed to be safe and reliable and, when asked, guessed that they cost something like $5,000. Brian picked up a telephone, recited Van Dyke's name and address to the person on the other end, told them to cut a check for five grand for delivery the next day, and that was that.

Not long after that they were settled in at the piano, where Brian pounded out the first chords of a song he'd been working on, a hurtling countrylike tub-thumper that reminded Van Dyke instantly of Marty Robbins's "El Paso." Yes, Brian said, nodding, he'd actually been thinking about the Old West when he wrote it. In fact, he'd been thinking of calling it "Heroes and Villains." Van Dyke picked up a pencil and paper and started to write, listening carefully to the meter of the melody Brian was la-la-ing over the chords, making sure the syllables he wrote coincided exactly with the rhythm of the music. Soon, he had an opening verse:

"I've been in this town so long that back in the city/I've been taken for lost and gone and unknown for a long, long time . . ."

Brian smiled and nodded, and Van Dyke turned back to his pad, one ear cocked to the music, the other tuned into the sound of his pencil scratching across the paper. They worked that way for hours, both of them feverish with the excitement of their new connection and the thrill of creation. "I have no idea if it was day or night," Van Dyke says. "Probably both. But we had the whole thing, apart from one section, in one sitting. That was the enthusiasm." As the lyrics took shape, the images that spilled out across Van Dyke's page seemed to take all of the feelings Brian sensed inside of himself and project them into vibrantly colored, abstract glimpses into another, parallel world. Set in a lawless boomtown somewhere out on the fringes of the Old West, "Heroes and Villains" described a world lit up by ambition and riddled with gunfire. The narrator speaks as a man who has become a part of the scene, but not of it, exactly, because he's still so thrilled and terrified by everything he sees. *"Heroes and villains, just see what you've done done"* he sings again and again, as the music pivots from minor to major and back again. The indictment, if that's what it is, later expands to take in the sweep of the nation around them: *"Bicycle rider, just see what you done done/To the church of the American Indian."* By the time it ends, the narrator has aged and seen his own children grow to adulthood. But if he has been transformed by the decades spent in the boomtown, has he become a hero or a villain? That's one question he won't, or can't, answer.

If "Heroes and Villains" seems set in the Deadwood, South Dakota, of the nineteenth century, the struggle it describes—modernity versus tradition, good versus evil, hope versus fear—fits just as easily into twentieth-century Hollywood. In a sense, it was a capsule version of American history and the lives of every striver who had tamed its wilderness, laid down its streets, or created the art that described it. It was all there, right down to the booze, gunfire, greed, and stubborn survival, against all odds, of innocence: *"She's still dancing in the night unafraid of what a dude'll do/In a town full of heroes and villains."*

"And that gave ignition to the process," Van Dyke says. "The engine had started. It was very much ad hoc. Seat of the pants. Extemporaneous values were enforced. Not too much precommitment to ideas. Or, if so, equally pursuing propinquity."

Other songs came nearly as quickly, and so Brian booked more studio time starting on August 3. He spent the first day back working on a marimba-dominated instrumental track for "Wind Chimes," another new tune he and Van Dyke had written. But the new burst of inspiration also prompted him to return to "Good Vibrations" a week later, winnowing his many hours of instrumental tracks down into the elusive mini-suite he'd been imagining since the middle of winter. He'd made enough progress by August 11 to dial his brother Carl in the Fargo, North Dakota, hotel where he and the rest of the band had just played a gig at the Memorial Auditorium and play him the edited instrumental track over the telephone line. "He called me from the recording studio and played this really bizarre-sounding music over the phone," Carl recalled. "There were drums smashing . . . and then it refined itself and got into the cello. It was a real funky track."

The touring group got back to L.A. in time for the first vocal session on the August 24, working from the set of new lyrics Brian had commissioned from

Mike Love, who wrote most of the new verses in his car on the way to the recording studio. Mike apparently thrived under deadline pressure—his words added a delicate sensuality to the track, while the bass vocal line he suggested for the chorus transcended its own verbal goofiness (rhyming "vibrations" with "excitations") by emphasizing the funky bass line already thrumming beneath the music. The vocal sessions would continue for nearly a month, with Brian once again monitoring every tonal and spiritual nuance of every note sung and double-tracked by every member. When Brian made his final mix on September 21 and then sat back in his chair in the control room at Columbia Studios and heard the finished song for the first time, he felt as if the skies above him had opened up. "I remember I had it right in the sack. I could just feel it when I dubbed it down, made the final mix from the sixteen track down to mono. It was a feeling of power . . . a feeling of exaltation. Artistic beauty. It was everything," he told *Rolling Stone* in 1976. "I remember saying, 'Oh my God. Sit back and listen to *this!*"

The song that emerged, finished in the last week of September and released to the public three weeks later, made an impact on popular culture that was both immediate and lasting. Shockingly, "Good Vibrations" blew past the standard sub-three-minute limit designated as the industry standard by record executives and radio programmers. Its contrasting moods and rhythms—veering from the delicate, flute-filled opening verses to the rumbling, wailing cello-and-theremin chorus to the Jew's-harp-and-honky-tonk-piano first bridge to the echoing, churchlike organ on the second bridge and the round of arching falsettos that lead to the final chorus—exploded even the most progressive notions of how a pop song could be written, constructed, and performed. "Good Vibrations" sounded like nothing that had ever been played on the radio before, and as it rocketed to the top of the *Billboard* charts—selling 400,000 copies in the first four days and one million in its first month—it came to summarize a feeling that had been building in youth culture throughout the mid-1960s.

In that sense, "Good Vibrations" functioned as a kind of mirror image to Bob Dylan's "Like a Rolling Stone," a similarly popular, catalytic, and even longer (though it had been sliced neatly in two for radio play) number one hit from the year before. Dylan was (and remains) a wonderfully musical songwriter, but the impact of "Like a Rolling Stone" comes most immediately in its lyrics, which string together surreal images—the chrome horse; the Siamese cat–wearing diplomat; the sad, yet sinister person known as "Napoleon in rags"; and the final rebuke, *"You're invisible now"*—with such striking authority that it forever transformed the vocabulary of popular music. And though the target of Dylan's six-minute chain of accusations was purposefully vague, its elusiveness only amplified the song's universality. Dylan might have been addressing a lover, the masters of a corrupt institution, his own arrogance, or perhaps some combination of them all. But as Greil Marcus points out in his book *Like a Rolling Stone: Bob Dylan at the Crossroads,* it was the overall sound that mattered most. Taken together, Dylan's slashing poetry, the screeching guitars, pounding drums, and wailing organ became a generational cry of frustration and statement of purpose.

And if the rollicking, roaring "Like a Rolling Stone" seemed determined to destroy everything in its path, the meandering, crystalline "Good Vibrations" stood on the same ground pointing blithely in the opposite direction, building a new utopia of its own. Where Dylan's voice was tart and piercingly intelligent, the Beach Boys were sweet and boyish. Where his music was visceral and rough, Brian's was sophisticated and honed to a high shine. And while it was the Minnesota poet's wild, psychedelic language that would transform the culture, it was the California studio whiz's equally wild, equally psychedelic music that sounded like a vision of the future.

At a moment in time when popular music meant more than ever, these songs meant more than any American rock 'n' roll tune ever had. They were the yearning of a new generation and signposts for a movement that would, for a time, promise to redefine the meaning and possibilities of American culture. As "Good Vibrations" came to dominate the sales charts and AM radio, Brian Wilson and the Beach Boys found themselves teetering unexpectedly near the leading edge of the burgeoning youth movement.

That said, the arbiters of serious culture were not prepared to speak of the Beach Boys in the same breath as Bob Dylan. Certainly, a significant percentage of the literati still dismissed the group as little more than candy-striped tools of consumerism. Skeptics were everywhere, particularly in the United States, where *Pet Sounds* had been much less popular than it had been abroad. But at least some corners of the youth demimonde—the hippies who hadn't yet been identified in quite that way—had been made to cock their collective ear. "They've found the new sound at last!" the London *Sunday Express* had raved above its ecstatic review of "Good Vibrations."

Like the *Sunday Express,* many musicians understood the significance of Brian's achievement on the album, as did a few members of the small but increasingly influential band of journalists and intellectuals who had begun to apply serious analytical thought to rock music. Not all were convinced, however. "I know L.A. hype when I hear it," snipped Ralph J. Gleason, a San Francisco–based jazz critic whose affection for Dylan had only recently steered him toward the wild and wooly latitudes of rock 'n' roll. Such attitudes dismayed Brian, if only because they reflected an image of the Beach Boys he was actively trying to leave behind, despite the stubborn efforts of his father, the Capitol Records executive suite, and a significant percentage of his own band, none of whom, it seemed, were convinced that the success of "Good Vibrations" hadn't been some kind of fluke. But it also inspired him, sending him back to the music, which drowned out even the most discouraging words.

Brian and Van Dyke worked constantly through the end of the summer and into the fall, usually recording with the studio musicians during the day and then reconvening on Laurel Way in the evening to write some more. High on Brian's Desbutols one night, they stayed up until dawn writing a stately, two-movement piece that began in the darkness of a crumbling, decadent society, then turned to face its inevitable destruction and the dawn that waited beyond. Most of the song was written during the summer, but it remained untitled and its last verse was still patchy until later in the fall, when Dennis Wilson returned from the band's British tour with tales of how some of the Brits had actually pointed and laughed at the band's striped shirts. Dennis's humiliation—he was near tears as he described it—touched Van Dyke deeply and crystallized the mood of sophistication-gone-cynical they were trying to express in the song. "We'll call it 'Surf's Up,'" he told Brian. And then he had the final lines: *"Surf's up, aboard a tidal wave/Come about hard and join the young and often spring you gave/I heard the word, wonderful thing, a children's song."*

Not that the paisley-bedecked Van Dyke was eager to pull Brian back toward the buttoned-down slickness those woefully out-of-step shirts represented. But the Anglophilia that had dominated American pop culture in the wake of the Beatles' invasion had always stuck in Van Dyke's craw. Particularly in the midst of a decade in which his nation was struggling to locate its moral bearings in the depths of the Cold War, the last throes of institutionalized racism, generational mistrust, and societal divides. The darkest side of that fight had come to his family's home just a few years earlier when his older brother

Benjamin, an up-and-comer in the US State Department, had died in mysterious circumstances while on assignment in Frankfurt, Germany. The family dealt with the blow as best they could, but the grief followed Van Dyke to Los Angeles and fueled his muse when he sat down at the piano with Brian. "I was dead set on centering my life on the patriotic ideal," Van Dyke says. "I was a son of the American revolution, and there was blood on the tracks. Recent blood, and it was still drying."

Four decades earlier, George Gershwin had set out to make his "Rhapsody" a portrait of the nation he knew. "I heard it as a sort of musical kaleidoscope of America—of our vast melting pot, of our unduplicated national pep, or our metropolitan madness," Gershwin had written. Now his two young inheritors had set out to do precisely the same thing. As the nights passed and the songs came together, the separate traumas that defined the two songwriters' lives and the stubborn hope for the future they refused to abandon came together into a series of musical vignettes that merged into an impressionistic portrait of the American past and present. "I'd just come off this personal Everest and was trying to make reason of my own life," Van Dyke says. "We were panning for good information, and it all felt very California and very frontier. The whole state of California felt like a frontier to us. And the whole record seemed like a real effort toward figuring out what Manifest Destiny was all about. We'd come as far as we could, as far as Horace Greeley told us to go. And so we looked back and tried to make sense of that great odyssey."

Some songs—"Heroes and Villains," "Surf's Up," and others—emerged whole, with verses and choruses that locked together in obvious ways. Others came out as individual episodes, each of them a discrete segment of the sepia-to-psychedelic collage of musical/lyrical moments that emerged from their shared vision. Some sections were as simple as a description of a barnyard or the cool air of a clear, country morning; others were more esoteric. "Cabin-Essence" contrasted placid verses describing a frontier home with a thundering chorus giving voice to the coming railroad. The song's climactic section zoomed skyward, simultaneously evoking the Grand Coulee Dam (and the electrified future it represents) and the eyes of a Chinese laborer as they follow the arc of a hungry crow circling a thresher working a cornfield. "Do You Like Worms" told the story of the Europeans sailing for Plymouth Rock, contrasting the hope that sailed with them to—in a reprise of the "Bicycle Rider" theme from "Heroes and Villains"—a glimpse of the damage they would wreak upon the unsuspecting natives, both on the mainland and then, later, in the Hawaiian Islands.

Another series of sections (including titles such as "Vega-Tables" and "Wind Chimes") described the transcendent beauty of the natural world, while several others ("Wonderful," "Child Is the Father of the Man") traced the pursuit of God in the face of an increasingly decadent civilization. Van Dyke's lyrics found an elegant balance between vivid down-home portraiture and a kind of James Joyce–inspired psychedelia that found its power well past the boundaries of traditional lyrical verse. Similarly, Brian's music contrasted traditional American instruments (banjo, steel guitar, fiddle, mandolin, harmonica, and tack piano) with symphonic arrangements and modern electric instruments.

"Surf's Up" was the locus for all these threads, but as they wrote and recorded more themes and vignettes, Brian couldn't resist taking apart the puzzle and putting it back together again in a completely different way. Should the end of "Heroes and Villains" be the middle of "Barnyard"? Would "Child Is the Father of the Man" work better as the climax to "Surf's Up"? Or was "I'm in Great Shape" actually part of "Barnyard"? The "Heroes and Villains" chorus—the *"just see what you've done done"* theme—became a recurring motif, a thread of doubt curling through multiple songs. But every time he'd make one decision, another section would get written and recorded and all of the options would change again. Brian would come home with more acetate records of the tracks-in-progress and spend hours playing the sections for his friends in different orders, searching for the most logical progression. The sheer number of sections and vignettes opened up a seemingly endless number of possibilities, and each seemed just as perfect as the next.

"[I'd say], 'God, Brian, why don't you leave it already? Just leave that. It's perfect that way,'" David Anderle recalled to David Leaf in 1978. Then Brian would spin the discs in a completely different order. "And I'd say, 'Well, of course, that's perfect, too.'"

And the music he was creating was only one facet of Brian's plans for the future. "The door has been opened for a whole universe of experience for me," Brian told a fan magazine interviewer that summer. To some extent, this was due to the books he'd been reading. Inspired by Loren Schwartz and the circle of young Hollywood sophisticates he had come to know, Brian had stacked his bedside table high with works ranging from the *I Ching* and Subud philosophy to tracts on astrology to the novels of Hermann Hesse to detailed charts of the stars and planets. And though Brian had never shown much interest in visual art, he was intrigued enough by the cartoon-style pop art he saw at the studio of an artist friend of Van Dyke's named Frank Holmes to let him take a shot at drawing a cover for the record Brian and Van Dyke had decided to title, with maximum hopefulness, *Smile*. The colorful, childlike drawing Holmes produced of a shop selling smiles (inspired by an abandoned jewelry store he'd seen near his home in Pasadena) appealed to Brian so much that he asked the artist to illustrate the twelve-page booklet he'd convinced Capitol to include with the album. The resulting illustrations were, like the songs themselves, abstract and a bit cryptic. But also like the songs, they projected a childlike sense of wonder that was poignant and just a little bittersweet.

Brian's intellectual inquiry was both fueled and muddled by the clouds of marijuana and hashish smoke that drifted in a perpetual haze over the Laurel Way social whirl. Tabs of acid were around too, though that was rare. "To the best of my knowledge, he may have taken LSD once," says Michael Vosse, a college friend of Anderle who would soon come to work for Brian. "He wasn't stoned all the time. Brian went through fads; he had hash because he could get it, and Van Dyke had plenty of pot. But really, Brian had a job to do, and he was a hard workin' guy."

So just to keep the ideas popping and the buzz going until the sun came up in the morning, there were Brian's ever-present Desbutols. Brian gulped fistfuls of the stuff, as it turned out, and his appetite for speed was matched only by his appetite for food. He'd have these enormous steak dinners, then roar off for midnight snacks at his favorite fast-food joints—Pioneer Chicken on Sunset or Dolores's over on La Cienega. Marilyn made cookies when he asked for them, and when those were gone, then there were always cartons of ice cream and Reddi-wip, the stuff in the spray can, which he would sometimes spray right into his mouth. Soon his once-wiry frame took on the bulk and presence of a real Beverly Hills pasha.

And just like a young royal coming into his own, Brian had begun to think in terms of empire. The Beach Boys had hired a young, ambitious new manager, Nick Grillo, earlier in the year, and he set up offices to oversee the group's career, plot their concert tours, and run their finances. Meanwhile, David Anderle was working to pull together Brother Records, the imprint they planned to use as a more sympathetic, noncorporate home for side projects. Brian also wanted to pursue film projects for himself and the group. Derek Taylor's contract had been extended for the foreseeable future, so he was busily spinning out his own brand of quirky, quicksilver hype. Brian had his cousin Steve Korthof as one personal assistant and another friend, Terry Sachen, performing a whole other set of vital chores and errands. As Taylor was ramping up the publicity to promote the release of "Good Vibrations" in October, he sent over Michael Vosse, then a young fan magazine reporter, to interview Brian in a coffee shop on Sunset Boulevard. Except once they got to talking, Vosse discovered that his subject was much less interested in talking about his new single than he was in his other interests. "He seemed to want to go off on a tangent about his theory on the divinity of humor, his idea that when you laugh, control goes out of the window. You're doing something you have no way to rein in, and so it opens the doors for epiphanies."

Vosse's enthusiasm for Brian's ideas seemed to inspire the musician. He called the writer the next morning and promptly offered him a job. "The next day I went to see him, and he gave me a really nice Nagra tape recorder, a big reel-to-reel job that you could use to record in sync with a motion picture camera, and sent me out to go around town and record water sounds. He explained that part of the new album would be a suite of elements, and so he wanted as many variations of how water can sound as I could come up with. He said, 'Take your time, go to oceans, streams, whatever.' So I did, and it was exhilarating! I'd come by to see him every day, and he'd listen to my tapes and talk about them. I was just fascinated that he would hear things every once in a while and his ears would prick up and he'd go back and listen again. And I had no idea what he was listening for!"

Vosse's duties expanded with their friendship, and he became a regular companion for Brian, accompanying him on his daily rounds of meetings and recording sessions, then going with him to East Lansing, Michigan, when he flew out to teach the other Beach Boys how to play "Good Vibrations" onstage. Brian had Vosse bring the Nagra on the airplane, and when they got to East Lansing, he had him tape a long, rambling conversation with their taxi driver. Back home, Brian had Vosse appear with him on Lloyd Thaxton's locally televised dance show, when he went to debut "Good Vibrations." The appearance turned odd when Brian insisted on bringing out an enormous basket of vegetables he'd had Marilyn prepare and spoke at length to a very confused Thaxton about the benefits of eating plenty of roughage. Later, Vosse came along with Brian to a meeting at the offices of the then brand-new A&M Records to talk about doing a deal. Label boss Chuck Kaye was clearly excited at the prospect of doing any kind of business with Brian Wilson of the Beach Boys, but his enthusiasm faded noticeably when he realized that Brian had come to pitch him a strange single called "Crack the Whip" he'd recorded for Jasper Dailey, an elderly photographer who had been shooting some pictures of Brian and the Beach Boys. Jasper, as it turned out, was a far better photographer than singer. "You could see the panic on (Kaye)'s face when he heard how awful it was," Vosse says, laughing. "This look of, 'What the *fuck* do I do?' He'd really wanted to romance Brian, but Brian only wanted him to like Jasper!"

To the uninitiated, Brian seemed to be veering between humor, eccentricity, genius, and incipient insanity. At one point during the previous summer, he decided it would be inspiring to feel the beach beneath his feet while writing at the piano in his living room, so he'd had a large sandbox built around the instrument, then had a truckload of sand shoveled in to fill it up. And there it would remain, at least until he figured out that his dogs, Banana and Louie, were also using the sand for their own creative purposes. A little later he decided it would be inspiring to have meetings and conversations within the confines of an Arabian-style tent. So he had an elaborate silk tent designed, constructed, and installed. Once the matching silk pillows were in place, he excitedly invited his inner circle through its elegant flaps to give the thing a test run. And they soon discovered that Brian's insistence that the thing be built without a vent at the top meant that the accrued body heat (to say nothing of the varieties of smoke generated) had no way to escape the tent, while fresh oxygen could not find its way inside. The gang tumbled out after an hour or so, all of them sweating, coughing, and choking, and the tent sat in the living room, mostly unused, for the next few months before Brian finally had the thing taken down.

Other passions rose to take the tent's place. When Capitol Records sent him an early home video camera and monitor as a Christmas present, Brian set it up near the sofa in the living room alcove and interviewed his friends Johnny Carson–style. (Michael Vosse: "His first show was with Van Dyke and then-wife Durrie Parks, and you can imagine how it went. They came on to show how to roll a joint. And it was like Albert Einstein shows you how to get high." Van Dyke Parks: "What? I would really like to see that. I'm surprised I'd be on film or tape. But who knows.") Shopping one day, Brian's eye was captured by a tall, rotating display of futuristic dolls that came in plastic bubble boxes. Entranced by the dolls' shimmering hair and sparkling eyes, he purchased the entire thing, spinning rack and all, setting it up just behind the organ in his music room.

He spent hours looking at the stars through his telescope and playing Ping-Pong, then replaced all the furniture in one room with gymnasium mats so everyone could exercise together—when they weren't smoking pot, doing speed, or eating one of the vast steak dinners Brian loved. Everything he thought of seemed to lead somewhere else. They should open a twenty-four-hour telescope store! Brian announced, sticking with the idea nearly as long as his whim to open a twenty-four-hour sporting goods store so L.A.'s other night owls would have somewhere to buy Ping-Pong tables at 3:00 a.m. Along with Vosse's water sounds, Brian also captured hours of stoned conversation he had with friends and colleagues, including party games, staged arguments, chants, and weird improvised skits. One night he became so enraptured with the sound of silverware on the table that he orchestrated his guests in a series of complex rhythms and counter-rhythms, looking for a perfect sound. "We oughta record this, make this part of the album!" he cried. "You didn't know if it was a put-on or if it was serious," says Danny Hutton, who sat at the table that night.

For Michael Vosse, it was all just another day at the office. "I'd been around a lot of people in showbiz by then, and nothing about his eccentricities struck me as unique," Vosse says with a shrug. "I thought he was funny. I mean, he used to write me memos on children's stationery, and he'd always address them to 'Clark Kent' and sign them 'Perry White.' People can look at that now and think he's wacko. But all those things that people looked back on later as quite alarming were all kind of funny back then."

If anything, the new atmosphere of creative and personal experimentation drew people to Brian's door. Brian's usual crowd of musician friends still came up, and with Anderle serving as a go-between, the crowd took on a decidedly intellectual air. Jules Siegel, an erudite magazine writer who had recently moved to Los Angeles from New York, was so impressed by Brian that he decided to not only hang around regularly but also document the scene in a long, impassioned article he'd presold to the *Saturday Evening Post.* Paul Robbins, who wrote for the *Los Angeles Free Press,* an alternative paper, also became a regular visitor. Still, Brian couldn't charm all of his guests. When Siegel brought his friend Thomas Pynchon up to the house one night, the famous hipster novelist sat in stunned, unhappy silence while the nervous, stoned pop star—who had dragged him into his then-new Arabian tent to get high—kept kicking over the oil lamp he was trying to light. "Brian was kind of afraid of Pynchon, because he'd heard he was an Eastern intellectual establishment genius," Siegel recalls. "And Pynchon wasn't very articulate. He was gonna sit there and let you talk while he listened. So neither of them really said a word all night long. It was one of the strangest scenes I'd ever seen in my life."

But no matter how odd things got at home, work on *Smile* continued at full throttle. Crafting instrumental tracks in the studio, Brian worked with just as much authority and creativity as ever, coolly directing the mostly older, almost entirely straightlaced musicians on songs that bore little resemblance to anything they had ever played. "It's gotta sound like jewelry!" he instructed a percussionist during a session for "Surf's Up." Later, he coaxed the musicians to let the rhythm dissipate naturally at the end of verses. "Don't worry about how it falls apart at the end of the verse. That's generally what it's supposed to do," he explained. When bassist Carol Kaye found this instruction difficult to reconcile with the standard perfectionism required of studio musicians, Brian eased her concerns with a smile. "Hey, but don't worry about it, Carol." "But I worry," she called back from the studio, only half-joking. "You mustn't," Brian said. "You mustn't worry." Not that sloppiness or imprecision was the goal, as Brian showed when he called the next take to a halt after only a dozen bars or so, pointing out a lapse by the drummer. "Let's have a little more foot pedal." The next take lasts about half as long before Brian punches in to stop it. "The *basses* aren't quite together!"

The article Jules Siegel wrote—ultimately killed by the *Saturday Evening Post* editors, but published in October 1967 by a magazine called *Cheetah*—described sessions for the "Fire" section of the elements suite that began when Brian distributed plastic fire hats to the studio full of musicians (including strings and horns), then had one of his assistants light a bucket of kindling on fire so everyone could smell smoke while they played. But all of that was dwarfed by the music itself, a screaming pictorial instrumental composition that combined pounding drums; a sinister, repeated bass line; wailing strings; and the high-pitched shriek of sirens to evoke the feeling of fire engines confronting a hellish inferno. At one point, Siegel wrote, a producer working down the hall poked his head in the control room to see what the ruckus was and ended up standing there, completely agog, for a long time. "This is really fantastic! Man, this is unbelievable!" Siegel quoted the guy as saying. "I don't believe it. I just can't believe what I'm hearing!" Even now Siegel recalls the incident clearly. "I still remember how dumbfounded he was just hearing the music come out of the speakers," he says, laughing.

Siegel's article would play a significant role in the legend *Smile* would eventually spawn. But it was the feverish testimony of observers like that pop producer—whose name no one can recall—that created the buzz that spread across the Los Angeles music scene with as much force and mystery as a new batch of Owsley's handmade LSD. "Have you heard it yet?" people asked one another, breathlessly. "Have you even heard ABOUT it?" And it wasn't just the fire hats and blazing buckets in the studio or the piano in the sandbox, the hashish tent, and assorted other oddities that excited them (though that probably didn't hurt). It was all that impossibly strange, yet amazingly beautiful, music that only a few, select people had been lucky enough to hear in the recording studio or from the acetate records Brian took home at the end of the day. Derek Taylor spread the word even further in the press, sometimes in stories he wrote himself, minus a byline but with all the charming hyperbole you'd expect from a Taylor piece. ("I have an idea. I'm not sure exactly how this is going to work, but we'll try it," Brian is heard declaring at the start of one experiment that comes to include layers of reverb, overdubbing, and other manipulations. When it's done, Taylor describes the session musicians shaking their heads in wonder, musing, "How did he do it?")

Word drifted to New York City, where David Oppenheim, a producer for CBS News at work on a special about rock 'n' roll to be hosted by Leonard Bernstein, decided to feature Brian and his new music on the show. Oppenheim and his crew came out in December and ultimately filmed a segment with Brian, sitting alone at his piano in a burgundy button-up shirt, playing and singing "Surf's Up." It was a moving, if understated, performance, and its power was amplified by the narration that described Brian as "one of today's most important pop musicians" and "Surf's Up" as ". . . poetic, beautiful in its own obscurity."

And though Brian had to back down from an original promise to deliver the album in time for the Christmas shopping season, Capitol Records took out ads in *Billboard* and other trade magazines promising *Smile* ("With the 'Good Vibrations' sound!") in January. Anticipation for the new album grew when Britain's influential music trade magazine, the *New Musical Express,* released its annual readers' poll. NME POLL SENSATION: BEACH BOYS BEAT THE BEATLES. True enough, with "Good Vibrations" still near the top of the charts, the magazine's readers proclaimed the Beach Boys "World Vocal Group" of the year with a hair more than 100 votes separating them from the hometown heroes, who scored 5,272 votes to the Americans' 5,373. The same poll showed Brian as the fourth-ranked "World Music Personality," his 3,028 votes landing him just behind third-place finisher John Lennon (3,515) and just ahead of Bob Dylan (1,931), braying his way into the fifth slot.

As 1966 whirled to a close, it seemed as if Brian had realized his most audacious visions. The moment he had created, starting with *Pet Sounds,* screaming into "Good Vibrations," and then vanishing completely into the sparkling, mysterious thickets of *Smile,* had become a perfect wave, a perfectly rigged custom machine. It was everything he'd ever wanted—commercial popularity, unbelievable artistic freedom, unimaginable acclaim from his peers. All the rules were gone now, all the expectations shaken into dust. Able finally to transcend pop's norms and his own limitations, anything could happen.

Anything, it seemed, except what did.

CHAPTER 7

J ust after the airplane roared off into the morning sky above the Chicago airport, Brian got an idea. He turned to Michael Vosse, recently hired and on his first trip with the boss, and chattered excitedly. "We've gotta get everyone together for a portrait!" They were still climbing into the clouds then, their backs pinned into their seats as Brian talked his way up to cruising altitude. They could get the pilot to call ahead to L.A. and tell Marilyn, he said. Have her book the Beach Boys' photographer, Guy Webster, and then call the whole gang together to meet them at the TWA terminal to take the photo when they stepped off the airplane at LAX. Everyone would show up, right? What else did they have to do on a Sunday afternoon in late October? Brian rang his call button and summoned the stewardess to his seat.

They had flown east a day and a half before so Brian could oversee the other Beach Boys' first performances of "Good Vibrations" at back-to-back shows scheduled for Saturday afternoon and evening in the gym at the University of Michigan. The performances had gone well, and the college audience had responded to the new song—released just two weeks earlier and already at the top of the *Billboard* charts—with such an ecstatic ovation that the other Beach Boys had pulled Brian onstage to take a bow and then join in on their encore of "Barbara Ann." Brian hadn't wanted to step back into the spotlights at first, but the cheers had followed him out of the hall and now onto this airplane, where the altitude had pushed his mood toward giddiness. "I need to get a message to my wife, right now!" he told the stewardess, filling in the details in a rush of wild enthusiasm. "We need to take a picture; the airport; just call my wife, she'll do everything else. . . ." The stewardess first tried to brush off Brian's demand, explaining that the pilot would have to call the airport control tower and have the message relayed from there via telephone, really only something they did in the case of emergencies. But Brian kept insisting, mentioning the Beach Boys, even, and the important business—show business!—all of this entailed. Had she heard "Good Vibrations" yet? What did she think? Finally, the woman agreed to take her famous passenger's query to the cockpit. And soon after that, the pilot radioed the message to L.A., where an airline official finally phoned Marilyn to transmit Brian's written instructions about whom to call and why. "As if," Vosse says now, "Brian was doing government business."

When the flight touched down in Los Angeles late that afternoon, nearly two dozen of Brian's closest compatriots were waiting: *Smile* insiders Van Dyke Parks and his wife, Durrie; David Anderle and his wife, Sheryl; Brian's driver, Terry Sachen; Marilyn and her sisters, Diane and Barbara; Carl Wilson's wife, Annie Hinsche; journalist Jules Siegel; musicians Danny Hutton, Dean Torrence of Jan and Dean, and Mark Volman from the Turtles, in addition to a handful of cousins and other friends, all waiting for him to join them beneath the colorful, childlike mural of airplanes soaring into a soft blue sky in the TWA terminal. Webster took a variety of pictures, the group expanding and contracting to form a variety of combinations. Throughout, the center of the galaxy was always Brian, dressed in canvas boat shoes, white jeans, and a light blue T-shirt, his reddish brown hair swept low across his forehead so that it nearly covered the eyes that regarded the camera so coolly. To look at the pictures now is to see a shy but powerful young man flexing his authority. He's distant but in command. Surely, "Good Vibrations" had something to do with that crooked smile that pulls at his lips. After all those months of work, all the anxiety, doubts, and stubborn belief, everything about Brian's vision was being confirmed in spades. And unlike *Pet Sounds,* which won him critical praise at the expense of sales, "Good Vibrations" hit the hipsters just as it did the millions of kids who were just in it for the fun, fun, fun. But if "Good Vibrations" was Brian's jet airplane, *Smile* would be a rocket ship, propelling him so far beyond the pop universe he had come to know that it was impossible for him to say where it would leave him.

Or if he even had the courage to go through with the journey. Because Brian had already started feeling doubts about *Smile*. They were glimmers of darkness he had been trying to fend off with the constant motion of a vast array of interlocking musical, visual, and completely unrelated projects. But he needed other people's enthusiasm to keep him going, and so every time he saw a flicker of doubt—as in the puzzled, unsmiling faces that greeted him in the TWA terminal—you could nearly see him recoil. And so once Webster had snapped his last photograph, Brian bid the crowd good-bye and left the airport with Marilyn to have dinner alone at an undisclosed location.

Later, when Webster showed him a contact sheet of the finished shots, Brian would post a blowup of his favorite shot on his living room mantel: the *Smile* class of 1966. And later, after he had discarded it, the airport photograph would take on a symbolic importance, as if it marked the point at which Brian's astonishing creative arc leveled off, nosing slowly toward a descent. It was hard to catch at first, if only because so many things seemed to be happening at once. "Good Vibrations" was still at the apex of record charts across the planet, while plans for *Smile* and all its related projects—the full-color booklet, the accompanying mini-films, the TV publicity, the articles already being written—were just ramping up into high gear. Capitol had printed up nearly half a million copies of Frank Holmes's sweetly psychedelic smile-shop album cover, a mountain of them stacked up and waiting to be wrapped around the brilliant new music. Then there were all the side projects, everything from the short films Brian shot with the other Beach Boys to promote "Good Vibrations," to his scheme for full-length features by, about, and starring the Beach Boys, to his ever-broadening plans for the group's own Brother Records and the various musical and comedic works it would produce.

And if that weren't exciting enough, Derek Taylor had started to lay even more of the group's public reputation on the shoulders of its semireclusive leader. "This is Brian Wilson. He is a Beach Boy. Some say he is more. Some say he is a Beach Boy and a genius," read the headline of one typical profile. And the text didn't let up: "This twenty-three-year-old powerhouse not only sings with the famous group, he writes the words and music then arranges, engineers, and produces the disc. . . . Even the packaging and design on the record jacket is controlled by the talented Mr. Wilson. He has often been called 'genius,' and it's a burden." It's the last line that's priceless (though the rest of it doesn't hesitate to stretch the facts up to and beyond the breaking point), given the expert way Taylor, working through a reporter (or alter ego) identified as "'60's Hollywood reporter Jerry Fineman," manages to both assert Brian's genius and then shrug it off as a nuisance in the same breath.

A canny publicist with a hipster's sensibility and a novelist's eye for poetic imagery, Taylor could sense how well the image of Brian as a solitary, quirky genius would play to the rapidly maturing, increasingly serious rock audience. What the recent L.A. transplant didn't understand was how such an accolade would echo in the ears of its subject. Certainly, Brian wasn't adverse to being celebrated. He'd even told Taylor that he knew he was better than his reputation gave him credit for being. But as with so many things in his life that pleased him, public acclaim had a way of tormenting Brian, too. Already the attention he had received within the industry for writing had become a point of contention between Brian and his attention-starved father. The other Beach Boys had long since come to resent that disparity too, particularly when they were the ones earning the cheers on stage night after night. And, Brian fretted, how could anyone live up to that kind of reputation? "I'm not a genius," he said to reporters back then. "I'm just a hardworking guy." Such understated humility fed Brian's reputation even more. Everything he touched turned to gold, and the best part was that he was too hip to care! "I never try the impossible, but I'm always aware of the workable," he said, summing up his approach to innovation at the end of the "Fineman" piece.

But if Brian's musical work inspired more people to regard him as a genius, his personal life spurred others to ponder the thin line between divine inspiration and complete lunacy. Consider his new, overwhelming appreciation for health food. What began with a slight alteration of his dietary regime (very slight, as it turned out) and a quirky song called "Vega-Tables" grew quickly into an obsession with fitness that led him to move the furniture out of his living room in order to make room for tumbling mats and exercise bars, none of which Brian seemed all that interested in using. Instead, the mostly sedentary, increasingly chunky musician contented himself with giving evangelical lectures about fitness—sometimes, as Derek Taylor recalled with a laugh to David Leaf, "while digging into a big, fat hamburger." Talking to Leaf in 2004, Brian rolled his eyes at his own youthful contradictions. "I wanted everyone else to exercise. I was too lazy."

He was far more willing to join his friends in exercising the outer reaches of their imaginations, particularly when it came to humor or other forms of verbal high jinks. All through that fall and winter, he kept his home tape recorder close at hand, spending hours recording himself and friends while they chanted, played games, had pretend arguments, or just shot the breeze. It was just like the old days with his Wollensak recorder, except much, much weirder. To dig through the tapes is to hear hours of chants about fishies going swim-swim and the need for beets and carrots, beets and carrots, beets and carrots. "Everybody talk like Smokey the Bear!" Brian commanded in the midst of one chant. Nothing but harmless fun, it seemed to most of his friends. "Maybe he wasn't as sophisticated as the sophisticates wanted, and he certainly wasn't as retarded as the surfer guys wanted," Vosse says. "But I thought he was funny. I still think he's funny."

But not to Van Dyke Parks, who sounds vaguely mortified while Brian, Vosse, and David Anderle pretend to order treats from a psychedelic ice cream wagon that plays a plinking version of "Good Vibrations" (Brian was at the piano) as it cruises the neighborhood. Later Brian changes the fantasy, pretending to have been swallowed by the microphone. "Van Dyke! You've gotta help me!" he shouts. "No names, please. The place might be raided," Van Dyke calls back, unamused. Even now he shakes his head at the memory. "I sensed all that was destructive, so I withdrew from those related social encounters," Van Dyke says.

Nevertheless, the silliness continued. Brian got the musicians at the recording studio involved in the fun too, at one point recording a long session in which the horn players talked through their mouthpieces, pretending they were trapped in their instruments. Intriguingly, given his own near-complete absorption in music, "falling into" instruments became a standard motif in Brian's comic tapes that fall and winter. Goofing around for the recorder at home, he and Michael Vosse took turns pretending to get stuck inside the piano or the tape player's microphone. And though at least one of Brian's sound experiments—the whirs, bangs, and grinding of people working drills, pounding nails, and sawing wood—would end up being used in a finished recording, other sessions seem to be inspired by something other than Brian's urge to create compelling new sounds.

One tape captures more than twenty-four minutes of dialogue after Brian ushered a group of friends and puzzled session musicians (who still seem to be getting paid, given the "When do I get my W-4?" crack one of them makes) into a pitch-black recording studio. The dialogue begins with Jules Siegel attempting to lead everyone in a dorm room–style party game called "Lifeboat," where the players portray survivors of a shipwreck who must decide who among them should be tossed into the water to save the others. But the game soon dissolves into random exchanges that veer toward frustration and then anger. Michael Vosse, who, for some reason, Brian sent to be by himself in a far corner of the studio, is the first to lose his temper when he gets lost in the blackness and collides with a piece of equipment. "Brian, I can't see!" he yells angrily, but his boss cuts him off: "Well, that's tough shit!"

Siegel pipes up, and the talk grows increasingly barbed between Vosse and the writer. "If you can't find your way out, why should any of us help you?" Siegel says. Vosse yells back an insult, and the tension infects the rest of the crowd. But perhaps Brian set them up to fight; when Vosse turns his anger on someone else, one of the women in the group says with a giggle, "This is *supposed* to be an argument!" But maybe she didn't know what was going on, either. "No, they're really into it," Siegel says gleefully. "What are we *doing* in here, Brian?" someone asks awhile later. "I want Michael to try to cheer everyone up," he responds, but the mood gets even worse when someone in the control booth starts playing the tape of the instrumental figure at the center of "Heroes and Villains."

"I feel so depressed. Really, seriously," Brian says, prophetically. "I keep sinking. I'm too down to smile."

———

No matter how frantically Brian worked to write and record his music, no matter how much free time he could consume with his comedy tapes and other enthusiasms, nothing seemed to hold back the shadow that was creeping over him. At times the darkness seemed to be coming from every direction at once. Nick Grillo's examination of the group's royalty statements from Capitol uncovered years of underpaid royalties. Brian, for instance, had never once been paid for his work as a producer. The group filed a lawsuit against the label, but the move only prompted more tension in his dealings with the executives already impatient to get *Smile* in stores. Worse, several of Brian's closest aides came to believe that Murry Wilson, who had negotiated and countersigned the first contract, might have had something to do with the situation. How could such a savvy, hands-on businessman have failed to recognize the disparity between what Capitol owed and what they were actually paying? They even speculated that he may have received some kind of kickback in exchange for not tipping off his sons that they were being ripped off. No one knew for sure, but Murry already frightened Brian, and such conjecture only exacerbated the anger, shame, and paranoia that infected his relationship with his father. And all of it only added to the weight of the creative burden he was already straining to lift.

That burden was only growing heavier, thanks both to the structural and thematic complexity of the new music and also to the reaction it had received from his family in and around the band. True enough, the guys always had to be pushed and dragged through any complicated new assignment. Brian expected that, particularly when they were squeezing sessions between dates on their near-endless tours. But it had gotten even worse during *Pet Sounds,* given their doubts about Tony Asher's lyrics. Brian had hoped the excitement about "Good Vibrations" might put them in a more cooperative mood, but he hadn't factored in how the presence of Van Dyke, along with all the other staffers and assistants and the array of friends that came along with them, would set off alarm bells in the ears of his bandmates and their family and friends. They'd always been suspicious of outsiders, and this crew of intellectual hipsters—who only encouraged Brian's wildest ideas and fueled his weirdest behavior—heralded the worst possible turn of events for a band of pop stars whose wealth and fame stemmed entirely from the songs their leader had once written about cars, surfing, and girls.

Still, the vocal sessions had started cheerfully enough back on September 19, with an evening session for "Prayer," the choral invocation Brian wrote to start the album. It's a beautiful piece, the unaccompanied voices traveling wordlessly through a series of complex harmonic modulations that rise and fall delicately. But as the group gathered around the microphone in the Columbia studio, Brian sounded too nervous to hear how delighted they were with the first song they'd attempt for their latest album. "This could be considered a track," Al Jardine mused, but Brian shook his head.

"Nah, we don't want to do that."

"But it's beautiful!" Dennis cried. And yet Brian still balked at calling "Prayer" an official song. "This is intro to the album, take one," he said to the engineer. There was an uncomfortable silence, and it took Carl, the unflappable baby brother, to stir the group's leader from his reverie: "Brian. Direct, okay?"

"Uh, okay," he responded hastily. "Let's try to really pull it off good, okay?"

The group began to sing, slowly finding their way through the intricate weave of voices in the first verse. A few broken takes later, Brian's attention wavered again, and he called to Danny Hutton, out in the control room. "Do you have any hash joints left, Danny? I know that you do." Hutton indicated that he didn't, because Brian groaned his reply ("Awwww!"). Nevertheless, drugs remained on his mind. When another take broke down, he turned to someone else and either joked or asked with striking directness: "You guys feeling that acid yet?"

The other Beach Boys were certainly not feeling acid in the fall of 1966. And to Mike Love, the hardworking front man who prided himself on being in touch with the tastes of the group's vast audience of clean-cut teenagers, no one but a tripped-out acid freak would ever come close to feeling the bizarre new songs Brian was crafting for the group. "Good Vibrations" had been weird enough, but at least Brian had had the good sense to let him put his own down-to-earth lyrics on top of all that crazy music. Anyone could understand a love story about two people. But what would anyone make of "Heroes and Villains," with its bizarre, purposefully nonsensical tale and its constant use of nonsense phrases like *"sunny-down snuff"*? What exactly was going on in "Do You Like Worms" with the *"Rock, rock, roll/Plymouth rock roll over"* line? And what kind of song title was "Do You Like Worms"? In a song that doesn't even mention worms once? And who but a drug addict would know what the phrase *"columnated ruins domino"* meant?

None of this made any sense to Mike, and when he saw how scattered Brian seemed, particularly when he came drifting into the studio in the company of Michael Vosse or Van Dyke Parks, his fury became obvious. Why were the Beach Boys, his group, suddenly being infiltrated by hippie weirdos? What sort of hippie bullshit, or drugs, or, more likely, both, were they feeding to Brian? And how could any of this end up producing the Beach Boys' next hit album?

Not everyone felt quite so strongly. Carl loved Brian's new music, so much so that he made a point of coming to the instrumental sessions when he was in town, adding guitar where he could and, mostly, watching his older brother work. Al Jardine was a pro, willing to do what he was told when the time came for him to sing. And even if Dennis Wilson was less engaged in the recording process (being far more involved with his various cars, motorcycles, and every other form of adult fun that fell in the lap of a sexy young rock star in Los Angeles in 1966), he was still supportive enough to talk the record up in the press. "*Smile* makes *Pet Sounds* stink, that's how good it is," he told one reporter. But Mike, on the other hand, was less convinced. More to the point, he was not content to trust his entire career to fan magazine hype and hippie bullshit.

"I called it 'acid alliteration,'" Mike says. "The [lyrics are] far out. But do they relate like 'Surfin' USA,' like 'Fun, Fun, Fun,' like 'California Girls,' like 'I Get Around'? Perhaps not! So that's the distinction. See, I'm into success.

These words equal successful hit records; those words don't.""

As Michael Vosse recalls, Mike's obvious distaste for the new songs hit Brian hard. "The vibe was getting worse and worse. Brian was trying to complete one of the most ambitious projects in pop music. But the people close to him were rolling their eyes and saying, 'Are you sure?' And that really got to him."

Brian began to dread the vocal sessions and often tried to soften his anxiety by getting high in the car while Vosse drove him down to the studio. His drug use only emphasized his other eccentricities and made it far more difficult for him to explain why it was so important for them all to crawl around and make animal sounds for the background of "Barnyard" or to groan and moan like primordial creatures to accompany one of the other sections that still didn't have a name or a discernible place in this (or any) rock 'n' roll record.

"Everyone was high but me," Al remembered in *Goldmine* in 2000. "Brian made us crawl around and snort like a bunch of pigs on a section of 'Heroes.' It was like being trapped in an insane asylum." The conflict simmered through the fall and into the winter, festering to the point that even the triumphs of the season—including their biggest hit single ever and months of playing to ecstatic crowds, particularly in Europe and England, where the new *Pet Sounds* material earned just as much rapturous applause as the earlier hits—did nothing to ease the tension. It all came to a head on December 6, in the midst of a recording session for the final movement of "Cabin-Essence," then known by its working title, "The Grand Coulee Dam."

The song had bothered Mike since he'd first heard it at a vocal tracking session in early October. Recorded in sections like "Good Vibrations," "Cabin-Essence" began with a quiet verse called "Home on the Range," which featured a tinkling piano, plucked banjo, bass, flute, harmonica, and a background vocal *doing-doing-doing*-ing up and down the scale beneath a sweet Carl Wilson vocal that described the frontier in terms only Van Dyke Parks could imagine: *"Light the lamp and fire mellow/Cabin-essence timely hello/Welcomes a time for a change,"* it began. This vignette lasted all of forty seconds, then gave way to the section called "Who Ran the Iron Horse?"—a thunderstorm of drums, fuzz bass, and cello against a shrieking tempest of backing vocals and a central chant of *"Who ran the iron horse?"* meant to evoke the coming of the steam engine and the spread of the railroad. Then it was back to another "Home on the Range" verse, into another "Iron Horse" segment, this time adding a barely audible chant performed by Dennis, describing the amphetamine-fired thoughts of a modern-day trucker zooming through the twentieth century.

They'd recorded most of that a few weeks earlier, but now Brian wanted them to voice the song's final section, which he and Van Dyke called "Grand Coulee Dam." This section, which took up the last minute of the song, began with two contrasting chants—*"Have you seen the Grand Coulee?"* and *"Working on the rail-road"*—that spiraled skyward until they gave way to the song's climactic chant, which Brian had asked Mike to sing as another whirlpool of backing vocals swirled above the backdrop of fuzz bass, banjo, clattering percussion, and cello: *"Over and over the crow flies/uncover the cornfield/Over and over the thresher and hover the wheat field . . ."*

The only problem with all of this was that Mike had no fucking idea what any of it meant. And frankly, Mike had no intention of singing a word of this until someone could explain it to him. And that someone was Van Dyke Parks. So Mike, lyric sheet in hand, stalked up to Brian and told him to call this Van-whoever-the-fuck to the studio to explain it to him, face-to-face. So Brian did exactly that, dialing his collaborator and asking him casually—a bit too casually, Van Dyke would soon come to understand—if he might be willing to pay a visit to the studio and help Mike with a lyric or two. Well, sure, Van Dyke said, not feeling the least bit of foreboding as he piloted his new Volvo sedan down to the Columbia studios in Hollywood. "The only person I had had any interchange with before that was Dennis, who had responded very favorably to 'Heroes and Villains' and 'Surf's Up,'" Van Dyke says. "Based on that, I gathered that the work would be approved. But then, with no warning whatsoever, I got that phone call from Brian. And that's when the whole house of cards came tumbling down."

What happened next has long become a central piece of the *Smile* legend, both because it marked a turning point in the album's progress and because it resonates with so much psychological and cultural subtext. On the most immediate level, the conflict between Van Dyke and Mike represents the fight for the direction and meaning of the Beach Boys. But in so doing, it reveals even more about Brian's own conflicted ambitions and impulses. When he pitted his new and old collaborators against one another, he was also setting up a duel between the opposing hemispheres in his mind. Was he going to be an artist or an entertainer; a cultural visionary or a pop music entrepreneur? Once music had been the only thing that made sense to him. No matter how bad things got around him, no matter how frantic he got in his own skin, Brian could wander off into his music and create a reality that didn't just make sense, but actually rang with beauty. Only now the music couldn't keep Brian's demons away anymore, because now they had gotten inside the music. What once was his escape had become the primary battleground, and so now he would have to summon all his courage and strength and face them down, man-to-man. Except Brian couldn't do that; instead, he got Van Dyke to do the talking for him on the floor of Columbia Recording studios, with Mike looming over him red-faced and fearsome.

"I want you to tell me what it means!" Mike demanded, pointing to the line about the crow and the cornfield. He was tall and sharply dressed, consciously hulking over the smaller, bespectacled Van Dyke, who wasn't about to be drawn into an argument about the quality of his work. Instead, Van Dyke dodged the issue entirely. "If you're looking for a literal explanation of that line, of any line of verse, I don't have it," he replied simply.

"You don't know what it means?" Mike laughed. "You wrote it and YOU don't know what it means?"

"I have no excuse, sir."

Feeling out of place, out of sorts, and unwilling to become a part of what he already suspected was a family feud with roots and motivations that had nothing to do with *Smile*, Van Dyke spun on his heel and glided out. Out into the control room, down the hall, and out to his Volvo, determined to never return. "That's when I lost interest," he says. "Because basically I was taught not to be where I wasn't wanted, and I could feel I wasn't wanted. It was like I had someone else's job, which was abhorrent to me, because I don't even want my own job. It was sad, so I decided to get away quick."

Van Dyke would be back, and work on the album would continue for several more months, but a chill had come into the air. Brian's energies grew even more scattered; his appetite for amphetamines and hashish accelerated, and his episodes of paranoia became more profound and frightening. One night that winter he attended a screening of John Frankenheimer's movie *Seconds*. Arriving a few minutes late, Brian had just settled into his seat when a voice from the screen seemed to greet him by name: "Hello, Mr. Wilson." And if that was freaky, the experience grew steadily more terrifying as Brian saw the other Mr. Wilson suffer a panic attack on an airplane (just as he had done two years earlier), attempt to reconnect with his past by touring an old family home (which Brian had also done down in Hawthorne immediately following his breakdown), and then discover a new self among a group of wild-hearted bohemians (just as Brian had done first with Loren Schwartz and now with his gang of *Smile* assistants). "Even the beach was in it," Brian fretted to a friend in Jules Siegel's article. "Birth and death and rebirth. The whole thing. It was my whole life right there on the screen." Couldn't it be a coincidence? he was asked. Brian shook his head. It was mind gangsters, probably in the employ of a wildly envious Phil Spector. "I've gone beyond Spector," Brian explained to Siegel. "I'm doing the spiritual sound . . . it's going to scare a lot of people."

Brian's friends managed to talk him down from that emotional precipice, but others loomed no matter where he wandered. After the session for "Fire," also known as "Mrs. O'Leary's Cow," in December, Brian noticed what he thought was a sudden spike in fires in and around downtown Los Angeles. Had his music created some kind of voodoo spell that was slowly setting the entire city ablaze? Brian found this prospect so terrifying that he destroyed his copy of the tape immediately and vowed that the music would never be aired in public. Not long after that, Brian became convinced that he was being followed and that someone was listening to his conversations on the telephone and perhaps in his house. Brian confessed his fears to Anderle and Grillo, and to put Brian at ease, they hired a team of surveillance experts to sweep his house for bugs. "These guys searched the house for hours and found nothing, nothing, and nothing," Michael Vosse recalls. "Then they drove off in his Rolls for like an hour, then came back saying, 'We found a microphone in there!' Honestly, I think it was a hustle. And then it became another distraction from the music."

The security guys started making regular checks of Brian's house and property, but the increasingly fearful musician took his own steps to ensure security. One day he called all of his friends and contacts and commanded them all to change their telephone numbers. Then he decided to move all of his important business meetings to the deep end of his swimming pool. This served two ends, Brian believed, since it was obviously impossible to bug a pool, and anyone floating half-naked in twelve feet of water would probably be more honest than someone hiding behind a suit and tie.

Were Brian's fears entirely misplaced? At least one of his friends still believes that Brian and perhaps Carl were being followed by detectives hired by Murry, who was eager to find out if his boys were taking as many drugs as he suspected. Still, Brian's fearful episodes worked their way from his immediate circle of friends and acquaintances into the media and then into legend. Jules Siegel's article made much out of one episode in which one of Brian's friends is greeted at the recording studio door by Vosse, who informs him that he won't be welcome at the session inside. "It's not you; it's your chick," Siegel quoted Vosse as saying. "Brian says she's a witch, and she's messing with his brain so bad by ESP that he can't work. It's like the Spector thing. You know how he is."

What Siegel neglected to mention in his story was that he was the guy being banned from the session and that the woman in question was his girlfriend and future wife, Chrissie. So, it seems fair to ask, was she a witch? Siegel says no but admits that she was a beautiful woman with a powerful personality who enjoyed flirting with other men. Indeed, Siegel would later write an article about his wife's affair with his famous novelist friend, Thomas Pynchon. "She was so beautiful she made Snow White look a bit crude. I'm sure this aroused such heavy fantasies that [Brian] felt like she was in his head," Siegel says. "You don't need any supernatural explanations for the effects of that on raging male hormones, do you?"

Another famous episode involved Anderle, an enthusiastic amateur painter who had been inspired to work secretly on a portrait of his boss for several months. Painting from memory, Anderle had produced a dark, moody vision of Brian, his skin the color of alabaster, his mouth bent in a curious smile, his blazing eyes peering out of a blackness that bristled with icons and figures. According to Vosse, who accompanied Brian to Anderle's apartment, the effect on the painting's subject was immediate and intense. He got right up next to it and stared for what seemed like hours, counting the objects that orbited his painted visage and tracing them with his fingertip. Everything about the painting struck him as extraordinarily significant, from the way the spray of icons hovered in the background to the numerological significance of their number and order. "He thought it captured his soul," Vosse says. And for a frightened young man who felt his soul was perpetually at risk of slipping away entirely, this was not a good feeling.

Van Dyke, who never recovered from his public dustup with Mike, left the project for good in April, bound for the peace and quiet of Palm Desert with a contract to produce his own solo album for Warner Brothers Records. Others were falling away, too. Vosse left in March, his relationship with Brian undone by the other Beach Boys, who resented paying the salary of an aide who worked only for one member of the group. Anderle would also be gone by the end of the spring, no longer willing to navigate the rocky straits between Brian's creative world and the professional one he refused to engage. Soon the Laurel Way house grew quiet, the happy chatter at the all-night rap sessions and pool parties replaced by the silent churning of Brian's thoughts and the circular patterns his fingers would make as they searched for melodies on the piano keys. Then Brian and Marilyn would leave the Laurel Way house altogether, abandoning the seat of *Pet Sounds,* "Good Vibrations," and *Smile* for a larger, even more elegant, tree-shaded Spanish mansion tucked into the gated community of Bel Air.

As winter became spring, Brian's work on *Smile* had slipped into a frantic pursuit of the single that would follow "Good Vibrations" and herald the album. He conducted an endless chain of instrumental and vocal sessions for "Heroes and Villains," searching desperately for an arrangement of melodies, sections, and moods that would give the song the coherence it seemed to lack. More sessions, more sections, more songs. An array of takes for the various pieces of the "Elements" suite (minus a new "Fire" section, which had yet to be composed). Run-throughs of other songs, some with titles, some without, then, curiously, a cover of Burt Bacharach's "Little Red Book." Then back to "Heroes and Villains" again. The Capitol execs were keening for the single, baying for a new album, desperate to come up with some follow-up to the multimillion-selling "Good Vibrations." But Brian could only keep tinkering, recording more and more music that made less and less sense to anyone but himself. Except he was just as baffled as anyone. Brian left the studio for a month starting in mid-April, then picked up again in mid-May, concluding with a session on May 18 for the water section of the "Elements," known as "I Love to Say Da Da." Another session was planned for the next day, but Brian failed to show up, and it was cancelled.

And then it was over, a year after Brian had first described the album he then called *Dumb Angel.* Eight months since "Good Vibrations" catapulted the Beach Boys into a whole new orbit of popular and critical acclaim. Six months since the music industry began to buzz about an album so powerful and revolutionary it would transform not just rock 'n' roll but all of popular culture. One month since Brian had been called a musical genius, nearly, in the Leonard Bernstein special on CBS. "In truth, every beautifully designed, finely wrought, inspirationally welded piece of music made these last months by Brian . . . has been SCRAPPED," Derek Taylor wrote in a British music magazine. "Not destroyed, but scrapped. For what he seals in a can and destroys is scrapped."

If Taylor's distinction between "destroyed" and "scrapped" seems unclear,

Brian must have felt the same way. In fact, there's reason to suggest that Brian didn't even know that Taylor announced the demise of *Smile,* a release that may have been authorized by other factions in the Beach Boys. After all, his final sessions for "I Love to Say Da Da" actually took place two weeks *after* Taylor's statement was published in early May. He finally completed "Heroes and Villains" in June, though the new, streamlined version—sliced down to 3:36 from versions that ranged from six minutes, to eight, to a rumored (and yet to be discovered) eleven-minute edit—did away with the song's more adventurous sections and leaned heavily on newly recorded, stripped-down instrumentation. Brian's *Smile*-era friends would spend decades bemoaning the loss of the original "Heroes and Villains," but in the summer of 1967, Brian felt strongly enough about the new version that he kept it to himself for weeks, waiting for his astrologer, a woman named Genevelyn, to identify the perfect moment to spring it upon the unsuspecting world. She came to Brian early in the evening of July 11, and what happened next would become yet another signal moment in the cultural legend that would come to grow around Brian Wilson and *Smile.*

As Terry Melcher told the tale to *Rolling Stone* in 1971, it all began just before midnight on the eleventh, when Brian gathered his remaining intimates into a flock of limousines and sped from the gates of his Bel Air home down into Hollywood and the studios of KHJ-AM radio near the Paramount lot on Melrose Avenue. A little fast talk got the flotilla past the guard at the parking lot, and soon Brian and his entourage were parading through the radio station and into the central on-air studio. Here, Brian pulled out his prized seven-inch acetate of "Heroes and Villains," the long-awaited follow-up to "Good Vibrations," the product of a year's worth of obsessive labor, and presented it to Tom Maule, the overnight disc jockey just then commanding the station's turntables. "Hi, I'm Brian Wilson," Melcher recalled hearing the pop monarch declare. "Here's the new Beach Boys single, and I'd like to give you and KHJ an exclusive on it."

Borne up by months of hype and now the assurances of his astrologer, Brian expected Maule to either burst into tears, fall to his knees in prayerful thanks, or perhaps faint dead away with the shock of his good fortune. Instead, the guy just kind of shrugged. "I can't play anything that's not on the playlist," he said, only sort of apologetically. At which point, Melcher recalled, Brian seemed to teeter on his heels, seemingly close to passing out. Maule ultimately was convinced to call his program director at home—"Put it on, you idiot!" Melcher recalled hearing the guy shriek—but by then the moment was gone, and Brian's fragile psyche had already been shattered. "It just about killed him," Melcher said.

Released officially at the end of the month, "Heroes and Villains" notched respectful, if slightly puzzled, reviews ("Weirdly fascinating," the UK's *New Music Review* decreed), but its stripped-down, Southwestern-meets-psychedelic-barbershop sound left listeners underwhelmed, particularly in the shadow of post–"Good Vibrations" hype. In a world still rocked by the Beatles' psychedelic masterpiece "Sgt. Pepper's Lonely Hearts Club Band," Brian's "Heroes and Villains" seemed beside the point. The song peaked eventually at *Billboard's* number twelve slot, which struck nearly everyone in the Beach Boys camp as both an unmitigated disaster and the final word on the misbegotten folly that was Brian's *Smile* era.

Wounded by the relative indifference to "Heroes and Villains," Brian started to plummet, and his flailing attempts to protect himself—mostly by falling back into the grasp of his family and the band they had formed—took on a desperation that soon bordered on self-immolation. Months earlier, when they were still riding high on "Good Vibrations," the Beach Boys had been tapped to headline the Monterey Pop Festival in mid-June. But as the day drew close and the event's cultural significance began to seem clear, Brian, who had also been asked to join Paul McCartney, Smokey Robinson, and Mick Jagger, among other youth culture leaders, in the festival's board of governors, began to worry. Once Brian had imagined Monterey as the perfect place to publicly unveil *Smile,* but in June, with "Heroes and Villains" still in shards and *Smile* in ruins, they didn't have anything new to play. To make matters worse, they'd be standing in front of a Bay Area audience drawn to hear younger, hipper bands like the Byrds, the Jefferson Airplane, and Moby Grape. How would the Beach Boys—still clad in their striped shirts and still boasting a set-list full of surfing, cars, and innocuous fun—go over with that crowd?

So, only two weeks before the event, Brian pulled the group out of Monterey. They needed to work on "Heroes and Villains," he said. What's more, he argued, Carl Wilson, just then fighting off the military's attempts to send him to Vietnam by arguing for conscientious objector status, might be too freaked out to sing in public. But neither of these excuses held much water for Monterey's counterculture audience, who might not have tuned in, turned on, and dropped out themselves but professed deep admiration for the pop stars who had. Pleading contractual obligations just didn't cut it. And while it was easier to sympathize with poor Carl and his draft board hassle, surely his darkest hour was a time to take strength in the community, not shun it. So you see, all "Good Vibrations" aside, the Beach Boys had just revealed themselves to be the surfing muscle-heads the hipsters had always assumed they were. And when 200,000 flower-bedecked, face-painted fans crowded Monterey's fairgrounds to groove to the tunes, inaugurate a new chapter in American popular culture, and provide the backdrop for one of the most successful, influential music films in the history of cinema, Brian and the other Beach Boys were shut into a room in his new Bel Air mansion, listening to the sound of their own voices echoing off the stucco walls.

Many years later, the Beach Boys–sanctioned documentary *An American Band* would play footage of Jimi Hendrix, perhaps *the* breakout star at Monterey, setting his guitar on fire amid its dying squeals of feedback beneath a snippet from his "Third Stone from the Sun"; "*. . . and you'll never hear surf music again! . . .*" added for emphasis. It's an unfair juxtaposition for Hendrix, since he bore no particular grudge against the Beach Boys and was, in fact, a huge fan of surf guitar king Dick Dale, whose then-ill health he might have been mourning (not celebrating) when he made that statement. But for the purposes of the Beach Boys' narrative, the imagery is too perfect to ignore: The coming of Hendrix and all his freaky pals spelled doom for the pink-cheeked boys from Hawthorne, who could have beat Hendrix to his pyrotechnics by several months had Brian not lost his faith in "Fire," the elements suite, and the revolutionary album that housed it way back in the middle of winter.

But Brian's angels were gone, and his faith had flown along with them. And though he was all but incapable of uttering this statement in plain English, he made it abundantly clear in the music he made to take the place of *Smile*. Recording almost entirely in the makeshift studio the group set up in the living room of his new Spanish mansion, Brian worked with the other Beach Boys to rerecord a handful of *Smile* tracks in spartan arrangements that leaned almost entirely on a three-tiered Baldwin organ someone had recently given him. The vocals come in simple arrangements with no audible double-tracking or echo beyond what can be found in a bathroom or—in the most elaborate studio trick on the album—the bottom of the empty swimming pool out back. A few glimmers of Brian's sonic experimentation come through, but save for the *Smile* rebuilds, Van Dyke Parks's elegant lyrics make room for the simple or the downright goofy, while Brian's sonic perfectionism bows to an *audio vérité* aesthetic of false starts, audible mistakes, and fits of stoned giggling. Such organic sounds have their charms, to be sure, but they paled considerably beside the culture-rattling promises that had accompanied Brian and the Beach Boys through the second half of 1966 and the first half of 1967. And those false promises were only emphasized by the new album's self-consciously silly, nonsense title, "Smiley Smile," and the cover illustration that portrayed Frank Holmes's smile shop lost and alone in a densely overgrown jungle.

Released in mid-September, *Smiley Smile* was the first Beach Boys album to credit the entire group for its production, rather than just Brian. It also didn't quite crack the top forty on *Billboard's* album charts, thus becoming the worst-selling album in the group's history. Perhaps anticipating this turn of events, Brian returned to the live band (replacing Bruce Johnston, who had sat out most of the *Smiley Smile* sessions too) for a pair of late-August Honolulu concerts the group had decided to record for a live album they had already named, puckishly, "Lei'd in Hawaii." Unfortunately, the group's performances were so flat the tapes were deemed unreleasable. But the band remained keen on the live album idea (and, perhaps, on the bawdy album title), so a few weeks later they all went into a Los Angeles studio to record themselves playing their set a bit more competently, with an eye toward pulling off the old trick of overdubbing cheers, applause, and between-song patter, then passing the thing off as an authentic live recording (see also the group's 1964 *In Concert* album and the Rolling Stones' ironically named *Got Live If You Want It*, plus too many subsequent "live" albums to mention). But while the stripped-down live-in-the-studio takes have some nice moments, the most important track to emerge from these sessions was an outtake of "Heroes and Villains" that probably wasn't meant to emerge from the studio in any form.

It begins at the start of the song's first verse, with the backing vocals over a simple, organ-dominated backing track. But just when Brian's lead vocal is supposed to begin, Mike Love starts to speak with false-stentorian authority.

"In every recording group's career there comes that moment when you realize you have a nuclear bomb on your hands. Right now, Brian Wilson, the leader of the Beach Boys, is about to unleash his nuclear power and sing for you the song that went all the way to forty!"

Shifting from mock-serious to bitterly sarcastic, Mike's rant becomes even more barbed as he goes on.

"It topped the charts at about forty, and the next week it just zoomed right off to, oh well, about 250. Right now it's lurking at about 10,000 on this year's top 10,000! Come on in here and sing! Wail your buns off!"

Mike hurls a few barbs at the other band members next, teeing off on Dennis's smoking, Carl's loud breathing, Al's obsessive teeth picking, and Brian's eating. But when "Heroes and Villains" moves to its final verse, he returns his attention to the song itself with added venom, particularly when he hears the group move toward Van Dyke's *"sunny down snuff I'm alright . . ."* line.

"Ah, this is probably my favorite part in all my career recording. And if it keeps up like this, it probably won't last much longer. Ah, sunny down you ol' snuff, you. If I ever sing anything like that again, I'm gonna . . ."

Mike makes a fart sound, then cracks up, suddenly aware of how bitter his rampage had become. From this point his voice lightens.

"Really folks, it's all in fun. Really, you've gotta figure on one hit well . . . I mean every six years you've gotta get a little animosity generated somehow. And besides, being basically masochists, we kind of enjoyed having this record bomb."

To hear this, particularly understanding the tension between Mike and Brian during the *Smile* era and the fairly obvious contempt Mike held for Brian's more artistic impulses, is a little terrifying. After all, Brian labored obsessively on "Heroes and Villains" for months on end, and Mike knew better than anyone how far Brian would push himself in pursuit of the right song, the right sound, even the right feeling behind the voice of one singer in the backing chorus. He knew how his cousin had been raised and knew how fragile his sense of himself could be. So could Mike really be so spiteful that he'd not only ridicule Brian's most recent attempt at a masterwork but also commit his words to tape? And then overdub his screed onto the song's musical and vocal foundation? How filled with hate would a person have to be in order to launch such a vicious attack at the delicate spirit of Brian Wilson?

Listen closely to the tape and an answer will begin to emerge. Listen for the high-pitched laugh that follows Mike's cry of *"Wail your buns off!"* Listen for the same voice's even louder guffaw when Mike ridicules *"sunny down snuff."* Then, when the backing track ends and even Mike has had enough, listen to that same voice punching in on the control room intercom: *"Okay, come on in!"* Because that's the voice of the ghoul who had first sketched out and then produced this brutal insult to the memory of *Smile*. And as it turns out, the voice of that merciless *Smile* basher belongs to Brian Wilson.

CHAPTER 8

I t's not the failure that kills you, as much as the hope. That's what gets under your skin and makes you believe that things can change, that life matters, that the distance between possibility and reality is nothing compared to human ingenuity, hard work, and a trace amount of God's grace. And it was in this spirit that Johnny Wilson built himself an airplane from scratch in the spring and summer of 1915.

As recounted by Timothy White in *The Nearest Faraway Place,* the great-uncle of Brian, Dennis, and Carl Wilson was a dark-eyed, sensitive adolescent whose preternatural ability to build gadgets both large and small had already made him something of a hero around Hutchinson, Kansas. Inspired by Orville and Wilbur Wright's 1903 flight in Kitty Hawk, North Carolina, the teenaged Johnny Wilson had designed and built a steam-powered biplane whose spruce-and-canvas body seemed so revolutionary that his neighbors would actually pay a nickel for the privilege of peeking through the folds of the tent he had pitched to serve as a temporary hangar. And though he was shy, Johnny thrived on the attention paid to his creation. As the afternoon of his first test flight drew near, he and his brothers distributed handbills to alert the townspeople of the coming event.

Here, Johnny Wilson's life took a turn for the worse. For

only thirty minutes before he was scheduled to climb aboard his hand-built machine and fly off into the air, the skies went black and the Midwestern breeze stiffened into a wind. Then it was a gale, whipping into a frenzy of dust and brush that swept just ahead of the funnel cloud blowing up from the south. The crowd bolted for cover, with Johnny and his brothers close behind, and it was all anyone could do to cover their heads while the twister raked across the field and headed straight for the gleaming new airplane. Soon the shrieking winds died down and the tornado was gone. But when Johnny emerged from hiding, he discovered that his treasured airplane had been torn to pieces, scattered willy-nilly over several miles of the rugged Kansas farmland.

Devastated by his bad luck, Johnny turned sullen and strangely preoccupied. He soon set to re-creating his treasured airplane, but he'd already spent much of his money on the first aircraft, and work on the replacement went fitfully for months, then years. It ended completely when Johnny signed up to be an army aviator in World War I. But Johnny didn't fly in Europe, either, and though his engineering ingenuity won him medals, the horrors he encountered in the trenches of France left him a nervous, tentative shadow of the charismatic young man he had once been. Married eventually and then relocated along with the rest of his family to Southern California, Johnny bounced from job to job in the aeronautics industry, seemingly on the brink of success before the shadow of that tornado would sweep across his mind and send his thoughts scattering in a hundred directions. "He was the hero of the family, full of ideas and dreams," Johnny's younger brother Charlie told White in his book. "Maybe if he'd gone slow, maybe he could have gotten well. But no one let him go slow."

The tornado that swept across Brian Wilson's life in 1967 was just as freakish and perhaps even more emotionally devastating, given the fact that it erupted not from the whims of nature, but out of the mouths of his friends and family. They were the ones, in his eyes, who had blown his masterwork to smithereens. Did they really expect him to just dust himself off and get right back to building their next profit-making venture? Obviously so, since they had celebrated the death of *Smile* by installing a fully functioning eight-track recording studio in the living room of Brian's house, the better to capture any stray musical notion he might produce the instant it rose from the lid of his shiny black Chickering piano. They wanted his music, but only if they could control it (and him), which is why the group had voted to relieve Brian of his sole authority over their creative affairs. Now they would all split the burden, the authority, the credit, and the money.

Brian didn't mind, he said. He'd worked so hard for so long, why not let the other guys see how easy it wasn't? At times he even liked the idea of having the studio right beneath his bedroom. Brian came home with an assortment of water-based acoustic paints so the guys could decorate the walls with colorful, psychedelic pictures. He also brought in a massive load of hashish to serve as a communal source of inspiration for the *Smiley Smile* sessions. They all partook—even Al and Mike—and its bonding effects can be heard both in the giggling fits and the glee they take in their simple, psychedelic doo-wop: *"On and on she go dum-be-doo-dah/On and on she go dum-be-doo,"* they sing on the doggerel-like "With Me Tonight," and with such conviction you'd think the words might hold the secret to the universe—a secret Brian figured could be unraveled even faster if they only *looked* happier while they recorded. "Hey, now, wait a minute. I have an idea!" He chirped half a line into one take, ignoring engineer Jim Lockert's grumbling, "Hey, what the hell is that?" as he bubbled on. "If you sing that with a smile, I swear to God. You wait and see what happens, I swear to God!" Everyone giggled some more, and Brian counted off the next take, his own face split open with a big, self-conscious grin.

But such moments of hilarity tended to be drug-induced and fleeting. For one thing, Brian couldn't help feeling stung by his reduced authority. He was supposed to be the group's visionary, but now they had rejected his vision, so why give them anything else to reject? It pissed him off, really, but that wasn't the sort of thing Brian could ever say. Instead, he'd stay in his room or else go off to a friend's house and drift off on a drug binge for a few days. "Sometimes he'd show up for sessions, sometimes not," recalls Stephen Desper, a young recording engineer who started working at Brian's home studio during the *Smiley Smile* sessions in the summer of 1967. "Sometimes he'd get all screwed up and disappear for a few days. That certainly impacted his creative abilities. And that made him feel guilty because there was so much pressure on him."

No longer able or willing to produce his usual torrent of new music, Brian filled in *Smiley Smile* with castoffs from *Smile*. But instead of using the intricately crafted tracks he had already recorded, Brian redid the tunes in slapdash versions that seemed to diminish or alter their original intent and meaning. The *Smile* recording of "Wonderful," for instance, had been a jewel-like ballad featuring an elegant arrangement of harpsichord, strings, horns, and blooms of delicate vocal harmony that celebrated the resilience of love and innocence even in the face of cynicism. The *Smiley Smile* version, on the other hand, featured a

CATCH A WAVE

tossed-off organ track, high-pitched backing vocals produced either by a sped-up tape or the voice box–shrinking effects of helium, and a midsong digression into an unstructured doo-wop sing-along, with much giggling and drugged-out whispering ("I can feel it coming on! I can feel it coming on!") until the verse briefly reasserts itself at the song's conclusion. "Wind Chimes" went through a similar transformation, losing its shimmering marimbas in exchange for a horror movie–like organ and a midsong blast of dissonant noise (immediately following the line, *"It's so peaceful, close to a lullaby"*) that twists the once-dreamy song into something more like a waking nightmare.

Was this Brian's conscious (or perhaps subconscious) commentary on what had happened to his music? Certainly, *Smiley Smile* was the first album he had been involved with that represented a step backward in terms of production values and songcraft. "It was a bunt instead of a grand slam," Carl Wilson would eventually complain, although he stopped short of acknowledging how the group production credit, to say nothing of some group members' vocal disapproval of the album Brian had intended to be his biggest masterwork, might have brought this about.

Still, even if *Smiley Smile* never became a hit, the album's reputation improved with hindsight, particularly when Bob Dylan and the Beatles went on to release their own stripped-down, warts-and-all albums in the next few months. But *John Wesley Harding* and *The Beatles* (aka *The White Album*) came without the self-destructive gestures that Brian wove into *Smiley Smile*. "Everyone was worried about how Brian seemed to be slipping back," Desper says. "But he didn't know what he wanted to do next. He didn't want to go back and make more surf songs. He knew he wanted to move on, but he didn't know the direction. He thought he knew what the new direction ought to be, but the (group) didn't go for it."

Some days Brian would stay in his bed, gazing vacantly at the ceiling while the sounds of music-in-progress filtered up through his pillow from the studio just beneath his room. Other days he'd jump out of bed with all the energy and enthusiasm he had ever had, suddenly exploding with his new riff or a song that had come to him while he was watching a bird flutter past his window. "The vibe was still great," Danny Hutton recalls of those days. "He'd have me over and he'd suddenly say: 'I've got this idea, man!' Then he'd point to a jar of wild honey. 'That's it! That's what the album's gonna be called!' And the other guys were thrilled."

They were less thrilled when Brian devoted his energy to Hutton's group, a three-singer outfit Brian had named Redwood, intending to sign them to Brother Records. Brian was so excited about the group's prospects, in fact, that he had not only given them two of his most recent songs, "Darlin'" (actually a rewrite of "Thinkin' about You Baby," a song Brian had given to a singer named Sharon Marie in the early '60s) and "Time to Get Alone," but also recorded the basic tracks in a real studio, with his old gang of studio hotshots putting their usual fire into the music. They were just starting to work on the vocal tracks when Carl and Mike walked through the door of the Wally Heider studio where they were working, looking anything but happy. "Mike got us outside and said, 'Hey, what's going on? We've got an album to do. Why don't you wrap this up?'" Hutton recalls. "And Brian was physically afraid of Mike. Not that Mike used to beat him up, but he's a tough guy physically, and Brian wasn't like that, so Mike could definitely push him around mentally."

Mike and Carl took the master tapes of the two songs for the Beach Boys' new album. Once they had put their own vocals on Brian's prerecorded tracks, they released "Darlin'" as a single, scoring themselves a top twenty hit. This last development stung, Hutton admits. "But if I were Mike, I would have done the same thing. It's like, Brian's our producer, he's our writer; (these other, unknown guys) are in the only studio we record in, and he wants to finish an album with them? Mike's like . . . *get out!* And everyone says shit about Mike, but if I were him, I would have said the same thing."

Still, Mike and Carl's latest intervention in his artistic decisions did nothing to enhance Brian's creative momentum or his sense of well-being. And Brian's chagrin would only grow more pronounced when the other Beach Boys vetoed his decision to sign Hutton's band to the Beach Boys' own Brother Records. Instead, Redwood signed a contract with ABC Records, where they changed their name to Three Dog Night and soon launched a run of hit singles and albums that by the early '70s would make them one of the top-selling rock groups in the world.

Despite, or perhaps because of, what he perceived as these ongoing affronts to his creativity, Brian's work in the last months of 1967 and the first half of 1968 at times edged back toward the fragile optimism that had always animated his best work. But just as his own creative horizons had receded, so too did Brian's vision of the western paradise. His psyche battered by its most recent journey into the wilderness, now Brian (often writing with the assistance of Mike and sometimes combinations of other bandmates) looked for transcendence in the textures of the natural world and the simple, homey life unfolding beneath its bowers. The *Wild Honey* album, recorded largely at Brian's house just after the *Smiley Smile* sessions had ended, added a driving rhythm-and-blues edge to the homegrown sound. This was particularly true on the theremin-laced title track (also featuring a screaming Carl Wilson lead vocal) and the purloined single "Darlin'," with its ascending horn lines and propulsive chorus harmonies. Both singles are vibrant and energetic, but it's the quieter, unassuming songs that reach for an entirely new aesthetic. "Country Air" describes a sunrise across the hills of rural America with a simple bass-piano-and-drums backing for a lyric that begins with a hummed verse (solo Mike) and then a richly harmonized chorus—*"Get a breath of that country air/breathe the beauty of it everywhere"*—that repeats several times with different concluding lines: *"Get a look at that clear blue sky"* the first time around; *"Mother Nature, she fills my eye"* the second; *"Rise up early the day won't let you sleep"* on the final repetition, with Carl stretching out the last word into a falsetto swoop that harmonizes, amazingly, with the sound of a crowing rooster. Recorded in a single three-hour session in mid-November, "Country Air" is both rustic and shimmering, the restraint of its instrumentation and block harmonies perfectly underscoring the simple perfection of nature.

Similarly, the sly love song "I'd Love Just Once to See You" begins with its narrator (Brian) poking around the kitchen to the tune of a strummed acoustic guitar and lightly tapped percussion: *"I drink a little of this and eat a little that/ and poke my head out the door,"* he talk/sings, before going on to wash the dishes, rinse the sink, and hum a little song to himself, musing on his absent beloved. Indeed, all this domestic activity is merely foreplay to a sexual proposition—*"I'd love just once to see you . . . in the nude"*—so disarmingly forthright that the chiming guitars and blossoming harmonies that fill the song's final twenty seconds sound just as sweet and fulfilling as a moment of spontaneous lovemaking.

"Let the Wind Blow" bridges the gap between the pleasures of nature and romance (although Mike's arch lyrics create a stumbling block that isn't truly overcome until Carl's magnificent, gospel-like performance on the 1973 *In Concert* album), and the idea is expanded upon in the harmony-filled, harpsichord-led waltz "Time to Get Alone" (first recorded in late 1967, then fiddled with in the succeeding months and released in 1969), in which one couple's romantic journey is reflected in a series of natural images, first as a speeding toboggan ride down a mountainside (the journey echoed in the chorus's descending chords) and, in the moments they spend, *"Lying down on our backs looking at the stars/*

looking down through the valley so deep and wide." The point is that as a loving couple, they are poised at the absolute center of nature, as perfectly interwoven as the voices weaving behind them.

What begins to emerge in this period—which extends into 1968's *Friends* with songs such as "Wake the World," then on through "Cool, Cool Water" and another bird song, "At My Window"—is an awe for the natural world that echoes ideals that found their first voice with the transcendentalists of the mid-nineteenth century. For like Thoreau at Walden Pond, Brian and, to an extent, the other Beach Boys created a vision of life in which beauty (interpreted perhaps as the presence of God or a connection to the sacred) becomes most vivid in the absence of the usual clamor of life. Dennis Wilson, working with a poet friend named Steve Kalinich, produced two elegantly understated songs for the *Friends* album in 1968 (his first original Beach Boy songs, if you ignore the space-filling solo, "Denny's Drums," on *Shut Down, Volume 2*) that pose variations on the same theme. "Be Still," with Dennis singing alone over the accompaniment of a single organ, sounds like a Unitarian hymn describing the sacred essence of life and the human potential to interact with God. *"You know you know you are/Be still and know you are,"* it begins. "Little Bird" strikes a more fanciful pose, with both its more realized production (courtesy of Brian, who also contributed the song's bridge, uncredited) and its vision of a natural world that provides both physical and spiritual sustenance. The birds provide music, the trees bear fruit, even an unsuccessful day of fishing has its reward: *"A trout in a shiny brook/Gave a worm another look/And told me not to worry about my life."*

And though this lyrical pose often put the group's music at odds with the reality of their own lives, it's the same contradiction that lurked beneath the Beach Boys when they were nonsurfers who just happened to be the nation's most successful purveyors of songs about surfing. What also remained consistent was the yearning that fired their dreams. For even if they couldn't quite attain the simple happiness they described, there was nothing phony about the desperation that animated their fantasies. Once again, the distinctly American texture of their visions emerged not from a conscious effort (surely they had no sense how closely the imagery in their songs resembled *Walden*) but from the reality of their experience and their tangled internal lives.

Naturally, the most striking examples in the group's surge of transcendentalist pop are both songs composed entirely by Brian. "Busy Doin' Nothin'" appeared on *Friends* as a breezy bossa nova–style song (richly orchestrated with clarinets, nylon-string guitars, and a loping acoustic bass) that describes what seems to be a typical day for a young, semiretired rock musician who, as the title implies, is not terribly busy. *"I had to fix a lot of things this morning, 'cause they were so scrambled,"* Brian sings in the first verse, his relaxed delivery growing even more placid as he eases into the next line, describing the stillness that comes with the setting sun and cooling breeze. Brian invites a friend to visit, giving explicit (and reputedly quite accurate, if you lived where his friend did) directions to his house on Bellagio Road. *"Drive for a couple miles,"* he begins:

> *You'll see a sign and turn left for a couple blocks*
> *Next is mine, you'll turn left on a little road, it's a bumpy one.*

The second verse climaxes with Brian's decision to call another friend. Only he lost the slip of paper he scribbled her number on, which introduces the conflict that drives the second half of the song. Once again, transcendence comes most readily in an absence of effort. Brian thinks about the number for a while, summons it in his memory, and then dials. Once again, all is right in the world—except it turns out his friend isn't home to answer. Again Brian eases into a solution that is so simple it would be absurd to mention, were it not for the ecstatic tone he brings to describing it: *"So I hung up the telephone . . . sharpened up a pencil and/Wrote a letter to my friend."* The clarinets rise up to herald this revelation, swooping and diving like a flock of birds through the trees while crickets chitter (drumsticks skittering across the hi-hat cymbal) and the dog lopes amiably in the brush (the stand-up bass solo). And none of these things matter, except for the fact that these tiny moments make up the essential fabric of existence, and this elegant recognition of their innate beauty is a small triumph not just in the career of Brian Wilson, but in the entire scope of popular music.

It's nice to think of Brian in this way, meandering alone through his mansion with a song on his lips and nothing—and yet everything—on his mind. For in "Busy Doin' Nothin'," he is the eccentric genius of dreams, entirely weird, but happily and productively so, nursing whatever psychic wounds he might carry in the balm of his own brilliance. But as in the early, heroic songs, the darkness that fuels his need for ecstatic vision is never far from the edges of his dreamed life. Another journal-style song recorded a few weeks later, the lazy waltz "I Went to Sleep," describes the events of a similarly leisurely day with a more detached tone.

The narrator (Brian again, at the crest of a block of harmonies) wanders into the park, goes home and listens to the radio, goes back to the park and watches a bird flying past. But rather than reveling in what he experiences—let alone interacting with it—he responds by falling asleep. The signal moment seems to come in the second verse, when Brian turns on the radio and feels completely disconnected from what he hears: *"Some group was playing a musical song/It wasn't too long/And I went to sleep."*

That Brian is growing increasingly interested in numbing his senses becomes all the more clear in "Sail Plane Song," cowritten with Carl and recorded days after "I Went to Sleep" in the spring of 1968 (though not released until 1998's *Endless Harmony* compilation). Here, Brian leaps onto a metaphorical airplane that, given the oddly circular chord pattern (played on piano and organ, with electric guitar and rudimentary drums keeping time) and remote sound of his vocal, is fueled by something more psychedelic than diesel jet fuel. *"Have you ever been on an airplane?/Up above the clouds there's no rain,"* he sings, neatly explaining why a person in pain might feel inclined to get high via any available means. And indeed, the journey he goes on to relate is both vividly described and entirely disconnected from reality, from his visit to the ocean to the skyward climb that ends when he turns off the engine and, instead of falling through the clouds, sails straight to the sun.

By this time, all the other Beach Boys had long since explored their own fondness for altered consciousness. They had all smoked pot to one extent or another (although Bruce Johnston generally preferred to keep his feet on terra firma, as did Al and Mike), while Carl dallied with an array of substances and the perpetually ravenous Dennis gobbled up whatever came within his reach. For Mike, the first reasonable path to the netherworld appeared courtesy of Dennis, of all people, in the last days of 1967, when the drummer came across the Maharishi, the Indian-born guru of Transcendental Meditation who had captured the interest of the Beatles during the summer of 1967. Impressed by the little Indian man's charismatic holiness during their meeting in Paris, Dennis summoned the rest of the group from London so they too could learn the joys of meditation. Mike, who yearned to explore his consciousness without surrendering control over reality, was struck immediately. An avowed materialist, Mike was even more intrigued when the guru told him that his pursuit of spirituality needn't require him to divest of all, or even any, of the exquisite accoutrements of his celebrity lifestyle. "That sounded pretty good to me," Mike said at the time. Now convinced that he had truly found the path to spiritual enlightenment meant for him, Mike jumped into TM with both feet, signing up immediately for an extended seminar to be held at the Maharishi's personal compound in Rishikesh, India. There his classmates would include all of the Beatles, accompanied by their wives and entourage, plus the British folksinger Donovan Leitch, American actress Mia Farrow, her sister Prudence, and a scattering of other spiritual seekers.

For Mike, the two weeks in Rishikesh would become a highlight of his life, both for the spiritual education he received and also for the glittering company he kept while he was there. For years he would describe how Paul McCartney came to him one afternoon, acoustic guitar in hand, singing the first verses of "Back to the USSR" and explaining how it was inspired by all those Chuck Berry and Beach Boys songs about traveling and girls. And as Mike always loved to point out, he had right at that moment told Paul exactly how he should write the bridge of the song, talking about how the girls in this place were so hot and the girls in that place were so cool . . . like "California Girls," geddit? And yes, Paul got it, all the way from the Moscow girls to the one named Georgia, so perpetually on his mi-mi-mi-mi-mind. The Beatles' recollections of Mike were just as vivid, even if most of them seemed to revolve around the way he had come equipped with crates of batteries, film, and other Western staples he was willing to sell to other campers for a premium. "He reminded me of a dealer," McCartney told his biographer, Barry Miles. "I think he might even have had booze in there. 'Hey man, come to Mr. Love!' . . . All in all it was good fun." And yet by the time it was all over, the musicians would come away with radically different opinions on the Maharishi himself; while the Beatles denounced their ex-guru in word and song, Mike would spend the rest of his days as a committed practitioner and tireless evangelist for the cause. But if TM can be viewed as a healthier alternative to drugs, Mike's passion for his guru would soon become just as damaging to the group's private fortunes and public reputation as their drug use.

Back in the United States in mid-March, Mike joined in the *Friends* sessions for a couple of weeks, then set out with the rest of the group on a self-financed tour of the American Southeast that began, as coincidence would have it, just two days before the assassination of the Rev. Martin Luther King Jr. in Memphis, Tennessee. The murder of the nation's most prominent civil rights activist sparked riots in some cities and gun-enforced martial order in many cities hoping to avoid the same plight. Naturally, the always tense urban areas of the Jim Crow South—

most of which the Beach Boys had been booked to play in the next few days—instantly became the epicenter of the nation's racial tension. Most of the shows were cancelled, and the ones that weren't drew only light crowds, including one show that according to the group's then-manager Nick Grillo (speaking to Steven Gaines) drew a total of twenty-five fans. "Devastating," Grillo told Gaines. "A fucking nightmare."

A month later the group set out on the road again, this time in a glossy package tour ("The Most Exciting Event of the Decade!" according to the promotional posters) with the Maharishi, who would open the show with lectures on the magic and wonder of Transcendental Meditation. As concocted by savvy spiritualist Mike, the tour would be a brilliant method to both spread the word about TM via their own mainstream popularity and simultaneously enhance their coolness factor thanks to their public association with the world's most prominent Indian mystic. The only problem was that the Beach Boys' fans were not only dwindling in number but also uniquely impatient when it came to sitting through long, generally unintelligible lectures on Eastern spirituality. As the guru sat cross-legged on the flower-bedecked stage explaining the utility of mantras and chakras and the like, the kids would bellow for "409" and "California Girls," thereby ruining the vibe entirely and prompting gales of high-pitched giggles from the ever-buoyant Maharishi. And once the Beach Boys did take the stage, they found themselves belting out their no-longer-quite-so-fresh hits to acres of empty seats.

Once at the absolute center of the American rock 'n' roll scene, the Beach Boys of 1968 found themselves woefully out of step with the mood and rhythm of the nation's popular culture. *Rolling Stone*'s Jann Wenner had anticipated this development as early as late 1967, when he wrote an editorial for his increasingly important youth culture journal castigating the Beach Boys and Brian Wilson for what he perceived as their artistic pretensions and overall phoniness. The performing group, Wenner wrote, was "totally disappointing," while all that *Smile*-era talk about Brian's genius was little more than a "promotional shuck" that had mesmerized the songwriter into a kind of creative paralysis. "The Beach Boys are just one prominent example of a group that has gotten hung up in trying to catch the Beatles. It's a pointless pursuit," Wenner concluded.

The fact that the Beatles themselves considered Brian to be not just a worthy rival but also an inspiring one didn't seem to matter. Nor had the fact that his post-*Smile* work had dialed back the group's ambitions considerably. And though

Wild Honey (and its single, "Darlin'") made respectable showings in the low twenties of the *Billboard* sales charts during the winter of '67/'68, the public antipathy for the Beach Boys grew stronger as they muddled into the spring and summer. The lovely *Friends* album, released at the start of the summer, stalled at number 126 on the *Billboard* charts, while the title track missed the top forty by a long shot, peaking at an anemic number 47.

And perhaps it was inevitable. In a year rent by public assassination, a bloody and controversial war, bitter protests on college campuses, and a racial divide that seemed only to grow more jagged as time went on, it's impossible to imagine how a group of sweet-faced boyish utopians—who had finally ditched their striped shirts but still insisted on wearing matching white suits, set off with hokey psychedelic neckerchiefs that made them look like vaguely groovy ice cream salesmen—could capture anyone's imagination. No, 1968 was the time for Jimi Hendrix's psychedelic guitar frenzy, for the windmilling rage of the Who, for the Doors' existentialist circus of horrors, and for the Rolling Stones, whose sympathy for the devil was rooted in the uncomfortable fact that He, so often, is We. Even the Beatles' eyes darkened as the year went on, moving from the psychedelic ecstasies of *Sgt. Pepper* to the monochromatic gloom of *The White Album* and its vaguely ominous songs that skirted the edges of sex, hard drugs, suicide, and violent revolution.

And even if the Beach Boys seemed determined to drift above the fray, no amount of cheerful harmony could keep the darkness around them from seeping into the sunny little world they continued to imagine in song. For Dennis, the chaos came to call one afternoon in the spring of 1968 when he picked up a couple of cute young hitchhikers and brought them back to his house on the western slope of Sunset Boulevard for what he hoped would be a quick three-way sexual liaison. Indeed, the two young women were more than happy to spend the afternoon rolling around naked with the hunky young drummer, and a good time was had by all. Later that evening, Dennis came home from a late-night recording session to discover that the girls had returned, only now they were accompanied by an entire flock of similarly freaked-out girls and the older man they called their guru: a dark-eyed, raven-haired drifter named Charlie Manson. Manson was even stranger and less clean than most people Dennis tended to hang around with. But he spoke of brotherhood and faith, knew where to get good drugs, and had such a hold over his flock of girls that when Charlie told them all to get naked, Dennis's living room became a writhing mass of pink, lithesome, submissive flesh. And for Dennis Wilson, this was all the transcendence he could ever imagine.

All Charlie asked for in return was a place for him and his family to live, food, drink, money, and access to everything else Dennis owned. Oh, and also a chance for Charlie to record some of his original music compositions, many of which elucidated his inimitable philosophies on life, love, and the inevitability of social conflict. And for Dennis, who had jumped from adolescence to wealth and fame without pausing to resolve the emotional toll of growing up in the shadow of Murry, the situation was just poisonous enough to feel right. Many young rock stars feel secretly (or not so secretly) guilty for their success, and Dennis experienced his guilt with the full-bodied enthusiasm he brought to his various indulgences. He was accustomed to giving away his money, cars, and clothes. Such sacrifices made him happy, so if he could satisfy both his conscience and his decadence in one mutually fulfilling relationship with Charlie Manson, that was fine by him, no matter how dirty and wild-eyed his permanent houseguest could be. "Fear is nothing but awareness, man," Dennis told a reporter from Britain's *Rave* magazine, going on to explain that he was quoting his friend, the Wizard, whom he described as being terribly wise and also, at times, quite scary. And he would grow even more so as the summer of Manson family fun went on.

Dennis brought Charlie up to Brian's house to record on several occasions, and the sessions produced everything from straight-ahead pop songs to more avant-garde tapes Mike Love described to a *Rolling Stone* reporter in 1971 as "...chanting, fucking, sucking, barking. It was a million laughs, believe me." Nevertheless, Dennis remained convinced of his pal's musical talent and took him to the Beverly Hills home of Terry Melcher up on Cielo Drive—the same house where Brian had asked Van Dyke Parks to help him write *Smile* a couple of summers earlier. The producer agreed to give Manson's music a listen. He decided against pursuing the project, however, thereby eliciting Manson's considerable rage. Manson never forgot where Melcher lived, either. And though the object of his hatred would soon move to another part of town, Manson's fury stayed focused on that house on Cielo Drive.

Dennis also wandered into Manson's sights by taking one of his songs, "Cease to Exist," smoothing down its bluesy edges, and recording it with the Beach Boys as "Never Learn Not to Love." Reportedly, Manson had written the song specifically for the group, imagining that his vision of love as a soul-consuming act of submission would make them feel better about themselves. *"Cease to exist,*

CATCH A WAVE

come and say you love me . . . *Submission is a gift/Go on, give it to your brother,*" Manson sang in his demo recording of the tune. And he's neither a terrible singer nor a bad songwriter, which may explain Dennis's interest in the guy. (Though at this point merely acknowledging this makes me feel like taking a hot, hot shower.) Dennis ended up revising the song's words, then removed Manson's name from the song's credit line, an affront Manson used to justify prying several more months' worth of goods and services from his rich friend.

Dennis eventually grew tired of Manson's parasitic ways, even if he had to move out of his Sunset Boulevard house in order to get the Wizard and family out of his life. Still, Manson's demands on Dennis would continue. And when they weren't satisfied soon enough, he or his minions would make threats, not just on Dennis's life, but also on that of his young stepson, Scott. The fear-slash-awareness would only deepen in the next weeks and months and not just because the Beach Boys, who put "Never Learn Not to Love" on the B-side of their next single, launched Manson's words and music onto the lower reaches of the *Billboard* charts. Soon the darkness of the age would seem to close in from every direction at the same time.

Up at Bellagio Road, Brian's eyes had taken on a curious glimmer. Sometimes this resulted from his long bouts with cocaine, which had come to join speed, grass, and the occasional dose of psychedelics on his menu of favored drugs. But such chemical indulgences offered only temporary relief from the demons that chattered away inside his ears. Some days their voices would overwhelm him so much that it was all Brian could do to lie in bed all day with the blankets pulled up to his chin, too depressed to climb to his feet and join in the work downstairs. "I feel like jumping out of the window," he confessed to Danny Hutton one day when his friend managed to get through the door and talk things over for a little while. "That was when the real decline started," Hutton recalls.

When Brian did get out of bed, his behavior grew increasingly strange and obsessive. He recorded dozens of versions of "Ol' Man River," from the Jerome Kern musical *Showboat,* constantly finding new combinations of chords, instruments, and voices to alter the feel of the old Broadway standard. "He was always working on it," Stephen Desper remembers. "I definitely recorded that song a lot of times." The guys eventually tired of that, though, and one day Mike announced that he'd had it, thank you very much, and now they were done wasting their time and money on Brian's "Ol' Man River" experiments. Brian left the studio with his eyes stinging. (And he still remembers how angry it made him: "Mike was really cocky about that one," he complains with a sour smile. "I remember that much about it.")

But even that obsession couldn't rival Brian's passion for Phil Spector's thunderous "Be My Baby," which he kept on the jukebox in his living room and would, when the mood struck him, listen to for hours at a time. One time, in the midst of a "Be My Baby" period, Brian had Desper make a tape loop consisting only of the song's chorus—the point at which all of the instruments and voices come together in the biggest blast of echo-heavy sound—and put it on the big ultra-hi-fidelity tape recorder in his home recording studio. It was an involved project, with much precise razoring of tape and then the elaborate threading of the twenty-five-foot loop around the room, placing chairs and tables at precise points in order to maintain the appropriate tension on the tape as it spun from and then back to the heads of the player. Then Brian put the speakers in the echo chamber, turned the lights out, and sat on the floor. Desper turned on the loop, made sure it was working properly, and then went out to run some errands, leaving Brian to the booming clamor of the Ronettes and Spector's wall of sound. "I must have been gone for about four hours," Desper says. "And when I came back, he was still listening to that loop over and over and over, in some kind of a trance. I opened the door and of course he was squinting, because he'd been in the dark the whole time. But he wasn't asleep, and when I said, 'Uh, are you sure you want to hear more?' he instantly said he did: 'Close the door!' Then he listened for another hour before getting up and asking me to turn it off."

Meanwhile, Marilyn had given birth to the couple's first daughter, Carnie. But while Brian loved his daughter as any father would, his own childhood weighed so heavily on him that he refused to take responsibility for raising his own child. "He once told me, 'Marilyn, I want you to discipline the kids. I'll do it wrong,'" Marilyn told *Rolling Stone*'s David Felton in 1976. "He backed out of it totally." Having an infant in the house is consuming enough for any parent, let alone one who knows she can't trust her spouse to help keep the baby comfortable and safe. And when Brian's behavior seemed so detached from reality that Marilyn began to fear for his safety, the family realized something had to be done. Though the facts are still sketchy (and hitherto unreported), several sources confirm that Brian, perhaps of his own volition, was committed for treatment at a mental hospital for a period of time in 1968.

"It was all very privately discussed," Desper says. "The sessions went on at the house without him. I just remember that it was a big relief, particularly for Carl. The feeling was that they'd finally admitted to [the problem], and now they were doing the right thing: 'Now he's gonna get some help.'" What that help might have entailed—Electroshock? Stiff doses of lithium or other antipsychotic drugs? Intensive talk therapy?—remains a mystery. But Brian couldn't have been in the hospital very long, judging by the pace of his work with the rest of the group in the studio; and the long-term salutary effects of his stay in the hospital are difficult to determine.

But whenever Brian was available and ready to work, the other band members would gladly drop whatever they were doing and do whatever they could to extract whatever musical gems their erstwhile visionary felt like scattering across the studio. "Do It Again," a nostalgic beach song with a funky backbeat that Brian cowrote with Mike at the latter's instigation, recaptured the *joie de vivre* of days gone by well enough to climb into the American top twenty (it hit the top of the charts across the sea in the United Kingdom). Pushed by Al to move back toward folk music, Brian produced an inventive cover of Leadbelly's "Cottonfields" that combined banjo, electric piano, Dobro, a horn section, and a thrumming electric bass line into a modern vision connecting the West Coast of the late twentieth century to the Louisiana fields of Stephen Foster's imagination. Al would eventually recut the song with a less imaginative, pedal steel–dominated arrangement, and his version would be a moderate hit in England. The musical quest for roots continued with Carl's cover of Phil Spector's "I Can Hear Music." Brian didn't participate in any of those sessions, but the song's thunderous sound revealed exactly how closely Carl had observed his older brother's production techniques. Bruce and Carl took a run at Ersel Hickey's "Bluebirds Over the Mountain," freshening up the rockabilly tune with marimbas and (less explicably) shrieking lead guitar riffs played by sideman Ed Carter. Brian experimented with a cover of Burt Bacharach's recent hit for Dionne Warwick, "Walk On By," and continued to fuss with "Ol' Man River," recording at least one version as a medley with Stephen Foster's "Old Folks at Home." He didn't get around to recording the vocals on Foster's tune, but its faux-nostalgic sentiment—the yearning for an idealized family home that never quite existed—struck a chord for a man still reeling from the dire circumstances of his own youth. Meanwhile, Murry seemed determined to make himself just as present in the lives of his grown sons as he had been when they were still living in his home.

It had been four years since the group had dismissed Murry Wilson as their manager. Most recently he had been keeping himself busy producing his own album of original jazz-pop instrumentals, "The Many Moods of Murry Wilson," released by Capitol (and paid for from the reserves in one of the Beach Boys' royalty accounts) in October 1967. The record didn't exactly launch a new music career for Murry. But he still owned 50 percent of Sea of Tunes, the company that owned the rights to Brian's songs. Given this authority and the fact that Brian, Dennis, and Carl could never really fire him as their father, Murry continued attending Beach Boy recording sessions on a regular basis. "Word would filter in, 'Oh, shit, Murry's here!' Brian would tense up, and then there'd be this mad dash to hide all the pot," Desper says. "Then Murry would come bursting in and everyone would say, 'Oh, hi Dad! How's it going? You can help us out!' But right before that they'd have said: 'Oh, fuck! Now we've lost two hours.'"

And though his sons had been hugely successful recording stars for years, Murry couldn't resist the temptation to exert his authority over whatever was going on, as Desper recalls: "He fancied himself the creator of the Beach Boys, and by rights, as their father, creator, and first backer, he'd take over. Brian found it difficult to stand up to him, so Murry would tell everyone what to do. He'd tell them to sing higher, tell them to sing something again, or point out the obvious stuff like, 'Okay, here's the count!' He just couldn't take his hand off the talkback mike." Murry was just as forceful with Desper, who usually found himself sitting right in front of where Murry liked to stand. "He'd put his hand on my shoulder and dig his nails into my shoulder, yelling, 'Surge! Surge here!' And he'd leave these marks in my skin—I mean, it hurt." The sessions could be bruising (literally, for Desper), but then Murry would make a grand gesture to smooth things over. "He'd ridicule me, then give me a lighter or something as if that would justify it all. He could be a very generous man. But he was just a kind of ornery fart."

Like a lot of men who came of age during the Depression and World War II, Murry had taken a few knocks in his life, and he emerged from the experience convinced that the best way to avoid more of the same was to swing first and take what he had coming to him before anyone else could grab it first. And once Murry figured out that his primary capital had come in the form of the three sons he loved so intensely, loosening his grip on them made no sense whatsoever. As far as he could see, he was just continuing his lifelong commitment to protect them, particularly against the weaknesses they still weren't mature enough to realize they had. "I've protected you for twenty-two years," Murry had railed during that notorious "Help Me, Rhonda" recording session four years earlier. "But I can't go on if you're not going to listen to an intelligent man. Against, against so many people who are trying to hurt you . . ."

And as the 1960s drew to a close, the sun-washed optimism the Beach Boys had once given voice to seemed to have been subsumed by the darkness that had always hovered on its fringes. What emerged was a nation that had splintered along every imaginable social fault line: black against white, young against old, rich against poor, students against their universities, women against men, humans against Mother Earth. You say you want a revolution? That's exactly what was going on in 1969, and every day it didn't erupt into bloody, hellish violence was kind of surprising. Then in late July of that year, the Los Angeles police got that call up to the house on Cielo Drive that Terry Melcher had recently moved away from, and what they found—apparently intended for Melcher by its master-mind—was so gruesome it seemed like that nightmare of violent revolution was becoming real.

The facts have been reported so often and so vividly it seems pointless to go into it all again. Suffice it to say that Sharon Tate, the pregnant wife of Roman Polanski, along with an array of friends and houseguests, had been murdered in the bloodiest, most heartless way imaginable. To make things even more lurid and awful, the murderers had scrawled vaguely revolutionary slogans—two drawn from the titles of recent Beatles songs—on the walls with their victims' blood. A prosperous, middle-aged couple who lived nearby, the LaBiancas, were murdered under similarly hellish circumstances the next night. And paranoia in Los Angeles, and everywhere else, ratcheted up to alarming heights. But nowhere more than in the heart of Dennis Wilson, Terry Melcher, and the various friends and associates who had come to know something about Manson's revolutionary fantasies in the last few months. Manson turned up at Dennis's door a day or two after the killings, looking even wilder than usual ("I been to the moon," he explained when asked what he'd been up to). Dennis gave him all the money he had on him that night, but not nearly the $1,500 Manson had asked for, which aggravated him to no end. And Manson was even angrier when he returned a week or so later to find that Dennis was up in Canada with the Beach Boys. That time Manson left something for Dennis: a .45-caliber bullet.

Dennis, Melcher, and their friends had whispered their suspicions all fall. But it took until mid-November for the authorities to build enough of a case to arrest

Manson and his family for the murders. And once the identity of the killers became known, it seemed clear to some people—particularly President Richard M. Nixon, recently elected on a strict law-and-order platform—that the murderers were hippie freaks bent on destroying society. Surely this was just another facet of the drug-fueled decadence that had first stirred in the Monterey fog in 1967, then burst into full, hideous bloom out of the primordial muck of Woodstock, New York, right when Manson was up to his hideous business in Beverly Hills. But the collision of his hippielike cult with Sharon Tate's new Hollywood crowd, Dennis and Melcher's L.A. rock scene, the LaBiancas' staid, upper-middle-class home, and then the many ambitions of L.A. prosecutor Vincent Bugliosi (who would leverage an entire second career out of his work on the Manson case) took in a much wider swath of American culture.

To some observers, the hideous crime seemed like the lurid apotheosis of two centuries of Manifest Destiny. To others it revealed the spiritual hollowness of the twentieth-century California Myth, which leaned so heavily on the phony ideals propagated in the false-fronted buildings posing as the real world in the Hollywood back lots. To others, the crimes of the Manson family merely revealed the dangerous amorality of the hippie movement. That the Beach Boys had stumbled into the affair, led on by some mixture of amoral lust and desperate, if confused, attempts at spirituality, only seemed to confirm their own essential hollowness and the emptiness of the mirage they had pursued from the hallways of high school to the white sands of the beach to the escape of the highway to the sonic pyrotechnics of *Pet Sounds* and "Good Vibrations." "Their vision had always been a passive one, and like many, they went from easy questions to easy answers," Greil Marcus wrote in his 1974 book, *Mystery Train*. The problem, Marcus continued, is that they were faced with the challenge of growing up: "A challenge they failed to meet," he concluded.

Still, even if he felt the group had faltered in their pursuit of the American Utopia, Marcus couldn't fault their intent or the spirit that drove them onward. "The Beach Boys were never fakes . . . (they) celebrated California hedonism, looked for its limits, experienced its failures. Their pleasures, as opposed to those claimed by such latter-day inheritors as the Eagles, have always radiated affection—because those pleasures were always rooted in friendship, or a memory of it."

Perhaps this was so because the world around them so often seemed to be bristling with thieves, con artists, and manipulators whose authority over their lives and affairs so often seemed inversely proportional to their concern for their well-being. Seven years since they had first signed with Capitol Records and nearly three years since they had started auditing the company's books, the group discovered that the company, which had earned a fortune from their many hit records, had spent the entire time skimming 10 percent off the top of their profits. This thanks to a record breakage clause buried deep in the contract that had been eliminated from most other deals when records ceased being made from (highly breakable) wax and were instead manufactured from (nearly indestructible) plastic. Just to add insult to injury, the company had also failed to pay Brian nearly $1.5 million in producer's royalties. The Beach Boys' company sued Capitol for all their back royalties, and though the case would eventually be settled in the Beach Boys' favor (the group got the rights to all of their albums from *Pet Sounds* onward), Capitol responded by deleting the group's entire catalogue from its backlist.

Meanwhile, Murry Wilson was busy working his own angles. Always the half-owner of Sea of Tunes, the publishing company that owned the copyrights to virtually all of the songs Brian had written in his career, he had at some point secured authority over Brian's 50 percent of the company. How he did this, exactly, would eventually become the crux of another Beach Boys lawsuit. But in 1969, Murry could make a believable claim that those songs belonged to him. And as the decade was drawing to a close and his sons' careers seemed to be drifting down for a landing, it occurred to him that the value of "Surfin' USA," "Help Me, Rhonda," and "Good Vibrations" had long since peaked. Eager to sell while the selling was even halfway good, Murry cast around the L.A. music industry in search of buyers. And after rejecting an initial offer that would have left the group with 50 percent control over their catalogue, Murry decided to accept a $700,000 offer from Irving-Almo, the publishing division of A&M records, for the songs, lock, stock, and barrel.

Brian's attempts to talk his father out of the sale (which may or may not have included the violent confrontation described in Brian's so-called 1991 autobiography, *Wouldn't It Be Nice*) went unheeded. Murry figured he knew what the sum total of his son's work was worth, and eventually Brian resigned himself to the inevitable. By the time Steve Love, Mike's brother and an assistant to Nick Grillo, drove up to Brian's house to collect his signature on the consent letter Murry needed to make the deal, the songwriter sat down and, with a heavy sigh, applied his signature. "He knew what he was doing," Steve says. "He wasn't happy, but he did it." Murry collected his $700,000 and according to both Grillo and Steve, he kept every penny for himself. Brian's catalogue of hits would eventually come to be worth tens of millions of dollars, but all that money went to the catalogue's owners over at A&M.

Not long afterwards, Hal Blaine, the man who had played the drums on so many Beach Boys hits, answered a knock on his door and found a downcast Brian standing on his doorstep holding a box of his framed gold records. Blaine was at first delighted to see his old friend, but happiness soon faded when he realized that Brian had come to give him the last physical evidence he had of his glory days. Blaine tried to talk him out of it, but Brian was adamant. And though Brian eventually agreed to take all but a few of the awards back home with him, it seemed clear to Blaine that Brian had no intention of ever looking at them, let alone hanging them upon the wall, ever again. "He was removing himself from his own past," Blaine remembers. "He was headed somewhere else, but I don't think he knew where that was, exactly, and right then I don't think he cared. And it was very, very sad."

CHAPTER 9

One afternoon in early 1969 the group was busy working on a track in the studio at Brian's house when he came rushing in through the bright blue, hand-painted door, still in his pajamas and holding a sheet of paper. "I've got a great idea!" he cried, waving the just-typed document in the air. Brian explained that he was holding a five-way agreement to declare that from this day forward, the group would be known not as the Beach Boys, but merely as the Beach. "We're not 'boys' anymore, right? We're *men*! So why do we want to call ourselves Beach Boys? All we've gotta do is sign this, and we'll change it for good. Look, I already signed it myself!" Brian held the paper in front of his face, pointing to the fresh ink on the line next to his name.

Whether Brian's impulse to create a new identity for the band stemmed from his reading of the marketplace or from a desire to disassociate himself from the past isn't quite clear. But he was obviously fired up about his idea and just as obviously deflated when the other guys brushed it off without much of a thought. "They all just kind of shrugged and said, 'Aw, come on, Brian, we don't wanna do that. That's how the public knows us, man,'" recording engineer Stephen Desper remembers. "And that was it. He put the paper on the piano, and it stayed there until I picked it up and took it away."

After dismissing Brian's proposal, everyone's attention turned back to the job at hand, which was finishing up the loose ends of the Beach Boys' last album for Capitol Records. Released in March 1969 and named *20/20* to note that it was the twentieth album they had released, the group's final original album for their label consisted almost entirely of uncollected singles, B-sides, and a handful of leftovers from the last few years. But whatever the album lacked in thematic coherence, it made up in the quality of the pieces contributed by each band member. Kicking off with "Do It Again," Brian and Mike's retro surfing single that had been a minor hit the previous summer, the album soared just as high with Carl's shimmering adaptation of "I Can Hear Music," took a slight turn with Bruce's quirky marimbas-and-shrieking-guitar cover of "Bluebirds Over the Mountain," then shot skyward again on the strength of Dennis's yearning "Be with Me" and his flat-out nasty rocker "All I Want to Do," which included the results of an actual recording of the drummer doing all he wanted to do with a groupie he had brought into the studio for that very purpose. The last track on the side, Bruce's keyboard-led instrumental "The Nearest Faraway Place," lost its way in a syrupy muck of harps and piano glissandos, but the second side kicked off in classic form with Brian's graceful production of Al's revamped Leadbelly tune, "Cotton Fields," and then waltzed through Brian's "I Went to Sleep" and the plangent "Time to Get Alone" before falling into a spiritual black hole with Dennis's Manson adaptation, "Never Learn Not to Love."

The bad vibrations from that tune don't linger, however, because the last two songs on *20/20* turned out to be two highlights from the *Smile* sessions: the wordless invocation "Our Prayer" and the frontier mosaic "Cabinessence." Carl had dug the songs out of the group's vault, mostly to give Brian a larger presence on the album. But Brian had complained bitterly about this violation of the stillborn *Smile* and then refused to participate in the vocal sessions Carl scheduled to add an extra layer to "Prayer." "He was superstitious about those tunes," Desper remembers. "He'd leave the house when the guys were working on them. He didn't want anything to do with them, really." But even if that glimpse at what might have been struck a sour note to Brian, the first appearance of tracks from *Smile* (as opposed to the rerecordings on *Smiley Smile*) struck a resounding chord with anyone who had heard about the ill-starred album. Because even two years later, in the season of the Grateful Dead's formless live album *Live/Dead,* the Who's conceptually ambitious rock opera

Tommy, and a hundred other expeditions beyond the known horizons of pop music, these two glimpses at *Smile* revealed a musical frontier that no one else had begun to imagine.

It's impossible to know what might have been had Brian found the strength to finish *Smile* while so much of the pop music world was still transfixed by the wailing theremin at the end of "Good Vibrations" and eager to hear what would come next. In any case, though, those days were long gone: *20/20* barely snuck into the top seventy on *Billboard's* album charts (although it conformed to the pattern of the previous few years by climbing into the top three in the United Kingdom). Beyond frustrated with their commercial circumstances, everyone in and around the Beach Boys was more than happy to be rid of their last major commitment to Capitol. But they still owed the label one last original single, and Murry Wilson took it upon himself to make sure it was a good one. Telling Brian it was up to him to give the group a lift to a new label, Murry sat down with his eldest son and helped him write "Break Away," an energetic, horn-fired pop single that can be read either as a declaration of independence for the entire band or a statement of purpose from its erstwhile leader: *"I'm gonna make away for each happy day/As my life turns around."*

Despite Brian and Murry's best efforts, though, "Break Away" stalled just south of *Billboard's* top sixty. This commercial disappointment did nothing to elevate the Beach Boys' stock among the record companies that band manager Nick Grillo was attempting to woo, but neither did Brian's antics. At times he seemed bent on ending the group's career before it could sign on with a new label. For instance, Grillo was very close to finalizing a fairly rich deal with the European label Deutsche-Gramophone in the spring of 1969 when Brian sat down with some European reporters, ostensibly to promote the just-released "Break Away." Instead, he spoke at length about the band's fading popularity and deepening financial desperation. "We owe everyone money," he said. "And if we don't pick ourselves off our backsides and have a hit record soon, we will be in worse trouble." As he went on, Brian seemed to relish being the bearer of such dire tidings. "I've always said, 'Be honest with your fans.' I don't see why I should lie and say everything is rosy when it's not."

The Deutsche-Gramophone offer evaporated soon afterwards, and it took Grillo another few months to come up with anything nearly as good. This time the offer came from Reprise, a boutique label in the Warner Brothers family. Founded as a jazz label for Frank Sinatra, Reprise had come to specialize in hip, underground-type artists such as the Grateful Dead, Neil Young, and Little Feat. Van Dyke Parks recorded for Reprise and also worked as an executive in the label's film division, producing a series of short films designed to promote the label's records and bands. Van Dyke was about a decade too early to make a dent with his proto–music videos, but he still had the ear of Reprise chief Mo Ostin. When Van Dyke heard that his Beach Boys–loving boss was hesitant to sign the group to the label, he made it his mission to make sure the deal came together. Ostin's biggest question, Van Dyke recalls, was if Brian still had what it took to make music. "Mo asked me specifically if Brian would be involved, and would I see to it," Van Dyke says. "I said yes, and I had a couple of opportunities to see to that in the next few years."

But first the Reprise executives wanted to see Brian, just to make sure the group's reclusive leader was up and around and not, as rumored, completely out of his mind. Grillo set up a date for the execs to tour the Beach Boys' studio at Brian's house on Bellagio Road, and he made sure the man of the house would be up, dressed, and ready to share his newest work when they all arrived. Brian promised he would, and so Grillo drove up to Brian's house with the other men in tow, leading them through the gate and down to the parking area at the rear of the house. The group had just emerged from their cars when Brian came out, his long hair combed, his clothes neatly pressed—and his face painted a vivid shade of bright green.

"He came out and said, 'Oh, hi!' and goes about the whole thing as if nothing is wrong," says Stephen Desper, who observed the entire scene from the opening handshakes to the farewells an hour or two later. "Brian was the perfect gentleman, very astute and very polite, only with his face painted green. And he knew damn well what he was doing. But the funniest thing was that no one said anything."

Not until the Reprise guys had left, at any rate. Then Grillo, sensing yet another all-but-signed record deal was about to fall through his fingertips thanks to Brian's efforts, went into full freak-out mode. "Brian!" he shrieked. "What the *fuck* are you doing? *What the fuck are you doing?*" Brian, Desper recalls, smiled innocently and shrugged. "Just seeing what would happen."

Or maybe he was looking for another way to control the fate of the group he had created and had lost his ability to steer. The deal the group eventually signed with Reprise hinged on Brian being an active participant in all their musical endeavors. But in typically paradoxical fashion, he both resented that burden and the fact that his brothers, cousin, and friends had in the last few years developed

Brian Douglas Wilson, 1942
(Collection of Brian and Melinda Wilson)

Brian, Carl, unidentified friend, and Dennis, in front of their family's home, circa 1950
(Author's collection)

Brian, Dennis, and Carl, circa 1954
(Author's collection)

Brian (bottom center), pitcher in American Legion ball, 1957
(Collection of Rich Sloan)

Left:
As a cross-country runner, fall 1959
(Collection of Rich Sloan)

Below:
Goofing around in the Sloans' yard
(Collection of Rich Sloan)

Brian (center) harmonizes with cousins Mike (far right) and Maureen (next to Mike) and other friends at the Loves' 1959 Christmas party. *(Collection of Stan Love)*

Senior Skip Day 1960. Brian is at far right, wondering why Rich Sloan (to his right) has just thrown ink on his shirt. He doesn't know that it's disappearing ink.

(Collection of Rich Sloan)

Freshly minted high school grad Mike Love had no idea what to do with his life in 1960.
(Collection of Stan Love)

Murry posts another hit on the Wilsons' music room wall as young stars Brian and Mike look on. *(Capitol Records archive)*

In the early '60s, the Beach Boys' parade of hit singles made them a hot concert draw.
(Capitol Records archive)

Portrait of the young hitmaker at work *(Capitol Records archive)*

With *Pet Sounds,* Brian pulled the group into new musical horizons.
(Capitol Records archive)

Brian and Van Dyke Parks look for the holy sound during a *Smile* session.
(Courtesy David Leaf)

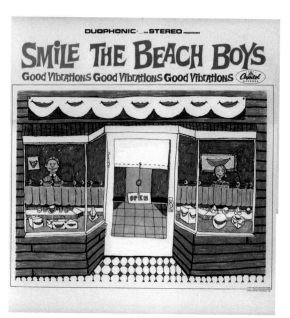

Brian expected his follow-up to *Good Vibrations* to be his greatest achievement to date. Instead, *Smile* fell to pieces. *(Courtesy Frank Holmes)*

As Brian stepped back, Murry made his stand. *(Author's collection)*

At home in Bel Air,
preparing for parenthood
(Capitol Records archive)

On the musical sidelines,
but always up for a game:
Brian in 1969.
(Courtesy Stan Love)

With his big brother out
of action, Carl helped lead
the group back from
obscurity.
(Courtesy Stan Love)

Driven and relentless,
Mike turned himself into
a prominent frontman.
(Courtesy Stan Love)

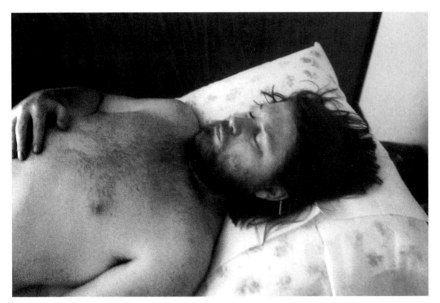

After years out of the spotlight, Brian (having an acupuncture treatment in '76) focused on coming back. *(Courtesy Stan Love)*

By the end of '76, Brian was back with plenty of new songs to share.
(Courtesy Stan Love)

When they earned their star on Hollywood Boulevard, the mayor declared Beach Boys Day in Los Angeles. *(Courtesy Peter Reum)*

By 1980, both Dennis (second from left) and Brian (third from right) were obviously losing control of their habits. *(Courtesy Ed Roach)*

Above:
His health restored again, Brian
(performing with the group in
'84) was happy to share the
spotlight with Dr. Landy.
(Courtesy Stan Love)

Left:
Brian's autobiography was meant
to showcase his new health and
independence. Instead, it did the
opposite.
(Courtesy Stan Love)

Mr. and Mrs. Wilson smile for the camera at their wedding.
(Courtesy Brian and Melinda Wilson)

With Landy out of the picture, Brian (working on *Orange Crate Art* with Van Dyke and
Lenny Waronker in '95) got back to work.
(Courtesy Van Dyke Parks)

A notoriously reluctant performer, Brian shocked fans when he hit the road in '99.

(Courtesy Ross W. Hamilton)

Back at work on *Smile* in 2003, Brian, Van Dyke, and Darian Sahanaja pause for a water break.

(Courtesy Brian and Melinda Wilson)

With Al Jardine and David Marks at the landmark dedication in Hawthorne, May 2005
(Courtesy Rich Sloan)

Just away from a nonbeliever…Brian performs the completed *Smile* in 2005.
(Courtesy Ross W. Hamilton)

songwriting and production chops that were strong enough to stand on their own. Indeed, by the end of 1969, the other members of the group had become so confident writing and producing their own tracks that they didn't really need Brian's help. Dennis in particular had developed a musical voice that was both distinct from his big brother's and also distinctly beautiful. When he showed up in early 1969 with his yearning ballad "Forever," he gave the band a love song that rivaled Brian's most melodic, emotionally complex ballads. "It wasn't like Brian was making a choice to be less involved," Desper says. "It's just that you've got limited hours in the day. Brian is a gentle guy; he doesn't like to hurt anyone's feelings, so if someone's working on something else, he wasn't going to jump in there and say, 'Look, this is my production and my house, so get outta here!' That's totally out of character for him."

Still, no matter how ambivalent Brian might have felt about the new balance of power in the group, he also couldn't help being swept up in the revived enthusiasm that the band felt as the new decade, a new recording contract, and a new beginning for their career came into view. Suddenly the failures of the last few years didn't seem to matter anymore. Maybe they were still the Beach Boys in name, but they truly were beginning to act and feel like grown men, working hard together to steer their ship back to the glories they had every faith they could reclaim.

All through the end of 1969 and into the first half of 1970, the music emanating from the studio in Brian's house gave the group even more reason to feel confident. Each member of the band had a pile of songs to offer, including an album's worth of songs Brian had either written alone or along with one or more of the other guys. By the end of spring, they had compiled a finished master for what they figured would be their first Reprise album, which they had decided to title *Add Some Music,* after a pop-folk tune Brian and Mike had written with friend Joe Knott, called "Add Some Music to Your Day." That song in particular seemed like a perfect statement of purpose to lead off the band's second decade, given the tune's shared, round-robin style lead vocal, full background harmonies, and a plainspoken lyric describing the ways music weaves magic through so many of the crucial and humdrum moments of daily life. *"You'll hear it when you're walkin' by a neighbor's home/You'll hear it faintly in the distance when you're on the phone,"* they sang, and when the Reprise executives listened to the tape, they tapped their feet appreciatively, noting how the acoustic guitars sounded so post-Woodstock and how the Boys' natural harmonic blend compared so favorably with the harmonies of Crosby, Stills, Nash, and Young and the Grateful Dead. But some of Brian's other tunes—particularly his diary-like love song "Two Can Play" and the workingman's tune "I Just Got My Pay"—were quirky at best and maybe just too weird, while Al's "Susie Cincinnati" sounded too much like "The Little Old Lady from Pasadena" to be part of the band's entry into the 1970s.

So Ostin and his crew rejected the Beach Boys' new album, telling the group to either come up with three or four stronger tracks or else risk losing their new contract. The group was furious, of course, but another dig through their pile of new material and another few days spent recording even newer songs, paved the way for the album Reprise was willing to release. They called the album *Sunflower,* and it featured on its cover a shot of six long-haired, distinctly adult Beach Boys sitting together on a grassy, sunlit hill surrounded by a flock of their own small children. And if that image took people by surprise, the music inside proved to be even more unexpected. Despite the fact that they were emerging from the darkest years of their commercial and personal lives, the group had produced a collection of songs that projected their utopian fantasies into a modern, adult context. The band's individual voices were more distinct than ever, but the rainbow of personalities still folded together into a sound that was sweet, surprisingly sexy, and, as ever, musically inventive.

The first side kicked off with Dennis's "Slip On Through," a tuneful, rhythmically complex rocker that featured densely layered vocals and a blazingly passionate chorus—*"Come on, won't you let me be/By your side, for now and eternity/Cause I love you, baby I do"*—that would inspire the most powerful lead vocal the drummer would ever commit to tape. Brian's "This Whole World" came next, a guitar-driven whirlwind of harmonies, chants, and chiming bells that was both deliciously melodic and dauntingly complicated, its melody spinning through half a dozen keys in less than two minutes. Meanwhile, Brian's lyric skipped merrily down the line separating the childlike from the transparently naive. *"Late at night I think about the love of this whole world,"* it began, going on to revel in the universal joys and sorrows of romance before concluding with a verse of wordless *oohs* and a final reprise of the opening verse sung over a backing chant that was part doo-wop and part Eastern mysticism: *"Om-bop-didit, om-bop-didit."*

"Add Some Music to Your Day" (the album's first single) came next, followed by Dennis's second tune, an R & B rave-up called "Got to Know the Woman," complete with Ike-and-Tina-style backing vocals from the Honeys and a strutting lyric so silly that Dennis even cracked himself up in the third verse (*"Come on!/Come on, come on and do the chicken!"* caused him to finally lose it), and his joy was too infectious to resist. Bruce's airy ballads, "Deirdre" and "Tears in the Morning," tethered themselves to enough real emotion to avoid floating off in the breeze, while Brian and Mike's dreamlike love song "All I Wanna Do" used synthesizers, a rotating organ speaker, and pillows of reverb beneath its drifting banners of harmony.

Dennis's tender "Forever" served as the high point of the album's second side, but Brian, Carl, and Al's gorgeously layered "Our Sweet Love" comes close on its heels. Al and Brian's "At My Window" was an oddly lovely paean to the birds in Brian's backyard. The album concluded with "Cool, Cool Water," an eccentric, three-stage tune that had been gestating in various forms since the last days of *Smile*. The brief chant in the middle was another *Smile* fragment, a leftover from the "I Love to Say Da Da" section of the projected "Elements" suite. Meanwhile, the ambient sounds of water that bubble and froth beneath the music were another *Smile* holdover, in concept at least, since capturing them required Desper to spend three days lugging his gear to the streams, rivers, and beaches near Santa Barbara. The final section featured Brian and Mike in a call-and-response that echoed the evangelical enthusiasm of their earliest surfing songs, only in the service of a far simpler kind of reverie:

When I'm thirsty and I reach for a glass—Cool, cool water tastes like such a gas,
When I'm just too hot to move—Cool, cool water is such a groove . . .

Delivered to the label during the first weeks of 1970, "Add Some Music to Your Day" inspired so much excitement in the promotions office at Reprise that its sales reps convinced retailers to take more copies of the Beach Boys' first Reprise single than they'd ever done from a label artist. But radio disc jockeys still couldn't be convinced to actually play the song, so it stalled in the mid-sixties of *Billboard's* singles list. The band and label maintained their high hopes through the spring, however, though these dimmed somewhat when Dennis's breathtaking "Slip On Through" missed the charts altogether in June. And though both American and British critics lavished praise upon the record (one British writer compared *Sunflower* to *Sgt. Pepper*), the album stiffed everywhere, getting no higher than the thirties on the British chart that fall and stalling at number 126 on the *Billboard* list. After all that work, creative excitement, and tingling sense of commercial potential, *Sunflower* turned out to be the worst-selling album of the Beach Boys' career to date.

Maybe Brian had been right about changing the band's name, after all. In the wake of Woodstock, with the country divided bitterly by age, race, and a bloody war that struck so many citizens as being as distant from the nation's democratic purposes as it was from the homeland itself, the very *idea* of the Beach Boys seemed embarrassing. Even if the actual Beach Boys had grown up too, even if their old music had never been quite as simple as it might have seemed, the intensity of their audience's youthful affections in the early sixties had become the same force that transformed the group into relics. The Great Society promised by the sixties had collapsed, and now the pop music that once gave voice to its hopes had become the soundtrack to an entire nation's naïveté. Sure, "Good Vibrations" had been revolutionary in its time. But at the dawn of the 1970s, that kind of glossy, dream-filled progressivism was lost in the prevailing currents of frustration and moral outrage.

Of course, the rock 'n' roll audience had all but ignored the Beach Boys' post–"Good Vibrations" work, and the songs that had connected in the previous two years ("Do It Again," for instance) had looked backwards for inspiration. But the Beach Boys' own conservatism on stage—particularly in their dress and rigidly constructed, hastily performed greatest hits shows—had also served to isolate them from current tastes. They had changed in recent months, to be sure. *Sunflower* proved that to the small handful of people who actually bought it. But now they had to get everyone else's attention too, and doing that was obviously going to take even more work than they had once imagined.

The process began with a call from Van Dyke Parks, who in the early fall of 1970 was serving on the board of the Big Sur Folk Festival, a days-long music festival being put together by Joan Baez. An annual event set in the same fairgrounds that hosted the catalytic Monterey Pop festival three years earlier, the 1970 edition of the Big Sur festival would feature Baez, Country Joe McDonald, Kris Kristofferson, a very young Linda Ronstadt, and several other artists. But another act or two backed out with only a few weeks to go, and with a sudden need to bolster the bill, Van Dyke proposed the Beach Boys. If his fellow organizers raised their eyebrows at the suggestion, they also didn't balk. The Beach Boys nearly did, however—reportedly because Mike Love feared aligning his band with radical leftists and/or full-blown communists, such as, he had always figured, Joan Baez. But memories of the last Monterey-based festival they had spurned—and the audience-building opportunities they had lost along with it—made them think better of refusing. The group accepted the offer, and four weeks later, they played back-to-back sets that opened with "Sloop John B." and included latter-day gems such as "Country Air," "Vegetables," and "Wake the World" before climaxing with a crystalline "Good Vibrations." Absent any songs about surfing or cars (the only pre–*Pet Sounds* song was "California Girls"), this down-home version of the Beach Boys, with their newly thick beards, shaggy hair, and fringed clothing, struck the surprised crowd as an entirely different band. *Rolling Stone*'s Jan Wenner, finally putting his seal of approval on the band he had dismissed three years earlier, wrote that the Beach Boys were ". . . the group that went right to the genesis of California music."

Determined to solidify their reputation in the post-Woodstock world, the group hired a new publicist, a former public radio newsman named Jack Rieley, who convinced them to make the leap into the '70s by playing longer, more varied shows, including regular appearances at benefit shows for antiwar and pro-environment causes. Rieley also urged the group to become explicitly political in the songs they wrote. That's what the band Chicago did, after all, girding their jazz-pop albums with quasirevolutionary slogans and ambient sounds of riots that gave them a kind of credibility they might not have achieved on the strength of "Saturday in the Park" alone. Now they were one of the biggest bands in the nation.

Rieley knew how to speak the Beach Boys' language. True enough, he was a bit of a huckster, at one point going so far as to claim that he had won a Pulitzer Prize for his work in NBC's Puerto Rico bureau. This was despite the fact that NBC doesn't have a news bureau in Puerto Rico, which Rieley apparently didn't know because he had never worked for NBC, and he had never been told that broadcasters aren't eligible for Pulitzer Prizes. But what are a couple of elaborate lies between people whose common pursuit is gaining some momentum? Soon Rieley displaced Nick Grillo as the group's manager, and as 1971 dawned, he told his new charges to roll up their sleeves and prepare to face a brighter, more prosperous future.

Rieley's prediction began to come true almost immediately, thanks to the work of three New York City music-industry neophytes who decided they'd like to see the Beach Boys perform at Carnegie Hall. First they'd hoped to produce two shows with the group, but the pace of ticket sales made them settle for one show on February 24. And though they came within eighteen tickets of selling out that show, the affair was still bare-bones enough that the producers couldn't afford to hire an opening act. Instead, they implored their headliners to come up with enough material to fill the entire night. Fortunately, the group agreed to take on that challenge. And from the moment WNEW-FM's star disc jockey Pete Fornatale walked onstage to introduce the band (holding a surfboard, much to the band's initial horror), the concert became a triumph.

If anyone had come expecting to see a group of neatly combed, striped-shirt-wearing, collegiate guys, they would have been shocked by the casually dressed men who came out to play. Mike, whose blond locks trailed to his shoulders, sported a foot-long golden beard. Carl and Al were similarly shaggy and bearded, while Dennis had a mane of hair and even baby-faced Bruce had a mustache and thick sideburns. The music they played was just as surprising. Stretching out to fill the two-hour program, the group dove deep into their modern catalogue, including two of Dennis's new songs, five *Pet Sounds* cuts, a few *Sunflower* songs, and a few quirky covers including Mike's favorite old R & B song, "Riot in Cell Block #9," and an ironic take on Merle Haggard's antihippie anthem, "Okie from Muskogee."

Reviews of the Carnegie Hall concert verged on the rapturous, but the group made an even bigger impact on New York and all of hippie culture a few months later when they paid a surprise visit to the Fillmore East. The moment came on April 27, three nights into the Grateful Dead's five-day stand at the city's rock epicenter. Six songs into the band's second set, lead guitarist Jerry Garcia leaned into his microphone and made the announcement: "We got another famous California group here," he said, his eyes sparkling mischievously beneath his wire-framed specs. This in itself wasn't a surprise to the Fillmore crowd, given the loose-knit cooperative vibe that bonded all of the San Francisco bands in those days. Was the Airplane in town? Quicksilver? The Burritos? Well, not exactly, as the crowd learned when Garcia finished his sentence: "It's the Beach Boys!"

On one level it made no sense whatsoever. The Dead, after all, were the very embodiment of the hippie counterculture: snaggletoothed, glitter-eyed weirdos whose acid-drenched anarchism was the antithesis of the Beach Boys' clean-cut image. And how could the Beach Boys' intricately structured pop even exist in the same cosmos as the Dead's musical journeys into the far corners of "Dark Star" and beyond? Still, *Workingman's Dead* and especially *American Beauty* had been full of traditionalist country tunes and harmony-packed pop numbers. You could almost hear the Beach Boys singing the Dead's "Attics of My Life," just as you could imagine Garcia and Robert Hunter writing a trippy frontier tune like "Heroes and Villains."

So if Garcia's announcement prompted a quick chorus of surprised hoots, this soon turned into applause and then a full cheering ovation when Mike, Carl, Dennis, Al, and Bruce bounced out onto the stage. After a few minutes of head-scratching and guitar tuning, the two bands launched into a ragged cover of Lieber and Stoller's "Searchin'," with the Dead's designated bluesman Ron "Pigpen" McKernan belting the lead over the Beach Boys' stacked harmonies. Pigpen got a little lost in the last verse or two, but the vibe felt right, and the bands slid easily into "Riot in Cell Block #9," with Mike taking the lead on his old favorite while also making siren noises on his Moog-built theremin. Then the Dead left the stage to their guests, who kicked off their solo slot with "Good Vibrations," then a self-consciously ironic "I Get Around." ("How about a car song?" Bruce whooped. "Take ya back to your adolescence," Mike said, dryly.) They called the Dead back to the stage for "Help Me, Rhonda," which the Beach Boys had rearranged for the occasion into a "Truckin'"-style shuffle. "We tried to kind of just make an arrangement as if it were written now!" Bruce explained. The new rhythm, though, only made the tune sound lugubrious, and though Garcia gamely added a few riffs into the mix, he sounded mostly puzzled by the song and ended up meandering aimlessly around his guitar's neck. At which point it was easy to wonder if the Beach Boys might be tripping over their own desire to win over the Fillmore crowd.

Already, Mike and Bruce's stage patter had betrayed some of their anxiety. Bruce in particular couldn't open his mouth without either apologizing ("I hope it's worth the wait!" during a tuning break), sounding out of touch ("I hope this'll be a good boogie"), or seeming just downright daffy ("We're glad there is something called the Grateful Dead, believe me, 'cause they're all *RIGHT*!"). But none of that sounded quite as desperate as Mike's attempt to curry favor with the freaks during the sing-along portion of "Good Vibrations" by recounting the time they had sung the song on a tour bus with the Buffalo Springfield, "all stoned and drunk and it sounded great." Hey, *groovy,* man. Or maybe not, because that's pretty much when you could hear at least one guy in the audience bellowing, "Bring back the Grateful Dead!"

But the Beach Boys stuck it out, and when they got the misbegotten "Rhonda" out of the way, the two bands came together in a way that was both unexpected and yet entirely right. The moment began with the first notes of

"Okie from Muskogee," which the Beach Boys had taken to using as a subtle commentary on their own retro image and, implicitly, the far more decadent reality beneath it. The Dead dug that joke too, and as their cover of Haggard's "Mama Tried" earlier that evening had made clear, they also got off on playing the role of the ornery outcast. Once Bruce hit the opening bass riff for "Okie," it took about two beats for the entire eleven-piece conglomeration to swing into the rhythm, and from that moment forward, the two bands were perfectly synchronized.

Mike sang lead with just the right ironic touch, his dry baritone a perfect foil for Garcia's curling, shimmering guitar lines, which twined around the Beach Boys' harmonized voices like an embrace. For this moment, at least, the two bands that had helped define their respective eras in California pop music could stand on the same stage, look out at the world around them, and sing the same song.

Just a moment later they slammed full-throttle into another mutual favorite, Chuck Berry's "Johnny B. Goode," interweaving Garcia's stinging guitar leads with a three-way lead vocal from Bobby Weir, Carl, and Al belting out the harmonized *"Go! Go Johnny go—wo-wo-wo-wo!"*'s" that the Beach Boys had used when the song was their final encore back in 1964. By the second verse, Carl and Al had improvised harmony parts around Weir's lead, and the energy in the final chorus nearly lifted the dusty old theater off of the ground before coming to an abrupt, ringing halt.

"Thank you, Grateful Dead!" Bruce yelled when it was over.

"Thank you, Beach Boys!" Weir shouted back.

"Let's hear it! Let's hear it!" Garcia said, standing back to join the audience's ovation as the Beach Boys walked off the Fillmore stage. And if Jerry's public benediction didn't carry enough weight in the pop culture climate of 1971, the more private one that took place in the Fillmore's sound booth surely would. That's where Bob Dylan had been watching the show, sitting with Jack Rieley and at least one reporter who happened to overhear the bard as he turned to Rieley and gestured to the five Beach Boys just as they were leaving the stage. "You know," he said, "they're fucking good, man."

———

As they went back into their recording studio, they were determined to come up with an album that would finally prove Dylan's point to the entire music world.

Following Rieley's suggestion that they take on political issues in their music, Mike and Al came up with "Don't Go Near the Water," a catchy plaint about water pollution that featured clever backing vocals and a textured instrumental track built from synthesizers, banjos, and an intriguingly dissonant piano part contributed by Brian. Carl came on strong with his first two significant compositions, a quasi-gospel number called "Long Promised Road" and the floating, synthesizer-laced "Feel Flows." Both featured lyrics by Jack Rieley, whose workmanlike verse tended toward simple rhyme schemes and imagery that was either a bit overheated (e.g., "Long Promised Road"'s *So hard to lift the jeweled scepter when the weight turns a smile to a frown/So hard to drink of passion nectar when the taste of life's holding you down*"), impossibly cryptic (*"Unbending, never-ending tablets of time/Record all the yearning/Unfearing, all-appearing message divine/Eases the burning,"* from "Feel Flows"), or both. Still, Carl's music was hard to resist, and the layered tracks he produced—combining his big brother's ear for sonic texture with modern instruments and recording processes—elevated the songs well beyond Rieley's literary limitations.

Al tossed in the folk-inspired "Lookin' at Tomorrow: A Welfare Song" and dusted off a charming *Sunflower* leftover called "Take a Load Off Your Feet," a whimsical argument for foot care that featured a vast array of sound effects and ambient noises, including Brian honking the horn of his Rolls-Royce, scraping a spoon on a cereal bowl, and skipping across the asphalt roof of his garage. Dennis came in with a variety of songs, including "4th of July," a protest song about the Nixon administration's attempts to silence critics of the Vietnam War that he had cowritten with Rieley, and "(Wouldn't It Be Nice to) Live Again," an intensely romantic love song that featured achingly beautiful harmonies from the entire group. Bruce came through with the tenderly nostalgic "Disney Girls (1957)," while Mike took on the fiery campus scene by transforming Lieber and Stoller's "Riot in Cell Block #9" into "Student Demonstration Time," a guitar-and-horn-fired stomper in which its author (his voice distorted by a bullhorn) recounted demonstrations and riots ranging from the antiwar riot in Isla Vista, California, to the shootings at Kent State before ending with the strangely hedged conclusion *"I know we're all fed up with useless wars and racial strife/But the next time there's a riot, well, you best stay out of sight."*

The band's new momentum on the road kept everyone fired up in the studio, where the atmosphere was, for the most part, just as collegial as it had been during the *Sunflower* era. The only exception, unfortunately, proved to be Brian, who seemed to spend most days alone in his room, either sleeping off whatever he'd done with his friends the previous night or just gazing silently at the ceiling above his head, watching the dust motes float through the shafts of sunlight. "He'd talk about being depressed, in his way," Desper says. "He'd say, 'Well, I just can't get with it today. I'm out of the loop.'" When the music coming through his floorboards excited him enough to draw him back into the loop, Brian would either clamber down to the studio in his striped pajamas or phone in an idea from the intercom on his bedside table. "He added a lot of parts, but more instrumental than singing," Stephen Desper recalls. Months of cocaine use, along with the corrosive effects of heavy pot and cigarette smoking, had also taken a toll on Brian's vocal cords. "He could do falsettos and stuff, but he'd need Carl to help him. Either that or I'd modify the tape speed-wise to make it artificially higher, so it sounded like the old days."

Even more important, the band needed to get Brian's original songs on the album. Unfortunately, he was either unwilling or unable to write new material for the band, at least not of his own volition. Still, he would respond to prodding on his up days, as when Rieley convinced Brian to collaborate with him on "A Day in the Life of a Tree," another environmental-themed song that described the world's plight in the voice of a slowly dying tree. Curiously, Brian asked Rieley to sing the lead vocal on the song, either because the manager's faltering delivery fit the emotional tone he was trying to create or because he was playing another one of his pranks, asserting his power over the commanding Rieley by fooling him into making an ass out of himself in the most public way imaginable. And while it could be true that Brian was about as fond of Rieley as he was of being forced to write songs, it seems more than possible that Brian was just as enthusiastic about Rieley's singing as he claimed. For one thing, he worked on the song for days, experimenting with a harmonium, an antique pump organ, and a smaller pipe organ to create the sounds that would illustrate the different phases of the tree's life. Brian also took the time to create an intricate, lovely vocal arrangement for the song's conclusion (featuring the entire group plus Van Dyke Parks), and according to more than one observer, he was moved to tears when the final vocals were recorded.

All of this makes it reasonable to assume that the song is as much about his own personal malaise as it is about the larger ecological one. When Brian lay in his bed for days at a time, listening to the music being recorded beneath his feet and pondering the distance between who he'd been in the mid-1960s and who he had come to be in the early 1970s, there could be no more accurate portrait than the lyrics of "A Day in the Life of a Tree."

One day I was full of life, my sap was rich and I was strong . . .
But now my branches suffer, and my leaves don't offer poetry to men of song.

From that point, when the music swells and the voices rise into the interlocking harmonies that Brian had once created so effortlessly, the conclusion they reach about the plight of the tree—or any sensitive creature—is chilling:

No life's left to be found,
There's nothing left for me.

Brian's sense of desolation might not have been quite so acute from day to day, but as he became less prolific, the songs he produced grew increasingly forlorn. One night in the summer of 1970, Brian drove down to the beach and went for a walk in the sand, pondering the thunderous roar of the waves and the endless expanse of inky water that lay beyond. Only a few years earlier, that same ocean had inspired nothing but a sense of possibility. But now, with so much music behind him, the fruits of his success all around (including the shimmering Rolls-Royce he drove to the beach), and the power to do anything he wanted with the rest of his life, Brian realized that he still felt as lost, alone, and terrified as he ever had. Back at his piano a few hours later, the feelings became a series of floating augmented chords, a melody, and then, finally, words.

I'm a cork on the ocean
Floating over the raging sea . . .
I lost my way.

The song had no chorus, just a series of verses that described Brian's angst with analogies drawn from the world outside his window. In the second verse, he imagines being a rock in a landslide, falling into a bottomless valley. In the third, he's a leaf on a windy day, wondering how long he can go on gripping the tree that holds him down. A brief instrumental passage led to the song's conclusion, a repeating chant of one phrase: *"These things I'll be until I die . . ."*

"'Til I Die," as Brian came to call the song, was another of his small musical miracles, so removed from traditional pop structures that the chords seemed to drift from key to key as if they were just as unmoored as the narrator. The lyrics, written without the assistance of a collaborator, are both straightforward and evocative as the physical analogies in each verse—the cork adrift on the ocean, the rock tumbling into the valley, the leaf losing its grip in a windstorm—conclude with a concise expression of the feelings the image represents: *"I lost my way," "It kills my soul," "Until I die."* Brian felt a little self-conscious about the song, considering how much of his wounded emotional core he revealed in its verses. But he also knew it was one of the best things he'd written in many years. So once it was finished, he sat down in the studio to sing it for the other guys, assuming they'd greet it with the same full-throated enthusiasm they'd shown for his efforts in the mid-1960s. But this time they seemed unimpressed. Those words are such a downer, Mike said. Aren't pop songs supposed to be fun? Who would want to listen to something that grim? Blinking with surprise and hurt, Brian shrugged. Stung by the criticism, he put the song away for a few months, then brought it out again for the *Surf's Up* sessions in early 1971, when the band came asking for more material. Brian cut an instrumental track—combining layers of vibes, organ, and an electronic drum machine—and ran the group through a rigorous series of vocal sessions so they could master the intricate vocal arrangement he had put together. But still conscious of Mike's criticism from the previous summer, Brian fiddled with the lyrics for days, going so far as to record a version of the song with more upbeat conclusions to the first two verses—*"It kills my soul"* became *"It holds me up,"* while *"I lost my way"* became *"I found my way."* But even the other guys recognized the thematic contradiction presented in the new lyrics, and so given the choice between having a new original Brian song on the album or not, they reverted to his original, darker lyrics.

The one track Brian would have nothing to do with would become the new album's title song. Carl, knowing that the Reprise executives expected more than two original Brian Wilson songs on a Beach Boys album, had ventured once again into the vaults in search of an unreleased song that would both fit the band's new sound and yet bear an obvious resemblance to Brian's classic work. With this in mind, Carl discovered the tapes for "Surf's Up," the song from the *Smile* sessions that created so much excitement when Brian first unveiled it on the Leonard Bernstein special in 1967. The only trouble was that the song had never been completed. Brian had long ago recorded a fully orchestrated instrumental track for the tune's first movement, but in the tumult of the era, he had never gotten around to recording the second half. In fact, the only reason that anyone outside of Brian and Van Dyke knew what the song was supposed to sound like was Brian's performance on the Bernstein show, a tape of which remained in the group's vaults. If not for that, the song might have vanished along with the rest of *Smile*.

Once he'd collected the few "Surf's Up" tapes he could find, Carl brought them back to Brian's home studio and worked with engineer Stephen Desper to figure out exactly how much of the song existed and what needed to be done in order to finish it. Hearing the song being played in the studio, Brian came downstairs and was both surprised and dismayed to learn that Carl was determined to put the song on the group's new album. No, he didn't want to help them on it. No, he had no intention of recording a lead vocal for the song. In fact, he wanted nothing to do with it. "Brian was afraid of it and refused to work on the song," Desper wrote in his self-published book, *Recording the Beach Boys*. "At times (he) left the house when production started."

Carl and Desper continued working on the song, adding a few keyboard and percussion parts and a new vocal by Carl to the instrumental section Brian recorded in 1966. To make Brian seem more present, they used his solo performance from the Bernstein special for the song's second half (which actually seemed to fit the section's more stripped-down mood), with a simple voiced chord to ease the transition from one to the next. A few Moog bass highlights accentuated the bass part Brian had played on the piano, and in the spots where his singing had grown shaky, Carl added some subtle vocal backing to give it more richness. When all that was done, the last remaining puzzle was the final section, just after Brian had sung, *"I heard the word, wonderful thing, a children's song,"* at which point the song took on the chord pattern from another *Smile* song, "Child Is the Father to the Man." Brian's original performance of the song ended with him singing a series of wordless *"Ahhhhh's,"* but Carl remembered a more involved vocal chant, and they were nearly finished pasting it all together when the studio door flew open and a slightly disheveled-looking Brian, his belly hanging out of his striped pajamas, stormed inside. As Desper recalled in his book, their jaws fell open when Brian announced that they needed to add something to the final movement of "Surf's Up." It was a lyric they didn't know, and if they opened up a track for him, he'd sing it right now. Desper set up a microphone and gave Brian a set of headphones, and they all sat back and gaped as he added the missing lyric—and the final piece to the "Surf's Up" puzzle.

A children's song, have you listened as they play?
Their song is love, and the children know the way.

The album, now called *Surf's Up,* was released by Reprise at the end of August 1971. It climbed into *Billboard's* Top Thirty, becoming the group's best-selling album since *Wild Honey,* and the reviews were even better. "After suffering several years of snubbing, both by rock critics and the public, the Beach Boys stage a remarkable comeback," *Rolling Stone's* critic declared. "The Beach Boys are back."

CHAPTER 10

Near midnight one evening in 1969, a young magazine writer named Tom Nolan wandered down a street in West Hollywood. As Nolan would write later, he had just seen *Skammen*, Ingmar Bergman's darkly surreal commentary on the psychological aftershocks of war. Still reeling from Bergman's disturbing, surrealist imagery, Nolan paused outside a health food store. Noting its whimsical name—the Radiant Radish—he pushed open the door and walked inside. Immediately, the place seemed a little off-kilter. The ceiling lamps had been switched off, so the only light was the ghostly fluorescent glow emanating from the shelves. The only other person in the store, Nolan noticed, was the baby-faced guy behind the counter, who gazed up silently from behind a thick curtain of long brown hair. He didn't say a word, at first, although he did manage a nod when Nolan came through the door. Also, he was wearing a bathrobe.

Actually, Nolan was less surprised by the robe than by the simple fact that the man wearing it was a millionaire rock star whose penchant for seclusion had become nearly as famous as the many hit songs he had written and produced. Just three years after writing and producing "Good Vibrations," Brian Wilson was selling vitamins out of a health food store in West Hollywood. As Nolan would later write in the two-part Beach Boys profile he published in *Rolling Stone* in 1971:

> He ran his fingers over the rows of bottles, seeking just the right supplement. "Did you get a call for B$_{12}$?"
>
> "A call?"
>
> "From your doctor. If you got a call—"
>
> "No."
>
> "Well, now, unless there's a call, we— You can't—" He would not sell me any B$_{12}$.

Nolan's sprawling story, published in what was then the journal of record of American youth culture, only began with that glimpse at Brian's quirky life. The first-ever unvarnished portrayal of the group's past, the piece was a mosaic of '60s-era sexual high jinks, memories of Manson, *Smile* legend, and a fractal portrait of the modern-day group as a six-piece ensemble of surprisingly sophisticated artists whose lead member just happened to be one of the greatest visionaries in pop music history, and maybe one of the strangest, too. "Yeah, he's out there," Carl confirmed with a laugh. "He's a very highly evolved person. And he's very sensitive at the same time, which can be confusing. Brian's Brian, you know?"

From there Nolan's story delved into the twists of Brian's secret and not-so-secret life, from the murmurs about the true cause of his deafness, to a vivid recounting of his first nervous collapse in 1964, to the years of drug-tinged musical breakthroughs and career breakdowns. There were disturbing anecdotes about his relationship with his children. ("She's not too bright, I'll tell ya," Brian said of three-year-old Carnie, going on to describe a series of her toddler-era sexual experiments he connected to things she had seen her parents doing. "It just goes to prove that if you don't hide anything from kids, they'll start doing things they normally wouldn't do until much later," he said, betraying no sense that this might not be a good thing.) And then there was Murry, perpetually intruding in order to take credit for the group's sound, songs, and, indeed, their entire career. "See, the whole trade has given Brian credit for everything," he grumbled. "I'm not beating myself on the back, but knowing them as a father, I knew their voices, right? And I'm musical, my wife is, we knew how to sing on key, and . . ."

On it went, exploring the murky currents of Brian's psyche. "I was called in to do some singing on a song," Van Dyke Parks reported of a recent session in the

Bellagio recording studio, where he pitched in on the chorale that ended "A Day in the Life of a Tree." "It worked out well. Of course I had to stumble out of the studio in pitch darkness. Brian turned out all the lights. Had to crawl out of there on the floor, clutching my wife . . . oh, it's a power trip all right . . ."

And Murry was ever-present, if only because Murry would not leave. "Write this down," he'd command. "You might want to put this in." Which Nolan did, much to Murry's pleasure—and his complete ignorance of how badly his bombast would go over with Nolan's readers. "I lost my left eye in an industrial accident at Goodyear . . . but I'd like to add that it made me a better man. I tried harder, drove harder, and did the work of two men in the company and got more raises. . . . And it isn't all talent—it's guts and promotion and just keeping at it even when you make mistakes. You can't be right all the time. But the ability to fight back, come back, and create again is America."

———

Brian had heard that speech before, of course. And now he was hearing a whole new generation of voices yammering the same old story at him, twisting his arm for more songs, more arrangements, more albums, more hits. "Or else you'll lose the house," they'd tell him. "The cars will be gone, you'll have nothing to eat . . . you'll be out on the street, headed back to Hawthorne, you lazy fuck." In Brian's ears the chant had become a dull roar, the rumble of the Beach Boys machine gearing up to run right over him.

Whatever the case, after a half decade in rock 'n' roll Siberia, the Beach Boys were back. The news was all over *Rolling Stone*—not just in the two-part cover profile, but also in the rave review that accompanied the release of *Surf's Up*. It was in the increasingly large, increasingly packed concert halls. It was even on the *Billboard* charts, which would show *Surf's Up* scaling all the way into the Top Thirty.

The only trouble was that Brian didn't want to be back.

The decade hadn't started that way. When Mike Love suffered a rather dramatic breakdown in February 1970 (spurred by some combination of overambitious fasting and what he liked to call his "tainted Wilson blood" and climaxing in a long, high-speed car chase through Hollywood as he attempted to evade cars driven by his father and brothers), Brian agreed to join the touring band for a handful of live shows in Seattle; Spokane; Vancouver, British Columbia; and Portland. The other guys were delighted to have Brian back on the road, of course, but they were also a bit anxious. Nearly three years since his last stage appearance and more than five years since his last full-fledged tour, it was hard for anyone to imagine Brian even making it to the airport on time, let alone forcing himself to step out into the lights and play music in front of thousands of people.

But Brian was up and ready to go to the airport when the time came to leave, and though he suffered a small panic attack between the early and late shows in Seattle's Opera House on February 28—muttering darkly that someone in the crowd was trying to kill him, then bolting out of the hall and sprinting partway up the face of nearby Queen Anne Hill before he calmed down—he was back in time for the start of the second show at 9:30. Introduced by the show's emcee at the top of the show ("We have another surprise for you," he declared, going on to explain Brian's years-long retirement from the road before proclaiming that "tonight, for the first time in four years, Brian is with the group!" Gasps, cheers, even a few shrieks. "So let's welcome Brian and the Beach Boys back to Seattle!"), Brian came out to a loud ovation, settling at a keyboard, where he played and sang for the entire forty-five-minute set of mostly recent hits and album cuts. The tape of the Seattle show is muddy, but even through the murk, it's possible to hear Brian's strong voice coming through the mix. And if he sounds a bit tentative on the bridge of "Surfer Girl," he nails his falsetto at the end of the song, covers Mike's bridge part on "Wouldn't It Be Nice" (Bruce did the verses, as per the usual stage arrangement), and transforms "Help Me, Rhonda" by hitting the high notes from the rarely played single arrangement. He's just as present on the then brand-new "Add Some Music to Your Day" and the climactic renditions of "Barbara Ann" and "Good Vibrations." "I was scared for a few minutes in the first show; it had been awhile since I'd been in front of so many people," Brian admitted on a radio interview during the '70s. "But after it started to cook, I really got with it."

But a more-hyped appearance with the group at the Whisky a Go-Go club in Los Angeles in November of that year didn't go as smoothly. The band was supposed to play a four-night stand, but Brian bolted after a night and a half, citing an array of physical ills that seemed, in retrospect, to be symptomatic of a panic attack ("There were faces out there swimming at me, and I had to stop singing . . . I had trouble focusing on anything and my right ear was killing me," he told *Melody Maker*).

The other Beach Boys still relied upon Brian's name and reputation in order to stay in business. "If we call it *Surf's Up,* we can presell 150,000 copies," Warner's executive Van Dyke Parks had said of the group's new release in Nolan's *Rolling Stone* profile, and indeed, the album named for one of the most legendary *Smile* songs had sold better than any Beach Boys album since *Pet Sounds.* But they had clearly lost their faith in their erstwhile leader's hit-making abilities, and Brian knew this. And though he couldn't put his frustration into words, Brian made his feelings clear by vanishing into the haze of his own eccentricity.

Later the other Beach Boys would talk about this period as the start of Brian's spiritual morass, a horrible time of emotional isolation and psychological desolation. But Brian's other friends recall him being more or less *compos mentis* pretty much all of the time. "He was a good football player," Dennis's friend and collaborator Stanley Shapiro recalls. "And a hell of a good hitter on the baseball field. And he was one of the funniest guys in the world back then." Crafty, too. Talking to Shapiro one day about shoes, they ended up agreeing that the most comfortable footwear either of them could recall were the ones they rented at bowling alleys. But where could a guy actually buy a pair of bowling shoes? Brian considered this quandary for a moment, then smiled. Maybe, he said, they didn't really need to *buy* a pair, per se. Ushering Shapiro into his Rolls-Royce, Brian piloted the limousine to a bowling alley in nearby Westwood, where he got a pair of shoes in his size and slapped down the usual ten-dollar deposit. Then he sat down, put on the shoes, walked out to his Rolls, and drove home. "And I thought that was hilarious," Shapiro says.

What was less amusing to the Beach Boys was how Brian's musical energies were focused on projects that had little to do with them. For a month or two he worked fitfully on a country album featuring longtime friend and Beach Boys concert promoter Fred Vail. Sessions for the album, named *Cows to the Pasture,* produced fifteen tracks, including C & W versions of "Kittens, Kids, and Kites," "There's Always Something There to Remind Me," and "Only the Lonely." Few were close to finished, however, and fewer still got far enough to include Vail's vocals. "Brian was only semifocused on that one," Vail says.

He spent more time on his collaborations with Stephen Kalinich, a gentle-natured poet and musician signed to the fledgling Brother Records back in 1967. Kalinich's career had never quite taken off, but he had contributed lyrics to both of Dennis Wilson's *Friends* songs, and he had orbited on the periphery of the Beach Boys' scene ever since. Brian had grown to love Kalinich's romantic poems, and as he shrank from the demands and indignities of pop music, he focused increasingly on his work with the poet, recording two full albums (*A World of Peace* and *America, I Know You*) in the early '70s that combined Kalinich's recitations with Brian's original music and backing vocals. "He'd do stuff combining music, percussion, with poems he'd recorded off the phone, or whatever," Kalinich recalls. "Adding in people singing stuff or weird sitar tracks. He was working on all this weird stuff with me, poems with strange backing music." The resulting tracks are quite striking, particularly "Lonely Boy," a vaguely Renaissance-inspired verse that Brian set to minstrel-like nylon-string guitars, percussion, and his own falsetto. A longer version of the "Be Still" poem Dennis used on *Friends* begins with a staged conversation in which Brian recalls the older song ("We had that on an album, right?") and then asks Kalinich to recite the longer version with his new, seemingly improvised keyboard accompaniment.

The poetry albums never came out, either because Brian lost interest in the project, lost his emotional bearings, or lost the support of his bandmates, who didn't want to invest their resources in a project that didn't seem to fit anyone's conception of a commercial enterprise. Still, Kalinich says, more than three decades later, Brian speaks enthusiastically about the work they did together. "Just the other day at breakfast, he sang the whole 'Lonely Man' thing for me: his part and mine. So how damaged was he back then, really?"

Some nights it was difficult to tell. When Paul and Linda McCartney came over to the Bellagio house one night, the party began cheerfully enough, with the usual array of friends, band members, and hangers-on gathering in the living room for beers, joints, and conversation. Always less than loquacious in social events he didn't feel completely in control of, Brian began fiddling with an empty fishbowl, peering through the glass at first, then flipping it upside-down and lowering its wide mouth over his head until it rested on his shoulders, like a deep-sea diver's helmet. This earned a laugh, so he began to clown around, stalking around the room like an astronaut or a robot. Only Brian couldn't see very well through the glass, and he collided with something hard enough to crack the fishbowl wide open, fracturing it into several pieces. And though Brian wasn't injured by the broken glass, the accident shattered his mood. Blushing bright red, he ran out of the living room, bounded up the stairs, and locked himself into his room, where he remained for the rest of the evening. When McCartney came knocking, asking his friend to come on down and hang out a bit more, Brian refused to answer. All McCartney could hear coming through the heavy wooden door was the gentle, heartbreaking sound of a deeply embarrassed young man snuffling softly to himself.

That same year, Brian's childhood neighbor, Mary Lou Van Antwerp, called out of the blue to say hi and see what her old friend was up to. She and Marilyn got to chatting, and soon Mary Lou, her husband, and their young kids were invited up to the Bellagio house for a big reunion dinner. At first the evening was relaxed and fun, with all the kids playing on the floor, Audree reminiscing about old times on West 119th Street, and Marilyn and Terry Melcher enjoying all the family legends. Then Brian came downstairs to say hello. "He had a beard and his hair was long and he was heavy," recalls Mary Lou. "As a kid, he was the skinniest thing you've ever seen. We never thought he would gain any weight. Now he seemed spacey and preoccupied, playing the piano and talking and not making much sense. He was just mumbling, really. And finally Audree told him, 'Brian, you're so fucked up!' He just walked out of the room, and the kids went right on playing."

What Brian did when he left the room wasn't clear. But the strangest thing about the whole evening, as Mary Lou recalls it, was how normal it all seemed to the people in the living room. No matter how detached from reality Brian seemed to become, their response was less sympathetic than confused and, it's hard not to conclude, resentful.

In retrospect, it's easy to see the family's flaws in their almost willful ignorance of his incipient psychiatric ills. But that ignores their own cultural and psychological foundations. Coming from a blue-collar culture that defined itself in terms of willpower and resilience *(Don't back down from that wave!)*, the eccentricities and emotional disconnection of one underperforming young man felt less like a reason for sympathy than for a good, therapeutic ass-kicking.

Whether Brian's flights of weirdness and his deepening detachment from the world inhabited by his father, his band, and the rest of his family were the result of a flaw in his character, misfiring brain chemistry, promiscuous drug use, or a deliberate, well-honed strategy intended to keep certain people away was never clear. What is clear, however, is that Brian often had plenty of energy and enthusiasm for those aspects of his life that had nothing to do with the Beach Boys. "Even in those years when he was supposedly in seclusion, Brian came downstairs all the time, this great big guy in a bathrobe," Stanley Shapiro says. "And we went places. Brian and I used to get into his Mercedes and drive over to the Radiant

Radish, or we'd go to Redondo Beach and hang out with his high school pals, or go look for Carol Mountain. Brian was as normal to me as anyone else."

Particularly in Hollywood, where a significant percentage of the moneyed, young entertainment figures of the early '70s had happily embraced cocaine. "Everyone was naive about it," says Danny Hutton, who then lived in a Laurel Canyon home whose most popular feature was the black-windowed party room on the lower level, where luminaries from every creative discipline would hang out, chat, listen to music, and, almost invariably, blow through the gleaming mountain of cocaine that usually rose from the coffee table in the center of the room.

Brian and Danny hung out regularly, and they usually weren't alone. "Everyone hung out there," Hutton says. "Harry Nilsson, John Lennon, Ringo Starr, Keith Moon. Elton John threw a surprise party for me at my house. And I had brought him over to the Bellagio house when he was just starting out. That was one of those great moments, when I told Brian, 'You gotta hear this guy!' So he said, 'Okay, play me something!' Elton started playing a tune and got about halfway into the first verse when Brian said, 'Okay, great. What else you got?' So Elton started another tune and again, once Brian got the gist, he's like: 'Okay, it's good! What's next!' And Elton wasn't used to it, and he was slowly getting frazzled." When louche punk rocker Iggy Pop showed up to party, he was at first entranced by Brian's charisma and fell happily into one of the complicated, multipart sing-alongs of "Shortenin' Bread" Brian loved to lead. What Iggy didn't know was that once a coked-up Brian got started with "Shortenin' Bread," he could go on for literally hours on end. And he still showed no sign of quitting when Iggy—who wore glitter makeup and slashed his own flesh with broken glass in the midst of his performances—backed out of the room and turned to Hutton, proclaiming: "I gotta get out of here, man. This guy is *nuts*!"

Tales of Brian's indulgences and eccentricities, along with his growing reputation as a commercial has-been, had spread like a bad odor around Hollywood. In fact, when Stanley Shapiro got Brian involved in rewriting the lyrics of his old Beach Boys songs (a project Murry initiated to sweeten the publishing deal he'd cut with A&M in 1969), the company brass was closer to furious than overjoyed. The whole story is pretty strange, not least for the fact that Brian (or any songwriter) would agree to participate in a wholesale rewriting of his or her works— particularly those works that had just been sold off by his father against his own most fervent wishes. To Brian, however, the opportunity to revise his own songs felt more like a way to reclaim his musical legacy from the family that had taken so much from him. So when he heard about Shapiro's plan, he jumped at it and even tapped his friend Tandyn Almer (a fellow drug enthusiast and Hollywood weirdo who earned showbiz spurs by writing the Association's smash hit "Along Comes Mary") to help. Focusing first on the *Friends* album, the trio worked together for a month or two, even composing original lyrics for Brian's airy instrumental "Passing By." *("I met you on the avenue/and stopped to say hello to you/and then realized I was just passing by . . .")* When they finished something to their mutual satisfaction, they'd record a demo version of the song, usually with Brian playing piano and singing lead over Almer and Shapiro's backing vocals.

After a few weeks of work, Shapiro took his stack of tapes over to A&M. At first, the execs were thrilled, not just by the songs' new lyrics, but also by the musicians playing them. "They were like: 'Wow, this is great! Who are those voices?' I said, 'Well, it's Tandyn Almer,' and they didn't like that at all." Almer, it seemed, had already worked for A&M and been fired for being, in official terms, "a disturbance" on the company's lot. But, Shapiro continues, they were even angrier to hear that the main presence on the tape was none other than Brian Wilson. "They said, 'What? *Brian Wilson!* There's no way we're gonna do work with Brian Wilson. He's crazy, number one. And if we accept anything with him, he'll be down at this lot putting up circus tents!' I was so pissed off, I quit on the spot." Shapiro took the tapes back to Brian, whom he found playing the piano at Almer's cluttered house, and set the only record of their work next to him on the piano bench. "And I have no idea what happened to any of it. It was never heard from again."

As distant as Brian had been from the Beach Boys in 1971, he was even more removed as the group prepared to record their follow-up to *Surf's Up* in the first weeks of 1972. But even as the other group members begged Brian for new material, they were rarely satisfied with the work he eventually gave them. For instance, when Brian submitted a quirky new rocker he'd written with Tandyn Almer called "Beatrice of Baltimore," the group balked at Almer's street poet–style lyrics *("She got a hole in her stockin'/She do a whole lot of rockin'/She do the shake down at Bumbles/She do the Chicano rumble . . .")* in favor of a new set of Jack Rieley originals that contributed the song's new title, "You Need a Mess of Help to Stand Alone." A second song written by Brian and Tandyn, an ode to a masseuse/hooker Brian knew called "Marcella," also got the Rieley treatment, though this time he kept enough of Almer's lyrics to share the writer's credit. But

Brian ended up being so absent during the recording of his songs, and on all the other songs on the new album, that the group actually had to edit his face into the group portrait that appeared on the inner sleeve of the album cover.

That Brian had become a Beach Boy in name only might have been more evident if the group hadn't been in the midst of several personnel shake-ups. Earlier in 1971, Dennis had capped a drunken tirade by punching through a bedroom window in his house and, in the process, severing a few tendons in his right hand. With his hand too damaged to wield a drumstick onstage, he had to pass his drumming responsibilities to a sideman, serving instead as a second stand-up singer or third keyboard player. This development only deepened Carl's resolve to shake up the group's lineup. Already, he and Jack Rieley had decided that the ongoing modernization of the Beach Boys might be enhanced by adding a couple of new voices into the mix. Eager to work with friends, Carl turned to Blondie Chaplin and Ricky Fataar, two members of the Flame, a South African group he helped bring to the United States and whose records he had produced. Both Blondie and Ricky could play a variety of instruments (Ricky being a particularly good drummer), sing, and write songs, which would help fill in the creative hole left by Brian. Both also came with a funkier, harder-edged music sensibility, which would shake up the Beach Boys' squeaky-clean image nearly as much as the fact that they were dark-skinned Africans who had clearly never worn striped shirts in their lives.

Brought in as full group members in February 1972, Blondie and Ricky added new gristle and bone to the group's stage show, but their arrival—and the deepening influence of Jack Rieley that it represented—also spelled the end of Bruce Johnston's seven-year tenure with the group. Announced in April, the longtime Beach Boy's departure was described as being "by mutual agreement," though his public critiques of the band (starting with an arch review of their next album he wrote for a British music magazine) imply something less amicable. Meanwhile, the rest of the group pursued their new album in factions, with Carl, Ricky, and Blondie in one studio; Mike and Alan working in another; Dennis off with Beach Boy sideman (and future member of soft-rock hit-makers Captain and Tennille) Daryl Dragon in still another; and Brian nowhere to be seen.

The album that resulted, named *Carl and the Passions: So Tough* in homage to the vocal quartet Brian had led to the Hawthorne High School talent show thirteen years earlier, was a schizophrenic affair. Brian's two tracks took some intriguing leaps, particularly in the instrumentation of "You Need a Mess of

Help" (including a fiddle, banjo, and tack piano), while "Marcella" boasted a relatively complex vocal arrangement, percussion, and an unexpected slide guitar break that would have had far more impact if they hadn't played the song at such a sluggish pace. (The song sounded far more vibrant on the *In Concert* album that would follow in 1973.)

Blondie and Ricky contributed one splendid song in the acoustic waltz "Hold On Dear Brother" and one funky love song, "Here She Comes," that would have sounded more at home on the album if the other Beach Boys (beyond Carl, whose voice can be heard in the backing chorus) had made audible contributions to it. Mike and Alan hopped on the early '70s Jesus-rock bandwagon, albeit with Transcendental Meditation overtones, with "He Come Down," a neogospel number that bore coauthor Brian's fingerprints on its surprisingly stirring gospel choir segments. Mike and Al turned to Carl to cowrite "All This Is That," which wove references to Robert Frost's "The Road Not Taken" and TM teachings into a somewhat awkward lyric *(I am that/thou art that/And all this is that . . .)* that didn't even come close to compromising the song's floating melody and the sparkling harmonies that—as Carl's falsetto soars away in the song's final moments—seem to drift off into infinity. Dennis reached for his own kind of spirituality with a pair of love songs whose elaborate orchestrations and unrestrained romanticism hearken back to the Hollywood of the '40s and '50s. Indeed, the more successful of the two had first boasted the working title "Old Movie" before Dennis settled on "Cuddle Up." No matter the title, the combination of strings and full vocal arrangement, played against Dennis's wavering voice, came closer to achieving the mood of passionate vulnerability he was after.

Released in May, the stylistically meandering *Carl and the Passions* would eventually become a cult favorite, with devotees including Elton John, who penned ecstatic liner notes for the album's 2000 CD re-release. But in 1972 the brief record (it was comprised of only eight songs clocking in at less than thirty-five minutes, which was short even in those days) proved underwhelming, particularly given the decision by Warner Brothers to package it as a double album with *Pet Sounds*, one of the five Capitol albums the company had purchased in the Beach Boys' contract. The pairing served not only to drag the group back into the past it had worked so hard to escape, but it also forced a direct comparison between the hit-and-miss fruits of the band's new, democratic era and the jaw-dropping glories of its Brian-led heyday. The contrast did not serve the new music very well at all, and the package stalled on the *Billboard* charts at number fifty.

If Brian noticed the album's middling performance, he wouldn't have cared very much. By 1972, the once hypercompetitive producer was happiest working outside the spotlight with people who made him feel comfortable. One of these turned out to be David Sandler, an aspiring young songwriter/producer he'd met at a recording session. Sandler, who had grown up in Minneapolis idolizing Brian, came to Los Angeles in 1970 hoping to make some connections. Happenstance led him to Bruce Johnston, who liked what he heard on Sandler's tapes and invited the young musician up to Bellagio to watch the group record at Brian's home studio. That afternoon they were trying to record a horn arrangement to go with "Good Time," but when Brian finally woke up and padded down to the studio, the eight horn players he found waiting for him didn't know what to play. "So he went to his office and wrote horn charts while talking to me," Sandler says. "It was an amazing horn line, with this overriding French horn riff, and he did the whole thing while having a conversation with me."

Sandler went back to Minnesota not long afterwards, but he kept in touch with Brian on the telephone. When he moved to L.A. a few months later, his idol gave him his first major break by tapping him to coproduce the debut album for Spring, the new duo act Marilyn had formed with her sister, Diane. Better still, Brian invited Sandler to move into a guest room in the Bellagio house, and he would remain there as the recording went on for the next two months. As a houseguest and collaborator, Sandler found himself living at the core of Brian's emotional netherworld, where the simplest tasks could become enormously complicated and the most ambitious projects rarely amounted to as much as you expected they might.

Still, sessions for the Spring album were relaxed and fun, Sandler remembers. And while Brian's energies ebbed and flowed from day to day, he ended up doing significant work on more than half of the tracks. "On 'Tennessee Waltz' he played the whole track, just stacking the instruments," Sandler recalls. "'Awake' was the same way, and on 'Sweet Mountain' we were standing side by side, doing bass parts on a synthesizer."

Other times, though, Brian wouldn't show up at all. On those days, Sandler and Steve Desper (credited as a coproducer) either ran the show themselves or with help from Rick Henn, who had followed Brian's musical example ever since he worked for Murry as a member of the Sunrays.

The self-titled album that resulted turned out to be an interesting mishmash of covers and a few Brian Wilson originals (though most were retreads from an earlier era). Brian's "Tennessee Waltz," for instance, juxtaposed the old-timey jangle of a tack piano against echoing percussion, a synthesizer bass, and a backing chorus of tightly woven harmonies. Brian's one new original song (cowritten with Sandler), "Sweet Mountain," featured neatly contrasting major/minor sections, while a slowed-down take of "This Whole World" came with a new and bracingly off-kilter vamp written by Sandler. Some of the song choices are a bit too pedestrian (Leon Russell and Bonnie Bramlett's "Superstar," for instance), and Marilyn and Diane sound more comfortable harmonizing than they do carrying a song as lead vocalists. But *Spring* had its charms, and when United Artists released it in the early summer of 1972, Marilyn made the publicity rounds on the Beach Boys' tour, promoting the album by talking about Brian's intense commitment to the project. "Sometimes he would cry at sessions because he liked a song so much he couldn't believe it," she said, going on to explain: "He's very emotional."

Throughout the recording of that album and then for months afterwards, Sandler saw all of Brian's emotions at close range. One night he took Sandler down to Hawthorne to visit an uncle who wasn't feeling well, then took him on a tour of old haunts that ended, at Brian's insistence, at the Foster's Freeze drive-in. A conversation about the sound of mission bells inspired Brian to drag his friend out one night to cruise old churches. "We've gotta get one! We're gonna steal one!" he kept saying, so insistent that Sandler didn't realize he was kidding until he turned the Rolls-Royce back toward home. But Brian could be deadly serious too, such as on the night when he began enthusing wildly about a particular kind of canned sloppy joe mix he enjoyed. "He was just dying for a sloppy joe, and he knew exactly which store had it, so we went out and bought it, brought it home, heated it up, and ate it. He was a really simple person, considering how successful he was. Just a very unfettered guy. But there was always a core of lucidity about him. He never seemed that crazy to me."

Sandler, on the other hand, was a perfect companion for Brian: a musical collaborator who appreciated his talents but neither demanded nor expected anything of him. So when Brian struggled out of bed in the late afternoon, he'd head down to his den and spend hours with Sandler, talking about whatever occurred to him. "We'd talk about arrangements and about girls. I'd bounce ideas off of him to see if he'd get interested." Sometimes Brian would merely gaze out of the window, saying nothing as Sandler described songs he wanted to record, with certain horns paired off against one another, the strings providing this texture while the guitars went this way and the keyboards went over here . . . and Brian would seem a thousand miles away until he'd murmur something—"You're gonna have a sonority problem there"—that cut to the heart of an issue Sandler wouldn't have started to perceive until he heard the music on the tape.

As Sandler came to understand, Brian's musical inspirations were just as overpowering as they were unpredictable. Musing one night on the titular similarities between the Four Tops' "Baby, I Need Your Lovin' " and the Spencer Davis Group's "Gimme Some Lovin'," Brian pulled Sandler into the studio and began to work out a medley arrangement. "It was really unusual, because he wanted to do a whole verse of one song, then a verse of the other," Sandler remembers. "He started with the drum machine, finding these two beats that sort of fought each other. I was playing the organ, doing these droning fifths, like bagpipes, and he was on the piano playing this really nice rhythm against the drum machine. Brian was very excited about it and called in Desper to come over and record it, and it went down perfect. Then he couldn't remember some of the words to 'Gimme Some Lovin',' so he called in Spencer Davis, who happened to be in town, and *he* came over and was listening to it, going, 'This is smashing! This is smashing!'" Later, Brian called in some of the Beach Boys to work out a full vocal arrangement. But, as Sandler recalls, they weren't crazy about the song, and their indifference cut the legs out from under Brian's enthusiasm.

A few months later, Sandler got a call from David Berson, a Warner's executive who had heard the Spring album and marveled at how the record (released on the United Artists label) sounded more like a Brian Wilson album than anything the Beach Boys had done for his label. "They had spent a lot of money on the group, and they wanted to do a better job getting a return out of them," Sandler says. "As it turned out, Warner's had just signed Phil Spector to a deal on one of its labels, so Berson said, 'You can obviously get Brian out of bed. I'll get Spector with him, and we'll get them to produce a record together!' I didn't know what to say, but I went to Brian's. It was late afternoon, and he was still in bed, but I went in and said, 'Hey, how'd you like to produce a record with Phil?'" But the prospect of working on a project with his own idol made Brian blanch. "He said, 'No! I don't wanna do that! I want to produce a record with you!' He just didn't want to get into a heavy situation like that."

At first it seemed like Brian was offering to coproduce a new Beach Boys album with Sandler. But the moment the talk began to revolve around contracts and other real-world commitments, Brian shut the discussion down.

"There were personality things, family things, going on," Sandler says. "I was orbiting out there as an outsider, so it was difficult to know what you're dealing with. But he was definitely trying to establish some independence from the group, and the Spring album was part of that. He still had a lot of music in him, but I think he was depressed. And maybe some of the people who were supposed to be helping him were hacking away but not helping him that much."

Despite the commercial disappointment of *Carl and the Passions,* the Beach Boys hatched an ambitious plan for the recording of their next album. Inspired by a copacetic visit to the Netherlands, the group decided to abandon Los Angeles in order to spend the summer recording in Holland, where the people were friendly, the living was relatively cheap, and the distractions few. With engineer Stephen Moffitt dispatched to find or build a suitable recording studio and another staffer charged with renting houses and cars for the band, their families, and assorted entourage members, the entire group decamped for Europe in early June 1972. Everyone, that is, except Brian, who really wasn't all that eager to leave home after all.

Not that there was anything he could do about it. Marilyn, Carnie, and younger sister Wendy (born in 1969) had left along with the other Beach Boys, and they all expected Brian to join them overseas as soon as possible. And as ever, the rest of the group—along with their employers at Warner Brothers records—expected Brian to kick up a few new gems so the new record would make at least as big an impact as *Surf's Up* had made in 1971. What's more, the other Beach Boys kept pledging that Brian was getting back on his feet and was ready to take the helm again. In fact, they had promised Mo Ostin, back when he was purchasing the rights to their post-1966 works as part of their record deal, that Brian would deliver a finished version of *Smile* for the label. That Brian had no intention of doing anything of the sort didn't stop the group from taking a $50,000 advance for the album or from hyping its imminent arrival to reporters and concert crowds, all of whom would gasp and applaud with delight.

To Brian, the thought of working on *Smile*—his stillborn paean to the vital core of love, hope, and terror beneath the American experience—made about as much sense as the thought of spending the next few months making music in a distant country that had nothing to do with the world he knew, as if his geography was the problem. It was the invasion of Brian's internal landscape that had shattered his will to create. The Beach Boys had done that, along with his family, again and again, stripping the soil, weighing the profit-bearing minerals, and shipping them off to be sold at market rates. And now they expected Brian to help them mine his depths again and were asking him to travel halfway around the world for the privilege? Just thinking about it made Brian sink into a bleak, desolate fog.

One voice came to him out of the darkness. It belonged to Randy Newman— that sad, teasing bray—singing the opening track and title song to his newest album, *Sail Away*.

On the surface, *Sail Away*'s title song presented the same misty vision of American freedom and opportunity Murry had always used to motivate his boys toward greatness—except that the song's narrator was an eighteenth-century slave trader easing one of his victims into a lifetime of bondage. And Brian could relate, on a spiritual level anyway. He knew how it felt to follow a dreamy vision, only to be sucked into the maw of a rapacious economic machine. As he listened to the album again—and again and again, as per his usual practice with records that struck his fancy—he heard a piece of himself in the rest of the songs, from the self-pity of a modern living legend ("It's Lonely at the Top"), to the self-deluded freak-show entertainer ("Simon Smith and His Amazing Dancing Bear"), to the unthinking xenophobia of modern America ("Political Science"), to the uncaring God who hovered coolly above it all ("He Gives Us All His Love" and "God's Song [That's Why I Love Mankind]"). A decade removed from the days when his utopian vision of America enraptured the world and transformed his family's American dream into mountains of cash, Brian could hear the story of his internal landscape in "Burn On," the song inspired by the plight of Ohio's Cuyahoga River, which, as Randy Newman sang, had grown so thick with petroleum sludge that it had actually erupted into flame.

In the end it took no fewer than three trips to LAX for Brian to board the airplane. Once the plane landed in Amsterdam, he snuck off without his ticket or passport and fell asleep in the duty-free lounge, touching off a brief panic for the greeters forced to wonder how their quarry could have vanished in midflight. They found him eventually, though, and once ensconced in Laren, a bucolic suburb of Amsterdam, Brian sank even deeper into anguish. Most days he avoided making the drive over to the studio in Baambrugge, choosing instead to sit in his house while peering out at the countryside, often dulling his senses with pot and glasses of hard apple cider. When Brian did drive off in his rented Mercedes, there was no telling where he might go or what condition he'd be in when he got back. One day he got so drunk that he wrapped the car around a telephone pole. The Mercedes was totaled, but Brian staggered out of the smoking wreckage without a scratch.

"He seemed to be going through a bad time, but I was really too young to understand it," elder daughter Carnie says. Still, Brian hadn't vanished entirely from his family. During the mornings he would take four-year-old Carnie and younger sister Wendy to feed carrots and sugar cubes to the horses that lived in a field down the road. When Wendy, then not quite three years old, accidentally sunk her foot into a bath of scalding water, Brian scooped his shrieking daughter up in his arms and sprinted her off for treatment at the small hospital across the road, with his wife and older daughter fast on his heels. The image of her father taking immediate control of the situation would never leave Carnie's memory. "I was running right behind him, thinking, 'That's my big, strong daddy carrying Wendy.'"

Sometimes the last thing Carnie and Wendy would hear at night would be the sound of their parents, standing together in the doorway of their room, twining their voices around the verses of "Frere Jacques." Once the girls were sleeping, Brian would descend again into his music room, to fall again into Randy Newman's world of dancing bears, buffoonish tycoons, and the dreamy, small-town America that never quite existed. Eventually, Brian felt his muse beginning to come awake. "If I kept playing the Randy Newman record, I could still stay in that mood," he said at the time. As Brian explored his feelings on the piano keyboard, the melodies that emerged seemed to trace the same tension between tenderness and violence, the innocence of youth and the inevitable corruption of age.

Brian crafted a story that was both fantastical and entirely personal, centering on a young prince whose life is transformed by the music that comes to him, along with a wizardly Pied Piper, through his magic transistor radio. Named "Mt. Vernon and Fairway," for the streets that met outside Mike Love's childhood home, and where the cousins spent many evenings singing along with the radio in the front seat of Brian's car, the piece became a parable about the role music played in Brian's life. It was all there, from the magical way the music descends upon the prince, to the spell it allows him to cast over his brothers and sisters, to the capricious way his mother (in a bit of role reversal) snatches the radio away and hides it where she thinks he'll never be able to find it. And yet the music and the magical spell it weaves never quite vanish. At the end of the story, he and his brothers and sisters can hear the joyous music playing in the wind that blows past their window.

Brian composed several musical sections for the piece, including the yearning keyboard figure that served as an overture, a couple of keyboard/synthesizer vignettes to go along with the action sequences, and some intricate vocal arrangements that evoked the sound of the magical music. Somehow, the other guys didn't get the gist of how the whole thing was going to fit together until most of the recording had been done, at which point news that Brian expected them to put a ten-minute-plus fairy tale about a prince and a magic radio on the new album came as something of a shock. "Nobody was ready for that. *Nobody!*" Brian told a reporter at the time. "I remember Carl said, *'WHAT?'*" Dismayed to have yet another one of his musical offerings slapped down, Brian retreated again to his house, where he soothed his hurt with apple cider, hashish, and *Sail Away*. Eventually, though, Carl, feeling guilty for his sharp reaction to his big brother's project, presented a second alternative: Why not include the fairy tale as a special bonus EP that would be packaged with the album? This notion assuaged Brian's feelings enough to draw him back into the studio, where he and Carl put the finishing touches on the music and Jack Rieley recorded the narration. Brian performed the role of the magical Pied Piper, whom he imbued with his looniest cartoon voice.

If the other Beach Boys didn't know what to make of Brian's loopy fairy tale, they were nevertheless pursuing many of the same questions in their own songs, albeit in the broader terms of culture and politics. Halfway across the planet, the record they produced—*Holland*—turned out to be almost entirely about California. But ten years after "Surfin' Safari," they had come to develop a more sophisticated understanding of the cultural currents that led their families to the Gold Coast and about the cultural and environmental undertow created in the stampede west. Dennis and Jack Rieley wrote "Steamboat," a dreamlike journey back to the mythic heart of Mark Twain's America, borne by the insistent chug of an actual steam engine, hurtling keyboard glissandos, and a wonderfully bluesy slide guitar break; while Carl, also working with Rieley, came up with "The Trader," a two-part exploration of Manifest Destiny as seen through the eyes of the conquering and the conquered.

Not all of the songs revolved around cultural themes, though. For instance, "Only with You" was another look into the romantic heart (and melodic inventiveness) of Dennis Wilson, only without Daryl Dragon's keening strings and horns and with a delicately understated lyric from Mike. "Funky Pretty," an eccentric rocker from Brian, Mike, and the omnipresent Rieley, climaxed in a whirring storm of synthesizers, guitars, percussion, and more interlocking vocal parts than one ear can track. Blondie, Ricky, and Mike produced the anthemic "We Got Love" and the brooding "Leavin' This Town." But the most ambitious work on the album was Al and Mike's "California Saga," a musical triptych that presented their home state's story in terms drawn from a chain of regional bards that included Walt Whitman, John Steinbeck, the great naturalist poet Robinson Jeffers, Country Joe McDonald, and, of course, Brian Wilson.

"California Saga" began with Mike's solo composition "Big Sur," an acoustic evocation of life in rustic Northern California. This segued into Al's "The Beaks of Eagles," which contrasted spoken verses from Robinson Jeffers's poem of the same name with Jardine's sung verses, expanding upon the poet's description of nature's resilience ("... *Lenin has lived and Jehovah died while the mother eagle/Hunts her same ills, crying the same beautiful and lonely cry . . .*") with original vignettes about the frontiersmen's struggles to settle the wilderness. The piece climaxed with Al's "California," a kind of "I Get Around" for the back-to-the-land era. As sung by Mike, with all the charismatic surfer-boy enthusiasm he brought to the group's earlier work, the song sounds like an invocation for the utopian world the Beach Boys had been pursuing for more than a decade:

> *And the people there in the open air, one big family*
> *Yeah, the people there love to sing and share their newfound liberty.*

A decade later, the search for the place where the kids are hip only begins where the highway ends. But the driving impulse—and the joyous music that springs from its description—remains the same. That the group could pivot from that moment of revelation right into Carl's "The Trader" and its clear-eyed acknowledgment of the awful price extracted from the natives in the white man's pursuit of paradise only lends the entire "California Saga" more depth. And, amazingly, they achieved that feat almost entirely without the magical ear of Brian Wilson—reaching creative heights that would have been unthinkable only two years earlier.

Still, when the group returned home, the master tape they presented Warner Brothers earned them another fishy stare and yet another variation on the age-old pop music demand: Where's the single? The real problem, as it emerged, was "We Got Love," the Blondie/Ricky–dominated tune that flew the furthest from the

Beach Boys' usual terrain. Granted, the studio outtake has only a glimmer of the explosive sound apparent in the band's live renditions, such as the one included on *In Concert*, the album that would follow in 1973. But what the execs really wanted, of course, was a brilliant new Brian Wilson song, and preferably one that wasn't part of a ten-minute fairy tale. Unfortunately, Brian had no evident interest in writing that kind of song—not for the Beach Boys, at any rate. That's how it seemed until Van Dyke Parks, still working his day job as a mixed-media exec for Warner Brothers records, showed up in the office of Warner's executive David Berson with a cassette tape of a song he helped Brian write a few months earlier. On a whim, Van Dyke had shown up at Brian's door, bearing a prototype Walkman tape recorder and almost no patience for Brian's usual dilly-dallying.

According to several published descriptions of the tape Van Dyke made (which he swears he turned over to the Warner's establishment in 1972 and hasn't seen since), it begins with Brian, sitting with Van Dyke on the piano bench in his home studio on Bellagio Road, begging his friend to "hypnotize me and make me believe I'm not crazy."

"Cut the shit, Brian," Van Dyke responds evenly. "You're a songwriter. That's what you do, and I want you to sit down and write a song for me."

"Convince me I'm not crazy," Brian says.

"Cut the shit, Brian, and play the tune."

Once again, Brian surrenders to the inevitable.

"What's the tune called?"

"'Sail On, Sailor.'"

And then he begins to play, a rollicking G chord capturing the insistent rhythm of a steamer plowing across heavy seas.

> *Fill your sails with fortitude*
> *and ride her stormy waves*
> *You've got to sail on, sail on, sailor.*

They had first written the song in 1971, and Brian had been tinkering with it ever since, airing it out at Danny Hutton's house. "He said, 'Hey, who's got lyrics?' and everyone fucking ran over there," Hutton recalls. Eventually, Tandyn Almer threw in a few verses, with an assist from pop poet Ray Kennedy. Van Dyke kept the cassette of the original song to himself for a few months, but he dug it out when he heard about the Warner executives rejecting *Holland*, presenting it to

David Berson as the one obvious solution to everyone's problems. Berson listened, and once he heard the song play out, he agreed: If the Beach Boys would agree to put "Sail On, Sailor" on *Holland,* the album could come out as scheduled.

Back in Los Angeles late that fall, the group set to work recording the song—which by then had been altered, yet again, with a new set of Jack Rieley lyrics. Brian refused to attend the recording sessions, but he did listen in on the telephone for a while and, as Ricky Fataar recalled in interviews at the time, suggested a guitar part that echoed the rhythm of an "SOS" Morse code distress call, while also fitting perfectly with the song's chugging beat and Blondie's fiery lead vocal. The group used the song as the album's opening cut, and though it flopped as a lead-off single that winter (rising only to *Billboard's* number seventy-nine spot), it climbed into the Top Fifty when it was rereleased two years later. *Holland* fared a bit better than *Carl and the Passions,* reaching the mid-thirties on the *Billboard* album charts. Even more encouraging, however, were the reviews, particularly the rave that ran in the pages of *Rolling Stone:* "Like the finest Beach Boys work, *Holland* makes me consistently smile," Jim Miller wrote. "They now play what might as well be described simply as Beach Boys music . . . *Holland* offers that music at its most satisfying." The reviews in England were just as laudatory: "I expect more from the Beach Boys than from anyone else," Richard Williams wrote in the *New Musical Express.* "*Holland* has the goods."

As the reviews made clear, the Beach Boys of early 1973 sounded like a rock 'n' roll group that had, at long last, found its way into maturity. Better still, they had done it without losing touch with the utopian spirit that had always guided them. By the winter of 1973, as the war in Vietnam ground on and Richard Nixon prepared to place his right hand on a Bible and swear once again to uphold the Constitution of the United States, the search for a place where the kids are hip took on even greater urgency. It wouldn't be long before the group's harmonized voices would once again seem to give melody to the nation's deepest frustrations and fondest hopes. But for all the Beach Boys would gain in the next few years, none of it could compare with what had already been lost and what they would be willing to sell off along the way.

CHAPTER 11

The one thing that never changed was Murry. He never stopped caring and never stopped pushing. He never stopped believing that he'd taught them everything they knew, given them everything he had, and he expected to be heeded. Though he had made mistakes, he demanded respect, not just for himself, but also for the United States, too. "It's one of those success stories that can happen in America," he said to *Rolling Stone*'s David Felton in the early '70s. "And it isn't all talent . . . They're just Americans; they're like any one of you. Got it? Got the message?"

Brian, Dennis, and Carl certainly did. Even as grown-ups, with years of success behind them, their own families to raise, and all the privileges of wealth and the obligations of adulthood, they never really got beyond the shadow their father's expectations had cast across their lives. Murry always told his friends that he was proud of his boys, but maybe it was more difficult for him to deliver that message to their faces. He didn't want them to lose their edge. Better to keep 'em on their toes and make sure they know what they're fighting for.

But Brian had already spent too much of his life trying to sing himself free of the emotional calamity his family had become. His music made him a success, but it had only made everything worse, turning his most intimate feelings into cash cows that were judged, manipulated, and exploited by everyone around him. If he'd used his music to escape his father, the empire it had created had, ironically enough, transformed everyone around him into a legion of Murrys. No matter where he went, Brian could hear variations of his father's insults. Nobody wants to hear this airy-fairy crap! Dust yourself off and write another hit! Ya gotta fight for success! All he wanted was to escape, but they would never let him go. The Beach Boys wanted—demanded—his songs, but then they rejected or rewrote whatever he gave them. They wanted his ears but not his head, let alone his heart.

So screw it. He'd slam his hands down on the keys, spin around on the bench, and dash out to the car, tearing out of the driveway and heading down the hill to Sunset Boulevard before making his way to Danny Hutton's place in Laurel Canyon, where the music played all night and the blacked-out windows kept out the light of day.

Not that Brian was the only Wilson struggling to adjust to the rigors and responsibilities of adulthood. Long known as the most coolheaded and reliable of the Wilson brothers, Carl had served as the band's onstage leader ever since Brian started skipping shows in 1963. Brian's baby brother had taken up even more of the burden in recent years, not just in concert, but also in the layered songwriting and production techniques he had developed. Carl had his own indulgences, to be sure. But the lessons of childhood had affected him as well, turning the quietest of the Wilson boys into the Beach Boys' pillar of common sense. Brian might seem nuts, Dennis might be raving drunk, Mike might snarl about cash flow, and Al might be somewhere out to lunch, but Carl would always be on top of the situation, his soft brown eyes placid and still behind his thick beard. What he didn't mention was that his back was killing him, the weight of responsibility grinding his vertebrae together until he could no longer bear the pain of standing on his feet. Sometimes Carl's spinal problems got so bad that he had to be carried from room to room in a chair. But it had fallen to him to hold the band together, and so he would, even while he raised his own boys and sustained a marriage pulled apart by the pressures of the road and the work-all-night, sleep-all-day rhythms of the professional rock 'n' roller.

All the Wilson boys heard their father's voice in their ears at night, but Dennis had always bucked the hardest against his reins. As a teenager, he'd escaped to the beach and the family of surfers he'd found there. That taste of freedom had led, ironically, right back to the bosom of his family when he became a part of the Beach Boys. But at least life as a rock 'n' roll star had allowed him to soak up the unquestioning, unconditional love he never felt at home. Into that internal void went the spotlights, cheers, girls, and entourage.

No matter where he was or what he was doing, Dennis always made sure to have enough drugs and booze to keep his restless body pain free and wired for sound. "There was never enough to fill him," Dennis's second wife, Barbara, recalls. "No matter how good-looking he was, no matter how successful, it didn't penetrate. There was a huge emptiness, a pain that he carried inside."

Dennis met Barbara Charen in 1969. He was sitting with Stanley Shapiro at the Hamburger Hamlet restaurant in Westwood when he noticed the petite red-head carrying bacon cheeseburgers and mugs of beer to the UCLA students at her tables. Struck as much by her intelligence and wit as he was by her physical beauty, Dennis became a regular at that burger joint, eventually working up the courage to ask the pretty waitress out on a date. From there they struck up a friendship, then a romance—he would meet her after every shift, usually in the most absurd way imaginable. For a week or two he made a point of showing up every night in a different car—borrowing them from his brothers, Mike, and Al, everyone he knew. Another night he tried to run into the restaurant at full speed, sprinting so fast that he didn't notice the glass doors were shut until he bounced off of them, landing in a dazed heap on the sidewalk. "These were things you don't see most adults doing," Barbara says with a smile.

But Dennis had needs most adults didn't have, and abilities, as well. He'd taught himself to play piano in the mid-1960s and then started composing songs whose plainspoken emotionalism and musical sophistication took nearly everyone by surprise. Just like his big brother's, Dennis's muse was inspired by desperation too overwhelming to confront head-on. So it was up to his fingers to find the chords and melodies that would trace the contours of his sorrows and hopes. "He was always writing. And he always wanted whomever he was with to be right next to him at the piano: 'Listen to this!'" Barbara remembers. "But my sense was that he never knew how beautiful his music was."

Now a practicing psychotherapist, Barbara can look back on the father of her two sons and on the family he never quite emerged from with at least a measure of professional remove. To see them now, more than three decades after the fact, is to see a family whose members have, like so many families, grown too accustomed to their roles to allow one another to change. "Brian's a genius, Carl's an angel, and Dennis is that kind of bad boy/imp/jester. So how can you ever get what comes from you taken seriously when that's your role?"

Dennis admired Brian too much to begrudge his brother the lion's share of the credit for creating and sustaining the Beach Boys. All he really wanted to achieve with his own music was a glimmer of respect from his father; and by early 1973, he had made some progress. The mutual disdain that divided Murry from his middle son during his adolescence and beyond had given way at first to tentative acceptance and then a real affection. The men would go fishing together when they could, and they found more common ground in the boxing matches on TV each Thursday night. "They'd be watching the fights together, talking on the phone while they both watched their own TVs," Barbara recalls. "It was a way for them to connect. I always sensed a certain excitement in Dennis when they talked on the phone. And when we'd go over to Audree's house in Whittier, which we did often, we always dropped by Murry's place, too. Dennis longed for Murry's approval. But my sense was that he never really got it."

Unconditional love had never come easily to Murry Wilson, and he was loath to dole it out as well. A heavyset man who kept the stresses of his life at bay by eating, drinking, and smoking with heedless abandon, Murry had grown an enormous belly in the last years of the '60s, and the weight of his girth put more pressure on a heart that was already dangerously overtaxed. When he got excited or moved too quickly, Murry's breath would come in gasps, his hands would shake, and he'd have to sit until his nervous system fell back into line. He'd come down with diverticulitis, a serious intestinal illness, in 1972, and the burden of this disease contributed to the fairly serious heart attack that felled Murry in the spring of 1973. Murry got out of the hospital a week or two later and seemed serious about changing his ways, but before he had time to get started, he suffered a sudden, massive heart attack on the morning of June 4. Audree was with him at the time and managed to call an ambulance within moments. But by the time the paramedics arrived, Murry was already dead. He was fifty-seven years old.

For all the years they had tried to escape the iron grip of their old man, Brian, Dennis, and Carl were all, in their way, devastated by Murry's death. Losing a family patriarch is never easy for anyone, but for boys who had spent their entire lives batted between the extremes of their father's outsized love and abuse, the loss was even more overwhelming. Until that day, their entire lives had been defined by the gravitational force of their father's stern authority. And though they had often struggled to stand on their own feet and move without feeling his weight upon their shoulders, he had also kept them connected to the earth.

Dennis burst into tears when he got the call, then refused to attend the funeral. "I'm sure he was home playing the piano with one of his buddies," Barbara says. "That's what he always did in times like that. But it seemed to me that when Murry died, something in Dennis died. It took a real toll on him. And I think that was really when he started deteriorating."

Brian also avoided his father's funeral that spring, flying instead to New York City with sister-in-law Diane Rovell in tow, ostensibly to promote Spring's new single, "Shyin' Away." But he was so detached from reality that he created less buzz about the record than confusion—and real alarm—about the state of his own sanity. Pete Fornatale, the WNEW-FM disc jockey whose Carnegie Hall introduction in February 1971 had launched the Beach Boys' renaissance with youth culture, greeted the prospect of a live, on-air interview with the band's reclusive visionary as a rare opportunity to meet one of his most treasured idols. When Brian finally appeared, led into the station's midtown studios by a couple of friends, Fornatale could feel his hands trembling with excitement. "I was really nervous, really wanting him to do well," he says. "Then I asked him what he was doing in New York City, and he said he was here to do the Ed Sullivan show, which had been cancelled two years earlier. He was either spaced out and weird or totally overhyped, saying things with the wrong inflection. I remember that when his handlers took him out of the studio, I walked down to the bathroom and threw up. It was that upsetting."

Was Brian really losing his grasp on reality, or was he signaling a new stage in his own retreat from the demands of adulthood? Certainly, his manner of thinking made him more ethereal than the average thirty-one-year-old husband and father. A decade of rock stardom and the riches and power that followed allowed (even encouraged) even more detachment from the humdrum existence that signified maturity to most everyone else. But most Baby Boomers weren't prepared to resign their claim to youth or their nagging sense that the New Frontier they had supposedly inherited had gone terribly awry. The grand call to national duty John F. Kennedy made in his inaugural speech had been subverted by war, assassinations, riots, and Watergate.

The sad distance between the early '70s and the early '60s was crystallized in George Lucas's movie *American Graffiti*, a bittersweet portrait of one night in the lives of a few high school–aged kids from suburban Southern California, circa

1962. The elegiac mood of the film was emphasized by a sound track that dug deeply into the hit songs of the era, starting with Bill Haley's catalytic "Rock Around the Clock," through an array of doo-wop and early rock 'n' roll hits, to "Surfin' Safari," the song that had lifted the Beach Boys to national prominence that very spring. And though Lucas readily acknowledged the three-year gap between the setting of his movie and the release of "All Summer Long" in 1965, he nevertheless staged his movie's climax, in which its various characters fan out to meet the future the world has in store for them, to the chiming harmonies of the song that cautioned repeatedly, *"Won't be long 'til summertime is through . . ."*

But even given the vivid descriptions of early '60s California youth culture that sparkle in the Beach Boys' earliest songs, the narrative and emotional complexity lurking just beneath their surface—the darkness that sparks their narrators' utopian ambitions—sounded just as vital in the early-to-mid 1970s. To old fans, it served as a bracing reminder of the musical and emotional wallop Brian's songs had. To younger listeners, the two Beach Boys songs included on *American Graffiti* were simply eye-opening. Who knew young men could sing like that? And why did their song about the joys of summer vacation end up sounding so joyous and so sad at the same time?

Meanwhile, the touring Beach Boys continued to draw larger, increasingly enthusiastic audiences to their shows in Europe and in the United States. Two years since they had committed themselves to playing longer, more varied shows, the stage band—which had expanded to include not just Blondie and Ricky but also a small handful of seasoned backing musicians—had become a crackerjack performance unit, as capable of pulling off a full-blown rocker (such as Mike's favorite new cover song, "Jumpin' Jack Flash") as they were of handling the tonal twists of "Good Vibrations" or the intricate harmonic shifts of "God Only Knows." The bulk of their sets was stocked with material from 1966 and beyond, with a healthy portion of originals from *Sunflower, Surf's Up,* and *Carl and the Passions.* Most often the only car and surf songs they would play would come in the encores, usually accompanied by one of Mike's wry jokes about "oldies but moldies." *The Beach Boys in Concert* album from 1973 (drawn from shows in 1972 and 1973) captured the band at its early '70s peak, finding connections between the new and the old ("Sail On, Sailor" into "Sloop John B."), showcasing Brian's most challenging *Pet Sounds* vocal arrangements ("You Still Believe in Me"), transforming old album tracks into standouts (Carl's gospel-like take on "Let the Wind Blow"), and injecting the encores ("Surfin' USA," "Fun, Fun, Fun") with a rollicking energy that edged toward the anarchic.

Back at the Fillmore East, the oldies earned as many hoots as cheers. But once *American Graffiti* became a hit, the older songs began to spur near-hysterical ovations. As the concert hall crowds that once greeted "Surf's Up" with standing ovations swelled into arena-size crowds, the enthusiasm for the band's more recent songs began to fade. They'd cheer for the surging rhythm of "Sail On, Sailor" and clap along to the countrified stomp of Al Jardine's "California." But when the encores came and "Good Vibrations" led into "I Get Around" or "California Girls," well, that was an invitation to pandemonium.

Picking up on the new surge of interest building around the band that had once been their most popular domestic product line, the executives at Capitol began to wonder if they were missing something important. Almost the entire Beach Boys catalogue had been out of print since the group left the label in 1969, and as the surge of *American Graffiti* mania spurred demand for the Beach Boys' early hits, it was obvious this would have to change. Drawing on the pre–*Pet Sounds* albums they still owned, the Capitol execs pulled together a twenty-song, double-album retrospective that featured the group's biggest hits ("Surfin' Safari" to "California Girls") and a handful of standout album tracks ("Let Him Run Wild," "Girl, Don't Tell Me") before ending with "All Summer Long." And if the label couldn't be bothered to find the right versions of "Rhonda" (they used the harmonica-led *Beach Boys Today* version rather than the more energetic hit single arrangement) and "Be True to Your School" (again, they overlooked the familiar single arrangement for the more static album cut), and even if they substituted their own phony stereo mixes over Brian's original mono, the Capitol execs made a few brilliant moves when it came to packaging. Listening to a canny suggestion from Mike, they rejected a predictable *Greatest Hits of the Beach Boys* title for the more evocative *Endless Summer.*

Even more crucial was the gatefold cover that included not a single photo of the band. Instead, the entire expanse was taken up with a colorful, cartoonlike painting that presented the Beach Boys as six long-haired, mostly bearded heads set in scenes at a lushly overgrown beach. Two seem to hover in the midst of a distant wave; another peers through the vegetation. The only one who seems to have a body wears a straw boater hat and sells balloons near a hot dog stand. Another reads a dog-eared copy of the comic book *Sgt. Rock;* and the last guy, blond, sun-kissed, and reminiscent of Dennis, gazes out through the racing stripes of a surfboard jabbed into the sand. Their individual features all but unrecognizable, the heads are impassive, less like pop stars than coastline oracles.

Unencumbered by any visual signifiers, the music on *Endless Summer* broke free of its early '60s trappings. For youngsters who hadn't heard it before, the spell it wove proved unexpectedly stirring. Divided into four vaguely thematic sides (side one is set on the beach; side two starts at school then zooms off onto the highway until the start of side three, when the album settles into a double-sided collection of ballads to girls real and imagined that ends with "All Summer Long"), the twenty songs contained none of the anger or irony that had dominated popular music ever since "Like a Rolling Stone" blasted across the mid-1960s. *Endless Summer,* on the other hand, presented starkly emotional tales of hope, risk, and loss, sung in plain language by young men whose clear, sweet voices were entirely free of cynicism or affect. *"Be true to your school, now/ And let your colors fly!"* they sang, exhibiting such belief in the American community that it seemed to come from an entirely different planet than virtually every rock 'n' roll song recorded since 1965. Consider, for instance, the striking contrast between "Be True to Your School" and Crosby, Stills, Nash, and Young's "Almost Cut My Hair," in which David Crosby declared that even in the midst of Nixon-era repression, he was going to let his "freak flag" flutter proudly in the breeze.

This sort of antiestablishment stance was a central part of the youth culture catechism in the early '70s, picking up even more momentum as Nixon's administration crumbled beneath the weight of its own desperate lawlessness in 1973 and 1974. And though a growing percentage of the population had come to yearn for the President's impeachment and conviction for his role in the Watergate break-in and subsequent cover-up schemes, such large-scale bitterness proved ultimately exhausting. Americans may not be fools all of the time, as Abe Lincoln pointed out, but even wised-up citizens yearn to feel good about their country and its leaders. That was hard to come by in the inflation-squeezed, war-blasted, gas-panicked, president-loathing early '70s, a fact that almost certainly enhanced the sound of those decade-old Beach Boys hits.

Released on June 24, *Endless Summer* climbed quickly into *Billboard*'s Top Ten, where it stayed throughout the summer. Two months after Nixon resigned the presidency, the album hit *Billboard*'s number one spot. It would stay on the charts for an astonishing 155 weeks, selling more than 3,000,000 copies, catapulting the Beach Boys from their summer spot as openers on the Crosby, Stills,

Nash, and Young reunion tour to selling out basketball arenas as headliners. *Rolling Stone* made the group's comeback official by declaring the Beach Boys 1974's Band of the Year, which was particularly striking given that they hadn't released any new music during the previous twelve months. But it was the power of their live shows that elevated the Beach Boys above the rest of the American rock 'n' roll scene. Even if their songs weren't new (by the end of 1974 the pre–*Pet Sounds* songs would take up half of their set, and the balance would continue to shift in the oldies' favor as the months went on), even if their vocabulary was tied to a consumerist lifestyle that struck some as archaic or even regressive, the spirit at their core—that mosaic of fear, hope, and ambition—was timeless.

Endless Summer was just the beginning. In 1975, the Beach Boys climbed back to the fore of the concert circuit, pushed ever higher by the success of *Spirit of America,* a second Capitol retrospective that climbed into *Billboard*'s Top Ten that summer, shadowed by the year-old *Endless Summer,* which bounced back into the Top Twenty for a summer-long stay. Warner's tried to get in on the action with *The Good Vibrations Best of the Beach Boys,* a single-disc collection of the group's most popular late '60s and early '70s singles. But the commercial dominance of the band's early '60s catalogue put the group's current label in an awkward position. They'd invested so much time and energy into rebuilding the Beach Boys into a hot-selling rock band, and that's precisely what they had become . . . for Capitol.

Unsurprisingly, Warner Brothers wanted some new product from their suddenly white-hot band, preferably from the hand of Brian Wilson. Unfortunately, the band was in turmoil again. Blondie Chaplin had left a year earlier, pushed out when he ran afoul of the group's business manager, Steve Love (Mike's brother, who joined the organization full-time after earning an MBA from the University of Southern California in 1971). Ricky Fataar stuck around for another year, but left in the fall of 1974, when he was offered a chance to join a new group being formed by Joe Walsh. On the plus side, the group had developed a relationship with James William Guercio, a musician-turned-manager who had steered the jazz-rock group Chicago to the top of the music industry, while also producing the group's multiplatinum albums. Guercio was a huge Beach Boys fan, and when Dennis told him the group needed a bass player to replace Blondie onstage, he packed up his instrument and hit the road eagerly. Soon Guercio began to advise the group on career decisions, proving so smart and sensible that they tapped him to be their new manager. When the group ended their summer tour in September 1974, Guercio sent them up to his Caribou Ranch studios nestled in the mountains of Nederland, Colorado.

Not much came of the sessions. While every member had been writing new songs, they all came expecting to focus on whatever music Brian had to offer, and what he had was, at best, quirky. Many sessions were devoted to his re-envisioning of the inspirational Civil War hymn "The Battle Hymn of the Republic." But Brian's arrangement of the song, which included electric guitar, drums, chirping synthesizers, and a rudimentary banjo line, was set at such a breakneck pace that Mike could barely spit the words out fast enough to keep up, let alone draw out the real emotion in the piece. The group had far more fun jamming on an early version of Brian's "Ding Dang," which in this rendition was a funky rock 'n' roll song with blazing guitar from Carl, in-the-pocket drums from Dennis, and full group vocals chanting a rudimentary but instantly memorable chorus of: *"Alley-oop—fuck her! Big tits!"*

The group also put down basic tracks for Dennis's lovely environmental ballad "River Song" (which would appear later on his 1977 solo album) and a song of Mike's called "Our Life, Our Love, Our Land." But the sessions fell apart after a couple of weeks, and the group went back to Los Angeles hoping Brian might feel more comfortable and willing to work in his usual stomping grounds. They tried again a month later, working this time in the group's new recording studio (Marilyn had finally put her foot down and reclaimed the Bellagio studio as family territory) on Fifth Street in Santa Monica. Here, more time was spent on the doomed "Battle Hymn" before Brian turned his attention to an original (and somewhat odd) Christmas song he'd written with Steve Kalinich called "Child of Winter," which came out sounding like a shorter, holiday-themed version of "Mt. Vernon and Fairway." Brian hoped to get "Child" out as a single for the holidays, but by the time Warner's actually got the record out into stores, Christmas was only a week away and the season of holiday cheer was essentially finished, as was the song's commercial potential. A Beach Boys take on "Here Comes Santa Claus" stayed in the can, while attempts at Brian's other new originals, a ballad he'd written with Carl called "Good Timin' " and a summery rocker Mike had written lyrics for called "It's OK," were tentative at best.

The tapes went back on the shelf and the group went back on the road, opening its 1975 schedule with a sold-out show at New York City's Madison Square Garden. They spent the rest of the winter and spring playing increasingly oldies-focused shows in the nation's basketball arenas and college football stadiums, then in May set out on a much-hyped twelve-city tour as coheadliner with Chicago. The so-called "Beachago" shows were particularly successful, thanks in part to the fact that the bands actually collaborated onstage, with the Chicago members adding punch (and horns) to "Darlin'," "California Girls," "Fun, Fun, Fun," and "Surf's Up" while the Beach Boys added vocals to "Feelin' Stronger Every Day," "Saturday in the Park," and "Wishing You Were Here" (the last of which had featured Carl, Dennis, and Al on its recorded version).

Though Chicago had been the nation's most popular rock band for most of the decade, most critics agreed that the Beach Boys' litany of decade-old hits blew the younger band off the stage. "There was an outpouring of emotion from the audience that surprised even the most regular attendees of Capitol Center concerts," the rock critic for the *Washington Post* wrote after a show in D.C. "There was a feeling in the air, pure, innocent, and without the false hipness that is standard at most rock shows, and even the Beach Boys themselves were amazed." The feeling followed the group across the Atlantic Ocean when they played at a daylong concert at Wembley Stadium headlined by the world's then-reigning king of rock 'n' roll, Elton John. "Unfortunately for Elton . . . the Beach Boys had stolen the show hours beforehand as they played their marvelous surfing songs under the blazing sunshine," according to *Melody Maker* magazine.

On the road, they were scaling peaks of public and critical acclaim that had seemed beyond reach even when their songs were brand-new. But if the Beach Boys were expecting to find their leader at home with a whole new collection of classics ready to record, they were in for a grim surprise. Because even as his old songs were bringing that old utopian spirit to a new generation of fans, Brian had gone farther down the rabbit hole. He gave up on regular bathing and grew his fingernails until they curved from his hands like talons. The hair he'd once kept immaculately styled became a greasy veil that hung to his shoulders. He smoked constantly and ate with a ravenous appetite that made his weight balloon more than 100 pounds in less than two years. As Carnie remembers, her father began most of his days with a dozen eggs and an entire loaf of bread. And to watch Brian eat his dinner was to see a man trying desperately to fill an internal void that must have felt bottomless. "He'd take his fork to his salad and he'd be like—bang! bang! bang!—spearing up as much as he could at one time," Carnie recalls. "Then he'd shove the whole thing into his mouth, close his eyes, and chew so fast, so intensely, he'd grab the table and grip it when he chewed. He'd

CATCH A WAVE

eat his entire steak in like two bites. And he'd be done and at the piano by the time the rest of us sat down to eat."

When he rolled out of bed in the afternoon or early evening, Brian would make a beeline to his jukebox and punch up "Be My Baby," listening to the song—or sometimes just the first verse and chorus—over and over again, as if he could absorb some vital energy from the sound of its thundering echo. When he tired of that, he'd settle at the piano to play another in his endless renditions of "Rhapsody in Blue" or the boogie-woogie piano riff from "Ding Dang." When he could no longer sit still, Brian might spend hours wandering aimlessly around the house, entering and leaving each room as if he were searching for something so important he couldn't bring himself to speak its name. There were days he'd spend alone in his new bedroom—far from the rest of the family in the chauffeur's quarters above the garage—listening to the radio and obliterating his thoughts with whatever combination of cocaine, speed, and pot he had stashed away. Back at the piano, he'd start playing the same songs again, and if Carnie or Wendy happened to sit down to listen, Brian would beg for a back rub. "I'll pay ya a nickel if you scratch my back!" he'd plead. "He just loved to be touched," Carnie says.

Marilyn, a young mother still in her midtwenties, would try to make her daughters understand why their father was so different from the dads they met at their friends' houses. "Mom would say, 'Your father's not like other dads. He'll never be able to be a father like your friends have. But he has this gift, and no one will ever be able to take that away.'"

At some point in 1974 he worked with Stephen Kalinich to write "California Feelin'," a lyrical paean to the beauty of the state's coastline. Melodic and yearning, the song seemed a perfect fit for the Beach Boys, and Brian even got Marilyn to drive him down to Western Studios to record a demo with his old engineer, Chuck Britz, manning the board. Brian threw himself into his performance, too, his voice soaring and falling through the octaves with all the power and grace he could muster. But near the end of the tune, Brian started goofing on the lyric, taking on the cheesy, overexcited croon of a Vegas balladeer. As the song thundered to a bogus, self-mocking climax, Brian jumped up from the piano and called out one last instruction to Britz: "Toss that one, Chuck." And then he was gone again.

Brian felt less constrained when it came to projects he knew would have nothing to do with the Beach Boys. In the first months of 1975, he signed a deal with

Equinox Records—run by Terry Melcher and ex–Beach Boy Bruce Johnston—to produce singles for the start-up label. Brian worked with Melcher to coproduce, play, and sing background vocals on covers of "Why Do Fools Fall in Love" (the Frankie Lymon and the Teenagers tune he had first covered for the Beach Boys in the early '60s) and "Jamaica Farewell," both of which were credited to the band California Music, a loose-knit group that included Melcher, Johnston, Gary Usher, Curt Becher, and a few other members of L.A.'s music scene. But the songs went nowhere, and when the Beach Boys got wind of Brian's solo project and the stream of cash it provided for his increasingly troublesome drug habit, they put an end to the deal. "Marilyn had me come in as the heavy," Stephen Love remembers. "We were under contract to Warner Brothers, and we couldn't have him going out on a tangent. If he was going to be productive, it's gotta be for the Beach Boys." But, Stephen continues, Brian was dead set against doing that. "He said to me, 'Don't try to reach me! Don't try to get to me!' He was so upset Marilyn didn't want [the Equinox deal] to happen."

Later that spring Brian got a call from Johnny Rivers, who told him he was putting the finishing touches on a cover of "Help Me, Rhonda." Would Brian like to come down to the studio and record the falsetto part of the background vocals? Brian came down the next night, Marilyn in tow, put the headphones on his ears, and knocked out the sky-high part in a single take, just like he'd done ten years earlier.

But such bursts of activity were marked exceptions as he grew almost will-fully detached from reality. By the fall of 1975, Brian's intake of food, alcohol, cigarettes, and drugs—now including occasional flirtations with heroin—had grown so frenzied that Marilyn began to talk openly about either divorcing him, putting him into a mental institution, or both. Meanwhile, the other Beach Boys had started to question the group's practice of giving Brian a full share of their touring income. After all, they had reached that deal back in 1965, when Brian was still writing and producing music for the group full-time. As of late 1975, it had been more than three years since he had made a serious attempt to record anything for the band. Why should they cut him in on such a large por-tion of their annual income when their onetime producer and visionary was spending all of his time—and their money—snorting coke and eating steaks at home? Rousing himself from his fog, Brian responded angrily to the band's threat when Stephen Love brought the news up to the Bellagio house. "[Brian] said, 'Well, don't play my songs then!' But anyone can play anything, as long as they pay the performance fees, so that wasn't gonna happen." The deeper motivation, Stephen continues, was really to get the group's erstwhile leader to get back to work. "If you've got a lot of dough rolling in and you just want to hang out, why change anything? He needed to be dislodged from his comfortable place. And Brian has a very precise inner sense of how much money he has."

To help guide Brian's transition back to the land of the living, Stephen appointed his brother Stanley—then at the end of a five-year career as a journeyman forward in the National Basketball Association—to serve as a full-time bodyguard, assistant, and minder. Stanley's first task, he recalls, was to sweep the property for Brian's drug stashes, particularly the daily drop-off made by a service-oriented dealer who used the family's curbside mailbox. Slowly gaining his charge's trust, Stanley worked to reacclimate him to day-to-day life, convincing Brian to bathe regularly, wear clothes during the day, cut back on his many indulgences, and even get some exercise.

At first, however, Brian refused to even consider the prospect of getting back to work with the Beach Boys. That changed when Marilyn called in the band's lawyers and accountants to explain the obligations he had taken on with the Warner Brothers contract and to make sure he understood that if he didn't get back to work writing and/or producing 70 percent of the Beach Boys' product, the label would sue him and take his house. Marilyn would leave with the girls, and he'd be out on the street, alone and hungry. Brian, she knew, hated to even think about the prospect of being homeless and hungry, but they'd keep on yelling at him, beating Brian down until he lay curled in the fetal position.

Other times he'd try to get away, literally crawling out of the room in an attempt to escape his tormentors. "They thought the tough treatment would scare him, that they could hammer him into shape. What they didn't realize was that he didn't like them anymore," Stanley says. "He'd write letters saying, 'Don't talk to me anymore. I'm withdrawing from the Beach Boys.' But they wouldn't pay attention and would just keep coming back."

Eventually Brian began to resign himself to the inevitable. "He decided to not fight it," Stanley says. "I talked him into having a sports mentality: This is what I do, this is the situation, so I'm going to fight my way through this and be a real competitor."

Called back into the NBA by the Atlanta Hawks that fall, Stanley left the Wilson house just in time to make room for the next stage in Brian's return to civilization. Hearing of a psychologist named Eugene Landy who specialized in treating the lifestyle dysfunctions of powerful showbiz personalities, Marilyn made an appointment and told him all about her problems with Brian. How could he seem so crazy and yet snap so suddenly into clear-eyed sanity? Why wouldn't he conform to anything like traditional social mores? And how could she stop him from eating, drinking, and drugging himself to death? Landy, a thin-faced man with long sideburns and thick-thatched hair, smiled and nodded. He'd heard all this before. "Right, I've treated a tremendous number of people in show business," he confirmed to *Rolling Stone*'s David Felton a few months later. (He specifically mentioned the notoriously boozy actor Richard Harris and had also been credited with treating the likes of Alice Cooper, Rod Steiger, and Gig Young.)

"For some reason I seem to be able to relate to them," Landy told Felton. "I think I have a nice reputation that says I'm unorthodox by orthodox standards, but basically unique by unorthodox standards." Felton pulled his string again, proposing to Landy that he was "a pretty heavy-duty Hollywood shrink." Again, Landy agreed, with maximum glee: "I'm outrageously expensive."

And all the more so when it came to Brian, who, Landy decreed, would require round-the-clock therapy for at least two years. The team of therapists—which included a psychiatrist, a physician, a nutritionist, and strong-armed minders—would help Brian become a resocialized, detoxified, superproductive artist and citizen. Better still, Landy could do all of it without ever acknowledging anything like serious psychiatric problems.

His initial diagnosis of paranoid schizophrenia had proven all wrong, Landy told *Rolling Stone*. "Brian was suffering from being scared," he said. "He was not able to deal with frightened, or even have a response to frightened, and therefore lived in the area of fantasy . . . He's in the process of returning from fantasy every day more and more."

It was an odd diagnosis, but not nearly as curious as the fact that licensed practitioner Landy was discussing it, along with many other intimate aspects of Brian's internal life, in the pages of a national magazine. But Landy, born in Pittsburgh, Pennsylvania, in 1934, had always been an eager promoter. Still unable to read when he dropped out of school in the sixth grade, he'd been hustling since before he'd started to shave. From there his autobiography, as described to various writers over the years, seems like a combination of Horatio Alger, Carl Jung, and Alan Freed, featuring stints in local radio, the music business, the movie industry, and then as the personal manager to a school-aged jazz guitarist named George Benson.

In the '60s he turned his attention to federal do-good agencies such as the Peace Corps, VISTA, and the Job Corps before enrolling in Los Angeles State College, from which he graduated in 1964 with a degree in psychology. Landy collected a master's degree and a PhD from the University of Oklahoma and then moved back to California in the early '70s and set up a practice that specialized in treating young people. He published a book, *The Underground Dictionary,* that helped straights to identify and understand hippie slang such as "kick stick" (marijuana joint) and "split beaver" (use your imagination). By the mid-1970s, the hustler-turned-psychologist had discovered an excellent way to combine his professional interests by focusing his practice on the treatment of Hollywood's most disconsolate stars and emperors, particularly those whose wealth and power invited the use of vast quantities of mood-altering substances.

"When I first met Dr. Landy, I knew I'd met someone who could play Brian's game," Marilyn told *Rolling Stone.* Landy's first step was to introduce himself into his patient's imagination, making regular visits to the Bellagio house to speak with Marilyn behind closed doors. Brian grew curious about his wife's visitor and eventually demanded to speak with Landy himself, declaring, "Something's wrong with me. I need help." From that point Landy moved his team in and took control of Brian's life. Friends known to use drugs were told to keep their distance. Brian was placed on a strict diet (Landy padlocked the family's refrigerator to keep him honest) and marched off for a daily regimen of jogging and weight lifting. Brian also had to satisfy requirements for songwriting and, eventually, recording. If Brian even thought about balking at these decrees, Landy would swoop in quickly to lay down the law. When Brian didn't want to get out of bed, Landy would drench him with water. When he claimed to be too nauseous to stay at a dinner party, Landy would command him to vomit on[to] the table. "I had to be crazier than Brian," Landy liked to say.

As the new year began, Landy's scheme seemed to be working. Brian got back into the habit of climbing out of bed in the morning, and once the effects of dieting and exercise began to manifest themselves, he showed real pride in his progress. When sessions for a new Beach Boys album began in early January, he not only showed up in the studio but also agreed to run the sessions, some of which included the same ace musicians he used on the Beach Boys' classic records from the mid-1960s. At first the plan was to record an album's worth of cover songs— '50s classics, mostly—to give Brian a chance to get his sea legs back. Once that was done, he'd move quickly into an album of new originals and, as the other

Beach Boys would tell the world repeatedly, "really stretch out and blow some minds."

By the summer of 1976, the news would be everywhere: in the pages of *Time* and *Newsweek*, on the covers of *People*, *Rolling Stone*, *Crawdaddy*, and *New West*, all over the arts sections of the *New York Times*, the *Los Angeles Times*, and every major newspaper in between. The idea that won their attention, summarized so deftly by Stephen Love as he dreamed up the PR campaign that winter, came down to one three-word headline: Brian Is Back.

CHAPTER 12

I t was the afternoon of December 18, 1976, and the Beach Boys were in Seattle, poised to play the second of two sold-out shows at the 12,000-seat Seattle Center Coliseum. Coming at the end of a year in which they had appeared in all of the leading national magazines, starred in their own network TV special, and seen their new album and single soar immediately to the upper reaches of the *Billboard* charts, the group's Seattle shows had touched off a small furor around the misty shores of Puget Sound. Then one day a news flash on the radio upped the voltage even more: "Great news for Beach Boys fans!" a KJR-AM disc jockey cried out. "Word from L.A. is that Brian Wilson will be appearing with the band when they come to town next week!"

If you happened to be in eighth grade that year, if you had dug *Endless Summer* enough to pick up a magazine or two that featured the Beach Boys on the cover, and if what you had read about the brilliant, troubled life of Brian Wilson had touched something profound in your own adolescent consciousness, the prospect of seeing it all come together right in front of you was almost too exciting to endure.

When the day finally arrived, overcast and damp as per usual in the Pacific Northwest during the holidays, my friend Tommy and I ditched sixth period together and hopped a bus for downtown. Once the bus crested Capitol Hill and shifted down for its descent into the city, we became silly with glee.

"I bet we go backstage. I bet you get to talk to Brian," Tommy said. Then he thought some more, no doubt considering the hours he'd spent playing his own set of just-purchased drums along with his copy of *Endless Summer,* imagining himself as the muscular, roguish, sandy-haired guy who held down the backbeat on the songs.

"I bet we meet Dennis."

All of which would be way too dumb to remember, let alone include in these pages, were it not for what happened less than five minutes after Tommy uttered those starstruck words. Because when the bus pulled into its stop on the corner of Fifth Avenue and Pine Street, and when we jumped down the stairs and began our walk to the monorail that would carry us directly to the Seattle Center, nearly the first person we saw strolling down the sidewalk in our direction was, in fact, Dennis Wilson.

"Peter, ohmigod, look!"

Tommy saw him first, snatching my arm and hissing into my ear. I assumed he was bullshitting me—turning his teenybopper fantasy into a practical joke—until I looked up and saw him for myself: the shoulder-length brown hair, the full beard, the sun-weathered cheeks. He wore one of those wraparound Mexican sweaters over a pair of jeans, and he had one woolly arm draped over the shoulder of a petite blonde I recognized from the magazines as Karen Lamm, his new, ex-model wife.

"Holy shit. What do we do?"

"Fuck if I know."

Well, I knew. Even as Tommy shrank back into the crowd (struck by a case of adolescent nerves he would regret from that moment on), I walked up to the guy, and in a voice squeezed about an octave above its normal pitch, I spoke to him.

"You're not, uh, Dennis Wilson . . . are you?"

"Yup."

He cocked an eyebrow in my direction while Karen Lamm looked down and smiled proudly, seeing what had to be a familiar sidewalk scene playing out one more time.

"Wow. Wow. I'm, uh, I'm going to the show tonight!"

"Hey, right on. I hope you have a good time."

I handed him my ticket envelope and the stub of a pencil, which he used to scrawl a signature. He gave them back, then held out his hand for a farewell shake. At which point the passage of time slowed; the ambient noise of cars, buses, and jackhammers faded; and I entered a Zen moment of adulation. With that gesture Dennis was literally pulling me into a live version of the Beach Boys fantasy I had concocted in my adolescent mind. Sex, adventure, friendship, sensitivity, and rock 'n' roll . . . that's what I heard in those songs, that's what I wanted to make my own someday. As Dennis let go of my hand, rested his other hand on the shoulder of his achingly beautiful wife, and ambled off around the corner, I knew it was all real.

Later that night when the lights dimmed and the five Beach Boys stood before us on a stage decorated with palm trees and a life-size sailboat, the opening bars of "Wouldn't It Be Nice" spurred an ovation that seemed to shake the Coliseum's concrete floor. People danced and screamed, their fingertips raking the smoky air. The band—Brian in a silk, body-length bathrobe; Carl in a white jumpsuit; Mike shirtless beneath a spangled gold vest; Al looking casual in white pants, blazer, and slouch cap; Dennis sitting behind a set of clear plastic drums—played two ecstatic sets, mixing a small handful of newer songs like "Feel Flows," "Sail On, Sailor," and "All This Is That" with a grand array of hits that sounded just as fresh and fun as they did on *Endless Summer*. It all sounded so beautiful I barely noticed how stiffly Brian sat at his piano and how awkwardly he stalked to center stage to take a bow. I had no way of knowing that the joyous music they made, even the gorgeous harmony that came when they leaned into their microphones and sang, described a vision of life they were in the process of abandoning and that soon even the memories would mean nothing to them.

———

In the fall of 1975, Stephen Love, who had recently replaced James Guercio as the group's manager, had concluded that the group had no choice: They had to get Brian back to work. Almost three years had passed since *Holland* had been released, and in that time the blockbuster sales of *Endless Summer* and its follow-up, *Spirit of America,* had only increased the pressure coming from Warner Brothers. The Beach Boys needed a new album soon, and it had to be good. More accurately, it had to be great, and everyone knew where great Beach Boys songs came from. Unfortunately, they also knew that the most vital man in their operation wanted nothing more than to be free of it as soon as possible and forever. Obviously, that would never do.

"Brian wanted to be left alone, but there was too much at stake," Stephen Love says. "If you've got an oil well, you don't want it to wander off and become someone else's oil well. There was always this sense that Brian could hit another home run, and so [the other Beach Boys] wanted to keep him on their team. They had a large appetite for what might be."

As Stephen knew, the other Beach Boys and the staff of Warner Brothers records weren't the only people craving new Beach Boys songs from Brian Wilson. All of those newly minted fans were surely eager to hear what truly modern Beach Boys music would sound like. Then there were the executives from the nation's other entertainment companies, all of whom had noted the success of *Endless Summer,* knowing full well that the group's deal with Warner Brothers would soon expire. So, Stephen Love decreed, the Beach Boys would indeed get their resident genius back in the driver's seat, and once he was there, they would throw open the studio doors and tell everyone who would listen that he was there. "The 'Brian Is Back!' idea was the perfect hook to get a new record contract," Stephen Love says. "Maybe it would have been more accurate to say, 'We think and hope Brian's on his way back!' But that's not gonna cut it for a professional [media] campaign."

It was, however, certainly more accurate, because once the tracksuit-clad, stringy-haired, thickly bearded Brian tiptoed back into the studio and sheepishly counted off the intro to his new arrangement of Fats Domino's "Blueberry Hill," it became quickly apparent that something had changed. The man who once had the most precise ear in all of the hottest recording studios in Hollywood no longer had the energy or desire to get anything right. "They were the fastest sessions ever," recalls Earle Mankey, the engineer who ran the board at most of the dates at Brother Studios. "The room would be full of musicians, all the old guys from the past, and there would be some acoustic basses and open mikes. I can listen back into the mix now and hear guys talking to each other and tuning up on the takes that ended up on the records. But at the end of the song Brian would say, 'That sounded great, guys!' and head for the door." A large part of the problem, Mankey continues, was that Brian was still terrified to be around people he didn't know. "He was scared to come into the studio, scared to talk to people. I don't think he was scared during the sessions—that might have been the most comfortable part of it, since he was so familiar with that process. I had the sense that Brian would have liked to have been into it. But he was too scared."

And once Brian felt comfortable enough with Mankey to sit and shoot the breeze for a while, the things the red-eyed, blank-faced musician said didn't bode well for his supposed return to glory. "He kept saying, 'Where's the fire? There's just no fire anymore. I can't get the fire to do this stuff!' It didn't matter to him anymore. He just didn't have the desire to get it done."

Obviously, the motivations that had kick-started Brian's therapy—getting him back to work ASAP—and his actual therapeutic needs were at cross purposes. What he needed was the time and space to recognize and confront the profound psychological problems that had afflicted him, to varying degrees, since his boyhood. What he got instead was all the creative responsibility he had spent most of a decade trying to avoid, plus the burden of a vast publicity campaign that would lean as heavily on his personal problems as the music itself would upon his talents. And if that wasn't enough to overwhelm his fragile circuits, Brian also had to weather the fairly obvious distrust and resentment of his bandmates. "They really had mixed feelings about [Brian's comeback] because they knew it would frustrate their own designs for their own music," Stephen Love recalls. "But they probably liked it economically, because they knew it was going to get them a bigger record deal."

The first glimmers of the story began to appear that winter, as word leaked that Brian was back in the recording studio producing the new Beach Boys album, or perhaps as many as three. "It's very possible that one will be an all-oldies album. We've wanted to do that for a long time, and Brian's into it," Dennis told Timothy White, then a staffer at *Crawdaddy* magazine. "The other two could take the form of a double album of all-new material that stretches from hard rock 'n' roll to these wordless vocals we've been doing that sound like the Vienna Boys Choir." Dennis went on to describe a dozen or so new originals penned by all the members of the band—his "10,000 Years" and "Rainbow"; Mike's "Glow, Crescent, Glow," "Lisa," and "Everyone's in Love with You"; Al's "Gold Rush"; and Brian's "Ding Dang," "Transcendental Meditation," and, most enticingly, "California Feeling," the ballad he'd written with Stephen Kalinich. It all sounded very ambitious and terribly alluring, and by the time spring began to tilt toward summer, a veritable army of reporters had already marched in, notebooks in hand, to cover the magic and wonder of the fabled Brian Wilson's return to active duty.

What they discovered was a band that was far less unified than they had been led to believe. Dennis and Carl had already been to enough sessions to figure out that Brian wasn't creating music that would stand up to *Holland,* let alone the classic stuff from the '60s. And now that *Endless Summer* had thrust all the old hits back into the public consciousness, how could they put out a record that so obviously wasn't even trying to live up to that standard? "Carl was dragging his feet, saying, 'This is a shitty record. This isn't anywhere near as good as it should be,'" Stephen Love says. "But the hard truth is that you don't have forever to tinker around with this stuff. The pressing demands of business sometimes interfere with artistic indulgence. Business-wise you want to get the goddamn album out when things are gelling. Commerce and art, man, that's a tough thing."

And for the Beach Boys in 1976, it was becoming extremely clear which of those two demands was going to take precedence—they already had the publicity campaign plotted out to the minute. And it all fit together so perfectly! Brian's comeback, the new album, the group's fifteenth anniversary—and the fact that this celebration of America's biggest rock band was taking place precisely as the nation's bicentennial celebration reached its own hysterical climax on July 4 was merely a bonus. By then the album's first single, "Rock 'n' Roll Music," was already flying up the charts toward the top five. The album itself—a fifteen-song set called *15 Big Ones*—was twenty-four hours from being released. NBC had already sent the white-hot creative team behind *Saturday Night Live* (that year's hippest new show) to helm the prime-time special already slated to air in August. An army of writers from virtually all of the nation's leading publications had already marched in, ready to unleash an even bigger publicity binge. Did it even matter that the stories that popped up to promote it weren't quite as cheery as their "Brian Is Back!" headlines?

Apparently not, because virtually every rendition made excellent use of the riptide flowing just beneath the glimmering surface of the Beach Boys' latest wave. "I'm not going out on the road like some broken-down rock star!" Mike had sniffed to *Newsweek,* contrasting his own stage-ready physique with the more humble condition of a certain comeback kid. Dennis and Carl, meanwhile, couldn't stop griping about the slapdash way Brian had gone about recording and compiling the tunes that ended up on the new album. "It was a great mistake to put Brian back in control," Dennis grumbled. "I hated to give [the fans] this." Brian himself proved a less-than-dependable interview, particularly when the subject was his own personal and musical renaissance. That same *Newsweek* story, published the week *15 Big Ones* came out, described his "blank" demeanor and "shaking hands." "We're going to do another 'Good Vibrations' next time. Another masterpiece," he said, by way of optimism.

Seemingly unwilling to get in the way of the redemptive narrative, most critics gave *15 Big Ones* gentle treatment. Even the *Newsweek* piece dropped its gimlet eye long enough to term the album "fascinating . . . [with] a curiously unshakable unity." True enough, Brian's arrangement of "Blueberry Hill" began with an intriguing dual-saxophone figure that built slowly from the first verse into a full arrangement with horns, bells, guitars, percussion, and thundering drums. Brian built a Spectorian roar almost entirely out of synthesizers and other keyboards in a moving cover of the master's "For Once in My Life," while the album's opening track, the hit revision of Chuck Berry's "Rock 'n' Roll Music," used fuzz-heavy guitars, a prominent walking bass line, organ, and dramatic pauses to carve out a distinct, if imperfect, take on a well-worn classic. "A Casual Look" boasted a nice a cappella intro and punchy horns throughout the tune, but that spark of vocal originality was an exception. The group vocals on the rest of the album are most striking for how simple—and sometimes close to inaudible—they are.

Of the original songs on the disc, Brian and Mike's "Had to Phone Ya" featured a full, clarinet-led instrumental arrangement and group harmonies that passed the lead vocal from member to member. The fun-in-the-summertime rocker "It's OK" had the *joie de vivre* and wailing chorus *("Gotta go to it, gotta go through it, gotta get with it")* of a classic car song, while "Back Home" (which had been curing in Brian's woodshed since 1963) had a throbbing bass, bouncing organ riffs, and a spirited vocal from Brian. Even more intriguing was "That Same Song," a whimsical history of world music that came close to sparking the gospel fire it set out to ignite.

But again, the vocals are mixed too low, too sloppily performed, or, in so many cases, arranged in such a slapdash manner that they sound like a bad imitation of Brian's joyous sound. Even more distressing was the tone of Brian's voice. Once the owner of a powerful but tender falsetto that could soar and swoop above even the most thunderous track, Brian now sang in a baritone croak. When the melody pushed him higher, his voice shattered into a squawk that was, as often as not, dismayingly off-pitch. It would have been bad enough from any professional singer, but to hear the man who had once revised the limits of rock 'n' roll harmony sing in that raw-throated croak sounded like a self-immolating gesture.

Brian's first wave of performances felt more like a strange kind of public execution: death by mass adoration. Starting with a vocal-free appearance at a pretour festival stop in Oakland on July 3, he made a more full return at the tour opener in Anaheim two nights later, shuffling to center stage to waggle his fingertips at the fans holding up a hand-lettered "Welcome Back, Brian" banner, then taking a mumbled stab at the solo in the middle of "Surfer Girl." And though his robotic movements and wide-eyed expression broadcast nothing short of barely controlled terror, the performances were heralded as triumphant.

Selections from the Anaheim show served as the centerpiece in the NBC special, which aired August 5 under the title "It's OK." As produced by *Saturday Night Live* creator Lorne Michaels, the hour-long show jumped from stage shots to band interviews to weird production bits designed to reveal something about the members' personalities. Here was Al Jardine at his hillside manse in rustic Big Sur, fending off a hostile goat long enough to describe his rural lifestyle like some kind of latter-day Thoreau ("It's not something everyone can do. Some of us are cut out for it; some of us have to live in cities") between dips in his hot tub and onstage performances of "Help Me, Rhonda." Carl Wilson motored coolly through Beverly Hills in a vintage Mercedes convertible; Dennis Wilson served enthusiastically as a judge at a local beauty contest; Mike Love did loop-de-loops as a passenger in a stunt plane. But mostly it was Brian Wilson: talking about his problems while lying in bed; performing a ragged, humorless "I'm Bugged at My Old Man" with Dennis and Carl on background vocals; looking grim while being feted by family, friends, and Paul McCartney at his own thirty-fourth birthday party. Most famously, Brian was rousted from bed by Dan Aykroyd and John Belushi, playing state cops determined to make the famed nonsurfer ride the waves, even if it meant shoving him into the water in his bathrobe. Brian was bowled over by the force of the waves, sputtering for air and holding onto his surfboard for dear life.

The show was celebrated roundly as a masterstroke for Brian and the group. But all that excitement—the silly skits, the up-close-and-personal confessions, the ecstatic performances of the oldies, et al—only distracted from the hour's one real moment of transcendence, when Brian and the rest of the group performed "That Same Song" with the help of the Baptist Double Rock gospel choir. Standing alone at a microphone placed just behind the pianist, facing up toward the thirty-piece chorus, Brian began his lead vocal as tentatively as ever. But once he hit the first chorus, the choir's voices echoing his own *("I know!—I KNOW!!/It took us a long time to go—TO GO!!/And build us a rock style . . ."),* an electric current seemed to pulse through him. He started to move, punching the air and slapping his hands together on the beat.

"I know—I KNOW!!/That we can take it one more miiiiiiile!"

The smoke was still in his voice, the layers of rust rattling away in his pipes, but he put everything he had into the last word of that line, drawing it out as long and as far as he could before the choir joined him for the final refrain:

"'Cause we're singin' that same song/We're still singing that saaaame soooong . . ."

As the summer moved toward the fall, the group's momentum continued to build. The regular touring band (minus Brian) played another dozen shows at basketball arenas and stadiums, then they all turned up looking tanned, fit, and tight on the cover of *People* magazine in late August ("Still Riding the Crest 15 Hairy Years Later," the article was titled). A few weeks later, *Rolling Stone* weighed in with another cover profile, this one focused almost entirely on Brian's resurgence. But while the cover of the magazine (which showed Brian on the beach the day he taped his surfing bit for NBC, wearing a blue bathrobe, a yellow surfboard tucked beneath his left arm) carried the hopeful title "The Healing of Brother Brian," the story by David Felton sank even deeper into the weird truth beneath the public relations campaign. The guys sat together for the story, cracking each other up. ("I'm Dennis, and I'm the cute one!") Brian spoke at length about his past work and his ambition for the future, then played some new compositions that left Felton swooning. "It just grabs you and follows you around like a little angel. It makes you feel good and gives you hope," he wrote of the love song Brian called "Marilyn Rovell."

But Landy and his army of minders scuttled through Felton's story, not just dictating Brian's activities and correcting his behavior, but also doing it in the most humiliating ways imaginable. ("This is embarrassing to me. I just feel brought down," Brian admitted in a rare private moment.) Brian spoke happily about the progress he'd made in the past year—he had lost quite a bit of weight, had a stylish new wardrobe and haircut, and was, it seemed, pleased to be up and around. But he also tended to act out—for instance, quizzing Felton in mid-interview about his ability to score cocaine or speed. "Do you have any at home? Do you know where you could get some?" he asked, and his query ended up in the pages of *Rolling Stone*. When the writer proposed that even making such a request would seem to defeat the purpose of his therapy, Brian shrugged amiably. "You just saw my weakness coming through," he said. Also his passive-aggressive response to Landy's bullying.

Still, as much as Brian resented Landy's relentless control over his life, being forced to answer to an aggressive, demanding authority figure also felt familiar and, as much as he might have hated to admit it, comfortable. Just like Murry had once done, Landy gave Brian boundaries and expectations. Now he had no choice but to get up in the morning, pull on some shorts and running shoes, and then drag his ass around the UCLA track for a half hour or so. After that his bodyguard would drive him home, where a nutritious breakfast was already waiting. Then came the shower, a fresh change of clothes, and the quick march over to the piano, where Landy or one of his minions made sure he fingered the keys and at least tried to pound out a new song or two before lunch. And no matter how tired or bored or anxious he felt, Brian was absolutely required to go to the recording studio, because the time was already booked. "He'd come in and say, 'Well, I've got to be here for the next couple of hours. What can I do?'" Earle Mankey remembers. "But that was the only way he'd get his dinner." And, surprisingly enough, Landy didn't hesitate to use his patient's ongoing appetite for drugs as a motivator, too. "He was also allowed to smoke one joint a day if he did his work," Mankey says.

Trish Campo (formerly Trish Roach), then Brother Studios' chief administrator, recalls Landy using less pleasant motivational methods. "He used to go out of his way to embarrass Brian. I remember he had a young kid working for him, and I remember seeing him standing over Brian with a fucking baseball bat, like if you don't knuckle down and do what we want, I'm gonna hit you with the bat." Was this really a recipe for creative inspiration? One afternoon that summer Campo looked into the studio and saw Brian at the piano gazing vacantly up at a decorative stained glass window that had planets and stars on it. Later that afternoon Campo heard a new song coming out of the studio: *What do the planets mean?/And have you ever seen/Sunrise in the mornin', it shined when you were born . . ."*

That song became "Solar System," and like most of the songs he produced that summer and fall, Brian created it almost entirely on his own, writing all of the music and words and playing almost all of the instruments—keyboards, synthesizers, and even the drums—himself. And though many of the new songs began as make-work tunes that sprang from his most familiar musical and lyrical touchstones, most of them ended up pirouetting through his quirky palette of melodic, harmonic, and structural tricks. Even if he started off writing simple me/you love songs set in classrooms, cars, and throbbing hearts, the years had warped his perspective in fascinating ways. "It's a frighteningly accurate album," says Earle Mankey, who engineered the sessions. "It may have sounded like a lighthearted album. But that's a serious, autobiographical album: Brian Wilson giving what he had. Sort of like *Eraserhead*."

To be fair, Brian's internal world wasn't anywhere near as horrifying as David Lynch's monstrous nightmare about sex and procreation. But the songs that made up the album he planned to call *Brian Loves You* (eventually retitled *The Beach Boys Love You,* though it was essentially a solo album with contributions from Carl, Dennis, and to a lesser extent, Mike and Al) projected a vision of life that was just as distorted and unsettling as the view from a fun house mirror.

The hard-rocking opening cut, "Let Us Go On This Way," kicked off the album with one of those tortured cries of joy that could only come in a love song by Brian Wilson: *"To get you babe, I went through the wringer/Ain't gonna let you slip through my fingers . . ."* From there the lyrics sketched a first-person tale of adolescent love—*"God please let us go on this way,"* the chorus pleaded—but the cracked harmonies behind Carl's forceful lead, particularly Brian's wavering falsetto, implied something far less innocent. That mood was only expanded in "Roller Skating Child," which pursued the same themes, only with a grown-up perspective that made it sound like a kind of musical interpretation of Vladimir Nabokov's novel *Lolita,* complete with vivid descriptions of adolescent sexuality (the ribbons in her hair, her devious wink, her preternatural facility on skates), careless parenting *("Her folks let me stay with her 'til late at night"),* and the lust-fueled escape that sounded so much like Humbert Humbert's scheme you can almost imagine him singing with Mike's voice. That these songs could only come from the imagination of Brian Wilson became clear with "Mona," a traditional, four-chord '50s-style love song whose grade school rhymes (movie/groovy, etc.) turned into a tutorial about Brian's favorite songs: *"Come on, listen to "Da Do Ron Ron now/Listen to 'Be My Baby'/I know you're gonna love Phil Spector . . ."*

Brian came up with a much more interesting musical track for "Johnny Carson," which transformed the album's standard instrumentation (organ, piano, synthesizer, and simple drums) into the relentless noise of industry—gears turning, belts spinning, steam hissing. Meanwhile, the lyrics elevated the then-reigning king of late-night TV into an icon of male strength, resilience, and charm. All of which was extremely strange, of course, and became stranger still in the refrain, which picked up speed as it shifted to a minor chord that emphasized the struggle behind the Carsonesque lines that followed: *"It's nice to have you on the show tonight/I've seen your act in Vegas—outtasight!"* The second refrain practically cried out with admiration: *"Don't you think he's such a natural guy?/The way he's kept it up could make you cry!"*

Musically inventive, instantly hummable, emotionally vivid, and well past the point that separates the normal from the freakishly bizarre, "Johnny Carson" served as the pivot point for the entire album. From there it just got weirder, starting with the nursery-rhyme erotica of the *Sunflower* outtake "Good Time" (*"My girlfriend Penny, she's kinda skinny/So she needs her falsies on . . ."*) and picking up speed with "Honkin' Down the Highway" (which anticipated a parentally instigated assignation the singer promises will end with him *"Takin' one little inch at a time, now!'Til we're feelin' fine, now . . ."*).

"Solar System" was a celestial variation on "California Girls" (*"Venus the Goddess of love/Thank all the stars above!"*), only with a fractured lead vocal (Brian again) that emphasized its core daffiness. "I'll Bet He's Nice" and "The Night Was So Young" reveled in traditional shades of self-pity, jealousy, and loneliness, but they were only brief diversions on the way to "Let's Put Our Hearts Together," a melodically tricky duet between a hoarse Brian and stiff Marilyn in which the lovers expressed dim-witted insecurities (He: *"I don't want to tell you that I care for you and have you just ignore me . . ."*; She: *"I know you've had so much experience that you don't need another person in your life . . ."*) before agreeing that they will *"See what we can cook up between us."* "I Wanna Pick You Up" followed, morphing the object of desire into either a disturbingly sexualized infant or a dismayingly infantilized adult. As sung in Dennis's whiskey bray, swooning observations such as *"I wanna tickle your feet"* lost whatever innocence they might have had. By the time he got to the final coda, *"Pat, pat, pat her on her butt, butt/She's gone to sleep, be quiet"* sounded nearly obscene.

"Airplane" spun a more mature perspective on romance, albeit from the suspended animation of 30,000 feet above the earth, where a man can muse on life and love without actually engaging in it. Back on the ground with the built-in Vegas encore "Love Is a Woman," the album staggered to a close in a hail of honking saxes, tootling flutes, and hoary crooning.

It wasn't "Good Vibrations." It was barely even the Beach Boys. But *Love You* was a mesmerizing and at times darkly lovely portrait of the world as viewed through the eyes of an emotionally fraught thirty-four-year-old rock star whose own success has become an inescapable trap.

But even as Brian seemed to resign himself to his new life as a creative functionary working under Landy's thumb, the shrink was wearing out his welcome with the rest of the Beach Boys. The breaking point came in late November when he encouraged Brian to accept an offer from Lorne Michaels to make a solo appearance on the November 27 edition of *Saturday Night Live*. The rest of the group was also in New York that weekend, fresh off of a pair of sold-out shows at Madison Square Garden, and they would have welcomed the chance to get their hipness ticket punched on the show that was seen as the TV zenith of mid-1970s cool. But Michaels only wanted Brian, and so Landy pushed for it to happen. Unfortunately, Brian's star turn was something less than an unalloyed triumph. Sitting petrified behind a grand piano that had been placed in a sandbox, smiling wanly whenever Landy, standing just off-camera, flashed a card instructing him to do so, Brian led the show's studio band through a sluggish "Back Home" and a magic-free "Good Vibrations" before climaxing with a shaky rendition of "Love Is a Woman."

Viewers at home, including this one, weren't sure what to make of it all. It still seemed amazing to see Brian Wilson performing anywhere, let alone looking so relatively fit and trim. And though it was painful to hear his voice shredding those once-crystalline songs, there was something romantic about the haunted look in Brian's eyes—if only because it confirmed the truth of the psychic melodrama at the heart of all of his songs. And in so doing, it made him seem heroic, not just for the rigors of the music's creation, but also for having the courage to sit at the piano and even attempt to play it in public.

If the other Beach Boys saw it that way, they didn't like it. On the contrary, they developed real concerns about the state of Brian's therapy. Stephen Love was particularly chagrined, since his suspicions about Landy dated back several months to the day when the shrink had proposed being paid with a percentage of Brian's earnings rather than an hourly rate. "It was like a brain surgeon saying, 'Well, if this patient lives, I get 10 percent of his income,'" Stephen says. Instead, Landy had increased his time and staffing so radically that the monthly charge had risen speedily from $10,000 to $20,000. Figuring enough was enough, Stephen—who oversaw all of the group members' incomes and expenditures—decided the shrink had to go. To make his case to Brian and Marilyn, he brought along Landy's most recent monthly bill. "And Brian was so appalled at how much he was paying this guy, he actually took a swing at him!"

Landy and company were gone by the beginning of December, making way again for Stan Love, whose pro basketball days had come to an end for good. Joined by a friend named Rocky Pamplin, a one-time *Playgirl* model who entertained secret hopes of starting his own career in music, the pair of live-in bodyguards/counselors did their best to keep Brian focused, busy, and relatively clean.

And for a time it seemed to work. Brian kept up his pace as 1977 began, cranking out a new batch of tunes that ranged from the lushly orchestrated ballads "Still I Dream of It" and "It's Over Now," to quirky observations on baseball ("It's Trying to Say") and movies ("Lines"), to loopy glimpses at his own life, such as "Life Is for the Living." Brian also declared his intention of returning to the road full-time, even pulling out his old Fender Precision bass to get his licks back in shape. "I feel more into it now," he told writer Harvey Kubernik at the time. "Rehearsals went real good, and I got some of the fire back."

To the surprise of nearly everyone, the "Brian Is Back!" campaign had actually worked. Brian Wilson was slimmed down, relatively clear-eyed, and back in action. The new record had been a hit; *Love You* was already in the can; and the album after that was close to finished. That would end their commitment to Warner Brothers, and so the nation's biggest record companies were lining up to offer the group lucrative deals for whatever they did next.

But even as Dennis Wilson walked away from me that afternoon in late December, with another sold-out show just ahead and the most profitable year the Beach Boys would ever have set to begin, he and his big brother, along with the rest of the group, were already veering toward a new set of disasters that would change their lives and the meaning of their work forever.

CHAPTER 13

As 1977 began, Stephen Love's plan moved easily into its next stage. The Beach Boys were the subject of a bidding war between record companies that resulted in an insanely lucrative deal from CBS Records, guaranteeing close to $1 million per album, plus bonuses for high sales, on top of a $2 million signing bonus. Wherever they went they played in the biggest arenas, were given the most generous guarantees ($50,000 per night) in the business, and sometimes earned two or three times that amount once the ticket sales were totaled. If that wasn't enough, they had reclaimed the pop world's respect, too, and not just from the Chamber of Commerce types, the beach ball–bouncers, the bunny-hoppers, and the pseudo-surfers who wore baggie shorts and huarache sandals to their shows in Nebraska. Thanks in part to the relentless chorus of "Brian Is Back" coverage, virtually every sensate person who cared about rock music had come to understand that the Beach Boys were serious musicians complete with serious angst and extremely serious appetites for sex, drugs, and all-around degeneracy. "A diseased bunch of motherfuckers if ever there was one," raved Lester Bangs, the snarling prince of the punk-rock writers. "But the miracle is that the Beach Boys have made that disease sound like the literal babyflesh pink of health. . . . Maybe it's just that unprickable and ingenuous wholesomeness that accounts not only for their charm, but for their beauty—a beauty so awesome that listening to them at their best is like being in some vast dream cathedral decorated with a thousand gleaming American pop culture icons."

If they had been different people, the Beach Boys might have taken up residence in that cathedral and stayed there forever. They would have realized that the transcendent beauty of their music had nothing to do with the surf, the cars, or the girls in the songs that made their audiences howl and everything to do with the way they sang about them. They would have understood that it was the *belief* in their voices and the friendship their harmonies signified that brought tears to people's eyes. It was the *idea* of surfing—the naked desperation that could drive you out into the waves or across a parched landscape in pursuit of something that's gotta be better than this—that registered in people's hearts and imaginations. To see the Beach Boys perform in the mid-to-late 1970s and hear this motley, bearded, paunchy, notoriously fucked-up group of nearly middle-aged men singing about school and cars and catching waves required a suspension of disbelief that was, in its way, daring.

On September 1, 1977, something like 150,000 New Yorkers crowded into Central Park to make that leap. All five Beach Boys came out for that muggy, late-summer afternoon, and together with their crack team of backing keyboardists, percussionists, and horn players, they lit up the Great Lawn with a three-hour extravaganza that began with "California Girls" and ended with "Fun, Fun, Fun," but also included four songs from *Love You* and key highlights from *Pet Sounds, Surf's Up, Holland,* and *15 Big Ones.* The throng danced and sang along the whole time, and if you'd been watching from a distance, it would have seemed entirely triumphant.

Only two days later, though, and unbeknownst to the cheering throngs, the Beach Boys were in an angry knot on the tarmac at Newark airport, screaming and gesturing and trading accusations that were so vile and livid that by the time the factions had stormed off in opposite directions, pretty much everyone who had been there suspected that the Beach Boys had sung together for the last time.

In a way it's not surprising to learn that it was their own appetites that tore the Beach Boys apart: They fought about money, who should be their manager, why that guy was taking such a big percentage of their income, and why they ought to pay anyone a premium rate just to field the offers the most popular band in America would get anyway. The fact that they were all making far more money than they ever had before only seemed to make them more bitter. No matter how much each of them had, they seemed to expect even more—more of their own songs on the album, more in the shows, more of their friends in the backing band or on the front office staff.

With Brian unwilling, unable, or unwelcome to take full control of the band's musical vision, that became a free-for-all, too. Carl and Dennis wanted to keep the Beach Boys contemporary by recording and then performing new, more adventurous songs. Mike, on the other hand, preferred riding the energy that erupted from the crowd whenever they kicked out another classic surfing or car song. Weren't they supposed to be in the business of giving people what they wanted? Al might have leaned more toward Carl and Dennis's side, except that both of those guys were such degenerate drinkers and dopers he had to vote with Mike, if only to keep the group from being consumed by chaos. In fact, the lifestyle conflict had grown so profound by 1977 that the group had fallen into the habit of leasing two separate airplanes for their tours, one reserved for those who preferred not to indulge in high-altitude smoking, drinking, and snorting and the other for those who did. If the profligate nature of this compromise bothered anyone, their complaints went unheeded.

As nonsensical as that solution was, the Beach Boys hadn't been raised to work out reasoned approaches to problems. Thus, they retreated to their respective airplanes, rode to the shows in separate limousines, took the stage by separate doors, and gazed beadily at one another from separate microphones even as their voices twined together in those old tales of fun and friendship. When the time came for the gang to sing together around a single microphone—as per their custom when they chimed so sweetly about *"Keepin' those a-lovin' good vibrations a-happenin' with you"*—chances were excellent that a knee might find its way, sharply, into the crotch of the guy standing next to its owner.

This was all merely a convoluted way for them to reestablish the fact that their own relationships were based less on friendship than on shared ambition, one of the many traits common to the Wilsons. "You know, there's a streak of insanity in that family. Their father was crazy, his father was crazy," Mike chattered happily to the *Washington Post* in the late '70s. He evidently thought no one would remember that he was talking about his own grandfather and uncle or that he'd had his very own rendezvous with a straitjacket following that breakdown in early 1970. "But along with that streak there's a real creativity," he added, as if that would make the foregoing seem less hostile.

Unfortunately, barely harnessed rage was a recurring feature of Mike's public persona. At the Big Sur Folk Festival in 1970—the group's first serious entrée into the peace-and-love subculture—he'd introduced "Cottonfields" by pointing out how big a hit it had been in Europe, even as "heavy AM radio" in the United States ignored it. "A lot of people thought it was too trite," he snapped. "So we all missed it that time, folks." Playing an international convention of CBS Records executives just after signing their big new contract in 1977, Mike again launched into an onstage diatribe inspired by what he thought of as Warner Brothers' lack of support for *Love You* (which had been released weeks after the Beach Boys had signed with the other label), leading him to refer darkly to "the things that have been done in the name of the music business." And though Mike had become rich and famous as a result of that business, thanks largely to his fellow Beach Boys, he had also come to resent the way his cousins overshadowed him so consistently during their climb to the heights of pop stardom.

He didn't mind following Brian's lead back in the old days. But then Brian had abandoned him for a succession of other collaborators and blown his own mind so thoroughly that he'd lost touch with what had made him—and them—so successful in the first place. Later, Mike had come to value Carl's skills as the group's onstage arranger and bandleader. But Dennis was a walking disaster. Not just because the middle Wilson was undisciplined and obnoxious (and had been ever since they were kids) but also because his looks and natural charisma let him get away with so much. "I could see the rivalry between Mike and Dennis for chicks," David Marks says, thinking back all the way to 1963. "Just dumb ego clashing, which escalated into dumb fistfights, typical shit." And if anything, the conflict had only grown worse. Mike could leap, spin, and wail his way through a two-hour show, but the moment Dennis stood at center stage during the encore to sing "You Are So Beautiful," the place would *erupt* just because he had that impish smile and all that sun-bleached blond hair.

Whatever motivated it, though, Mike had a point about his middle cousin's penchant for obnoxiousness, and once Dennis had truly discovered the joys of cocaine and vodka in the mid-1970s, his onstage and offstage behavior grew even more mercurial: smashed cars, days-long binges, wired-up temper tantrums, sexual liaisons in the candlelit meditation room Mike had set up at Brother Studios. Dennis's romantic exploits were another story entirely, though his two marriages to Karen Lamm (another drug and alcohol enthusiast) featured maximum fireworks, as would a long-term romance with Fleetwood Mac's Christine McVie (then also a coke-and-booze enthusiast).

The drummer also maintained a more-than-healthy sexual interest in basically any woman who meandered in his direction. "Dennis was all about sex," says Trish Campo, the Brother Studios administrator who had been the drummer's friend and confidante since they met in 1970. "He called his penis 'The Wood,' and it had its own identity. It really ran him. But he wanted everyone, especially women, to totally love their moment with him."

The Wood notwithstanding, Dennis's behavior would present a challenge to even the most sympathetic business partner. Though Dennis could write and produce songs that all but rivaled Brian's for emotional power and melodic grace, the perpetual state of hysteria he tended to operate under made him something less than an ideal session leader. As a sad result, even a beautiful song such as "Wouldn't It Be Nice to Live Again" (recorded during the *Surf's Up* sessions in 1971) went unfinished.

The fact that he managed to score a solo deal with Caribou Records (courtesy of old pal James Guercio) and then produce an album, *Pacific Ocean Blue,* that notched surprisingly strong sales and far better reviews than either of the group's mid-1970s efforts only further rankled Mike and Al. Maybe, they hinted in not-so-subtle ways, it was time for Dennis to pursue his solo career full-time and leave the Beach Boys to more stable heads. But even if Dennis yearned to strike out on his own, he'd never been anything *but* a Beach Boy. Everything that mattered to him—music, public adoration, endless streams of cash—flowed directly from the group that had defined his existence since he was sixteen. Indeed, the prospect of appearing anywhere without his usual safety net proved so terrifying that Dennis balked at making any solo appearances to promote his album. A planned club tour was cancelled only days after it was announced.

Still, the professional and emotional strings that kept Dennis locked into the Beach Boys didn't necessarily reflect an abiding closeness between the three Wilson brothers. While Brian, Dennis, and Carl certainly shared a fraternal bond, the blistering environment created by their father had burned away some essential connective material. For all the time they spent singing, playing, traveling, drinking, drugging, and puking together, the Wilson boys never seemed to feel truly at ease with one another. "If there wasn't the Beach Boys and there wasn't music, I would not even talk to them," Dennis observed at one point. "But through the music, I fell in love with my brothers."

But as ever, love in the Wilson family tended to be a mixed blessing. Dennis often showed his love for Brian by sharing his drugs with him, which was obviously not a healthy prospect for either of them. Carl may have been more circumspect about using with or around his emotionally fragile brother, but no amount of brotherly love could make him feel happy about stepping aside to let Brian assume control of the band's musical output. Carl felt he had, in the decade since Brian had left them all high and dry, earned the right to take the reins. What's more, he didn't believe that Brian had the fortitude—let alone the exposure to the outside world—to create new music that would fit on modern radio. That the "Brian Is Back!" campaign had reestablished him in the public eye as the genius responsible for all of their careers rankled Carl just as much as it did Mike.

But they didn't seem to have a choice in the matter, which may explain why the dedication the band wrote to Brian on the inside dust sleeve of *Love You* managed to be as condescending as it was outwardly fawning. Printed beneath a large picture showing him beaming happily at a party while Marilyn whispers in his ear, the writing begins with an all-caps headline: "TO BRIAN WHOM WE LOVE WITH ALL OUR HEARTS."

From there the whole thing just got surreal:

> "We wish to express our appreciation, and acknowledge your willingness to create and support totally the completion of these songs. We thank you for sharing yourself and your music with us, and all those who love you as well. An unspeakable joy being with you (sic) in your expression of the music you put out there for everyone. Brian, we feel honored and grateful and we love you."

Their mood changed noticeably after *Love You* failed to make much of a dent on the charts that spring. Unsurprisingly, given its odd sound and feel, *Love You* jumped into the Top Fifty, sputtered for a month or two, then sank without leaving so much as a ripple. The band continued to play a handful of Brian's new songs in concert ("Honkin' down the Highway" could really rock), but the commercial failure struck the others, and particularly Mike and Al, as an affront. They had told Brian that his new songs were too weird, too *out there,* to appeal to the mass market, and though the CBS contract required Brian to write and/or produce 70 percent of the group's music, that didn't mean they had to let him produce whatever he wanted. From now on they would record and release music the fans wanted to hear—and because they were the ones up in the front lines onstage every night, they would be the ones to judge what would appeal.

First off, the group shelved Brian's planned next album, *Adult Child*. Much like *Love You,* the songs Brian had recorded in early 1977 veered between boyish musings and devastatingly personal statements of loss and regret. That might have been fine, except that a significant number of the songs (including a cover of the '30s big band classic "Deep Purple") had been gussied up in elaborate swing arrangements by Dick Reynolds, the Four Freshmen's arranger whom Brian had last commissioned to do some string arrangements for the Beach Boys' 1964 Christmas album. So, even if Brian's rusty baritone on "Deep Purple" hadn't made him sound like Tom Waits on quaaludes, even if Carl didn't sound quite so drunk on "It's Over Now," nothing about those jaunty horns, the sighing strings, and the whacked-out spirit of *ring-a-ding-ding* struck anyone in the Beach Boys organization as being even remotely radio-friendly. Or, as Stan heard his brother Mike ask Brian the moment he heard the new tracks: *"What the fuck are you doing?"*

Not making the next Beach Boys record, as it turned out. And perhaps that didn't bother Brian. He'd already coasted on his '60s reputation for more than a decade, and it was easy to conclude that his new styles—heavy on the whirring, belching synthesizers one minute; overloaded with cheesy strings and horns the next; and always so light on the lyrics, vocals, and polish—were *intended* to show that he was coasting. Or even, in his passive-aggressive way, that they were a hostile gesture toward the bandmates who made a habit of rejecting his most personal work. "Carl took his productions seriously and did really careful mixes," Earle Mankey recalls. "When Brian came in, he'd say, 'Let's mix this,' and after one pass, like five minutes later, he'd say, 'That's good!' Or maybe he'd say, 'More bass! More vocal!' But that was it."

So now that they wanted to take back control, Brian could shrug it off and hit the road, playing and singing when it suited him or sitting mutely in front of an unamplified piano when it didn't. If they were desperate to get his name on some new songs, he'd toss off something in ten minutes or maybe dig through the cobwebs for some old tune he could pass off as new. What did he owe the Beach Boys, beyond what he had already given them, and what had they ever done for him? Just thinking about it made him furious. "The Beach Boys were pissed at him, and he at them," says Stan Love, whose role as Brian's caretaker continued into the late '70s. "He wasn't going to produce a song for them, because he didn't like them as people anymore. The major conflict was with

Mike. Brian didn't want to write with him anymore, but of course Mike tried to hang on, doing his arrogant pressure trip on him. And Brian didn't dig it."

Inevitably, Brian's attention reverted to the chemicals he had turned to in order to replace the comfort and euphoria he got from his music. Though his trio of bodyguards tried desperately to keep his most destructive habits at bay, Brian excelled at concealing his stash and sneaking off to use it; and before they realized their backs had even been turned, he'd have vanished—off to a bar, off to wherever Dennis and his reliable array of substances might be. Hours later Brian would stagger home, eyes pinwheeling in his head. From that point on, life around the Wilson house on Bellagio Road would go from weird to worse. Lunging once to give Carnie a hug, Brian forgot that he was holding a burning cigarette in his hand. The ember sizzled into her skin, and her screams were still echoing in his ears the next morning when the hungover, horrified Brian locked himself in the bathroom and shaved his head as a badge of shame. Still, when Carnie took matters into her own hands by throwing her old man's vodka and cigarettes down the toilet—"None of my friends' parents smoke and drink!" she'd hollered at him—Brian was so enraged that he spun her around and gave her bottom a hard whack. It was the one thing he swore he'd never do, and after gaping at his daughter for a second, Brian burst into tears. He spent the rest of the evening wandering from room to room, weeping mournfully.

If the other Beach Boys noticed his ongoing dysfunction, they were either too preoccupied with their own problems or too satisfied with the status quo to do much of anything about it. They'd managed to broker a tentative resolution to their September 1977 blowup, but that had been motivated less by a real desire to maintain their creative collaboration than by an unwillingness to lose the extremely lucrative CBS contract. Needing to produce the final album owed on their Warner Brothers contract before they could really cash in, the group decamped to Fairfield, Iowa, where Mike had secured recording space and living quarters in the meditation-friendly dorms of Maharishi International University. Getting away from L.A. and its many distractions (in other words, drugs) would help them focus on the project, he had argued. That might have been true, but the increased focus did nothing to enhance their creativity, and what eventually emerged from the Iowa sessions turned out to be the most cynical, spiritually void work the group ever produced.

In fact, *M.I.U. Album,* as the record was called, may be one of the worst records ever made by a great rock band. Coproduced by Al and backup keyboardist Ron

Altbach, with Brian credited as executive producer (almost certainly for contractual purposes), the record had a generic easy-listening sound, heavy on the tinkly keyboards and sweeping strings, with nary a trace of Brian's ear for quirky texture. As for the songs themselves—the horror, the horror. Consider the point at the end of the first verse of Mike and Al's "Kona Coast," when Mike declared, with all the authenticity a bald, middle-aged, nonsurfer could muster: *"I wanna go surfin' where I dig it the most, in Hawaii!"* Such an obvious echo of Brian's far superior 1964 tune "Hawaii" would have been bad enough were it not for the tune's plodding rhythm and limp guitars. That Brian, singing in the strongest falsetto he'd delivered on record since 1970, had been pressed into reprising the swooping falsetto from the earlier tune just added insult to injury.

That's not to say that everything about the album is a disaster: "She's Got Rhythm," the opening song, boasted an energetic verse and bracing falsetto lead from Brian, even if the tale of the "foxy girl" who gets away during a night of "disco dancing" made about as much of an impact as the barely audible drums and generic bass line. Al's pair of '50s covers ("Come Go with Me" and "Peggy Sue") went down easily enough, but that can't be said for "Hey Little Tomboy," an *Adult Child* leftover and certainly the worst of those songs, which reveled uncomfortably in an adolescent girl who is putting away her skateboard and baseball mitt in order to get hot and heavy with the swain portrayed by Mike. *"I'm gonna teach you to kiss/It's gonna feel just like this,"* he crooned in what may be the most unsettling moment in the entire recorded history of the Beach Boys.

Still, "Tomboy" got stiff competition when Brian and Mike's "Belles of Paris" popped up a few songs later. Here, Mike's attempt to graft some *tres chic francais* into his overview of Parisian delights descended quickly from ridiculous to unintentionally comic. *"C'est tres jolie en Paree in the spring,"* he sang, sounding about as sophisticated as Pepé Le Pew. *M.I.U.*'s final insult was the concluding track, the Altbach-written "Winds of Change," whose soupy strings and reverb-heavy piano were meant to underscore the emotional impact of lines about cosmic oceans that flow into hearts and quiet dawns that sing songs to everyone. And just in case that weren't aggravating enough, Brian reprised yet another fragment from one of his far better songs, in this case the bittersweet cry, *"won't last forever . . ."* from "When I Grow Up."

Unsurprisingly, the gruesome album topped out at number 151 on *Billboard*'s album chart, a failure in every respect. But even *M.I.U.* wasn't quite as sad, cynical, and wrong as the Christmas-themed songs the group created for the holiday album they gave Warner Brothers as a final kiss-off. It was largely a combination of lightly rewritten *M.I.U.* songs—*"I wanna spend Christmas where I dig it the most, in Hawaii!"* they declaimed in "Melekalikimaka," actually a revised "Kona Coast," and leftovers from earlier projects (1970's "Loop De Loop" = "Santa's Got an Airplane," 1976's "Hey There Momma" = "I Saw Santa Rockin' Around the Christmas Tree"). Apart from a pair of good new originals (Carl's punchy, horn-driven "Go and Get That Girl" and Dennis's meditative "Morning Christmas"), the album—which was swiftly rejected by Warner Brothers—represented an even more hideous new low for the Beach Boys (though some of the tracks were, inexplicably, released on the CD release of the group's 1964 album).

As 1978 began, the Beach Boys were headed in a distinctly hellish direction. A hugely successful tour of Australia nearly resulted in another breakup when Dennis, allegedly working with Carl's money, bought some heroin that ended up making Brian sick. When Stephen Love called a meeting to figure out exactly where the drugs had come from, Brian's bodyguard Rocky Pamplin ended up punching a drunk Carl in the face, knocking him unconscious.

"Mike levitated off his chair, he was so jubilant that Rocky smacked Carl like that," Stephen Love recalls. "We were so shook up that Dennis had even scored the heroin, so we were making a stand against hard drugs." Not that it made much of an impact. Carl got so wasted before the next night's show that he slurred his words noticeably and then nearly fell over during "Good Vibrations." And just when it seemed like Carl was going to drag the *"Gotta keep those a-lovin' good vibrations a-happenin' with you"* sing-along into bedlam, it fell to Brian, of all people, to pull it back by launching the band into the *"Hum-de-dum"* chant he'd pulled off the original recording before completing the final mix in 1966.

But if Brian had moments of clarity, the larger fabric of his life was fast unraveling. Unable to build a trusting relationship with a new therapist, his mood swings grew more pronounced. He slid back into despair, and his drug use only exacerbated his emotional problems, while his deepening emotional isolation tore at the already-stretched fabric of his marriage. The alienation had drawn both husband and wife to take comfort in other partners, and during the late summer of 1978, Brian finally told her the marriage was, at long last, over. He moved into a rented house near the Riviera Country Club on Sunset Boulevard, and his trio of helpers came along to help him set up housekeeping. But while Stan, Rocky, and Steve Korthof tried to instill a kind of normalcy and structure to Brian's life, the dark tide in his brain pulled him even further into the looking glass. Many days he'd lie on the sofa staring up at the ceiling for hours, smoking cigarettes down to the filter and then flicking the butts onto the floor, where they'd burn holes into the hardwood floor. Sometimes a curl of smoke would rise from the floor and Brian would watch it go, wondering if the house might finally burn down. Would that finally put an end to the darkness in his head?

When he got too hungry or bored to stay on the couch, Brian had rituals he'd use to keep his demons at bay. He'd eat steaks for every meal, then polish off entire cakes and sacks of cookies or vats of ice cream for dessert. After that he'd sprint out to the pool, then walk around it as fast as possible for as long as possible. He'd go until he was drenched with sweat, until his leg muscles were shaking with the effort of propelling his increasingly blubbery body through the late afternoon heat. Physically drained, he'd limp back into the house and play "Be My Baby" for a few hours. Or sometimes it'd be "Rhapsody in Blue" that he would play again and again as he sank into the cushions, the ember of his cigarette glowing red as the house fell once again into the dark. If the panic gripped him again, Brian would cloud his mind with whatever chemicals he could introduce into his haunted cortex. If there was nothing in the house, he'd sneak out the door and wander down to Sunset Boulevard, where he'd get so drunk that he'd wander out into traffic, almost as if he hoped some speeding bus would do for him what he didn't have the courage to do himself.

The guys tried to help. Steve Korthof, a former US Marine, would make like a drill sergeant, bellowing at his cousin to get the fuck out of bed, get his clothes on, and make something of his life. Rocky—the muscle-bound ex–male model—followed suit, using his sheer physicality to intimidate Brian into motion. Brian would do as he was told, getting out of bed, pulling on his clothes, and then sitting at the piano to write some music, all the while planning his next bolt for freedom, his next score. "It was terrible for him, because the doctors gave him these pills that made him sluggish. But Rocky and Steve were screaming at him all of the time, and he just got fucking sick of it," Stan Love says. "He was a grown man, and he didn't like it. You wouldn't like it either, no matter how crazy you were."

The band would lean on him for new songs, citing the demands of their new CBS contract, but they wouldn't let him write what he wanted to, so what was the point? "He hated the pressure," Stan Love says. "Mike was pressuring him to write with him; Marilyn was on him about the money thing." Even his moments of enthusiasm for touring had been stymied. "Carl wouldn't let him play the bass for the entire show, which is what Brian wanted to do. He didn't want him to sing out onstage, either. Carl really stymied him, because he didn't want to be overshadowed." Or maybe Carl just knew that Brian's performances could be as erratic as his emotional condition, and he didn't want to risk the embarrassment of having his brother lose it onstage during a key moment.

As the months passed, Brian's moods began to edge toward anger. He'd storm around the house throwing things at the wall or kicking out the windows. He'd bellow at his helpers or at no one and storm off to sit alone in the dark for hours on end. Pushed to wit's end, Stan and the others would take Brian to see a psychiatrist and beg to put their hulking charge into a mental hospital for observation. One psychiatrist was evaluating Brian in his office when he made the mistake of taking out a pipe and lighting it, just like Murry used to do when he was lecturing his sons. Suddenly Brian snapped and came at the guy across the top of his desk. Stan Love was in the waiting room at the time and had just leaped to his feet when the panicked doctor burst into the waiting room. "He was screaming, 'Help me! Call the police!'"

Brian went to the hospital after that. But if Brian was crazy, he wasn't dumb, and he could always talk his way out again. Even if he seemed resigned to staying in the hospital for a while, then the Beach Boys would come calling, wondering if he felt well enough to make the next concert tour. And then he'd be off on the road for a month or so—doing a little better, perhaps, thanks to the rigid schedule and discipline of touring—but then that would come to an end and he'd be back on the couch at home again, with the cigarette-scarred floors, the worn-down couch, the shoe-scuffed patio, "Be My Baby," "Rhapsody in Blue," and the recriminations in his head.

One day Brian wandered off again and didn't come back, which would have been scary even if he hadn't left his wallet, keys, and identification at home. He was missing for days before a call finally came in from a man in San Diego who had seen him in a gay bar, playing the piano for drinks. What happened before then—what he'd eaten, where he'd slept, whom he'd been with—was a mystery no one was particularly eager to unravel. But at least that shook everyone up enough to get Brian back in a mental hospital for an extended stay. And he was, by all accounts, making progress. Then the Beach Boys called again to check in: They were already overdue to start making their first album for CBS. How would he feel about heading over to Florida to help them? Brian signed himself out of the hospital, hopped a flight, and was back with them again, back at work in the recording studio.

The sessions did not go well. Neither did the meeting/listening session when CBS chief Walter Yetnikoff flew out to check in on them. Brian put together a reel of songs they'd been working on, some still in production but nevertheless a pretty good picture of what they'd been doing. "It was the first time [Yetnikoff had] come to see them at work, and they were excited," Stan Love recalls. "He showed up, and he was obviously excited about it. But then they played him what they thought was the album, and when it was over, he turned to the group and said, 'I think I've been fucked.'"

Realizing they had a lot more work ahead of them and that he was in no shape to lead any group, let alone the fractured, fractious Beach Boys, Brian called back to Los Angeles and summoned Bruce Johnston back into the fold. Bruce was only too glad to heed the call, and now that he had his own earth-rattling hit (he had written Barry Manilow's schlocky 1975 smash "I Write the Songs"), the group was more than willing to let him try his hand at producing the album.

Amazingly, the album that resulted was a big improvement over *M.I.U.* Called *L.A.: Light Album,* a title that evoked both Los Angeles and the city's long-standing position as a capital of vaguely mystical New Age religions (the liner notes explained the title *Light Album* as referring to "The awareness of, and the presence of, God here in this world as an ongoing loving reality"), the album's strength came largely from its diversity of voices. Kicking off with "Good Timin'," a pretty, harmony-rich ballad Brian wrote with Carl in 1974, the album skipped right to Al's slight "Lady Lynda" before easing into Carl's lovely maritime ballad "Full Sail." Carl also contributed "Angel Come Home," a tale of heartbreak and remorse sung by Dennis with great, shambling feeling. Things turned even funkier with Dennis's brooding, pulsing "Love Surrounds Me," a reggae-laced ballad that may be the most underrated song of his career. Mike checked in with "Sumahama," rescued from its faux-Japanese strings and bursts of phonetic language (shades of "Belles of Paris") by its bittersweet melody and the sensitivity he brings to his tale of the girl searching for her missing father.

The album's flip side featured Dennis's lush ballad "Baby Blue," then eased off with Carl's "Goin' South" and a good-humored version of Brian's boogie-woogie arrangement of the folk standard "Shortenin' Bread." Unfortunately, all of these—and perhaps the entire album—were overshadowed by the album's lead single, an eleven-minute reworking of Brian and Mike's R & B workout "Here Comes the Night." The song first appeared as an album track on *Wild Honey* in 1967, but now Bruce and his friend Curt Becher—a pop producer called in for this sole purpose—had decided to turn the song into a full-fledged disco tune, complete with throbbing bass, shrieking strings, wah-wah guitars, and layer upon layer of synthesized beeps, whirs, rattles, and clanks.

If the group was worried about the prospect of leaping onto a commercial bandwagon that diverged so completely from their previous influences and innovations, they were even more eager to score a hit single. The band (and particularly Carl) worked hard to give the song their distinctive vocal flair, but no one seemed to have figured out that the disco tide that had swept across the culture in the mid-1970s had crested, which cast the Beach Boys' unexpected sashay beneath the mirror ball into the worst light imaginable. And you didn't have to be violently opposed to disco to feel dismayed by what "Here Comes the Night" represented—the Beach Boys had apparently come up so short in the search for market-friendly gimmicks that they couldn't even find a new way to steal from themselves. Observant fans also noticed that the best songs on *L.A.* sounded suspiciously like the work of solo artists. Indeed, both of Dennis's songs had been plucked from a stockpile he'd been building for his second solo album, tentatively called *Bamboo.* The vocals on Carl's songs seemed limited entirely to layers of his own voice with occasional help from Dennis and Bruce. And if Brian sang a note anywhere on the album, his voice is so far down in the mix as to be completely unidentifiable.

They continued to tour, taking the stage to the symphonic overture of "California Girls," then spinning their voices into the same harmonies, throwing their bodies into the rhythms they knew as intimately as the pulse in their veins. The new "Here Comes the Night" nearly got them booed off stage the night they debuted it at Radio City Music Hall that spring, but they had long since learned how to adjust their own interests to suit the audience's expectations. The song was history by the next night, and the other new songs rotated out of the set soon after, and then they were back to singing the same old songs in the same old way, reliving the same old fantasies and harboring the same old fears. Only now they all seemed to be doing it alone, standing at their own microphones in their own spotlights, no longer talking between songs or even glancing into one another's eyes when they sang the same old unifying prayer about *"Keepin' those a-lovin' good vibrations/a-happenin' with you."*

When the band came home to play the Universal Amphitheater that summer, Rich Sloan—Brian's childhood friend and high school teammate—came up to see them play, the first time he had had the chance to see the Beach Boys perform in person. He was even more excited to go backstage before the show and spend some time catching up with his old friends. But when he got to the bungalow that served as the band's dressing area, Sloan found that the enthusiastic group of strivers he'd known in 1962 had faded over the years. The rambunctious Dennis the Menace he had once known now stumbled through the door with red-rimmed eyes and hair so unwashed it looked like dreadlocks. In his hand Dennis carried a liter-size Coke bottle he had filled with milk and rum. "Dennis and Carl were a pair," Sloan recalls. "Mike and Al did their thing, and poor Brian was somewhere in the middle. Actually, Al didn't even want to go into the bungalow. I had to go outside to talk to him, and he was saying that they never saw each other anymore, except at recording sessions and onstage."

Sloan could hear the rumble of stomps and cheers as the hometown crowd geared up for the Beach Boys to take the stage, but even as curtain time came and went, the group sat in their dressing room, staring mutely at an episode of *Mork and Mindy*. "I'll never forget that," Sloan says. "Their manager kept rushing in saying, 'Guys! We've got to get out onstage!' Finally they took us out to our seats and they came out to play." Dennis, visibly drunk, came trailing a substitute who sat nearby in case he passed out or just decided to walk off. Brian sat mutely at his piano for most of the night. The crowd cheered just the same, although Audree Wilson never quite got in the spirit. "She'd been saying that it was so sad. The guys had had so many highs over the years, but now all three of her boys were getting divorced at the same time. What was going to happen to them now?"

For some people the answer seemed all too obvious: Brian was going to die. His family and the Beach Boys—as if you could find a distinction between those two entities—either felt powerless to do anything to change his direction or didn't have the energy to try. What they did do, however, was book him for another recording session. Only this one was going to be in Western Studios in Hollywood, literally in the same room (studio number three) where he'd once wielded sound as masterfully as Galahad had wielded his sword. And it would be just like it had been fifteen years earlier. The original Steinway piano would be there. Hal Blaine would marshal a band of Brian's favorite musicians. Up in the control room, the modern seventy-two-track digital gear would be covered with plywood upon which they would set up the old four-track Ampex recorder, Urei tube console, and original Altec 604e speakers Brian had used in the '60s. Chuck Britz, always Brian's most trusted engineer, even agreed to come out of retirement to run the vacuum tube mixing board they'd managed to dig up for the sessions.

For all the elaborate planning, the sessions took on the feeling of a wake, albeit one with a living corpse. "They figured this was the last time Brian would record at Western," says Bellagio-era engineer Steve Desper, who had also been called in to consult. And with an eye toward posterity, the group also arranged to set up an old Studer recorder to get a fly-on-the-wall perspective on everything that happened once Brian started to work. Still, some held out hope that maybe, just maybe, the experience of being back on his old turf surrounded by all his old colleagues would stir something in the thirty-eight-year-old ruin of a man. "They wanted to see if Brian could be motivated to get back into his old self, back when he was recording *Pet Sounds* and all that," Desper says. "But getting into Brian's head is a lot more difficult than getting that old sound."

Particularly when he feels the glories of his past starting to weigh down upon him. And that was precisely what happened the moment the overweight, heavily bearded musician walked a bit unsteadily from the white light and heat of a July afternoon through the doors and into the hermetic darkness of the studio. "From the moment he walked in through the door, everyone stood up and applauded," Desper recalls. "And what was he supposed to do? Record another 'Good Vibrations' on the spot? You could see he was uncomfortable, and nothing Marilyn (who had come down to offer support to her ex-husband), Carl, Chuck, or I tried to do was going to help."

Brian had a couple of new tunes—just trifles, really, a few changes he'd been messing around with—but he didn't want to pull those out while everyone was staring. Instead, he suggested a couple of oldies, and in the next few days they ran through takes of Chuck Berry's "School Days (Ring! Ring! Goes the Bell)," the old R & B song "Stranded in the Jungle," and "Jamaica Farewell." He relaxed enough to work on one original song, a mostly improvised, three-chord reggae-lite tune they eventually called "Sunshine." "He just didn't warm up to the effort," Desper says. "Even if you went back and tried to make everything work, you couldn't take Brian back. He was a different person. You couldn't go back and revisit those times."

CHAPTER 14

Ronald Reagan, the Midwestern boy turned actor turned TV pitchman turned governor of California, rode for the White House wearing a white hat (literally, in his ads) and wielding a misty vision of the American Dream. "Some say that spirit no longer exists. But I have seen it—I have felt it—all across this land," Reagan declared as he accepted the Republican nomination that July. And Americans figured they saw the same things reflected back to them in Reagan, so much so in fact that they were willing to overlook his rather obviously dyed hair and seemingly rouged cheeks. And that the old-fashioned family man had not only been divorced but also enjoyed only the most distant of relationships with his two sets of children. Oh, and then it turned out that a lot of his public pronouncements—about the Cadillac-owning welfare sponges bleeding the nation dry, about the mountains of pollution caused by trees, about his own experiences liberating the prisoners of Nazi death camps, and about the inevitable trickle of money from the investment accounts of the leisure class into the pockets of the working poor—never quite penciled out, either.

But Reagan sure seemed to believe it. And after four years of Jimmy Carter's stern lectures about sacrifice and failure, Reagan's optimism, no matter where it came from, was intoxicating.

Years of revising his own life in and out of the movies had taught the glamorous Californian a valuable lesson: An appealing fantasy can be far more powerful than an inconvenient truth. "We have every right to dream heroic dreams," Reagan told the nation during his first inaugural speech in January 1981. "Those who say that we are in a time when there are no heroes just don't know where to look." Or, perhaps, where not to look.

In a sense, the Beach Boys of the early 1980s provided a perfect sound track for the Reagan era. While Carl's fight to earn conscientious objector status during the late 1960s prefigured the progressive tilt of their work in the early 1970s and the frank environmentalism of the mid-1970s, the increasing dominance of Mike—always the most politically conservative member of the group—in the late 1970s carried them, along with the country, farther to the right. By early 1980 they had played a benefit for the presidential campaign of George H. W. Bush. And though group members (particularly Mike, oddly enough) still spoke up often and loudly for the same environmental programs the Reagan/Bush ticket was determined to do away with, the group jumped eagerly at the chance to perform at one of the inaugural balls thrown to hail the new administration when it took office that next January.

"You know, we're not so politically savvy and all that," Mike says. "But I think we liked Reagan quite a bit. And Mrs. Reagan, you know, nice people. And we liked the association of him being governor of California." The Reagans liked being associated with the Beach Boys, too, a fact that would eventually become a point of national politics. "We did a benefit at the White House when the Reagans were there," Mike continues. "I have a photo of us there; Nancy had her arm around me, and Brian, and everybody are all together there."

So even as their lives spun out of control and even as their commitment to their work ebbed and their own relationships grew cold and jagged, they continued to present themselves, in the words of Mike, circa 1983, as ". . . really positive and wholesome and fun. All our adult lives we performed to totally project a good time. And that's what we're going to do in the future." Soon they came up with a new way to position the group for public consumption, a kind of self-generated honorific that seemed to summarize the place the Mike-led, eighties-era Beach Boys yearned to have in the cultural fabric: America's Band.

The album they released in the spring of 1980, *Keepin' the Summer Alive*, came with a cover painting that portrayed the full group in their onstage formation performing for an audience of polar bears and a solitary penguin in a dark,

CATCH A WAVE

icy tundra. Only the group is living inside a large glass bubble—its sand, palm tree, surfboards, and bikini-clad beauty kept at what one presumes is a warm but breezy eighty-five degrees. Safe in their own simulated environment. And completely out of touch with reality. As was the music that came inside the wrapper. Desperate to justify the fat advance they'd taken from CBS but unable (or unwilling) to blaze a new trail to the creative horizons that spawned their best work, the only thing they could think to do was to mimic the successes they'd had so long ago. So the group—actually Bruce, Carl, and Alan, with occasional visits from Brian and Mike and one brief appearance from the increasingly bedraggled Dennis—continued to produce songs, many of which were designed to be sung by boys half their age. *"There's nothin' like a-romancin' in the stands/Walkin' down the hallways holdin' hands . . . ,"* the thirty-nine-year-old Mike sang over the four chords Brian bothered to toss into "Some of Your Love." Carl's "Keepin' the Summer Alive," which became the new album's title track, also featured a high school–aged narrator, as did the group's cover of "School Days," the one oldie that survived from the Western sessions in July. Of Brian's other originals on the album, only the rollicking first single "Goin' On" betrayed a trace of his usual sparkle, and some of that came from the whirlpool-of-harmony bridge he'd adapted from the 1964 outtake "All Dressed Up for School."

Still, the album contained at least one piece of work that was, despite itself, revelatory. The tune was one Bruce had brought in, a retelling of the band's history he had first written after leaving the group in the early '70s. Now renamed "Endless Harmony" (the original title "Ten Years Harmony" clearly being no longer accurate), the song came in two parts; the first, longer piece featured Bruce singing alone above a series of jazzy minor chords descending across the keys of a shimmering Fender Rhodes piano. The music is a bit melodramatic (à la Bruce's "I Write the Songs," which had proved such a natural fit for a moist-eyed Barry Manilow), but that's a perfect fit for lyrics that begin describing the teenaged Beach Boys as carefree nature lovers who loved to sing until the onset of fame transformed them into iconic figures with the power to turn their own simple pleasures into a vast fortune. Most of this is complete hooey, which may be why Bruce is so stumped at the end of the verse when the lyrics pose the existential query: What does any of it mean? Why, it's the beginning of an endless harmony! he declares. Which seems willfully naive at best, given the state of the band's relationships, never mind their physical health. Nevertheless, the entire group joins in at full force, while the rest of the guys weave a wall of harmony behind him, oohing and ahhing behind a first-person verse that salutes the motherland ("God bless America!") while also thanking its citizens for their patronage, then shifts back to patriotic gratitude before settling on traditional showbiz self-congratulation: Everyone loves the Beach Boys! At which point the song deserves to come sputtering to a dissonant, discordant end.

Instead, something kind of magical happens. The background chorus turns rich and full, each voice finding its own line of perfectly woven melody until they all join a wordless, skyward progression of *dah-doo-dah, dah-doo-dah, dah-doo-dah* that comes to a sudden stop, leaving only one aching falsetto to trace a sad arc down until he falls once again into that billowing cushion of voices. For in those moments, in that one sighing chord, you can hear all the hope and beauty they put into every great song they ever made. And you can also hear the sorrow, because that one mournful voice, engineered to sound exactly like Brian, is actually Bruce mimicking the sound of the man who had envisioned the Beach Boys but now couldn't even be bothered to make the session. The horizon he had created had become a mirage. And that didn't bother the other Beach Boys at all.

Every so often they actually seemed to be having fun. An enormous show at the Knebworth Festival in England that June brought out 100,000 fans on a rainy night, and their enthusiasm in turn brought out that old playful spirit. The entire six-man band was there, with a seemingly clear-eyed, playful Dennis thrashing the drums while a clean-shaven, freshly shorn Brian played the grand piano, managing sharp (if joyless) vocal turns on "Sloop John B." and "Surfer Girl." Visiting Seattle six months later, the group played another basketball arena show, this time only days following the murder of John Lennon. Brian seemed dazed that night, sitting mutely at the piano, sucking on his endless procession of Marlboros with an out-of-body intensity. But only a few feet away, Dennis reigned supreme on the drums, barely looking up from the task of holding down the rhythm. He was particularly in-the-pocket on "Good Vibrations," laying back on the beat to emphasize the psychedelic funk that had always hidden just beneath the surface of its chorus. "Say a prayer for John," Carl had called out at the end of the show, and the roar of approval that came back seemed to rock the entire group back on their heels. Carl smiled, nodded, and then began applauding himself, leading the others as they joined the spontaneous ovation for their one-time rival.

Such moments of unity were rare. *Keepin' the Summer Alive* earned miserable reviews, spun off no hit singles, and then peaked at number seventy-five on the *Billboard* charts. That failure—along with the usual array of backstage habits, problems, and conflicts—cooled whatever remnants of creative fire might have remained in the group. And more than half a dozen years since they had settled on their oldies-based repertoire—and grown accustomed to the wild ovations it earned them night after night—they began to balk at the notion of rehearsing or showing up for preshow sound checks. Why bother, some band members argued, when they could just roll in at showtime, crank out the usual two dozen songs, and leave eighty minutes later to the same raucous standing ovation? "The Beach Boys set plays itself," Carl told a reporter at the time. "We can play a real turkey of a show and then people will still come back afterwards and say, 'That's the best concert I've ever seen in my life.'" To the others, that realization was liberating. But it was beginning to drive Carl nuts.

"They wouldn't rehearse or try doing new material," he complained to the *New York Times*. "It was disturbing to get up onstage and not feel the energy, the joy you expect from the Beach Boys."

Carl was only thirty-four. A recent move to the mountains of Colorado had helped him kick most of the bad habits that had been fogging his vision for much of the second half of the '70s. So why should he stick with the Beach Boys if they wouldn't follow his lead to new music, or—at the very least—back to a tighter, more musically precise show? The more he thought about it, the more Carl realized that he didn't want to be a part of it anymore. So he left to start a solo career. Writing primarily with Myrna Smith-Schilling (wife of his manager, Jerry Schilling, and a member of the gospel group Sweet Inspiration that had once backed Elvis Presley) that winter, he made a moderately successful solo record, *Carl Wilson,* that leaned heavily on the rhythm-and-blues tunes he'd fallen in love with when he was first learning to play guitar in junior high school. That spring he formed his own band and hit the road, playing clubs in the Northeast and then touring the state-fair-and-arena circuit as the opening act for the Doobie Brothers. Sometimes the tour would nearly cross paths with the Beach Boys, who continued to tour without him, playing the same songs in more or less the same order to the same delighted crowds, few of whom seemed to notice that the band's usual lead guitarist, bandleader, and lead voice on a dozen of its most popular songs had been replaced by an anonymous musician.

Meanwhile, Dennis had fallen even further into alcoholism, devolving from the muscle-bound sex symbol he had once been into a rheumy-eyed, bloated hulk who had trouble sitting upright on his drummer's stool. Often the middle Wilson brother would behave so badly onstage that the group would exile him for weeks or months at a time, instructing him not to return until he could walk a straight line and play a simple four/four rhythm without falling over. Pared down to only Mike, Al, and Bruce, the stage group would be forced to drag Brian out onto the road in order to get at least one Wilson brother onstage. The fact that the group's onetime leader could barely hit the piano keys in time to the music, let alone be bothered to play the correct chords, didn't seem to matter. ("I play in the key of BW," he shrugged one night to a roadie.) When the houselights dimmed and the arena filled with the wistful opening chords of "California Girls," the shared dream the song evoked seemed to overwhelm whatever familiar faces or spirit might have been absent onstage.

At a show in St. Paul, Minnesota, in the early fall of 1981, the crowd of high school kids and ruddy-faced young families roared happily the moment the Beach Boys took the stage. Dennis wasn't there either that night, and with only three original members, plus Bruce, to carry the load, the band resembled a wounded duck in flight. Mike—dressed in his now-standard costume of white tennis clothes and a truck driver's cap—paced the stage wildly. And though Brian was immensely overweight and visibly unhappy, Mike seemed to relish directing the spotlight at him—" . . . and now we're gonna hear it from my cuz, Brian Wilson, the man who wrote 'God Only Knows' waaay back in that faraway land called the 1960s . . ."—time and again prompting the overwrought man to turn his cracked, ruined voice to the looping, soaring melodies he'd long since surrendered to Carl. Finally, as the band came back for its encores for "Good Vibrations," Brian only made it through the first two lines before calling out, sadly: "Help me on this one, guys, please help me now, I can't . . ."

Beyond the footlights, the beach balls continued to fly and the chain of bunny-hoppers twined up and down the aisles, easily a thousand people strong and all of them bouncing happily to the dreamy, joyful music Brian Wilson had written but no longer had the ability to sing.

As they reached the twentieth anniversary of the Labor Day weekend that marked the beginning of the group that became the Beach Boys, the creative dissolution visible on stage and audible on record radiated into their increasingly shattered lives offstage. Brian had started a relationship and then moved into a house in the Pacific Palisades with Carolyn Williams, a nurse he had met during his last stay in the mental hospital. She was, by all accounts, a sweet, well-intentioned woman. But even given her professional training, Carolyn was overwhelmed by the severity of her man's dysfunction and the strength of his desire to warp his tortured consciousness. In this he found ready companionship, along with a seemingly bottomless supply of cocaine and vodka, in Dennis. Often Dennis would come over to see Brian, luring him to the music room with a sack of McDonald's hamburgers and a few grams of cocaine.

One tape from the era reveals the brothers switching off between piano and Hammond organ, collaborating on a sad, drifting spiritual-style tune called "Oh, Lord," then pounding out a spirited rendition of Brian's "Peter Gunn"–style stomper, "City Blues." As the night wears on and the pile of cocaine begins to shrink, the mood turns more manic. Song fragments trail on forever, leading nowhere except the same "Heart and Soul"–style changes, with a few words or a phrase scatted over the top. At one point they play the same four chords together, over and over, while Brian sings lustily: *Oh, oh, I feel so fine/I feel so fiiiine today, I feel so fiiiine . . ."* It's a nonsense song, the sort of thing you or I could write merely by putting our hands on the piano keys and playing the most basic chords in the rock 'n' roll songbook. But after a minute or so a coked-to-the-eyeballs Brian stops and exclaims loudly, "Whoa! *Wow!* You were really getting into that! I was feelin' so good on the organ!" The writer and producer of *Pet Sounds,* the creator of some of the rock era's most elaborately orchestrated music, is so thrilled by the four chords he's managed to string together that he's screaming at the top of his lungs. "I made that song up! I made it up! I was so *into* it, I can't believe it!"

True enough, the distance Brian had come was hard to believe.

"Everything I am or ever will be is in the music," Dennis had said once. "If you want to know me, just listen." When the Beach Boys sent him away, he would make occasional attempts to clean up, checking into detox programs and swearing that he was going to see it through. But he never could find the resolve to stick with it, and soon he'd be back on the streets of Venice again, wandering from liquor store to bar to crash pad. And though he would beg the others to let him return to the group, once Dennis was back on the road, he'd soon start drinking again, sometimes collapsing onstage, other times picking fights with Mike, who made no secret of his contempt for his cousin's inability to control his own appetites. That Dennis was also going out of his way to share his drugs and booze with Brian only made things worse.

Carl came back to the Beach Boys in time for their summer tour in 1982 and just in time to see Capitol's "Beach Boys Medley," a Frankensteinian stitching together of original "Good Vibrations," "Surfin' Safari," "Help Me, Rhonda," "I Get Around," and "Shut Down" sounds into one 4:08-long mess. And though the "medley" (which was actually one in a chain of similarly awful, record company–created mash-ups to hit the charts in the early eighties) was all but unlistenable, it only just missed *Billboard*'s Top Ten (peaking at number twelve), thereby becoming the group's biggest hit since "Rock 'n' Roll Music" hit the top five in 1976.

If the success of the "Medley" enhanced the group's income or brought more crowds into the shows, it did nothing to alter the darkening relationships within the band, to say nothing of the accelerating emotional and physical declines of both Brian and Dennis. And while the Beach Boys continued to tour and had in fact helped pioneer the lucrative double-billing of major league baseball games and rock shows (thereby becoming a sort of official companion to America's pastime), their real lives had taken on a surreal darkness that was nothing short of cinematic. And then some.

One night at the Universal Amphitheater, the usual backstage tension between Mike and Dennis followed them onstage, where an off-mike comment from Mike enraged Dennis so much that he kicked over his drums and flew off the riser at the group's lead singer, spurring a fistfight that raged in full view of the increasingly horrified arena. "They had security usher Dennis offstage and lock him into a closet so he wouldn't come back," Trish Campo recalls. Fortunately, they still had enough percussionists onstage to have one ready to jump into Dennis's seat for the rest of the show. Eventually the group made it a policy to keep the cousins apart, using roadies to make sure Mike and Dennis stayed out of one another's sight until the moment the show began. Even then they were steered to separate doors on separate sides of the stage. And just when the cousins' relationship had fallen to its nadir, Dennis's teenaged daughter Jennifer introduced him to a girlfriend named Shawn. She wasn't quite twenty then, this short, pug-nosed blonde with the dimples and ready smile. But there was something very familiar about her face—the angular shape of her jaw, the thin aqualine nose—and when Dennis learned her last name was Love, he thought back to the little-known paternity case Mike had faced in the mid-1960s. The child in question belonged to a twenty-two-year-old secretary with whom Mike had apparently spent some quality time. And though the comparatively unsophisticated blood tests of the era indicated that Mike *could* be the girl's father, a judge ruled that the woman had failed to prove her claim "by a preponderance of the evidence." Whatever that means. Nevertheless, Mike paid out $9,500 to get the woman to renounce any future claims that might be made on behalf of the child, and everyone went on with their separate lives. Except for baby Shawn, who was only starting hers.

Nearly two decades later, she met Dennis and, with the spark she ignited in his bloodshot eyes, gained entrée into the world of the man she considered to be her father. Dennis always had a weakness for young women—and had in the late 1970s been busted for keeping company with a wayward teenager in a Phoenix hotel room—so perhaps it wasn't surprising that he would start flirting with his daughter's friend. Or that he would see his way clear to seducing her and then impregnating her. But was he truly in love with Shawn when he asked her to marry him? Or did he just relish the prospect of seeing the look on Mike's face when his cousin realized that Dennis was not only his son-in-law but also the father of his first grandchild? In all the drugs, booze, insanity, and long-festering hatreds that had subsumed the band, no one had the energy or focus to confront Dennis about how disturbing the rocky romance with the much younger woman truly was. "There were never any repercussions for things," Trish Campo says. "I'd get into a car with Dennis, and he'd be going 120 miles an hour down the Pacific Coast Highway, literally bouncing off the walls, and the cops would just shrug and say, 'It's Dennis Wilson, leave him alone!' And it was the same thing with Shawn. He could do anything he wanted, and nothing bad would happen to him."

Mike, for his part, had by 1981 been married and divorced six times. That seems a fairly phenomenal track record for a man just approaching his fortieth birthday, but he was soon married again, this time to a woman named Cathy Martinez. The elaborate ceremony was held outdoors on a beautiful afternoon at his sprawling home in Santa Barbara, with Mike dressed in a white top hat and morning coat and his bride in a white silk wedding gown that trailed down nearly to the middle of her thighs. The couple gazed deeply into one another's eyes while they recited their vows, following the prompts laid down by their chosen officiant, legendary rock 'n' roll disc jockey Wolfman Jack. Mike's seventh marriage lasted less than a year, but it wasn't long before he was married again.

On another night in early 1982, Brian's former helpers/handlers Stan Love and Rocky Pamplin found themselves at a Super Bowl party, tossing down a few drinks and kicking around the dismal state their former employer had fallen into. Brian had always had his problems, sure. But the more they talked about how things had turned out for him, the more it all seemed to come back to Dennis. After all, he was the guy who was giving Brian his drugs these days. And the more Stan and Rocky drank, the more unacceptable that seemed. Eventually it struck them both that the time had come to dispense some vigilante justice. "We'd had friction for years and it finally exploded," Stan says of his cousin. "Dennis was so arrogant and wild; he thought he could fuck around with a professional basketball player, you know? And I wanted to point out to him what happens when you do that." What happened was this: Stan and his partner burst into Dennis's house, scaring off the small coterie of friends who were hanging around by pretending to be narcotics officers. When the bystanders scattered, the ex-bodyguards turned their wrath on Dennis, throwing him to the floor and using their fists, feet, and the handset of a nearby telephone to conduct a beating that didn't end until Dennis's face was battered and bleeding, his ribs broken, and his voice a nearly incomprehensible cry for mercy.

But after years of living at full-throttle, steamrolling every physical, professional, legal, and moral boundary he could see, pausing only to point and laugh before roaring off again, Dennis had already burned through the world's mercy. Certainly, the other Beach Boys and their various managers/helpers could see where he was headed. They even tried to help, in their emotionally distant way, signing him up for detox and even hiring a private jet to take him away in style. But when he wouldn't go or when he went for two days before making a break back to the streets of Venice and all his usual hook-ups and turn-ons, they just sighed and shook their heads. "I don't think he ever thought seriously about cleaning up. He was gonna do what he was gonna do," says Trish Campo, who finally resigned her position as Dennis's personal manager in the spring of 1983, even though she could never stop being his friend. "He basically wanted to challenge life at every moment: How fast could you go, how crazy could you be, how far could he get away with something? The drugs and alcohol did something for him."

The drugs and alcohol were doing something for Brian, too. By the end of 1982, his weight had reached 340 and was still climbing, along with his seemingly unquenchable appetites for food, booze, and other, even more dangerous, substances. At the rate Brian was going, it was clear that he would be, as one insider put it to another, "the next headline in *Billboard*." So now they were at a crux in the road. Either they could let Brian continue on his path to self-extinction or else they could force him to confront his problems once and for all. But what could work? As much as they hated to admit it, there was only one doctor who had ever really worked his way beneath Brian's skin. His name was Eugene Landy and, as luck would have it, he was willing to take Brian on again. But only with certain restrictions: This time, Landy declared, there could be no interference from the Beach Boys or anyone else. The program he described to them conformed exactly with the description he'd contributed to the *Handbook of Innovative Psychotherapies,* published in 1981: "The success of twenty-four-hour therapy rests on the extent to which the therapeutic team can exert control over every aspect of the patient's life." Thus, Landy would set up a house for Brian to live in, along with a full staff of helpers, bodyguards, and attendants. The goal, he'd written, was to "totally disrupt the privacy of [the] patient's [life], gaining complete control over every aspect of their physical, personal, social, and sexual environments."

Landy, in other words, would be Brian's ultimate authority. A father figure, if you will.

Carl and the rest of the group accepted Landy's proposal that fall. But because they didn't have the authority to commit Brian to treatment, first they had to maneuver the ever-resistant musician into a position where he could not say no. To do this, they settled on a ruse, sending a letter to Brian in early November to notify him that he had been "fired" by the Beach Boys. What's more, they lied to him and Carolyn Williams, his live-in companion, claiming that his profligate spending had drained all of his savings accounts. Brian had no money to pay his rent or grocery bills, they said, and soon he'd be out on the street unless, of course, he and Carolyn agreed to meet with Dr. Landy and at least talk about rejoining his program. Seeing no other option, Brian acquiesced. Landy didn't actually attend the December 1 meeting but sent in his colleague, Arnold Dahlke, who secretly taped the goings-on until Carolyn noticed the recorder and snatched the tape away. "No one told me we were being taped. Things sure are strange around here these days," Brian observed.

They got even stranger when Carolyn, in a heated moment, told Dahlke that Landy could "go to hell." Somehow, this random curse became a large point of contention, as the still-absent Landy had Dahlke and his financial administrator Sally Steinberg tell Carolyn that nothing could proceed until she let him come back from hell. "We can't go ahead until this is resolved," Dahlke said. "Landy is very stubborn and he has to sit down and discuss Brian with you, but right now he's in hell and no one can bring him back but you." Eventually Carolyn sent the psychologist a hand-drawn "Get out of hell free" card, and later that evening another staffer showed up with a note from Landy saying he'd been awarded a prize ". . . for outstanding temper-control-of-the-year," which he wanted to share. What he'd taped to the card was a half-smoked joint.

Like the Wizard of Oz, Landy continued to remain in the shadows, fluttering just beyond the fringe of the meetings until mid-December, when he put in a three-minute appearance at a conference between his assistants and Brian and Carolyn. Just after New Year's, Brian agreed to check into Cedars-Sinai for a weeklong battery of physical tests. Both he and Carolyn were expecting that he'd be returning to their Pacific Palisades home, but by the time she came to pick him up, Landy and company had already taken him off to Hawaii, leaving only a legalistic letter Brian had signed instructing her to move out of his house immediately.

Holed up in a remote beach near Kona, Hawaii, the psychologist rolled up his sleeves and set on the task of rebuilding Brian Wilson's fragile psyche in a whole new way. Soon Brian would lose weight, steer clear of drugs and alcohol, and regain the kind of self-discipline he hadn't displayed in nearly twenty years. His eyes would seem clear and focused, and he'd speak again of writing songs and making records. And no matter where he went, Eugene Landy or his representatives would be there, watching his actions, recording his statements, noting who he was with, what they did, and what he said he wanted to do next. And just in case he slipped out of sight for a moment or two, he wore a beeper so Landy could summon him to the nearest telephone. "I influence all of his thinking," Landy told *California* magazine in 1984. "I'm practically a member of the band."

─────────

And though no one knew it at the time, the band was about to feel the influence of a few very unlikely fans in Washington, D.C. It started in the spring of 1983 in the office of the Secretary of the Interior, then occupied by James Watt, whose market-friendly approach to guarding the nation's public spaces had already made him anathema to environmentalists of every political stripe. What's more, Watt was a fundamentalist Christian and fierce social conservative who could not abide the thought of promiscuous drug use or worse taking place on the very National Parks property he was charged with overseeing. And after catching a whiff—literally—of the massive free rock concerts staged near the Washington Memorial on Washington's Mall starring the Beach Boys in 1981 and the Grass Roots in 1982, he figured he'd smelled enough. The free concert would continue in 1983, Watt announced. But this time around it would feature the US Army's Blues Band and the Las Vegas showroom singer Wayne Newton. "Patriotic, family-based entertainment," according to Watt, and not the bands that attracted what he called "the wrong element" to the celebration. "We're not going to encourage drug abuse and alcoholism as was done in the past," he decreed.

Granted, Watt's statement included neither the word *beach* nor the word *boys*. But the Beach Boys had loomed so large across Washington's Fourth of July in the last few years that it was fairly obvious whom he was talking about. And though Watt had provided an unwittingly accurate portrait of the Beach Boys' more private indulgences and problems, he had failed to note the group's connections to both the president and the vice president. These became clear the next day, when Bush stood up to defend his one-time supporters. "They're my friends and I like their music." Reagan made no official comment at first, but his chief of staff, Michael Deaver, declared that his entire family and in fact most of his neighbors had ventured to the Mall for the last Beach Boys concert there and had "a wonderful time." Finally sensing the dimensions of the political disaster looming ahead, Watt's office backpedaled frantically, terming the group "solid, middle-class family people." Which of course was far less accurate than the secretary's earlier implication about drugs and alcohol.

But by then Reagan—still skating through his Teflon era—had compelled his Secretary of the Interior to appear at a sort of public humiliation ritual, dragging him into the White House for a good talking-to and sending him away with a larger-than-life statue of a bullet-pierced foot meant to represent his own gaffe-scarred extremity. Meanwhile, Mike had already leaped to take advantage of what he had already figured for a uniquely double-sided publicity opportunity. On the one hand, he could play the renegade, shaking his head at Watt and all the clueless straights who thought they could knock the rock. "I thank all you undesirable elements for coming!" he'd yell at concert crowds that spring, always earning a massive ovation. But he also accepted Nancy Reagan's apology when she called to make amends, and even now he revels in the small talk they shared that afternoon. "I said, 'Well, that's okay, Mrs. Reagan, it's not the last time James Watt is going to say something silly,'" he recalls cracking. She invited the group to visit the White House the next time they were in Washington, and two months later they took her up on the offer, performing on the South Lawn at a party for the Special Olympics. And it was all so chummy and sweet (Reagan: "We were looking forward to seeing them on the Fourth of July. I'm glad they got here early!" Mike: "For undesirable elements, I think we have a lot of desirable elements here.") that no one seemed to mind or even notice that Mike's hat advertised Chevrolet, the company that had started sponsoring some Beach Boys concerts. Or that Dennis seemed pretty obviously drunk. Instead, they all sang along to "California Girls" (dedicated by Mike to Mrs. Reagan, of course), and later that night the group played a private birthday party at the vice president's residence, where they helped the VP celebrate his fifty-ninth birthday with an hour of greatest hits that climaxed when the birthday boy leaped up onstage to help sing "Barbara Ann," specially dedicated to his own favorite Barbara, the white-haired woman who was beaming regally from her seat just beyond the edge of the stage.

America's Band, indeed. And yet this public anointment by the highest offices in the nation's power structure did nothing to inform or deepen the Beach Boys' artistic vision or the sense of possibility they brought to their music. Once it was over, they just packed up their gear, as they had done so many thousands of other times, and moved on to the next venue, where they could parcel out the usual portion of surf/car/girl hits, tart it up with a few jokes and generic exhortations, and then collect a rather large check and get back to their hotel.

They performed in Atlantic City, New Jersey, that Fourth of July, all of the original Beach Boys plus Bruce, performing on a ten-foot stage built on the sand, halfway between the rumbling ocean and rattling, chiming slot machines in the casinos on the boardwalk. The crowd was enormous, a galaxy of boats moored just beyond the breakers, all of them bathed easily in music so loud it drowned out the sound of the planes buzzing overhead. The Playboy casino twinkled just over the horizon. Was this Dennis Wilson's vision of heaven? Perhaps. But Dennis was a wreck that night, sweaty and shirtless, his booze-swollen gut rippling as he flailed unsteadily at the rhythm he could no longer nail down for his own. And when he got to his traditional spotlight number, "You Are So Beautiful," his voice was so wrecked by the years of booze, cocaine, and cigarettes that he could only launch into a meandering rap about how it felt to stand up there on the stage, looking out at all the faces that were looking back up at them. "If you only knew," he wheezed. "If you only knew how it felt to be up here singing and playing . . . the joy it brings to us . . ." The audience screamed its approval, as they always did, and

Dennis stood silent for a moment, letting the cheers wash around him, waiting for the love to drizzle into that part of him that was too empty to ever be satisfied, no matter how much music, love, sex, drugs, booze, or applause he poured inside.

"Happy birthday, America!" Carl screamed, and then they were off again, ripping through another "Surfin' USA," another "Fun, Fun, Fun," another "Barbara Ann." This was the music Dennis had inspired, echoes of the world he had first glimpsed during those stolen teenaged hours on the beach and then brought home to deposit into his big brother's unbounded imagination. Now, nearly a quarter century later, it still had the power to enrapture people, still had them dancing and screaming on this beach 3,000 miles away. *If you only knew, if you only knew.*

The people kept cheering for the Beach Boys, but they didn't know anything. Five months later, on a sunny but chilly December afternoon just a few days after his thirty-ninth birthday, Dennis was drinking with some friends on a boat moored in Marina Del Rey, near the slip where he had once moored the *Harmony*, his beloved teak sloop, since repossessed for lack of regular payments. Restless as ever, Dennis had strapped on a diving mask and jumped into the ocean, swimming down to sift through the sand in search of relics from his earlier life. He came up with a silver picture frame he had once hurled off his boat, laughing in triumph as he tossed it up toward his friends. Then he went down again, slipping out of the sunshine and back down into the greenish depths where it had all started for him. Dennis had always been a strong swimmer, which is what puzzled some people later. But he was a different person now. "That last year it was like he was alive, but he wasn't there," Trish Campo says. Barbara Wilson, who last saw the father of her sons at a party celebrating his youngest son's first birthday in the summer of 1983, had reached the same conclusion. "Dennis was so far gone, it was as if he had already died."

So there he was in the chilly water, using all of his remaining strength to push himself even deeper, searching for something just beyond the tips of his fingers. Did he realize how cold the late December water had grown? Did he struggle against the end, or did it simply ease him away, off into a light that would, finally, ease that terrible emptiness?

Forty-five minutes later the Harbor Patrol discovered Dennis's body on the floor of the harbor. An autopsy performed later revealed that his blood alcohol level was twice what the police would need to declare him legally drunk. A day later the surviving Beach Boys gathered before the press, looking sad, if not all that surprised. "We are not disbanding," Carl declared, firmly. "We know Dennis would want us to continue in the spirit and tradition of the Beach Boys."

Which is precisely what they did without missing a beat. The group played its usual schedule of shows in 1984, including a triumphant return to the Washington Monument on the Fourth of July. Meanwhile, they had also started work on their first new album in five years and the first in eight years to feature the contributions of a healthy Brian Wilson. But fearing that even a clear-eyed Brian might not, at forty-two, have the right sensibility for the modern market, the group chose instead to hire Steve Levine, producer of the then-popular British band Culture Club, to steer their new project. It was, in many ways, a very odd pairing. Culture Club, fronted by the heavily made-up cross-dresser Boy George, performed mostly dance-friendly tunes played almost entirely on synthesizers and other electronic gear. And this was precisely the technique Levine brought to the Beach Boys. As Carl said when the album came out in 1985: "Almost everything on the record was programmed note-for-note, sound-for-sound, beat-by-beat, and then we wouldn't hear it until we sent it through the computer," he said. "The digital approach is so new, and it can be quite tedious until you learn it."

Not surprisingly, the record that emerged turned out to be an awkward, if occasionally engaging, blend of eras, styles, and cultures. Titled simply *The Beach Boys* and dedicated to "the memory of our beloved brother, cousin, and friend," the record kicked off with a few bars of booming, straight-ahead drums: precisely the sort of boom-boom rhythm Dennis might have played. The brief intro (actually a digital program) led into Mike and Terry Melcher's faux-1950s ballad "Getcha Back," which was most notable for its multitiered harmonies and particularly the familiar falsetto wailing over the top. Carl's R & B–inspired "It's Gettin' Late" made excellent use of Levine's layered keyboards, while the youngest Wilson's graceful love song "Where I Belong" featured full group harmonies that were richer than anything they had attempted in fifteen years. From there, however, the record suffers from all the usual conceptual flaws that mark the group's post–*Love You* albums. "California Calling" strip-mined the memory of "Surfin' USA" to predictably lame effect, stringing together references to surfing, boogie boarding, woody station wagons, and the expression "totally rad" with all the grace and passion of one of Levine's computer programs. Conversely, many of the other songs tried too hard to echo the contemporary pop charts. Carl's hard-rocking "Maybe I Don't Know" got tangled in a generic hair-metal guitar solo, while "Passing Friend," contributed by Boy George and Roy Hay, sounded just like the Culture Club outtake it was. Stevie Wonder's "I Do Love You" came off a bit better, if only because it's a much better song that combined its author's musical chops (Stevie played all of the instruments himself) with Carl's voice at its funkiest.

Brian's reinvigorated voice added a richness to the blend that had been missing for years. But his own songs sounded more like exercises than the product of inspiration, both in terms of their simple music and lyrics (composed in part by Landy) that had none of the goofy poetry Brian invested in even his most tossed-off songs. *"I'm so lonely/Really, really so lonely/I wish that you'd come comfort me, oh yeah"* was about as deep as it got. The one new original that did contain more than a trace of Brian's musical and lyrical touch was the silly, modularly structured "Male Ego," which was relegated to semi-existence as the "Getcha Back" flip side and as a bonus track on the CD.

Released during the spring of 1985, *The Beach Boys* benefited from yet another wave of publicity pegged to a Brian comeback and the curiosity/sympathy that lingered from the Watt affair and Dennis's death. "Getcha Back" jumped into the midtwenties on the singles charts, propelled in part by a video that earned light rotation on MTV, despite its portrayal of the group as cool security guards at a teenaged pool party and then as the groovy, ageless surfers they never really had been. The album stalled at number fifty-two, however, and soon the group was back to its primary occupation of finding new ways to repackage and sell off the shards of the pure, windswept horizon they had helped Brian bring to life two decades earlier. If they had ever felt moved by the beauty of what they had once created, if they had ever connected the quest for physical transcendence the songs described to the spiritual one that linked them to their ancestors and to the gleam in the eyes that sparkled beyond the footlights every night, it had clearly ceased to matter to them. For now the Beach Boys, like so many other middle-aged businessmen in Ronald Reagan's go-go 1980s, were committed to making money.

And maybe this was exactly what America's Band was supposed to be doing. After all, America's entertainment industry never shied away from naked greed, either. The traveling circuses of the nineteenth century actually sold grifters the right to fleece their crowds, contracting with them just as they did with food and drink concessionaires. And though the popular entertainers of the twentieth century have historically presented themselves as transgressive types aligned with society's downtrodden rank and file, their success has most often been determined by their relationships with the rich and powerful.

So the Beach Boys took care of business, accepting a deal from Sunkist to record a revised version of "Good Vibrations" for a multimedia ad campaign promoting orange soda. They observed the group's twenty-fifth anniversary with a concert on the beach in Hawaii, where guests including Ray Charles, Glen Campbell, Belinda Carlisle of the Go-Gos, and the Fabulous Thunderbirds played along on the greatest hits, with the Beach Boys providing (largely overdubbed in postproduction) backing harmonies. Taped by NBC, the show aired in the prime-time horse latitudes of mid-March, where it failed to make much of a splash. The group's first single in 1986, Mike and Terry Melcher's "Rock 'n' Roll to the Rescue," spoke both of "surfer girls" and "high school days," while their next release turned out to be a far-too-faithful cover of the Mamas and Papas' "California Dreamin'," chosen both for its harmonic possibilities (which they barely bothered to explore) and the irresistible pull of the word "California" in its title. A year later the group hitched a ride on the hip-hop bandwagon by providing instrumental and vocal backing to the Fat Boys' rap version of "Wipeout," which was a minor hit in the summer of 1987.

The short-term result was a series of medium-size hits that kept the group's new music on the radio. But the longer-term result was that they had willingly made the final leap from serious artistry to self-parody. To watch the Beach Boys performing now—chauffeured across baseball infields in woody station wagons, performing on stages crowded with unironic surfboards, all of them dressed in clothes that had come to resemble an eccentric cross between high school letterman's garb and geriatric leisure wear—was to see a group of musicians who no longer had any idea what their songs meant or why they were still so important to the people who came to hear them sung.

When the group played a show following a minor league baseball game in Portland, Oregon, in August 1987, they worked with all the smooth detachment of men running an assembly line. Backstage before the show, Al chatted warmly with radio contest winners, showing them his guitars and urging them to hang around, grab a soda or some chips off of the banquet table, whatever. "You don't have to go anywhere," he said. Mike stood with his assistant, another balding man named Mike, and loosened up for the show by downing a procession of Heinekens, which he poured carefully into a tall soda cup between visits with admirers. Asked to pose for a picture, the self-proclaimed teetotaler would make sure to hide his beer behind his back. Bruce occupied himself with the matter of the *Billboard* charts, which just then were showing the progress of the "Wipeout" single. Or that's what he wanted to do, anyway, but now it turned out that his assistant had forgotten to bring the latest issue of *Billboard,* so everything they knew was a week old. Now Bruce, who wore a white shirt decorated with thick vertical stripes, much like the Beach Boys' early '60s getup, only multicolored, was visibly angry, shaking his head and reminding the woman that it was the one thing he'd asked her to do. How was it, again, that she'd forgotten to do it? She asked him if he wanted a Coke or some tea with honey, but he didn't. What he wanted was the new *Billboard,* but it wasn't here. Was it? No, she had to agree. It wasn't.

Carl came in later, looking tired and preoccupied, wanting only to loosen up for the show. But when cornered by a reporter wishing to request several obscurities, he shrugged off the whole subject with a worn-out sigh. "This is kind of the meat-and-potatoes crowd, you know?" he said, gesturing toward the rumble coming from the nearly filled stands outside. "They don't have the patience for the quiet stuff or more than a new song or two. Maybe another time we'll come back and play a smaller hall for the real fans."

He didn't sound convinced. And why should he? When the Beach Boys climbed out of their woody wagons half an hour later and fell into the opening chords of "California Girls," the stadium went up like a rocket. They danced, they cheered, they sang along. The beach balls bounced, the couples hugged, and the kids ran up and down the aisle, pretending they were surfing down the concrete stairs.

But how long could that last? Mike had already started to fret about the group's advancing age—and the effect that might have on their aggregate sex appeal—when, just a few months after the Portland show, the group got a call from an administrator at University of Nevada at Las Vegas. They were about to play a casino show at Caesar's, and so the athletic department was wondering: Might the group be willing to invite the school's cheerleaders onstage to dance when they played "Be True to Your School" at Caesar's Palace? Well, Mike always liked having young girls around, and the closer the better. The cheerleaders were duly invited, and they put on quite a show up there, jumping and wriggling and pom-poming for all they were worth. All of which led Mike to a revelation: They ought to hire their own troupe of cheerleaders to dance onstage every night! Bruce agreed instantly, though Carl thought it was the stupidest thing he'd ever heard, and Al nearly went ballistic when he realized that now they could never change the set list because that would screw up the girls' wardrobe changes. But Mike was determined, and so they spent the entire summer and then a few subsequent tours playing and singing some of the rock era's most influential songs amid a throng of young women, all beaming and jumping and waving pompoms like each night was the big game and the dorky, middle-aged Beach Boys were about to be crowned homecoming kings.

The group did have an award coming, as it turned out, and it was a big one. Now twenty-five years past their first recording, they had become eligible for induction into the new but already influential Rock 'n' Roll Hall of Fame. And it was a measure of the ongoing acclaim for Brian's best work that they—along with the Beatles, Bob Dylan, and the Supremes—were afforded the honor the first time they were eligible to be nominated. The black-tie ceremony, held in late January 1988 at the Waldorf-Astoria hotel in midtown Manhattan, also featured appearances by Mick Jagger, who inducted the Beatles (represented by George Harrison and Ringo Starr); Bruce Springsteen, celebrating the work of Dylan; and Elton John, who was slated to bring up the Beach Boys. So even if Paul McCartney skipped the party to protest some ongoing intra-Beatle feud and Diana Ross turned her nose up at appearing on the same stage with her former partners, the crowd that did turn up at the Waldorf's ballroom (which also included Paul Simon, Billy Joel, Neil Young, John Fogerty, and Little Richard) represented the very heart of the Western world's popular music in the second half of the twentieth century. It was a wonderful if occasionally bittersweet night, and the vibrations were even better than good, right up through Elton John's introduction and the standing ovation that greeted Brian, Carl, Al, and Mike as they walked up onto the stage.

Perhaps Mike had been enjoying the champagne. Maybe he hadn't slept well the night before. At any rate, there was a weird glint in his eyes, and the moment Brian finished his scripted speech and Mike had a clear shot at the microphone, his anger boiled over in public once again. After a brief salute to the inductees who had died, Mike tossed a jibe at the absent McCartney, wondering pointedly how a lawsuit could keep someone away from such a lovely evening. "Now, that's a bummer 'cause we're talkin' about harmony in the world!" he said. The small ripple of applause that elicited only fired him up all the more, and then he was lashing out at Diana Ross, which led him to boast about how the Beach Boys still played 180 dates a year. "I'd like to see the MOPTOPS match that!" he roared. "I'd like to see MICK JAGGER get out on the stage and do 'I Get

CATCH A WAVE

Around' versus 'Jumpin' Jack Flash' ANY DAY NOW!" By now the crowd was tittering uncomfortably, and a few hisses snaked up from the tables. And still he went on, complaining that people were going to say he was crazy. "Well, they been sayin' that for years! Ain't nothin' new about that!" Meanwhile, the other Beach Boys had begun to look increasingly uneasy, alternately blinking at each other and gazing down at the tips of their shoes. "It was kind of a blank moment," Jardine says. "Like, whoa! Where's this coming from?" But Mike was still rolling, trying to make some point about how we're all one world, and now we need to do something beautiful with all the talent here. But somehow he still couldn't shake the impulse to taunt: "I'd like to see some people KICK OUT THE JAMS!" he yelled. "I challenge The Boss to get up onstage and jam!"

Finally, Paul Shaffer signaled the band to kick into "Good Vibrations," and the crowd was up on its feet again, this time cheering the fact that Mike, finally, was finished talking. Instantly, Mike's speech became a recurring joke for everyone else to play off of. Walking offstage, Elton John switched into diva mode, demanding in a mock-petulant voice: "Why didn't he fucking mention *me*?" Dazed and horrified, Al walked up to where George Harrison and Ringo Starr were sitting. "I said, 'Geez, guys, I really want to apologize for that speech. My partner's not feeling well.' Then Ringo put his head on my shoulder and said, 'It's okay, we love you guys.' George's classic remark was, 'I guess Mike didn't listen to the Maharishi, did he?' Then he put his head on my shoulder too, and it was really quite sweet." When Dylan got up to accept his award a little later, he lobbed a gentle barb back at the Beach Boys' perpetually seething singer. "I'd like to thank Mike Love for not mentioning me," he said, smiling puckishly. "Peace, love, and harmony are important, indeed. But so is forgiveness."

Ironically, Dylan's admonition echoed the feelings contained at the heart of many of the same songs the Beach Boys had just been honored for creating. And though there was something sad about how far they had drifted from the central spirit of their music, the mere presence of Brian Wilson—looking fit and relatively clear-eyed, no less—hinted that even now, in the wake of so much sorrow, self-abuse, death, and soul-killing commercialization, it was still possible to find a little love and mercy.

CHAPTER 15

By the time *The Beach Boys* was released in the spring of 1985, two things were beginning to become clear: Eugene Landy had saved Brian Wilson's life. And having done that, he was in the process of making it a mess.

Only two years past the day he had been shipped to Hawaii in near-fatal condition—his body swollen beyond recognition, his lungs choked with chemicals, his heart struggling to keep up, his eyes pinwheeling with drugs and unrestrained craziness—Brian stood tall, trim, and healthy. He would run six miles in the morning, lift weights, and then cool off with herbal tea and a restrained, healthy breakfast. After that he'd go willingly to his piano to work on songs that gave him evident pleasure. In the evenings he'd get dressed up and hit the town, taking in concerts, showing his face at the right events. Sometimes he even played music in public, albeit at small charitable events; and even though you could see anxiety in his eyes, the clear, youthful tone of his voice made it obvious that the forty-two-year-old Brian Wilson wasn't just alive . . . he was thriving.

Or that's how it seemed until you noticed whom he was with. Because someone was always there, and whoever that someone was, they were always watching him. Sometimes it was Dr. Landy, Brian's smaller, rangier, hard-eyed doppelgänger, the guy who was always running up a little too fast to shake hands, looking up at you a bit too intensely, demanding too much information. Other times it was one, or more often two, of Landy's helpers: that weird crew of silent watchers who were constantly taking notes, unless they were running their little pocket-recorders, which they would do until they started pointing their video cameras around. What they were looking for and why they needed to capture every stray moment of Brian's social interaction was a mystery.

The closer you got, the weirder it became. When Timothy White went to Brian's new Malibu house to talk about *The Beach Boys* that winter, he discovered a reborn man whose new lease on life seemed to come with some deed restrictions. The 24/7 minders, for one thing. And then, as Brian showed him, the beepers they all had to wear in order to be within a heartbeat of Landy at all times. "I have a sudden sense of airlessness in the room, as if the oxygen is being sucked out," he wrote, describing the moment Brian showed him the beeper. "And then I'm filled with an odd sadness."

And for Brian, perhaps, it was also a feeling of déjà vu. He had long since come to learn how it felt to be the subject of someone's proprietary sense of discipline. Murry had steered him until his early twenties, when a brief window of near-total independence was slammed shut by the other Beach Boys, along with their various owners, managers, and agents. No amount of wanting to leave the band had given Brian the courage to actually do it in the late 1960s and early 1970s. Instead, he allowed them to pull him all the way back in during the mid-1970s. It took a painfully slow, excruciatingly public march toward death for the Beach Boys to finally leave Brian alone in the early 1980s, and then they had turned over the keys to Landy, who said he had no intention of sticking around for more than a couple of years, even as he was adding his name to Brian's financial and professional documents.

It was strange and sad and almost entirely soul-killing, even when viewed from a distance. And it was also what Brian wanted. Or maybe not what he wanted as much as what he needed. For unless he had that stern authority figure telling him when to wake up, what to do, and then when to stop doing it so he could go to bed, nothing else in the world made sense. That externalized authority was like gravity to him, keeping his feet on the earth, giving him something to push up against. Brian might say that he hated it, and he certainly enjoyed finding subtle new ways to rebel against it. But even while he grumbled and moaned, he did what he had to do to make sure it was always there, keeping him from drifting off into outer space. So Brian kept Landy's beeper clipped to his belt. He posed for publicity pictures showing the two of them pretending to ride surfboards, and he didn't complain when Landy told one reporter that they had become, as he put it, "partners in life." Landy continued: "We've exchanged names. He's Brian Landy Wilson and I'm Eugene Wilson Landy."

Landy apparently didn't notice how much like *Invasion of the Body Snatchers* that sounded. True enough, his particular form of treatment had dictated that he assume control over virtually every aspect of Brian's life. But even that arrangement did not necessitate becoming his patient's professional and artistic partner, let alone having the power to control the man's artistic output. Or, for that matter, becoming his financial partner and being richly compensated as a result. For Landy had obviously never lost his appetite for a life bathed in the spotlight. And now that he held the reins to one of popular music's most sought-after living legends, he was going to hold on with the sort of white-knuckled intensity that hadn't been seen since Murry Wilson had worked his magic during the "Help Me, Rhonda" session twenty years ago.

No wonder Landy referred so constantly to the abuses and manipulations levied by Murry Wilson. But the ferocity of the psychologist's denunciations only put the similarities between biological father and his therapeutic heir into higher relief. Both were pugnacious go-getters; both had long cultivated showbiz dreams that bore fruit only through the talents of Brian Wilson. It's also safe to say that both Murry and Landy loved Brian in their way. And Brian would never deny that they had both fulfilled an important role in his life. "I loved my dad because he knew where it was at. He had that competitive spirit which really blew my mind," he said during the spring of 1998. A few months later, Brian confessed to National Public Radio's Terry Gross that he still thought fondly of Landy. "Yeah, I miss him. I miss his personality."

It was an amazing admission, but not really all that surprising. For just as the younger Brian had depended on his father to fend off the Capitol Records execs and keep his own feet to the fire, the middle-aged artist relied on Landy to keep him sequestered from the more troubling members of his family (virtually everyone, now that you mention it), the Beach Boys organization, and whoever else made him feel uncomfortable. Landy's aggressive insistence sparked Brian's creativity, just as Murry's perpetual demands got him going back in the early '60s. Landy also put the spurs to Brian's athletic ambition, setting up a rigid schedule of workouts that transformed Brian's body. And once Brian dropped weight,

Landy sent him to get his face touched up surgically in order to revive the boyishly handsome look of his youth. Now when Brian looked in the mirror, he took pride in his appearance, and rightfully so: He hadn't looked this good since he was twenty-two.

"People say that Dr. Landy runs my life, but the truth is, I'm in charge," Brian wrote in a statement to the *Los Angeles Times* a few years later. And in a weird way he was telling the truth: As passive as Brian could be, he had also maneuvered Landy into being precisely the same father figure whose loss had so devastated him. But just because Brian craved the relationship still didn't make it a healthy one.

Once *The Beach Boys* was done, and especially after it failed to light the charts on fire, Landy and Brian set out to start his solo career. Sensing that Brian would work better with a collaborator, Landy set him up in 1986 with Gary Usher, the guy who had knocked on the Wilsons' door back in late 1961 and gone on to cowrite "409," "In My Room," and a handful of Brian's other early hits. The ever-suspicious Murry had shoved Usher aside before he and Brian could form a lasting professional bond, and though Usher had gone on to become a prominent record producer (working with the Byrds and the Surfaris, among others), they hadn't seen one another in many years. Still, it didn't take Brian and Gary long to become reacquainted, and soon they hunkered down in Usher's studio, writing songs and recording demos, which they then began to sculpt into more sophisticated master tapes. And they were having a ball, according to Usher's account (subsequently published in book form as *The Wilson Project* by the Australian writer Stephen J. McParland), until the interference started.

The way Landy's system worked, Brian never went anywhere without one of his minders—usually Kevin Leslie, whose muscular physique and mane of blond hair earned him the nickname "the Surf Nazi" from one of Brian's friends. Scott Steinberg or Landy's twenty-two-year-old son, Evan, also became regular companions. Most often they would sit silently in the corner, observing and taking notes. But then the psychologist began to make his presence known, first by demanding that Brian and Gary work on one song instead of another, then by sending Brian in with new lyrics written by Landy and/or his live-in girlfriend, Alexandra. Unfortunately, Landy's actual poetic sensibility was quite a bit shakier than his self-confidence, and his words tended to revolve around sentimental love tales or psychobabble that was as dull as it was obvious. *"In my car/I'm captain of my destiny . . . /Pretty baby, come cruise with me"* went one typical chorus.

Actually, Landy preferred to steer Brian's destiny, particularly when it came to the women he cruised with. All of which became evident to Melinda Ledbetter the day she met the shy rock star on the sales floor of Martin Cadillac, where she was working in 1986. He had come with Landy in search of a new car, and once the blonde former model pointed out a town car nearby, Brian decided to buy it on the spot. "It was the first car I showed him," she says. "This brown Seville, and it was just ugly." They got to talking back in the sales office, and Brian was soon telling his new friend about his brother Dennis and how two years had passed since he'd drowned, but that still didn't change how terribly upset he was about it. "My first impression was that he was someone who was troubled," she says. A couple of days later, Landy called Melinda at work to ask if she might want to go out on a date with Brian. Understandably, being asked out by a man's therapist struck Melinda as a trifle bizarre. Nevertheless, she agreed to the date, and a few nights later Brian came to pick her up at the apartment complex where she was living. And though he had apparently forgotten the exact number of her apartment—Melinda realized he'd arrived when she noticed that he was standing in the middle of the building's courtyard shouting her name—they were soon in the back of a black stretch limo, cruising up through the Hollywood Hills to the Universal Amphitheater to see the Moody Blues perform. And the more they talked, the more she became enamored of Brian. "He was so different from anyone that I'd ever met. Just the sweetest, most naive guy—so honest and sincere."

And so closely monitored. In addition to the two attendants who were accompanying the couple, Landy himself called in every hour or so to hear the latest on how it was going. All of which struck Melinda as a bit unsettling. But what really mattered to her was that the open, soft glow in Brian's blue eyes had warmed her heart. He called back a few days later, and they went out again. And soon they were fast friends, talking on the phone and going out to dinner or to the movies on a fairly regular basis. But they were never alone.

If Brian had grown resigned to Landy's omnipresence in his life, he couldn't always feign enthusiasm for it, particularly when it came to his music. As Gary Usher noticed, whenever Landy decided to take over writing lyrics for a particular song, Brian's interest would diminish almost immediately. And just as he had complained about Murry's overbearing ways in 1961 and 1962, Brian spoke often to Usher (when Kevin Leslie was out of the room) about how much he wanted to break free of Landy's grasp. "I live in a strange hell," Brian reportedly said. "I'm a prisoner and I have no hope of escaping." Usher also described Brian's tales of feeling so trapped when he woke up in the morning that he would scream into his pillow until his voice was too raw to talk. He also claimed to have attempted suicide in the summer of 1985, diving into the ocean and swimming straight out to sea until one of Landy's men chased him down and pulled him back to shore.

And yet Brian persevered, and eventually one of the Wilson/Usher songs, "Let's Go to Heaven in My Car," ended up in the sound track of the *Police Academy 3* movie. But when Seymour Stein, the president of Sire Records, saw Brian induct Jerry Lieber and Mike Stoller into the Rock 'n' Roll Hall of Fame in early 1987 (singing an a cappella version of "On Broadway") and signed Brian to a solo contract, he insisted that he be allowed to appoint his own coproducer to help Brian stay organized and on-task. Landy accepted Stein's conditions—particularly since Stein agreed to let him take an executive producer's credit, too—and Stein tapped staff producer Andy Paley, a multi-instrumentalist/producer who had been a Brian fanatic since his grade school days in Boston. Later he'd formed the Paley Brothers with his brother, Jonathan, and recorded an album at Brother Studios in the mid-1970s. Ten years later Paley had become a full-time producer, working on albums for artists ranging from Patti Smith to Jerry Lee Lewis. But when Stein called to tell the Boston-based musician about his new opportunity in California, Paley didn't hesitate. He jumped on an airplane for the coast and was soon installed in an apartment building in Burbank, from which he commuted every day to Brian's house in Malibu to help his hero write and record a batch of new songs. "We started writing pretty much right away," Paley recalls. "Brian's house was right on the water, and the atmosphere was pretty cool. Except that Landy was checking me out, trying to use me as someone he could manipulate to help him get stuff out of the record company."

Generally, Paley would get to Malibu somewhere between 9:00 and 10:00 in the morning, usually finding Brian drinking tea out on his porch. They'd go running, then sit in the hot tub for a while and talk. Like the work he'd done with Tony Asher and Van Dyke Parks, Brian's work with Paley sprang largely out of conversations they'd have about whatever was on their minds at the time. "My job was to kick him in the ass and get him going," Paley says. "It was difficult because he was medicated, and that slowed him down a bit. He was also in mid-career and didn't have anything to prove anymore." So they'd shoot the breeze or sometimes go off to see a movie just for a change of pace. Even more often they would sit in a quiet room and meditate together, both of them chasing the elusive sparks of inspiration that might lead to a song. Often, Paley would show up with a riff or a verse and play it for Brian, asking what he thought of it—did he think he could come up with a bridge or a chorus? If Brian heard something that excited him, he'd jump onto the piano bench and start pounding away, and a few minutes later they'd have the rough outline for a song.

Such moments were often punctuated by strange intrusions by Landy or his minions swooping in to maneuver Brian into doing whatever the doctor wanted. Paley recounts one vocal session where Brian's minder interrupted a take to tell Brian that he was singing the wrong words. "The guy was saying something like, 'Brian, don't you think the lyrics would be better if Alexandra fixed them?' And Brian said, 'No, I like them the way they are.' Then the guy's like, 'Well, what did you tell me last night when I said you could have that milkshake if you switched the lyrics?' And then Brian said, 'Oh, okay. The new lyrics are better than the old ones.'"

When Landy was determined to get his way, the team of producers and engineers in the studio had to come up with subterfuges to keep him from undermining Brian's work. At one point they were working on "Meet Me in My Dreams Tonight," a song Brian had written with Paley. But Landy had composed another set of lyrics to the tune—something about experiencing a "love attack," Paley recalls—and ordered Brian to sing the song again using the second set of words. Landy had forbidden the engineers from even mixing the original "Meet Me in My Dreams," but when he flew to Hawaii one morning for a vacation, they lured the day's bodyguard out of the studio for a Ping-Pong game, mixing the original lyrics into the tune when he was down the hall. Once that version made the rounds of the executives at Sire, Landy's "love attack" was never heard from again.

One of the biggest struggles involved the *Smile*-like suite that Lenny Waronker, Sire's secondmost senior executive, had asked Brian to prepare for the album. A longtime fan of Brian's more artistically ambitious work, Waronker was particularly eager to see Brian complete at least one new example of the extended, modular style of recording that had represented the step beyond *Pet Sounds* and "Good Vibrations." Brian had been cool on the idea at first, but he liked the name Waronker had suggested—"Rio Grande," from the movie of the same name—and spent the next few days with Paley composing a few new pieces and stringing together a bunch of previously unrelated bits into an impressionistic frontier-style narrative. They were nearly done writing when Landy walked in with a new set of lyrics that revised the piece into a psychology-themed epic called "Life's Suite." But even if Brian couldn't muster the strength to tell Landy to back off, Waronker—who was coproducing the "Rio Grande" sessions—

rejected Landy's "Life's Suite" lyrics out of hand. Once again, Landy grew apoplectic, but Waronker would have none of it, and they completed the frontier-themed piece as composed by Brian and Paley.

Landy found other ways to assert his control over the recording process, often moving sessions from one studio to another at the last minute and then confiscating all of the master tapes when they were done working. His helpers used the studio's intercom system to eavesdrop on sessions when they were in another room—though the engineering crew soon figured this out and thus stopped using the intercoms. Often, Landy's meetings with Stein, Waronker, or Russ Titelman (an old friend of Brian's who had gone on to become an influential producer and was now coproducing several tracks on the album) devolved into screaming matches, with the pugnacious psychologist bellowing the loudest. Landy's fits weren't only about significant artistic decisions: One magazine article from the era portrayed the engaging sight of Landy pitching a major fit when Sire arranged for him to be met at the airport by a Lincoln Town Car rather than the stretch limousine he had been expecting.

"Anything good we got out of those sessions was done totally on stolen time," Paley says. "Landy was always checking in, phoning in directions, basically never wanting to give Brian any breathing room. It was a hassle and many times heartbreaking because we'd do something good, finally, and then Landy would swoop in and dive-bomb it." But when they did have peace in the studio, Brian could work with amazing speed and precision, often dreaming up and singing complex, multipart vocal arrangements while standing alone at the microphone. When Titelman requested a revision to the lyrics of "Melt Away" in midsession, Brian stepped away from the microphone and paced across the studio floor, muttering, *"I'm gonna get it, I'm gonna get it, I'm gonna get it."* About a minute later, he put the headphones back on and sang a new line—*"I feel just like an island/Until I see you smilin'"*—that so perfectly fit the mood and meter of the song that Paley could only gape with wonder. "He was under pressure, but what he came up with was just such a beautiful, cool twist."

The moments of creativity could be magical. But as Landy continued to do battle with the Sire Records team, most often using Brian as his cudgel, the recording process dragged on for more than a year. Star collaborators—Jeff Lynne, Lindsey Buckingham, and Terence Trent D'arby, among others—shuttled in and out. As time passed and the bills began to pile up, pressure from the record company only increased. Still, as Paley recalls, Brian's sense of humor remained intact.

Once, after they had taken one of their meditation retreats in a nearby studio, Brian turned to Paley and noted, "The only way this whole record is gonna work out is with medication and meditation." On his way to the men's room on another day, he noticed a group of young musicians hanging out in the lounge at the A&M studio and walked up to a pay phone near where they were sitting. After picking up the receiver, he pretended to listen quietly for a moment, then began to wail. "What? A plane crash? No! NO! Don't tell me that! It can't be true! Okay, bye-bye." Brian hung up and walked to the bathroom without saying another word. When he came out a few minutes later, he approached the group of guys and shrugged apologetically: "You know, that was just a bogus call." Paley watched the whole thing unfold from down the hall, barely able to contain his laughter. "The best part was, they had absolutely no idea who Brian was."

As the record finally neared completion in early 1988, Stein and Waronker made sure that everyone at Sire Records knew how vitally important the record was to them and to the company. Actually, their colleagues had already figured it out—both execs had been so wrapped up in the micro-details of Brian's recording sessions that many of their other tasks had been left undone for months. But now that *Brian Wilson,* as the album was now called, was on its way, they made certain that every conceivable publicity tool would be wielded to maximum impact. A vast ad campaign was set into motion. The most elaborate promotion kits in the history of rock 'n' roll—including lengthy historical essays by David Leaf, a step-by-step recounting of the album's birth, a probing Q-and-A with the artist, and a detailed career-long discography—were mailed to virtually everyone in the entertainment media. Once again, word of a Brian Wilson comeback drew immediate attention from the nation's biggest publications. And when advance tapes of the album went out to critics, the excitement became even more intense: This was no lame, latter-day Beach Boys album. *Brian Wilson,* the critics began to whisper to their friends and editors, was the real deal: melodic, poetic, full of extravagant arrangements and unexpected instruments. And, of course, wave after wave of those beautiful harmonies. Titelman was going around calling it *Pet Sounds '88,* and to everyone who had heard the album, even that assertion didn't seem terribly outlandish.

So once again, the reporters and the writers came storming in. But not all of them were being guided by the sound of the music. Early that spring, the gothic side of the Brian Wilson saga had also come floating to the surface, this time in the form of charges mounted against Landy by the California Board of Medical

Quality Assurance. Some of the assertions were actually about another patient—a woman alleging that Landy had given her cocaine and other drugs while also compelling her to have sex with him. Landy called the charges "frivolous and malicious," but when giving a sworn deposition in an accompanying civil suit, he limited his responses to repeatedly pleading his Fifth Amendment right to not incriminate himself. Those unrelated allegations added a little zest to the story, but the real attention-grabber had to do with Landy's relationship with the client who happened to be a multimillionaire rock 'n' roll star. According to the state's complaint, Landy had created ". . . various dual, triple, and quadruple relationships [that have] caused severe emotional damage, psychological dependency, and financial exploitation to his patient."

Unsurprisingly, the writers charged with reporting on Brian's new life and career all wanted to get to the bottom of the matter. Unsurprisingly, what they heard veered wildly from one extreme to the other. One minute, Brian was mounting stirring defenses of his psychologist-turned-friend-turned-partner-and-collaborator. "Right now I'm in the best emotional, physical, intellectual, and financial shape I've been in for many years, maybe my whole life," Brian wrote in a statement to the *Los Angeles Times Magazine* that was meant to refute an investigative piece written by Nancy Spiller. "I want to publicly thank [Landy] for helping me regain control of my life and art." But only a day or two later, Brian told *Rolling Stone*'s Michael Goldberg that he heard voices in his head threatening to kill him. "I get calls in my head from people in the vicinity or maybe ten, twenty miles out," he whispered to Goldberg. "They get to me." Talking to Timothy White (writing this time for the *New York Times Magazine*), Brian first defended Landy. "I don't know what I would have possibly done without him." But when Landy left the room, his client's tune changed dramatically. "I have to stand on my own two feet," he insisted. "Especially when it comes to my music or the Beach Boys' music."

Whether the thrum of controversy helped or hindered the buzz surrounding the album is unclear. But when the album finally did arrive in early July, critical response ranged from ecstatically positive ("A remarkable work that recalls the exhilarating sweep of the Beach Boys' most endearing recordings," Robert Hilburn sang in the *Los Angeles Times*) to something less than that ("Let's be honest . . . *Brian Wilson* can't compare with any of the early '60s Beach Boys classics," opined the AP's David Bauder). Other critics hailed the mere fact of the record's existence ("Despite all he has been through, the mood of *Brian*

Wilson is disarmingly innocent and optimistic," wrote Paul Grein in the *Los Angeles Times*), while still others looked at the vast team of producers, coproducers, and collaborators who shared credit on the cover with Executive Producer Dr. Eugene E. Landy and figured the whole thing for a scam. ("The first solo album by Wilson . . . is often appalling," concluded *People*'s Ralph Novak.)

If some reviews were obviously softened by the critics' sympathy for Brian, and others were made more jagged by suspicion about Landy and the star chamber of producers and executives, the album itself existed somewhere in between, veering between moments of sweet, redemptive beauty and songs that were overwhelmed by their own ambition, to some that actually did combine the tactics of the past with the tools of the present into a wholly new sound. And then there were a few that seemed either so out of character or so desperate to be in character that they sounded like the product of extremely talented forgers.

But for anyone who had despaired of ever hearing another structurally inventive, harmony-rich Brian Wilson song—let alone one featuring multiple layers of his own soaring falsetto—*Brian Wilson* defied expectations twenty seconds into the album's opening song, when the opening verse *("I was sittin' in a crummy movie with my hand on my chin . . .")* gave way to a chorus whose plea for spiritual generosity *(". . . So love and mercy to you and your friends tonight")* described the very heart of what Brian's life had been lacking for so long. To hear him singing it in his clear, boyish tenor was breathtaking enough, but after its third verse, "Love and Mercy" shifted to a completely different pattern of descending instrumental/vocal chords, which gave way to an entirely a cappella section whose wordless voices traced still another series of descending chords, meandering slowly back to a reprise of the *"love and mercy . . ."* chorus.

The second song, the stompingly rhythmic "Walkin' the Line," was another of Brian's deceptively autobiographical songs, combining the percussive sound of footsteps, drums, sleigh bells, synth bass, synthesizer, electric guitars, and three layers of interlocking voices into a description of his own impossibly rigid life *("I walk the line, I walk the line every day for you . . .")*. The tune climaxed with a statement of purpose *("If I don't get my way this time I'll die, and that's no lie")* that Brian spat out beneath a sharp-edged falsetto wail that echoed the cry of freedom at the end of "Fun, Fun, Fun." The gentle, lovely "Melt Away" borrowed the sleigh bells and percussive blasts of snare from "God Only Knows" but blended them into an entirely different feeling, with words that emphasized the scars of experience while the interweaving paths of the bass and melody conspired with the billowing *ooohs* and *aaahs* to describe the soothing balm of love. Similarly, the booming, blasting "Baby, Let Your Hair Grow Long" updated the mournful first line of "Caroline, No" (*"Where did your long hair go?"*), only with the voice of a seasoned veteran who knows that innocence and hope can be regained. Brian emphasized the climactic bridge—*"I can't wait to see that change in you/You can do it just the way you used to do"*—by singing it in a falsetto (just the way he used to do), then swerving into a four-bar string interlude that swerved unexpectedly back to the root chord of the verse.

From that solid opening quartet, the album turned quirkier and less satisfying. "Little Children" lifted the chorus of "Mountain of Love" (last heard on the *Beach Boys Party* album) for a calliope-like dash through Brian's dreamy/nightmarish reflections on childhood. "There's So Many" played off the same celestial/romantic images introduced in 1977's "Solar System," only with a much better vocal and lyrics from Landy and his girlfriend Alexandra Morgan that have the clunkiness of the earlier song but miss its wide-eyed charm. The full-bore rocker "Nighttime" weighed down an engagingly layered backing track with a dull melody and rote lyrics, while the Jeff Lynne collaboration "Let It Shine" was so dominated by its guest that it sounded more like an Electric Light Orchestra outtake than a new Brian Wilson tune. "Meet Me in My Dreams Tonight" fared better, thanks largely to its indelible melody and loping rhythm.

The eight-minute-plus final track, "Rio Grande," was meant to be the album's standout and perhaps a signpost to what would lie ahead on future albums. Building from Waronker's suggestion of a frontier-themed suite (much like the *Smile* tracks "Heroes and Villains" and "Cabinessence"), Brian and Paley had constructed a series of musical vignettes that portrayed a trip across a frontier filled with marauding Indians, terrifying thunderstorms, and sweet, unspoken mysteries as a metaphor for life. Recorded with different groups of musicians in different studios—including a bluegrass group Paley recorded during a trip to Boston—the piece strived for the same picturesque sound as the *Smile* songs, with the same jarring shifts in tone and texture. The opening sequence had the chugging rhythm of a riverboat, then faded to a brief campfire vignette that drifted into the sound of a Native American rain dance. The sound of thunder and rain signaled the plucked mandolins and guitars that led off the "Take Me Home" segment, with its layers of soft harmonies. But then the "Night Bloomin' Jasmine" section took one last look back at the erotic mystery of the unknown, before the opening "Rio Grande" theme came back for a brief reprise. And even if "Rio Grande" lacked the wild inspiration of Brian's *Smile*-era work, along with the elegant abstractions in Van Dyke Parks's lyrics, it succeeded at giving *Brian Wilson* the forward-looking perspective of a legitimate comeback. Brian had finally delivered on his oft-given promise to "really stretch out and blow some minds" with his sheer ambition. When the needle finally lifted at the end of side two, it was easy to imagine that he really might be back on his journey to the distant frontier.

But now that the record was done, the daily schedule of writing and record-ing—which came with its own crew of non-Landy collaborators—gave way to the treadmill of interviews, record signings, and other public appearances. And these were controlled almost exclusively by Landy, whose taste and needs dictated many of the key decisions made during the vital period of post-release publicity. Anticipating solo performances of the new music, Landy had the stage-shy Brian drilled in the ways of lead singer–dom, with an emphasis on dance. Thus, when Brian was booked to play the popular *Late Night with David Letterman* show on NBC in August, he sang "Nighttime" in tight leather pants, lurching across the stage with all the grace of a traffic cop whose jockey shorts have caught on fire. Other TV performances went just as badly, with Brian too obviously terrified, his hands shaking and his eyes darting around like a guy with fear in his heart and ghosts on his mind. Nothing about it made him look like the brilliant but reasonably sane guy audiences seem most comfortable seeing in front of them. All great reviews and geysers of publicity aside, *Brian Wilson* stalled at number fifty-two on the *Billboard* charts and sank quickly from there.

The Beach Boys, meanwhile, were on the verge of hitting a surprising new high point. Asked to come up with a beachy song about the Caribbean to go along with a scene in *Cocktail,* a movie starring Tom Cruise as a celebrity bar-tender, they had gotten their hands on "Kokomo," a song former Mamas and Papas leader John Phillips (who had also been a neighbor of Brian's in Bel Air) had written several years earlier with Scott McKenzie, whose song "San Francisco (Be Sure to Wear Some Flowers in Your Hair)" had been a smash in 1967. The existing song had a pleasant, Jimmy Buffett–like sensibility, but as Mike gave it a listen and took up his pen, he made a few changes, shifting the lyrics into the present tense and adding a bass vocal part that gave the song the percussive,

Chuck Berry–like alliteration he'd put into so many of his early collaborations with Brian. As produced by Terry Melcher (who also had enough of a hand in revising the song to earn a composing credit), the song had a layered, Brian-like sound, thanks largely to the unlikely combination of steel drums and accordion (played by Van Dyke Parks, oddly enough) that leads the ensemble. Better yet, the group's vocals—particularly on the Carl-led chorus—sound as rich as they had been on a single since "Good Timin'," and perhaps as far back as "Do It Again." Released in late summer with the momentum of *Cocktail* behind it, "Kokomo" rode all the way to the top of the *Billboard* charts. It was the group's first number one single since "Good Vibrations," almost exactly twenty-two years earlier. And Brian Wilson had nothing to do with it.

Perhaps this shouldn't have been surprising. Although Brian was still an official Beach Boy, his burgeoning solo career—fed by Landy's hostile relationship with the other group members and his increased power over his patient's creative life—had created an even larger than usual gulf between the Beach Boys and their original visionary. Naturally, the production of "Kokomo" and its unexpected success left plenty of room for the usual hurt feelings and outrage on both sides. According to Landy, Brian's absence on the song was a result of the group's deliberately keeping him away from the session. According to the group, it was Landy who had kept Brian away to avenge the group's unwillingness to give him a producer's credit on the song. As usual, interpretations of what had actually happened varied wildly.

But as the group rode its latest burst of glory to a new album contract with Capitol, you might have expected them to invest themselves into making a killer album that would leverage "Kokomo" into a full-fledged commercial renaissance. You would be wrong. Instead, the group cobbled together three recent singles ("Kokomo," "Wipeout," and "Make It Big," which had appeared in a movie called *Troop Beverly Hills*) with three oldies ("I Get Around," "Wouldn't It Be Nice," and "California Girls," all of which had been featured in recent movies) and four highly mediocre new songs, two of which, including the title track, "Still Cruisin'," were part of an endorsement deal they'd reached with Chevrolet to feature the car maker's Corvette sports car prominently in their work. The Love/Melcher–written "Still Cruisin'" was an obvious "Kokomo" rewrite, though the punch line of the chorus depended on a reference to Paul Simon's "Still Crazy After All These Years" for its wit. The other song in the commercial deal was Brian's "In My Car," which had a few interesting chord changes and rhythmic ideas, but these were buried beneath a frantically busy synthesizer arrangement and Landy/Morgan–written lyrics that featured magical lines such as, *"I'm master of my fate/When I accelerate/My new 'Vette is my throne."* The album's two remaining songs, the Jardine-written "Island Girl" and a Phillips/Melcher/Love/ Bruce Johnston collaboration called "Somewhere in Japan," sounded just like anyone else's late '80s synth-pop. Who needed it? More than 750,000 record buyers, as it turned out, though most of them were probably trying to find an LP version of "Kokomo" for their collections.

If the Beach Boys had squandered yet another opportunity to reestablish themselves as contemporary musicians, it certainly didn't seem to bother them. They could always go back to touring on the same set of oldies, which was far easier than writing and recording new songs, anyway. And whenever the subject of new records came up, that would bring Brian back into the mix. And as it turned out, none of the remaining band members were particularly eager to see that happen. By 1989 the touring Beach Boys had achieved a balance of egos and interests that was delicate, yet functioning. Adding Brian, particularly when he was feeling his oats, only threw everything back into chaos. As a result, the one song Brian did contribute to *Still Cruisin'* was essentially a solo track with an obviously overdubbed vocal from Carl. And while Brian felt the same ambivalence about the group that had spent twenty years rejecting his most personal work, he also couldn't bear the thought that they didn't need him. When he realized in the spring of 1990 that the group had started scheduling their recording sessions deliberately so he wouldn't be able to attend, Brian felt, as his lawyer, John Mason, wrote, like "a very depressed and demoralized Beach Boy." As Mason recounted in a letter to Brother Records president Elliott Lott, Brian complained that he had twice offered to write and produce albums for the group in the late '80s, only to be sent away. "This kind of treatment hurts me very much in my chest," Brian told Mason. "It's obvious the boys don't want me . . . I am very hurt."

And it wasn't just a professional divide. As the letter went on, Mason recounted Brian's attempts to go out to dinner with Carl, only to be stood up twice in one week. "Both times Carl left Brian alone and waiting for a phone call," Mason wrote. Perhaps Carl was reluctant to go to dinner with Brian because he knew that he was about to enter the legal battle being waged to separate his brother from the psychologist Brian credited publicly with saving his life. Maybe Brian didn't really believe Landy was the all-knowing visionary he described to reporters. Or maybe

Landy had him so doped up he had lost track of what he did and didn't believe. Either way, Carl obviously wasn't eager to explore the issue with Brian over sushi. Already, the California Board of Medical Quality Assurance was moving forward with its case against Landy. And it was only a matter of weeks before the extended Wilson/Beach Boys family was going to file a case in the civil courts. And though Carl had avoided getting involved for months, he was beginning to realize he had no choice.

Strangely, it had been left to Stan Love, the cousin who had served as Brian's assistant/keeper in the months before Landy's first appearance in late 1975 and then for several years after the psychologist had been dismissed in late 1976, to pursue the case. The ex-pro basketball player had moved up to Oregon by then, living with his wife and kids in Lake Oswego, a leafy suburb about fifteen minutes south of Portland. He had settled down quite a bit by then, but Stan still hadn't found a career that fulfilled him. So when he got a call in 1987 from Rick Nelson, another former Beach Boys staffer, and heard all the whispers about Landy's financial and psychological abuses, Stan had both the outrage and the time to do something about it. "The real killer was that Audree kept calling me in tears, saying, 'I can't call Brian. The girls can't call Brian. Landy tells him we're bad influences and won't let him talk to us,'" he says. Stan might also have identified a win-win type of situation in which he could simultaneously help a cousin he cared about while also working his way back into the lucrative family business. No matter his motivations, Stan found a lawyer in San Diego who not only specialized in psychological abuse but also turned out to be a fan of Brian's music. The lawyer, Tom Monson, waived his usual retainer, and together they began turning up a trail of witnesses and documents that confirmed all of their worst suspicions.

The medical board's investigation ended in the spring of 1989 when Landy finally agreed to surrender his license to practice psychology. Still, that had no effect on his relationship with Brian (with whom Landy was vacationing in Hawaii on the day he resigned his license) because, as they had both asserted during the interviews accompanying the release of *Brian Wilson* a year earlier, Landy had ceased being Brian's therapist of record back in 1987. Now they were creative and business partners, the cofounders of a company they called Brains and Genius, in whose Pico Boulevard headquarters work continued apace. They had hired Mark Linett to build a studio in their offices, where they had started working on Brian's second solo album. Brian's long-delayed tell-all autobiography was shifting into higher gear. Meanwhile, they also launched a $100 million civil suit against A&M's music publishing arm, Irving Music, alleging an array of crimes and abuses in the original 1969 deal Murry had struck when selling the rights to Brian's many hits.

What all of these projects had in common was the way they girded Landy's connections to Brian. The album, titled *Sweet Insanity,* was being coproduced by Landy, this time without the interference of the Sire hotshots who had shepherded Brian's first solo album. Landy also cowrote virtually all of the songs, pushing Brian to try his hand at rapping in a song called "Smart Girls" *("My name is Brian and I'm the man/I write hit songs with a wave of my hand . . .")* and to sing about his current travails with a therapist's keen analytical eye, as in "Thank You (Brian)": *"They're not happy, 'cause I'm different/More creative, independent/Ah-ouuu."* Brian seeps through every so often, usually in an unexpected twist of melody or a sudden burst of unrestrained, propulsive rhythm. But Landy's sense of instrumentation was every bit as lyrical as his way with words, which may explain the album's flatly undifferentiated, synth-driven sound. And also why Sire's executives found it to be unreleasable.

Nevertheless, *Sweet Insanity* was celebrated richly in the pages of Brian's autobiography (now titled *Wouldn't It Be Nice)* being written with the help of *People* magazine correspondent Todd Gold. Here Brian would examine his entire life through the lens Landy had provided, with an emphasis on Murry's wickedness, the other Beach Boys' stupidity and greed, and the heroic ministrations of the therapist who helped Brian regain his sanity and artistry. And if much of the material in the book happened to reinforce the assertions made in the $100 million lawsuit and/or refute the accusations made by the California Board of Medical Quality Assurance, well, so much the better.

But Brains and Genius wasn't the only office keeping busy. Stan flew down to Los Angeles in May 1990 to file a petition asking the California courts to supplant Landy's control by appointing him Brian's legal conservator. A crowd of reporters came to cover the filing, and they weren't disappointed when Stan's press conference was interrupted by the sudden entrance of Brian Wilson, who stalked angrily to the podium to dismiss everything his cousin had just told them. "I think [the charges] are outrageous . . . out of the ballpark!" Brian declared, his hands trembling as he read from a statement scrawled on a dog-eared piece of notebook paper. "I feel great and my life is back on track. I see who I want to see and I am in charge of my own life."

Whether Brian had penned those words or even agreed with their sentiments is debatable. For even though Brian had craved the authority and structure Landy provided and truly did credit him with instilling the self-discipline that had saved his life, the sad fact was that Brian was no longer in a position to comprehend how he felt about much of anything. For one thing, Landy had moved to cut off virtually all of the people with whom Brian had a personal connection that the psychologist couldn't control. Melinda Ledbetter, who had been seeing Brian on and off for three years, had seen her access to Brian suddenly and inexplicably cut off in late 1989. And when circumstances required Brian to have face-to-face contact with old friends or family members, they often came away dismayed to discover that he could no longer remember some longtime friends and would often lapse into incoherence or even fall asleep in midconversation. Brian had also taken on some disturbing facial tics, which were often accompanied by shaking hands and a visible trembling in his legs.

Some observers concluded that he had suffered a stroke or was showing the latter-day side effects of the mountains of cocaine and rivers of alcohol he had ingested in the 1970s and early 1980s. But when Brian made a surprise appearance at a Beach Boys' fan convention in the summer of 1990, it didn't take long for Peter Reum, a longtime fan who happened to work as a therapist in Colorado, to realize something else. Reum had met and spoken to Brian on several occasions during the previous fifteen years, and so he knew that the man standing before him in San Diego had changed in distressing ways. Given his professional training, Reum suspected that Brian's twitching, waxen face, and palsied hands pointed to tardive dyskinesia, a neurological condition that develops in patients whose systems have become saturated with psychotropic medications, like the ones Brian had been taking in quantity ever since Landy had taken over his life in 1983.

Reum's suspicions were heightened by the many acquaintances who had seen Landy and his helpers dispensing pills to Brian. When Michael Vosse—Brian's aide-de-camp during the headiest days of *Smile*—came to visit the Malibu house, their two-hour conversation was interrupted three times by assistants bearing pills. "They said something about allergies, but his speech was slurred and his eyes were fucked up," Vosse recalls. "I was surprised he didn't nod out." When one of the Surf Nazis (as they had all come to be known) accidentally left the medicine bag in the recording studio during the recording of *Brian Wilson* in 1987, a couple of the engineers couldn't resist taking a peek inside. What they found resembled a portable doctor's office, Mark Linett says. "It looked like every pharmaceutical on the face of the earth."

Those stories and the many others that confirmed and expanded upon the dizzying quantity of drugs that had been prescribed to control what Landy often described as paranoid schizophrenia mixed with manic-depression added up to what Reum feared was a potentially dire situation. If Brian continued to ingest drugs at the current rate, his system would grow so overloaded that he would deteriorate into "a drooling, palsied mental patient," as Reum puts it. And by that point, the damage to his nervous system would be irreversible, leading to physical degeneration that would escalate steadily until, in the not-so-distant future, it would stop his heart once and for all. Reum called David Leaf, the Beach Boys biographer who had somehow managed to maintain his friendship with Brian throughout Landy's regime. Leaf had known Reum through Beach Boys circles for several years, and he relayed Reum's information to Carl, who realized that the time had come for him to get involved.

And yet Landy continued to fight off the charges. In the spring of 1991, he agreed to separate himself from Brian for ninety days in hopes of proving claims that the musician was every bit as independent as they claimed. Still, the separation agreement apparently didn't cover Landy's assistants, who continued to guide Brian's daily activities as per the program that had been established by Landy. When called to account for the millions of dollars he had been paid by Brian over the last eight years, Landy pointed out that the $35,000 he had billed Brian for professional services each month through 1986 had also paid the salaries of the many assistants who worked for him. Asked about the 1984 deal he had negotiated to take 25 percent of whatever money Brian earned for writing and producing new songs, Landy told the *Los Angeles Times* that because the musician was so damaged at the time, ". . . they never expected Brian to produce (or) to write anything again." Once it became obvious that Brian would become a productive musician again, Landy incorporated them both as co-owners of Brains and Genius. At the same time, Brian also paid Landy an annual $300,000 for giving him career advice, which came on top of the annual $150,000 the Beach Boys' partnership (Brother Records Inc., or BRI) paid him for serving as Brian's representative at their corporate meetings. Nevertheless, Landy said he was as surprised as anyone to learn that a 1989 revision of Brian's will had named him the primary beneficiary, inheriting as much as 70 percent of his ex-client's fortune.

Landy also insisted he had nothing to do with the writing of Brian's autobiography. But when *Wouldn't It Be Nice* was published in October 1991, the words on its pages sounded nothing like the voice of its supposed author. In some places this seemed to be because the stories being related had been lifted nearly word for word from earlier biographies, only with the pronouns changed to reflect Brian's first-person perspective. In other sections the narrative read like depositions for their various court cases, while others ripped the Beach Boys for various personal and professional shortcomings ("I was unsettled by the Beach Boys' ragged musicianship," Brian notes after sharing the stage with them in one late '80s concert). Some of the assertions were merely mean-spirited. Others, such as the observation that the touring Beach Boys had by the late '80s forgotten how to sing "Their Hearts Were Full of Spring," were demonstrably false. But the book became particularly fantastical whenever Landy entered the picture. In these pages, the notoriously tempestuous psychologist is always the coolest head in the room, dispensing philosophical wisdom as easily as he whips off lyrics so brilliant that the so-called pros—Waronker, Titelman, Paley, you know who you are—can only clench their fists with impotent fury. The book ends with Brian in tears, asking the departing Landy why, if he's in such great shape, and so productive, and happier than ever, why did they have to part?

> "Why is Carl doing this to me?" I asked. "Why? Why the fuck is he doing it?"
>
> "Why?" Gene said in a voice that was soft and calm, a voice that was in sharp contrast to my anguish. "I think it's because Carl's been jealous of your talent and fame all of his life . . . and because your brother hates me more than he loves or cares about you."

The Superior Court of Santa Monica disagreed. Presented with evidence detailing Landy's many conflicting roles in Brian's life, the court ordered Landy to remove himself from the musician's life. All financial and personal ties would be dissolved, and if Landy even attempted to contact Brian, he would be fined or sent to jail. Stan Love had already agreed to stay in Oregon, leaving Brian's affairs in the hands of a conservator, Jerome S. Billet.

The ruling came down on February 3, 1992. The next morning the phone rang at Andy Paley's house. When he picked it up, he heard the familiar sound of Brian's voice. "I can do anything I want to now," he said cheerfully. "Let's make some music."

CHAPTER 16

Don Was tells the tale with the passion of the converted.

It was the fall of 1989, and he was dug into a recording studio in Los Angeles, producing an album for the Knack, the neo-power pop band that enjoyed a brief, exciting moment of fame in the late '70s and early '80s. Was has an encyclopedic knowledge of popular music, with an expertise ranging from jazz to country to hard rock to the grittiest Detroit rhythm and blues. He had heard all of the Beach Boys' hits and knew enough about Brian's more adventurous works to understand that there was something going on that went beyond "Surfin' USA" and even "Good Vibrations."

But Was hadn't imagined how far it went until the guys in the Knack put on their bootleg of the *Smile* sessions. "Like a musical burning bush, these tapes awakened me to a higher conscious in record making," Was would eventually write. "I was amazed that one, single human could dream up this unprecedented and radically advanced approach to rock 'n' roll." When Was got a chance to see the latter-day Brian play his own songs, his knowledge of the man's struggle only deepened his sense of the music. "I hear the weary voice of a man who's been hurled through the emotional wringer, and yet one can plainly discern the youthful sweetness, optimism, and goodness that characterize Brian's soul. It's that very dichotomy that makes him one of the most enigmatic and endearing characters of these times."

And so inspiring that Was temporarily abandoned his musical pursuits in order to produce and direct a documentary about Brian's life. The film, *I Just Wasn't Made for These Times,* would go on to win rave reviews and film festival awards. But it wasn't the first time the paradoxes of Brian's life and music had inspired someone to alter the course of their life and career. In 1971 a young Beach Boys fan from New Rochelle, New York, named David Leaf came away from Tom Nolan's *Rolling Stone* profile with a fascination for Brian Wilson that grew even more intense during his years at George Washington University. When he graduated in 1975, he packed up his belongings and moved straight to Los Angeles. "I had this idea I was going to write a book about Brian Wilson," he recalls. Leaf started a Beach Boys fanzine he called *Pet Sounds,* and sure enough, it led to a publishing contract to write *The Beach Boys and the California Myth,* a biography that told Brian's story in near-Shakespearean terms of innocence, hope, greed, and brutality. "I came to California to test the myth, to meet the Beach Boys, looking for symbols," Leaf wrote in his introduction to the 1978 book. "It wasn't long before my journey went too far. My journalistic investigations and excavations discovered more human suffering than I really wanted to know."

Leaf's detailed portrait of the *Smile* sessions and the weirdness that surrounded them inspired a new generation of music-minded kids who were just then coming of age. One of his readers in the Mount Washington section of Northeast Los Angeles was a high schooler named Darian Sahanaja, whose interest in the Beach Boys began with *Endless Summer,* the first album he'd ever bought, in 1974. Sometimes the Led Zeppelin/Rolling Stones–obsessed neighborhood kids would beat him up for liking the Beach Boys, but Sahanaja didn't care. He taught himself to play Beach Boys songs on the piano and later silk-screened himself a T-shirt based on the original *Smile* cover art. He was still wearing it a few years later when he was introduced to Probyn Gregory, another musician and Beach Boys fan. They became friends and later musical collaborators, eventually finding a network of similarly Brian-fixated friends and acquaintances. One of these turned out to be another native Angeleno named Domenic Priore, whose dedication to Brian's music had led him to collect a vast library of bootleg session tapes. When it turned out that both Probyn and Darian had their own *Smile* bootlegs too, the threesome got together for a marathon listening session. They spent more than twelve hours in the same little room that day, rolling the tapes in different sequences in search of the melodic and thematic connections that linked them into the whole Brian and Van Dyke had intended to create. "It got so intense in there, we didn't even want to go out to get food," Probyn recalls. They ordered in two meals, not leaving their little room until late in the evening.

Priore followed Leaf's example a few years later by starting his own fanzine called *The Dumb Angel Gazette*. This too led to a book, *Look! Listen! Vibrate! Smile!*, which consisted entirely of writings about *Smile*. Much of the text was actually photocopied pages from period magazines, newspapers, and industry advertisements. But taken with the original essays by Priore and friends, LLVS presented the lost album as nothing less than a missing keystone in the development of twentieth-century popular culture. "It is only the fault of bad business that we were not fortunate enough to hear this stuff at the time of its creation," Priore wrote in his introduction. "Most of US know that Brian Wilson was on the ball and way ahead of the rest of the music world at the time when it was reaching its peak. (It's been all downhill since then, face the FACTS!)"

And it wasn't just the high school kids and superfans going out of their way to celebrate Brian's vision. Fleetwood Mac's Lindsey Buckingham had produced his group's multiplatinum 1979 album *Tusk* with an ear tuned to Brian's quirkiest sonic experiments, then included a lovely, stripped-down cover of "Farmer's Daughter" (recorded during a preconcert sound check) on Fleetwood Mac's 1980 live album. In 1981 the former Eagle Don Henley wrote a *Pet Sounds* sound-alike tune, "Love Rules," for his contribution to the sound track of the hit comedy *Fast Times at Ridgemont High*. Some of the most popular bands of the 1980s and 1990s would record their own homages—R.E.M., Bruce Springsteen, Barenaked Ladies, the Jayhawks, Wilco, the list goes on and on. But none would write *about* Brian as perceptively as John Cale, the former bass/viola player for the late '60s New York demimonde favorites the Velvet Underground, whose song "Mr. Wilson" celebrated the dreaminess in Brian's music even as it acknowledged the horrors of his life. Even from as far away as Wales, the beauty and honesty of those old Beach Boys songs had always rung true. And no matter what happened, Cale sang, he couldn't believe it was all still real and always would be.

Cale wrote "Mr. Wilson" in 1974, years before hype, circumstance, and critical hindsight would expand Brian's myth to the epic dimensions it would later take. But the Welshman had already identified one of the most important elements in Brian's legend: his inability and/or unwillingness to make new music. For the silence that had come to define *Smile*, along with the obviously halfhearted sound so much of his latter-day music had taken on, had enhanced the meaning of the music that had come before. *"I guess I just wasn't made for these times,"* he had declared on *Pet Sounds,* and the song had become the overture for a decades-long saga that would be, in its way, just as influential as *Pet Sounds* had been. The decades he spent lost in the wilderness, the years he spent sitting glumly onstage like the world's saddest performing bear, presented a dark vision that made the utopian dreams in his music all the more poignant. Now you knew how dangerous those waves had really been and how close the darkness looming just beyond the frame of "Good Vibrations" really was. Better yet, you could listen to *Pet Sounds* and hear Brian's sad wail as the voice of your own wounded inner self. His suffering became your own, only larger and more beautiful.

Ultimately, Brian's public suffering had transformed him from a musical figure into a cultural one. Like the mythical railway man John Henry, he had invested so much of his heart, soul, and God-given talent into his work that it had risen up and consumed him. And while this was obviously tragic, it was hard to miss the romance in the story. For having given himself entirely to the laying of the rails, the dead man's voice rumbled and sang in every passing train.

The Beach Boys, meanwhile, continued moving from city to city with all the cool precision of the evening express. Their feelings for and expectations of their erstwhile leader weren't always clear. But it's compelling to note that back during the legal battle to eject Landy, Mike had been interviewed on *A Current Affair,* where he mostly reiterated the boilerplate issues of psychological abuse and financial misdeeds that made up the heart of the case. And as the reporter nudged him back to the emotional heart of the story—the sorrow of having a family member allegedly kidnapped and brainwashed by a manipulative malefactor—Mike fell so thoroughly into the moment that his sharp blue eyes glistened and his voice pitched higher with emotion. "I just want to see my cousin," he wailed. "I want to write hits with my cousin!"

Mike's emotion seemed genuine. But his choice of words was revealing. For while there is no reason to doubt that Mike and the rest of the extended Wilson/ Beach Boys family loved Brian as any family loves one of its members, it's easy to suspect that the same behavioral eccentricity and emotional trauma that had made Brian famous had rendered him virtually unknowable to his relatives. As a result, they had also come to think of him less as a member of the family than as a key executive in the family industry. Because even when the guy wasn't writing hits, he was usually at the center of some kind of media frenzy that enhanced the value of the business. Whether he deserved it or not—and the other Beach Boys clearly believed that Brian had absorbed an outsize portion of credit for their success—the media, and thus the world, saw him as the center of it all. And as much as that aggravated the other Beach Boys, they also knew they could profit immensely by embracing it. And if Brian was unwilling to hug back (or incapable of doing so) in quite the way they had hoped, well, there were other ways to profit from the Brian Wilson machine.

Mike had taken particular interest in his cousin's lawsuit against A&M's publishing company. And when Brian took home a $10 million settlement in 1992, Mike got in on the celebration by filing a $3 million lawsuit claiming that he had been uncredited for work on seventy-nine of the songs in question. And if some of Mike's claims were legit—Brian never debated that Mike had written the lyrics to "California Girls," though he also didn't do anything to get his cousin's name on the popular song's royalty statement—others seemed slightly less convincing. For instance, Mike's claim for credit on "Wouldn't It Be Nice" pivoted off of his studio improvisation of a single couplet *("Good night, baby/Sleep tight, baby")* at the very end of the song. Perhaps anticipating that this wasn't a very strong case for cowriter status, Mike also asserted he had helped write or at least edit other lyrics on the song. This news surprised Tony Asher to no end, if only because Mike and the group had been in Japan when he and Brian had written the *Pet Sounds* songs. How could the absent Mike have been pitching in on songwriting sessions at the same time? As Tony recalls, the lawyer representing Mike focused on the occasional trips to the bathroom Brian had made during those afternoons. Wasn't it possible, he proposed, that he had secretly been dialing Mike in Japan to get his advice? "[That argument] was so absurd I didn't know how to answer," Tony says.

That same October Mike also filed a defamation lawsuit against Brian, claiming that his autobiography had not only demeaned his professional abilities but also referred to him as "a violent, sex-crazed maniac," a description of his character that struck Mike as something less than accurate. And he wasn't the only Beach Boy looking to vent some rage about *Wouldn't It Be Nice*. In the fall of 1994, the entire group (in the guise of Brother Records, Inc.), plus Carl and the boys' mother, Audree, filed multimillion-dollar lawsuits against Brian, Landy, and Todd Gold, seeking to assuage their own wounded feelings, reputations, and careers.

If the group was united in their pursuit of Brian's riches in the courts, they were growing much less harmonious in virtually every other way. A simmering personality clash between Mike and Al first erupted into open warfare in 1990 when Mike enlisted Carl in an effort to oust the group's founding rhythm guitarist from the lineup. The dustup was resolved fairly quickly, though the conflict would continue to fester throughout the decade. And the absence of group cohesion could be heard quite clearly on what passed for the group's next album, *Summer in Paradise,* which was produced by Mike and Terry Melcher. Recorded with only the most fleeting help from Carl and Al and no contribution from Brian, the album was most notable for its absence of new ideas. A pointless cover of the group's first single, "Surfin'," led things off, while even the new Love/Melcher originals were built largely from musical or lyrical references to the group's earlier hits (e.g., one couplet in the album's title track found a way to name-check "Help Me, Rhonda," "Barbara Ann," "Fun, Fun, Fun," *and* the term "America's Band," all in the space of twenty-four words). Celebrity fan and occasional touring drummer John Stamos (best known for his role as Uncle Jesse on the TV sitcom *Full House*) was allowed to cover Dennis's "Forever," which now came with the heavily processed sound of modern easy listening. But even the lite-metal guitars on Dennis's once-understated ballad weren't quite as painful as Mike's "Summer of Love," which climaxed, so to speak, in a hail of yucky sexual references (Mike in Senor Suave mode, crooning about the joys of doing "it" in disparate, summery venues, including a beach and a swimming pool) that seem designed to excite the wrath of the same Parents Music Resource Center Mike had once supported. The music failed to gain any interest from the record industry, forcing the group to release it on their own Brother label with independent distribution. The few reviews that were printed were scathing, and only a scattering of the CDs was sold.

The group fared better in 1993 with *Good Vibrations,* a five-CD box set that gathered virtually all of their singles with loads of the stronger album tracks, a few lesser-known B-sides, demos, live tracks, and nonhits from the '70s and '80s and a generous helping of outtakes from throughout their thirty-year-plus history. The entire collection was well reviewed, but the real attention-getter was the thirty-minute stretch of *Smile* music that dominated the set's second disc. Starting with the previously released "Good Vibrations" single and "Our Prayer," the album headed for deeper waters with an alternate version of "Heroes and Villains" that had surfaced as a bonus track on a CD reissue in 1990. Apart from the *20/20* version of "Cabinessence," the other *Smile* stuff was completely unheard: nearly seven minutes of discarded instrumental and vocal sections from "Heroes and Villains"; then the original, fully orchestrated versions of "Wonderful" and "Wind Chimes"; followed by a brief fire engine–style intro to yet another version of "Heroes and

Villains." Next came "Do You Dig Worms," with its mysterious references to Plymouth Rock, Native American chants, and Hawaii; then the original, sound effects–laden "Vegetables"; followed by "I Love to Say Da Da," which had been intended to be the water segment of the Elements Suite. The *Smile* pieces concluded with Brian's studio demo of "Surf's Up," performed solo at the piano. Not every critic was wowed. "What one mostly hears in the *Smile* music is an unfocused, confounding sifting of ideas," Billy Altman wrote in the *New York Times*. But others pronounced themselves flabbergasted. ". . . The music is mystic, mad, wild, and gentle, quite unlike anything anyone, including Wilson, had ever tried in pop music before," wrote *Time*'s Jay Cocks, concluding: "The songs seem random at first, off-beam and crazy, but they haunt."

The burst of acclaim for the rarities on the box set even inspired the touring Beach Boys to shake up their usual act. That fall they mounted a theater tour that stretched their set to nearly 150 minutes, including a twelve-song set that highlighted exquisite performances of such ambitious songs as "Wonderful" (in its original *Smile* arrangement), "All This Is That," "Add Some Music to Your Day," and "Caroline, No," most of which hadn't been heard onstage for twenty years. Again, reviews veered toward the ecstatic. But the flirtation with the more esoteric corners of their catalogue didn't last beyond that stretch of relatively intimate shows. When they got back to their usual schedule of casinos, state fairs, and baseball games in 1994, the all-hits-all-the-time format was back, too.

His legal woes notwithstanding, the post-Landy Brian seemed more centered and happy than he'd been in years. He had a good circle of friends (including *Beach Boys and the California Myth* author David Leaf, who had become particularly close to Brian during the recording of his 1988 solo album) to keep him company. Even more importantly, he finally had consistent, competent psychiatric care. His new doctors learned quickly that Brian had never been schizophrenic, as Landy had asserted (and medicated him for) during the '80s. Instead, Brian was mildly manic-depressive with a schizo-affective disorder that presented itself in the form of those disembodied voices Brian had been hearing for so long. New medication helped keep them at bay most of the time, and the more stable and productive his life became, the less likely he was to be derailed by their appearances. Now on a much more moderate diet of medication, Brian began to shed the more troubling symptoms of tardive dyskinesia, and his good days soon came to outnumber the bad ones.

Still, he remained as spaced-out as any creative person, and when he was crossing Pico Boulevard in West Los Angeles one morning, Brian had to jump fast to avoid an oncoming car he hadn't noticed. Just another day in the life of Brian Wilson, until the driver stopped to make sure he was okay, and the unrolling window revealed Melinda Ledbetter, the woman he'd dated for a time in the '80s. Soon they were dating even more seriously than they had done before. "It was a really cute, all-American courtship," says Andy Paley. "They'd go out to dinner and go to the movies, and sometimes they'd have spats, like all couples. But we double-dated a lot, going skiing for the weekend or over to Vegas. Brian had his doubts, like everyone does: 'Oh, I don't know if I can sustain a relationship,' that sort of thing. Mostly it was great." Indeed, the couple was married on February 19, 1995, a day Brian chose because it was also his first wife's birthday, which meant his anniversary would be easy to remember.

Meanwhile, Brian's daughters, Carnie and Wendy, had teamed with their childhood friend Chynna Phillips (John's daughter) to form the pop trio Wilson-Phillips. The group's first album sold four million copies, propelled by a handful of hit singles, many of them cowritten by the girls themselves. The trio broke up a few years later, but Carnie and Wendy continued as a duet. In the mid-1990s, they asked their father to join with them on an album of new songs. The work continued on and off for a while, and Brian's initial vision of making the album a sequel of sorts to *Pet Sounds* (including a couple of new songs he'd written with Tony Asher) didn't come together. But the joint project allowed the girls, and particularly Carnie, a chance to reconnect with their father. That opportunity proved just as fruitful—perhaps even more—than the sessions themselves.

Brian's renewed collaboration with Andy Paley also reached for new heights. Getting together to write or record most days, they worked quickly to put together basic tracks for an album's worth of songs Brian kept talking about in terms of the Beach Boys. "He'd be arranging their voices in his head, saying, 'Okay, this is Mike, and here's Carl, and Al and Bruce, and this is me up here,'" Paley says. And if Brian's new songs bore none of the stamps that had come to define latter-day Beach Boys songs—no references to beaches or surf, no self-conscious attempts to seem younger than the singers' actual years—they did reflect more of Brian's musical, emotional, and intellectual interests than any series of songs he'd recorded since *The Beach Boys Love You*. Ranging from full-blown rockers to delicate ballads, the basic tracks—some nearly finished, others with spare arrangements and scratch vocals—set a new standard for Brian's solo work.

The lushly romantic "Gettin' In Over My Head" built its verses on suspended chords that underscored the uncertainty of a narrator who, in typical Brian fashion, is so swept up in love that *"it's scarin' me right out of my mind."* "Slightly American Music" retold the nation's history as a surreal parade of presidents, Indian chiefs, and military generals, all of them marching side-by-side with George Gershwin, Fats Domino, and Phil Spector. The rhythmically complex "Chain Reaction" and rollicking, bare-bones "I'm Broke" rocked as hard as anything Brian had written. "You're Still a Mystery" was another wondrously melodic ballad about the gray areas of romance, while "It's Not Easy Being Me" revisited "I Just Wasn't Made for These Times" terrain, only with youthful disillusionment replaced by twenty years of bitter experience. *"The same fears haunt me endlessly/It's not easy bein' me . . ."* wailed the chorus. Still, redemption is just around the corner—literally—in the jazzy shuffle "Marketplace," which described the corner market as a soul-affirming cornucopia of flavors, cultures, and experiences. *"The world's a zoo, what can we do?/But try some, buy some,"* he sings.

And that was just the beginning. Brian got so heated up about a New Orleans–style stomper called "Soul Searchin'" that he followed his collaborator all the way to London (where Paley was doing some production work on another record) just so they could keep working on the song in the hotel. Brian also spent hours working on variations of John Fogerty's "Proud Mary," with at least one version combining guitars, organ, synthesizer, horns, steel drums, a Jew's harp, and a choirlike chorus that teased out the tune's innate funk until its final chorus sounded like Sunday morning at the Double Rock Baptist Church. "Desert Drive" built on the propulsive sax riff from "Salt Lake City," and "Frankie Avalon" declared so much wide-eyed enthusiasm for the '50s-era teen idol that it's half naive, half crazy, and almost entirely adorable.

At the same time he was writing and recording with Paley, Brian was working with Don Was on his documentary, filming interviews and preparing to perform live versions of ten of his classic Beach Boys songs with a handpicked band of Was's favorite session pros. And if that weren't enough, Brian had also agreed to sing virtually all of the parts on Van Dyke Parks's new album *Orange Crate Art,* an affectionate exploration of California history. Which isn't to say that Brian was always the most reliable or enthusiastic collaborator. He refused to do Was's film at first, mostly because he didn't like the songs the producer had chosen for him to perform at its conclusion. But he changed his mind eventually and grew comfortable enough with Was to enjoy the sessions. Similarly, Brian dragged his feet into Van Dyke's first session, interrupting the start of his first take to ask an excruciatingly simple question: "Wait a minute. What am I even doing here?" Van Dyke hit the talk button without missing a beat. "You're here because I can't stand the sound of my own voice!" Brian thought about that for a second, nodded his head, and stepped up to the microphone. "Well, that makes sense. Okay, take one!"

Released in early 1995, the Don Was movie, *I Just Wasn't Made for These Times,* proved a remarkably probing documentary, combing home movies, vintage performances, contemporary interviews, and expert testimony from a galaxy of unlikely witnesses (ranging from Sonic Youth's Thurston Moore to Linda Ronstadt) to describe Brian's life and the significance of his work. Brian's filmed musical performances might have been rough in places, but as Was noted, the cracks in his voice told a story, too. *Orange Crate Art* emerged later in the year, earning solid praise for Van Dyke's elegant, lyrical songs and Brian's richly layered vocals.

Warner Brothers' advertisements for *Orange Crate Art* made rich use of the *Smile* legend that linked the new album's pair of creators. And it was hardly surprising that Brian and Van Dyke's renewed collaboration would lead to hopeful speculation about the likelihood that the fabled album would finally be released. Indeed, the success of the *Good Vibrations* box set had inspired Capitol to turn engineer Mark Linett and others loose in the tape archive, with an eye toward compiling the *Smile* tapes into another multi-CD set. Don Was played Brian one of Todd Rundgren's interactive music CD-ROMs and suggested that he release it that way—pull together a few hours' worth of session tapes and let the listeners "finish" the album themselves. Brian evinced enthusiasm to Was ("He's into it," the producer assured the *New York Times*), but when questioned by reporter Neill Strauss, the always-mercurial musician made a sour face and dismissed the entire album. *Smile,* he said, was "too weird" to contemplate.

Instead, Brian turned his attention to creating new music with the Beach Boys. Brian and Mike, fresh from the resolution of Mike's copyright lawsuit, teamed up briefly in early 1995 to revise a Wilson/Paley song, "Dancin' the Night Away," into "Baywatch Nights," which the Beach Boys intended to record for the sound track to the popular lifeguard show. The song was never finished (though the group appeared on the show, frolicking in the surf with Brian and then miming a performance without him), but the group nevertheless prepared to start working on a new album with their old leader at the helm. Andy Paley, for one, was astonished. "I learned early on that it's a bad idea to make any kind of plans with Brian, if only because he's had his plans shattered so many times." Nevertheless, Mike and the other guys seemed genuinely eager. Don Was had signed on to produce the sessions and had already sifted through the pile of demos Brian and Paley had provided, pulling out "Soul Searchin'" as a potential single. "Don was excited about the new stuff," Paley recalls. "We had meetings and everything was getting rolling."

So the group convened in the studio, first laying down group vocals behind Carl's lead on "Soul Searchin'." They all came back a day later to sing the background parts behind Brian's lead on "Still a Mystery," their voices merging easily into the intricate structure Brian had arranged. Things were moving so quickly and easily that it seemed like the old days. "Everyone was so happy to be there," Paley says. "First I thought: 'Wow, this could really happen.' And when Carl sang 'Soul Searchin',' it was like . . . wow, this really *is* going to happen!" But then something changed. And just like the still-unreleased song says, it's still a mystery.

"I have no idea why that didn't come together," Mike says. "I think everyone was willing to do it. I'm not sure how eager, but certainly willing." In 1998 Brian pointed the finger at Carl. "Well, a month after Carl sang 'Soul Searchin', he said he didn't like it and didn't want it on an album. That he didn't like it and had changed his opinion." According to Melinda Wilson, the real problem was that Carl didn't think Brian's new music was commercial enough. As a counterproposal, he and the other Beach Boys proposed teaming Brian with Sean O'Hagan, the leader of the British avant-pop band the High Llamas. But Brian wasn't interested in doing that. "He didn't pick up a positive vibe," she says. "And Brian was really hurt that he had gone to them and asked them to work with him, and they had turned him down."

But given the excitement the new songs had already drummed up—Don Was's enthusiasm might have been a tip-off—why didn't Brian just finish the songs on his own and release them as a solo album? At this, Paley doesn't seem mystified, as much as purposefully mystifying. "A lot of people didn't want it to happen. I can't really go into it." You might think that Brian would be crushed that his latest project for the Beach Boys—the product of months of writing, arranging, and recording—had withered on the vine. But he was remarkably sanguine about it—as if the prospect of releasing an elaborately staged album full of his best work might put him into the position of competing with his own legacy. And for a man who had spent nearly three decades hiding in his own shadow, that was not something he felt prepared to do.

Instead, he drifted happily into the next Beach Boys project: a Mike-led journey to Nashville to help a handful of popular country musicians (Lorrie Morgan, Kathy Troccoli, Collin Raye, and so on) put their stamp on the group's biggest hits. It was an interesting idea, and certainly Willie Nelson did a splendid job of making "The Warmth of the Sun" his own, while T. Graham Brown added impressive fire and grit to "Help Me, Rhonda." But the vast majority of the songs were less inspired, with most being simplified versions of the original arrangements, with only the occasional fiddle or pedal steel guitar to place the recordings somewhere south of the Mason-Dixon line. The financial backers of the album had insisted that Brian be a visible part of the project, and he was credited as a coproducer, along with pop-country producer Joe Thomas. But according to Melinda, the other Beach Boys could never bring themselves to take him seriously. "They treated him like an invalid, all the time saying, 'Do this, don't do that, are you okay?'" They became particularly tense, she says, when the time came for the band to perform at Nashville's annual Fan Fair concert. "Basically, they were afraid he was going to sing. They were worried he was going to embarrass them, somehow."

Still, some of the footage captured by Alan Boyd for a companion video certainly made it seem like the guys were enjoying one another's company. In one hilarious moment, Brian compels Al to help him imitate Mike's nasal voice by pinching his nose shut while he sings a verse of "Fun, Fun, Fun." "Mike's not gonna like that!" Brian giggles at the camera. Unfortunately, neither country nor rock fans liked *Stars and Stripes Vol. 1,* and the projected *Vol. 2* never materialized.

Neither did the "*Pet Sounds* Sessions" box set that Capitol had planned to commemorate the thirtieth anniversary of the landmark album's release in May. Although Brian couldn't bear the idea of moving beyond the shadow of his 1960s legacy, the latter-day Beach Boys could no longer bear having it loom over them, too. And though the group had agreed to let Brian oversee the preparations for Capitol's four-CD set of *Pet Sounds* session tapes and alternative mixes, Mike, Carl, and Al were something less than enthusiastic about the prospect of yet another project that would emphasize Brian's role as the Beach Boys' sole visionary. Mike, in particular, freaked out when he read the elaborate liner notes that had been prepared by David Leaf, whom he had despised ever since the writer had portrayed him as a mean-spirited troglodyte in the pages of *The Beach Boys and the California Myth*. And just when the box set was put in turnaround, Carl vetoed an offer that had been made for the group to play a ten-show tour that would feature full performances of *Pet Sounds*. Brian's elaborate studio arrangements would simply be too hard to play onstage, Carl said. And besides, his big brother would never be able to recreate his own vocals on the stage. "He told me he didn't want to see Brian embarrassed in public, and there was no way Brian would be able to do it," Melinda says. "I never told Brian that. But he picks up on things, you know. No one had to tell him anything."

Still, Capitol was determined to get the box set out. They negotiated a compromise with Mike, allowing him to preface Leaf's writings with his own original essay. He led the piece with his recollection of the day he actually suggested the new record be called *Pet Sounds* and emphasized the other members' contributions to the group's sound. "Brian, for certain, was the master gardener," Mike concluded. "Without him, the fruits of our efforts would never have been so distinctive or prolific." The *Pet Sounds* box set came out in late 1997, a year and a half after the album's actual anniversary. By then the Beach Boys were confronting a far more devastating crisis.

Late in 1996, Carl, who had been feeling sluggish and dizzy as of late, went to see his doctor. He emerged from the hospital with a devastating diagnosis: He had lung cancer, and the disease had already spread its tentacles into his liver and his brain. His prospects were grim, but Carl stayed hopeful, figuring the best medicine for him would be to go right on living as he always had. This meant going on the road with the Beach Boys, of course, so though the disease had sapped his strength and the chemotherapy had taken his hair, Carl went right back out with the group in the spring of 1997 and kept right on going through the summer tour. Performing at the Jones Beach amphitheater outside New York City that August, Carl came out to a rapturous ovation, which he greeted with a big smile and bows. And though his voice was breathier than usual on "Sail On, Sailor" and though he had to lean on a stool at times to preserve his strength, the lead guitarist was all business, belting out the old songs with all the sleek professionalism he'd shown for so much of the last thirty-five years. The group's next concert, held in New Jersey the next night, would be Carl's last. His strength depleted, Carl headed home to rest, leaving the group to cancel their next few shows.

Carl intended to get back on the road with the group when their next set of shows began in October, but at that point Mike said he would no longer appear in public with a bandmate who was so obviously ill. "Carl was very sick," the group's manager, Elliott Lott, explained a year or two later. "He had lost his hair and had to wear a wig. He needed oxygen after every song. Mike didn't want to appear with Carl out of love for him." And yet, Mike still wanted to play those shows. So with an eye locked simultaneously on the glories of the past and the promise of the future, he managed to get in touch with David Marks, the first-ever replacement Beach Boy. Marks hadn't been a part of the group for more than thirty-five years, and though he'd been a member of several other bands, pursued his musical education at the Berklee Conservatory in Boston, and worked with a lot of leading musicians (Warren Zevon, for one), he'd wasted quite a few years indulging his own appetites for drugs and alcohol. Nevertheless, when the curtain came up on the band in October 1997, David Marks was standing in Carl's spot, playing his guitar parts and singing into his microphone. Just like old times, Mike was heard to say.

Audree Wilson, who had been noticeably enfeebled for the last few years, passed away in late December 1997 at the age of 78. Carl made it to the funeral, looking so vibrant that some observers wondered if all the talk about his meditating his cancer into remission was actually true. But when Brian and Melinda went to his house to watch the Super Bowl a few weeks later, Carl was obviously nearing the end. "We just knew," Melinda says. "When we left, Brian said, 'I don't think we're ever gonna see him again.'"

The brothers had been distant for years—they'd never really regained the closeness that had evaporated when Brian abandoned his post and ceded control of the group to Carl in the late '60s. "We didn't really talk to each other for twenty-five years," Brian said a few months after his brother's death. "We couldn't deal with each other, so we didn't talk to each other." But that last day gave the brothers a chance to move beyond the professional and personal frustrations that had driven them apart for so long. "They came from a family that had a hard time communicating with one another," Melinda said a few months after Carl died. "I think the only real tension they had was trying to figure out how to love each other." Brian had already written a musical elegy for his brother, an affectionate farewell he'd called "Lay Down Burden." He'd hoped to record it as a duet with Carl, but fate had conspired against him. And when he got to his baby brother's funeral, the enormity of Carl's absence overwhelmed him. "I'd never seen my mom and dad cry together like that," Carnie Wilson says. "He just fell into her arms wailing, 'He's gone! Carl's gone and I don't know where he went!'"

Suddenly, Brian was the only surviving member of the Wilson family that had lived on West 119th Street. "I'm the last of the Wilsons," he said that spring, heaving a big sigh toward the ceiling. "It's tough, sure. But I have plenty of will in my name. That's what I call myself, the Great Will. I will. I will. I WILL!" Hearing the ferocity in his own voice, Brian laughed out loud. But Carl's death had changed something. For the first time in his life, Brian no longer had to measure up to—or feel guilty about disappointing—his family's expectations. It was terrible to feel so alone in the world. But in a strange way, the death of his brother had also made him free.

CHAPTER 17

On the verge of restarting his career yet again, Brian Wilson is in his basement recording studio, listening to the Four Freshmen. A young recording engineer is sitting next to him; a guest is walking in through the office door. But Brian is alone, his eyes staring off into the empty air in front of him. Except to him the air isn't really empty. It's full of voices singing "Day by Day," and now Brian's eyes are closed, his face tilted upward as if the music were washing over him. When the song ends, his eyes flicker open and he smiles. After a while the interview starts.

It is the spring of 1998, and he has a new record coming out in just a few weeks. It's called *Imagination,* and he's very excited to talk about it. "I think this album represents a rebirth in my life," he says. "I was a little bit scared, but after ten minutes, it was a breeze. I'm a little happier than I used to be. It's a pretty big thing for me to have a family and know that my wife loves me, trusting her and everything. There's no way to describe how comfortable I've been feeling."

He's accustomed to retailing his personal life in exchange for column inches—that's been part of his job for more than thirty years. But Brian works hard to keep things light and simple. Once his relationship with his older daughters was screwed up, he says. Then they recorded some songs together a couple of years ago, and everything changed. "Three cuts on their album healed my wounds. Theirs, too. *Three bitty songs!*" Now Brian is talking about his toddler daughters, recently adopted from an unwed mother somewhere in the Midwest. "Little kids are an inspiration. As soon as we had Dari, I started writing tunes. Three or four songs right after she was born. Really, there's no way to describe how comfortable I've been feeling."

Then he starts to relax, his gestures becoming more expansive, his sentences growing longer. He looks deeper into himself and can't help but tell what he sees. "I'm the last of the Wilsons, I call it, and it's scary. I keep thinking I'm going to get assassinated like John Lennon did. I manage to get through my fears, but sometimes I get these crazy notions that someone is going to kill me or something. Then I have to go somewhere and think about that for a while and say, 'Well, is that really probable?' I have to use logic in my thinking."

Logic is a circular thing for him. A few minutes after he celebrates the joys of his life in St. Charles, he mentions how desperate he is to leave. "It's peaceful here. But now and then I feel a little bit like I really want to go back to L.A. Sometimes I really feel like I need to get away from here. All the phones and all the recording and all the practice sessions." Asked about *Smile,* Brian makes a face and rolls his eyes. "I thought too much. *Smile* was just a bunch of weird stuff that didn't even amount to anything." Noting the aghast expression on his guest's face, he shrugs. "But I guess we did that album pretty good." Asked to name his favorite Beach Boys albums, he lists *15 Big Ones* and *The Beach Boys Love You.* "That's when it all happened for me. That's where my heart lies. *Love You,* Jesus, that's the best album we ever made."

At one point Brian gets up to help himself to a soda and returns with a can of Diet Rite, which he drains in two long gulps, then discards with a wickedly accurate line drive into a garbage can sitting against a wall thirty feet away. When he wants to have fun, he says, he goes to see a movie. "But most of the movies I see are for shit. Same old bullshit. Explosions, gun fights, chases. It's ridiculous. I don't go to too many movies anymore." Instead, he goes to his piano and tries to find a new song to sing. "You have to live up to your name. I have to make music to keep people satisfied, but my particular fans aren't ever going to be satisfied. It's like a mom taking care of her baby. It's a basic life idea."

Later he sums up the prospects of his future. "I think there's going to be plenty of scared feelings to have, plenty of being scared of this, plenty of being scared of that, and plenty of trying to live up to my name." He pauses to consider this. "What a mess, huh?" Then he laughs and jumps to his feet. "Hey, thanks a lot, man. This was, like, the best interview I've ever done!" He heads up the stairs, taking them two-by-two, and a moment later the family room TV blazes to life.

It's hard to know what to believe. "You know what? It's all true," says one friend. "Brian never lies. When he tells you something, that's what's true for him at that moment. It might change a moment later, but when he says it, it's the absolute truth to him."

Brian's 1997 move to St. Charles—a rural village about an hour west of Chicago—had been spurred by his new partnership and friendship with Joe Thomas, the coproducer of the *Stars and Stripes* album. A onetime professional wrestler (he worked with the stage name "Buddy Love: The woman's pet, the men's regret"), Joe had jumped to the music business in 1984, opening a recording studio/record company called River North. Joe focused first on commercial jingles, then moved into pop music, signing and producing artists ranging from country balladeer Kathy Troccoli to ex-Chicago singer Peter Cetera to British art-rocker Alan Parsons. A tall, sturdy man with a waterfall-like mullet, the Chicago-bred Thomas made yet another unlikely musical partner for Brian. Particularly considering the vast majority of the records he'd produced, which tended to slide down the glossiest lanes in the middle of the road. But the slick sound of Joe's work—and the entrée it might allow Brian into the lucrative adult contemporary market—was a large part of his appeal. The Wilsons and the Thomases found homes next door to one another in a deluxe hillside subdivision outside of St. Charles. When a 102-track recording studio had been installed in the Wilsons' basement, they moved in and started to work.

From the beginning, the goal was to make a hit record. "Brian said, 'You know, I want to make songs that I can hear on the radio,'" Joe said, sitting in Brian's studio in St. Charles that spring. "Back when he was happiest, he'd get into his '65 'Vette and go down the street hearing 'California Girls' and 'Don't Worry, Baby,' and all these things. That's what he wanted." They began to think of the new record as a modern approximation of the *Beach Boys Today/Summer Days (and Summer Nights!)* era of late-1964 to mid-1965, when Brian's ear for sonic innovation was still tuned to the pop music mainstream. With that in mind, they covered two Beach Boys oldies ("Keep an Eye on Summer" and "Let Him Run Wild"), along with a mid-1960s outtake ("Sherry, She Needs Me") with lyrics revised by the top adult contemporary songwriter Carole Bayer Sager into "She Says That She Needs Me." One new song, the "Kokomo"-like "South American," had lyrics written by Jimmy Buffett. Another had lyrics by occasional Eagles collaborator J.D. Souther. Of the songs Brian wrote alone or with Joe, the chiming "Your Imagination," the lover's lament "Cry," the bittersweet "Lay Down Burden," and the mini-suite "Happy Days" all contained Brian's unlikely chord progressions, graceful rhythms, and uncanny melodic twists.

But given a directive to make hits—underscored by the participation of former-Eagles-kingpin-turned-label-chief Irving Azoff, who signed Brian to his new record label, Giant—Joe took it upon himself to make sure that the new songs sounded as close to adult contemporary radio as possible. Most were dominated by tinkling keyboards, with plenty of melodic interjections from a gently plucked nylon-string guitar. If Brian tried to use an instrument or an arrangement that might not fit into the soothing blend, Joe would shake his head and slice it out of the picture. And if this bothered Brian, he didn't show it. He enjoyed Joe's warm, blue-collar sensibility and had grown so close to him that he'd swim in his pool and then let himself into the kitchen to fix himself a tuna salad sandwich, even when Joe and his wife were out. ("We'd come home and find these dishes in the sink and puddles on the kitchen floor," Joe recalled with a laugh.) And Brian was happy to defer to his new partner. "We call it a Brian Wilson album, but it's really a Joe Thomas/Brian Wilson album," he said that afternoon in his studio.

But was that his way of distancing himself from the record? Not that *Imagination* didn't have its charms. Some of the new songs were lovely, and "Happy Days," the two-part suite with movements contrasting Brian's bad old life with his easygoing new one, was structurally daring and, in its second half, ebullient and sweet. The prominent viola on the new version of "Keep an Eye on Summer" was inspired, as was the elegant woodwinds arrangement on "She Says That She Needs Me," a song that also meandered from section to section in ways unheard of in most pop tunes. The complicated tumble of vocals that trace the downward chord progression on "Cry" could raise the hairs on the back of your neck. And Brian's multitracked vocals sounded like the aural equivalent of buttercream frosting—thick, sweet, and delicious. Throughout, he sounded relaxed, focused, and emotionally present: a man whose head might still get lost in the clouds, but whose feet were now rooted firmly on the earth.

Or maybe that was just more of Joe's sonic airbrushing. For many listeners who had come to associate Brian's best work with his most idiosyncratic sounds and notions, *Imagination* bore many distressing signs. The real Brian Wilson would never homogenize his music to sound exactly like every other song on the radio, they complained. For even if he didn't mind spinning reporters with meaningless happy talk, you could always tell a real Brian Wilson song by the piercing, often uncomfortable honesty he injected into its grooves. How could you know that, then hear the lite-metal "Dream Angel" *("We can fly forever, never wonderin' why!")* and even imagine that it emerged willingly from the same man?

Maybe it would have felt different if *Imagination* had actually scaled the charts. Instead, the album stalled in the number eighty-eight spot, while the lead single, "Your Imagination," only just grazed the adult contemporary Top Twenty before slipping back into obscurity. With a veritable platoon of writers shuttling in and out, some of them finding Brian in a less-than-cheerful mood, the buzz in some corners of the media took on the familiar gothic ring. A blistering, if desperately overheated, exposé in Britain's pop culture magazine *Uncut* called on a vast array of anonymous sources to describe the "predicament" Brian had landed in, "relinquishing" his hard-won liberty to a "blonde phantom, shades of [Gloria] Swanson in *Sunset Boulevard*."

Awash in rumor and unsourced accusations, illustrated with a rich variety of extremely unflattering photographs, the *Uncut* story set the standard for brutality-masquerading-as-concern. Others would follow, many of them written by people who found Brian's two-word answers, occasional memory lapses, and flights into fantasy to be evidence of the misery being inflicted upon him. "I was discomfited for days afterwards about having been a part of a process that I cannot believe he enjoys," the *Guardian*'s Ginny Dougary wrote after her audience with the troubled wizard. "And I wonder whether, even now, Wilson is being leaned on to conform to other people's demands."

Only a few years earlier, Mike had been weeping with rage on *A Current Affair,* wishing death upon the man who he said had kidnapped his defenseless cousin. "I'd like to kill him with my bare hands!" he snarled. But by 1997, Mike had found a new malefactor, hinting darkly to a hotel ballroom full of onlookers at the Rock 'n' Roll Fantasy Camp in Miami's South Beach that while all the Beach Boys would love to reunite, "Brian usually has someone in his life who tells him what to do. And now that person kinda wants to keep him away from us. I don't know why. You'd have to ask her, I guess." Actually, Brian was the one who rolled his eyes when asked if he even considered himself a Beach Boy anymore. "No," he said. "Maybe a little bit. But as far as a new album, I don't know. I don't really know for sure if I even want to do one." Nevertheless, observers from every corner of Brian's life continued to insist that he was being bullied and abused by, well, *someone*. A year later, another unnamed source in the *Uncut* story fingered Joe Thomas, asserting that "Brian is too scared, and too lazy, to say 'Fuck you.'" Or maybe he was just saying it to the wrong people or in the wrong ways.

━━━━━━━━

At first Brian didn't want to do any concerts. "He'd been told for years how bad he was onstage," Melinda says. And it became a self-fulfilling prophecy, particularly at the one-off show they did in a theater in St. Charles during the spring of 1998. It was a short concert, just a handful of Beach Boys songs and a few selections from *Imagination* performed with an all-star backing band (Bruce Johnston, Christopher Cross, the Eagles' Timothy B. Schmit), mostly for the benefit of the video cameras. And though the audience gave him a standing ovation the moment he walked onstage, Brian was so terrified that he could barely open his mouth. Much of the performance seen and heard on the resulting promotional video was recorded later, with the close-ups captured after the audience had left the building—and even those vocals were overdubbed a few days later in the studio. "He's just a shy kind of guy," Melinda says. "But I was pushing him to tour because he never really got to realize the impact that his music had on people. I just felt he needed to go out and see how much people loved him, because he didn't know."

Once the *Imagination* publicity had run its course, Melinda and Joe began putting together the infrastructure for a full-fledged solo tour. Joe recruited a few of his Chicago-based musicians, while Melinda called on some of the Los Angeles people Brian had expressed an interest in playing with. Primary among these was the Wondermints, the avant-pop group Darian Sahanaja had gone on to form. Brian had met the group in 1995 at a tribute show for Brian where they performed a set of his more obscure songs. Andy Paley had brought Brian to the show, slating him for a surprise appearance at the end of the night. So Brian had been sitting backstage during the acts, nervously checking his watch, when the Wondermints struck up "This Whole World," the sound of which caused Brian's ears to perk up: "Whoa," he cried. "Who's THAT? That sounds great!" When he met the group later, he nodded toward them and said to Andy, "If I'd had those guys in '67, I could have taken *Smile* out on the road!" So when it was time for him to actually hit the road with a new band, Melinda called to see if Darian and his bandmates might be interested in helping out. Darian, Nick Walusko, and Mike D'Amico signed on, along with Darian's friend and occasional utility Wondermint Probyn Gregory, and in January 1999 they flew to Brian's house in Illinois to start rehearsing.

Seasoned Beach Boys sideman Jeff Foskett was there too, playing guitar and handling the high falsettos, along with singer/multi-instrumentalist Scott Bennett, reed player Paul Mertens, bassist Bob Lizik, drummer Todd Sucherman, and background singer Taylor Mills, the lone woman in the outfit. And while Brian stayed out in Los Angeles, the musicians worked together in his basement recording studio to come up with stage arrangements for their leader's songs. Joe Thomas served as bandleader and had some strong feelings about how Brian's classic songs might be enhanced for a modern audience. "He had a lot of ideas," Darian recalls. "He played the piano, so he loved embellishing things. Lots of little riffs. Basically, he wanted the show to sound like *Imagination*." None of this sounded quite right to Darian, who recalls that he reached a breaking point when Joe instructed the rhythm section to play "Caroline, No" as a "sexy, Sade kind of thing." Darian complained to his manager that night, saying he was considering calling it quits. "And apparently he called Melinda, who called right over to Joe and told him that unless the Wondermints were happy, Brian wasn't going to come out to work on the show." The next morning's rehearsal began with a brief confrontation between Joe and Darian, but they soon agreed to find a way to make it work. "It was almost as if I'd gained some respect," Darian says, recalling how from that point onward, Joe made a point of asking for his feedback.

When Brian finally did fly in to join the group, Darian paid careful attention to his responses. "When liberties were taken, his response would be, 'Uh, cool.' Or he wouldn't respond at all, so you'd have to ask, and he'd say, 'I think it sounds, uh, good.' But as soon as we did a song close to his original arrangement, he'd go *nuts:* 'Wow! Outtasite!' And then he'd want to hear it again. And that made perfect sense to me, because in my mind, Brian has always been about doing parts, and how the parts come together and create this gorgeous feeling. He's always hid behind this wall of sound. That's what he wants . . . the strength came in the overall ensemble."

The rehearsals continued for the next few weeks, leading up to the tour's scheduled kickoff in Ann Arbor, Michigan, on March 9. The band was certainly ready, but once again, Brian was clearly terrified. "He was absolutely gray," Darian recalls. When the time came to board the bus for the long drive to Michigan, a blizzard struck the Midwest. The bus turned out to be a regular passenger bus rather than the luxe touring bus most bands travel in, and to make things even less pleasant, its heater was broken. "We were all trying to keep warm, and Mike D'Amico was sick, so we were trying to keep him bundled up. And Brian was in a really bad way—cold and miserable and just frightened beyond belief."

The group finally got to Ann Arbor, where an eager audience awaited at the 1,700-capacity Michigan Theater. The show began with a twenty-three-minute video retelling of Brian's musical and personal past. Pictures of Dennis and Carl incited huge ovations, as did shots of the *Pet Sounds* album and, even louder, a picture of Frank Holmes's *Smile* artwork. The only sour note was the resounding boo that echoed through the hall when Mike's face filled the screen. But that was long forgotten by the time the film climaxed in a series of still photos that illustrated audio of the young Brian leading a studio full of musicians through "The Little Girl I Once Knew," the avant-pop single that signaled the start of the *Pet Sounds* era. The sound of one take breaking down led to another count-off ("Here we go!"), and that led, incredibly, to the sound of the live band playing the song's opening bars. When the lights came up, Brian was at center stage, dressed all in black and sitting stoically behind an electric keyboard, surrounded by an eleven-piece band. *"We met when she was younger, annnnnd I had no eyes for her . . ."* And the crowd went berserk.

It was hard to pick out Brian's voice in the group harmonies on "She's Not . . . ," particularly because he was singing the midrange notes rather than the falsetto. But he took a definite, if shaky, lead on "This Whole World" and then another one on "Don't Worry, Baby," and then the show started to roll. "I was constantly looking over thinking, 'Okay, this is where he bolts!'" Darian says. In fact, the band had already assured Brian that he could leave whenever he felt overwhelmed—they'd just keep right on playing until he was ready to come back out. "And I figured ''Til I Die' would do it; he'd be gone. But he stayed, and then we got through the whole show." The set list touched all of the eras in Brian's career, including six selections from *Pet Sounds* (including both instrumentals), two from *Sunflower,* a few '70s songs (including "Back Home"), three songs from *Imagination,* and an array of the more interesting, if lesser-heard, songs from the early days ("All Summer Long," "Kiss Me Baby," and so on). And though Brian barely touched his keyboard, and even if his voice would occasionally wander away from the notes he was intending to hit, he served as the center of the entire two-hour-plus show, singing lead on each of the twenty-seven songs, rattling off introductions, and even cracking a joke or two. Darian recalls, "I remember thinking, 'Wow! He did it!' It didn't matter if the show was any good, *he didn't bolt!* And that was huge."

The first tour was actually just four dates in the Midwest. But the band reconvened in June for a six-stop swing through the Northeast, then flew to Japan—another hotbed of Beach Boys fans—for a night in Osaka and then a three-night stand in Tokyo. Those dates became another turning point when Joe Thomas, who didn't like to fly, chose not to make the trip. He was already pressuring Brian to start work on a new album, but according to Melinda, the joys of performance had already turned Brian's head away from the studio. "It gave him so much confidence. He'd get offstage and say, 'I got ten standing ovations!' After all those years, he still had no idea how people felt about his music." And though he'd valued Joe's support during the making of *Imagination* and during the first tour, not having him around in Japan felt surprisingly okay, too. "We were having our preshow circle, where we each say something," one band member remembers. "It was the first show in Tokyo, I think, the second night in Japan. And Brian said, 'Hey, not having Joe around last night worked out okay! I think we're gonna keep on rolling without him for a while.'" They never saw Joe again. But the band did indeed keep rolling, first with a nine-show swing down the West Coast in the fall, then ending the year (and the century) with a New Year's Eve show at the Redondo Beach Performing Arts Center.

As surprising as it was to see Brian performing entire shows onstage and eventually seeming relaxed and even happy up there, it was even more bracing to see the fruit of his career presented in such a serious way. For more than two decades, the Beach Boys had played Brian's music as if it were the sound track to an All-American pep rally, complete with cheerleaders, flags, and fireworks. But as its inside-the-recording-studio opening made clear, Brian's show was entirely about the music and the warm, adventurous spirit that linked "Fun, Fun, Fun" to "Let's Go Away for Awhile" and "Love and Mercy." As Dave Hoekstra wrote for the *Los Angeles Times:* "At the end of the evening Wilson stood triumphant on the stage—a man who has emerged from his darkest, most paralyzing blue period to again celebrate his music—and the human spirit—for his fans."

Energized by the experience, Brian began to consider even more daring ideas. The crowd had loved the *Pet Sounds* songs so much—they even gave standing ovations to the two instrumentals—that Melinda, Brian, and his managers talked again of performing the entire album onstage. Certainly this band wouldn't feel intimidated by the album's intricate arrangements, the many exotic instruments, and the breakneck shifts in rhythm and tone. They'd already played half of the album, for one thing. And this time around they could do themselves one better, hiring an orchestra to add elegance and power to the presentation. And if anyone in the group doubted that Brian was capable of singing the songs he'd written, they kept their doubts to themselves. This was Brian's music, his legacy, his life. As far as this band was concerned, anything he wanted to make of it was exactly the right thing to do.

The *Pet Sounds* tour traveled the United States in the summer of 2000, splitting the evening into four parts: First came an opening orchestral suite of Brian's music, as arranged by Van Dyke Parks; then came an hour-long set of Brian's hits and rarities, performed by the band without the orchestra; then the band and orchestra would team up on *Pet Sounds,* climaxing with the bonus single, "Good Vibrations." After that, the band would come back for a mini-set of big hits, ending with Brian's near-solo rendition of "Love and Mercy," the song from his 1988 solo album that had become his regular show closer. The tour traveled abroad in 2002, and a four-night stand at London's Royal Festival Hall attracted sellout crowds that included the glittering likes of Elvis Costello, Roger Daltrey, Eric Clapton, and Paul McCartney. Wrote David Sinclair in the *Times* of London: "Such was the emotional fervor generated by the performance that a substantial section of the audience rewarded him with a standing ovation after every single number."

———————

If Brian had taken control over his music in the last years of the 1990s, Mike was doing his best to solidify his control over the Beach Boys. With Carl gone, he had also moved to rid the band of Al Jardine, his perpetual annoyance for the past decade. Exactly what led to the split, who did what to whom and why, and the legality of it vis-à-vis the group's long-standing corporate structure, is far too conflicted, confusing, and tied up in litigation to explain in detail. Ultimately, Mike ended up making a deal with the Beach Boys' corporate parent, Brother Records Inc. (BRI, one of whose owners continues to be Al Jardine), for the right to tour under the name the Beach Boys. Which is precisely what he did, performing the group's biggest hits with Bruce Johnston joining him on the stage-front keyboard while the rest of the vocal and instrumental parts were handled by a rotating band of hired hands. Al stewed on this for a while, then set up his own alternative Beach Boys act, joining with Brian's daughters Carnie and Wendy, his own sons Matt and Adam, and longtime sidemen Billy Hinsche, Ed Carter, and Bobby Figueroa in a group he called the Beach Boys' Family and Friends. Unfortunately, Al had neglected to secure a license from BRI, so another storm of litigation ensued, mostly revolving around Al's use of the words *beach* and *boys* in such close proximity. The notion of "friends" and "family" didn't enter into the discussion, but that had been the case for a long time.

Mike's contract with BRI allowed him to use the Beach Boys name for the time being; but with one century ending and the vast future sprawling ahead, he had started to think in terms of history and his place in it. Mike's 1992 lawsuit for song copyrights had been fueled in part by his desire for fair and equitable credit for what the Beach Boys had achieved artistically. And when he was interviewed a few years later for 1998's *Endless Harmony*, the group's official documentary, Mike argued aggressively for his importance in the Brian-Mike songwriting team and thus in the creative development of the Beach Boys. "Ultimately, I think the Beach Boys meant so much to so many people because of the positivity," he declared to filmmaker Alan Boyd. "And that was *me*. Brian was melancholy. I was Mr. Positive Thinker." Mike's assertion had a whiff of truth to it, particularly when it came to the cousins' public personalities. But Brian's music has rarely been dirgelike (even the saddest songs on *Pet Sounds sounded* ecstatic), and songs he wrote solo or with other collaborators were (and continue to be) upbeat to the point of giddiness. (*". . . And when I go anywhere, I see love, I see love, I see love . . ."* he wrote in his solo 1970 composition "This Whole World.")

Mike's desire to revise the group's history could be viewed even more clearly in the next major project, a two-part biographical drama aired on ABC in early 2000. Produced by actor, celebrity, and occasional onstage drummer John Stamos, the movie was intended to improve upon a 1990 TV miniseries, *Summer Dreams*, which had been based on Steven Gaines's 1986 tell-all bio, *Heroes and Villains: The True Story of the Beach Boys*. That movie had been truly ridiculous, complete with absurd caricatures of the major characters (the Hawthorne-era Brian had been presented as a dork who wears loafers to the beach and can only gape in wonder as far cooler brother Dennis surfs, swains, and barks out ideas for hit songs), hippie-style wigs and beards that seemed to have been designed by J. Edgar Hoover, and cover versions of the group's songs that hurt to listen to. *An American Family,* on the other hand, boasted the group's original recordings (including unreleased rehearsals, outtakes, and the like), the expertise of group archivist and in-house filmmaker Alan Boyd (who earned a production credit), and creative input from all of the guys. But Mike enjoyed the closest relationship with Stamos; as a result, the film that aired, and particularly the section that touched on the more controversial aspects of the group's history, appeared to reflect only his version of events.

For instance, the personal devolution of the Brian character coincides almost exactly with the moment he stops writing with the Mike character. Virtually all of fake Brian's non–Beach Boys friends and collaborators are portrayed as hippie goofballs, dope fiends, and/or thieves. Primary among these is the faux–Van Dyke Parks, a character whose name had to be changed at the last minute due to the savagely fictionalized nature of his portrayal. Here, the coauthor of *Smile* is seen mostly as a part-time drug dealer and full-time rip-off artist whose high-handed nonsense (composed for the movie by a subsequently aghast Beach Boys insider, who had yet to understand exactly how these scenes would go down) was every bit as ridiculous as fake Mike said it was. So how delicious it was for America to see fake Mike literally shred the lyrics while denouncing the pretentious freak's work with Mike's favorite put-down of the real *Smile* lyrics: "acid alliteration." Those who were acquainted with history or had given even the most cursory listen to the commercially available "Good Vibrations" session tapes found it less appetizing to see Brian portrayed as being so helpless in the midst of recording that he needs Mike to tell him how to identify "the hooks" in his masterpiece single. And that was just one episode in a four-hour portrait of Mike as the more level-headed, yet equally creative, half of their hit-making duo.

A few years later, Mike was steadfastly unapologetic about that chapter in Beach Boy history. Or anything. "A lot of times people see something in print that I've said and they say, 'That Mike Love is an asshole!' And I can appreciate where they're coming from. But I look at it as humor. I have a sardonic sense of humor."

In December 2000, nearly a year after *An American Family* had aired, Brian was at a Christmas party at the house of band member Scott Bennett. He sat behind the piano, where he chatted with friends and teased out a few songs. He's often most comfortable behind a piano, but there are always limits to Brian's patience for anything; so when David Leaf's wife, Eva, called out for Brian to play a verse of "Heroes and Villains," everyone knew that she was wandering out onto very thin ice. Brian had not played the first song he'd written for *Smile* in public in more than thirty years. "If you had even mentioned it to him a month earlier, he would have *freaked*," says Darian Sahanaja, who was astonished by what happened next.

Brian shrugged. "Oh, I guess I'll do it for you," he said, hitting the rolling C chord that launches the first verse. *"I been in this town so long that back in the city I been taken for lost and gone, and unknown for a long, long, time . . ."* When he was done, the room broke into cheers. The reaction stunned Brian so much that he agreed to play the song again, this time with the band behind him, during his mini-set at a tribute concert for him being staged for the TNT cable channel's cameras at Radio City Music Hall that next March. Brian had invited his *Smile* collaborator to see the show that night and had him take a bow—"Van Dyke's here tonight!" Brian cried. "He's here, and he's *happy!*"—before the band launched into a driving rendition of the song, which prompted a standing ovation from the capacity crowd once it was done.

Paul Simon played a song that night, too (a beautifully reenvisioned "Surfer Girl," performed solo on acoustic guitar), and he was so delighted by Brian's performance that he invited him to join his summer tour of arenas and sheds as a featured opening act. Sensing that Brian's resistance to *Smile* was ebbing, Melinda and Darian appealed to him to incorporate more of the music into the summer shows. Didn't he see the ovation Vince Gill, David Crosby, and Jimmy Webb got at Radio City when they sang "Surf's Up"? And wasn't it beautiful when the Boys' Choir of Harlem opened the show with "Our Prayer"? Brian conceded both points, and soon both of those songs were in the set list. "It was like little baby steps all the way," Darian says. "Then we were looking for something that could follow the *Pet Sounds* show, and one day we just looked at each other and said, 'How about *Smile*?'" And the weird thing was, Brian didn't say no.

For years, the album had represented everything bad that had happened in his life. Intended as the pinnacle of his artistic/spiritual exploration, *Smile* had instead become his biggest disaster. Previously Brian had been able to take all of his inner turmoil and project it into music that was even more powerful than the darkness that had inspired it. But with *Smile,* the process went so sideways that the turmoil had not only overwhelmed the music but actually colonized it. From that point forward, Brian had never committed himself so entirely to any piece of music. And when he even got close—with "Ol' Man River," or "'Til I Die," or even the "Mt. Vernon and Fairway" fairy tale on *Holland*—he had been made to feel precisely as rejected and brutalized as he had felt when *Smile* was withering on the vine. "It was too painful for him to talk about," Melinda says. "Let's just say you wrote a book thirty-eight years ago; it was the best thing you ever did; you figured it would change your career. You show it to your family, and they do nothing but belittle it. It was his baby, something he created, and they didn't like it. But he wasn't strong enough to say: 'Okay, I'll get someone else to sing it.' It was devastating for him. How would you react when someone mentioned it to you?"

Here's what Brian said in 2001, only a few weeks before he played "Heroes and Villains" at Radio City. "I don't really ever want to put out the *Smile* stuff. It's just not appropriate music." He was talking on the phone, peering out of the window and feeling antsy. "Look, *Smile* scared me. We were taking drugs at the time. It was a very druggish kind of trip. But it definitely had the feeling of America in it. Van Dyke is into that, and he did a great job. I know it's a legendary thing. The *Smile* trip is a legend."

Therein lay yet another excellent reason to leave that particular box in the attic. So many articles had been written about the album; so many books, documentaries, and docudramas had pivoted off of the legend of the Great Lost Album. How much of that frantic myth-making would have happened if *Smile* had actually come out? Nearly four decades since it failed to materialize, you could almost argue that the album's absence had made a larger impact on the world than the presence of any music album could ever make. All those writers and filmmakers; all the musicians who wrote and arranged their own songs to sound like Brian's; all of the superfans who communed with one another on the Internet, obsessing over micro-details of "Surf's Up" tracking outtakes as if they were the very fibers of the Shroud of Turin—none of them was really thinking about music. In their minds, *Smile* had become a metaphor for every other fragmented dream and broken ambition in the world. It was the song "I Just Wasn't Made for These Times" played out as conceptual art: a human installation on permanent display wherever Brian Wilson happened to be standing.

But Brian had never intended to sacrifice his art in the pursuit of legend. "I didn't want to think about it at all, but it was the only thing anyone wanted to talk about!" Brian said a few months into 2004. And though things had changed a lot by then, even the memory of the myth surrounding *Smile* made him visibly uncomfortable. He fidgeted, peered out of the window. His sentences became abrupt, his face impermeable. "I said I'd junked the tapes, 'cause I had a real negative attitude about it. I didn't want to talk about it anymore. But that didn't change anything. Which was a *pain,* actually. You want to move on, ya know?"

And Brian wasn't the only man feeling overshadowed by the failure of what so many perceived as his greatest achievement. "That was just a few months of work I did as a contract employee many, many years ago," Van Dyke Parks said in 1998. He was having breakfast in a New York hotel, trying to be polite to his guest, but there was no mistaking the firmness in his voice. "Life goes on. I had other opportunities and I took them. Really, I think it means a lot more to other people than it does to me." Which was understandable. For while Van Dyke had grown easily into the profile of a true gentleman of the southern fashion, complete with elaborate manners and a mischievous twinkle in his eye, he was also a hardworking musician, producer, and arranger who didn't necessarily appreciate how his decades of work with the likes of the Byrds, Little Feat, U2, and Rufus Wainwright, among many others, plus his own albums and movie sound tracks, still resided in the shadow of something that didn't quite get finished in 1967.

Other currents swept just beneath the surface, too. Van Dyke had to resent seeing some of the songs he cowrote with Brian subsequently appearing without his name on them. And if Van Dyke felt guilty about abandoning his *Smile* partner just as the going was getting tough, he was also a hardworking professional who believed that Brian's surrender, followed by decades of near-complete withdrawal, mounted to another kind of betrayal. All of those conflicting impulses had long since blended together into something so hard to confront that Van Dyke, just like Brian, just didn't want to try anymore. Even in 2004, Van Dyke continued to distance himself from the legend that, he said one more time, meant so much more to everyone else.

So, you might wonder, why did he keep his copies of Frank Holmes's original *Smile* lithographs framed on the wall of his music room, hanging right above the keyboard where he works every single day? When asked this question, Van Dyke was silent for a moment. When he opened his mouth, his wife, Sally, interrupted him: "He's got you there, Van."

———

At first the band figured they'd just play the existing *Smile* tracks onstage. Take what had been released and figure out how to present it as a live performance. Brian clearly wasn't thrilled with the notion—"It was still hard for him to come to grips with *Smile,*" Melinda says—but everyone else was so gung ho that he just shrugged and resumed his course down the path of least resistance. In this case, that meant allowing his managers to book the Royal Festival Hall for a few nights in early 2004 and announce that the shows would include the live debut of *Smile*. At that point, Brian's anxieties became immaterial. "It was tough to pick up again. Brought back bad memories, you know?" Brian's eyes darkened, and he looked down at the table in front of him. "But my wife helped me get into it. She said, 'Look, don't worry about it. Just go ahead and do it, it's gonna be great.' So I did, and it changed for the positive." As if reviving the rock generation's most notorious unfinished album could be that easy.

Early in the fall of 2003, Brian sat down and wrote out a list of song titles that he remembered from the *Smile* era and faxed them over to Darian, who had been appointed "musical secretary" for the project. The keyboard player took the list into the Beach Boys' tape vault, downloaded all of the available material into his laptop, and took it up to Brian's house. Soon Darian was driving up into the hills every morning, joining Brian at the piano in his music room, where they would listen to the original songs and snippets and figure out how they were originally intended to go together. Sometimes the complexities would overwhelm Brian, and he'd curl up in an armchair, moaning hopelessly, "How are we gonna do this, Darian? How the hell are we gonna do this?" Then he'd hear something that tickled him, and he'd jump up again. "What was that? How'd we get *that* sound?" and the work would continue. "I could tell he was already freeing himself," Darian recalls. "He'd be saying, 'Oh yeah, that's supposed to be a part of this song,' or 'Use that bit to connect these two songs over here,' and it was really neat."

One morning, as they played the original instrumental track for "Do You Dig Worms," whose words and melody had never been known, Darian got to pose the question every *Smile* obsessive had wanted to ask for more than thirty-five years: "I said, 'Brian, was there anything else that was supposed to happen here?'" Brian dug through the faded scraps of paper he had before him, found one with Van Dyke's handwriting on it, and then started to sing: *"Waving from the ocean liners/Beaded, cheering . . ."* Then he was stuck. What was the next word? He couldn't read the writing. After a moment or two spent attempting to decipher the phrase, Brian picked up the phone and dialed his old collaborator. They hadn't spoken in a few years, but Brian got right to the point. "Hi, it's Brian. Do you know that song 'Do You Dig Worms'? What's that word in the first verse right after 'cheering'?"

The question pushed Brian into a ticklish situation. Up until that point—several months since the announcement that he intended to perform *Smile* in Europe—Brian had yet to say a word to Van Dyke about his new plans for their old collaboration. This left his former partner feeling aggrieved and more than a little hurt. "I didn't want to hear about its reemergence from the press," he said. "But of course I did." Which awakened memories of seeing "Wonderful" turn up on *Smiley Smile* without his name on it. Much like "Sail On, Sailor" had made its much-trumpeted debut with a veritable laundry list of coauthors (Jack Rieley, Tandyn Almer, Ray Kennedy), none of whom had been sitting with Brian and Van Dyke when they had actually composed the original song in 1971. Even at the Radio City tribute in 2001, when Brian had flown Van Dyke and Sally out to New York to see the show and be singled out for an ovation, the Wilsons had neglected to invite the Parkses to join Ricky Martin, Billy Joel, and the Go-Gos, among others, to the exclusive after-party thrown in a swank midtown restaurant. Instead, Van Dyke had invited a few friends back to his hotel suite and toasted the evening in more intimate surroundings. "This was Brian's night," he said. "That's important. He's a good man and he deserves to be celebrated." But the thought of Brian tinkering with *Smile* (the spectral presence of which he would eventually compare to Miss Havisham's rotting, rat-filled wedding cake in Dickens's *Great Expectations*) on his own was more than his erstwhile collaborator could stomach. When Melinda had called one day to invite him to the *Smile* premiere in London, Van Dyke had refused. This clearly wasn't his project anymore, he said.

And yet, Van Dyke did not want to impede the process, either. So when Brian called that morning, he told him to fax the "Worms" lyric sheet over. He called back a few minutes later to declare that his original handwritten word had been "Indians." *"Beaded, cheering Indians behind them . . ."* Brian and Darian finished the morning's work session, and later that day Brian called Van Dyke again. This time they talked for quite a while. And when Darian drove into Brian's driveway the next morning, his boss was standing on his doorstep, rocking back and forth on his heels. "Van Dyke's gonna be here in fifteen minutes," he said. From that point, Van Dyke was a part of *Smile* again, recalling the lyrics that hadn't been written down, composing new ones to fit holes he hadn't quite filled in 1967, and adding his part to the new melodies Brian was composing. Gradually the old and the new folded together so effortlessly that even Darian couldn't tell where one began and the other left off. "Brian would sing a melody, and I wouldn't know if it was new or something that had always been there," he says. "Van Dyke would listen, look up, and then point up in the air and nod his head, like confirmation of some thread he'd left behind. It was really weird and beautiful to see at the same time. Consistency questions went out the window. They're the same guys! Though Brian has gone through hell and back, but something about their flow, their rapport, seemed exactly the same. For them to come up with ideas now, whether they were there all along or if they were new, it was seamless to me. They created their own universe."

He'd only just managed to tiptoe back in, but as happy as he was to be looking at the world again from the inside of *Smile,* Brian could feel the familiar terror welling up inside. Once again, he was preparing to introduce his baby to the world. What made him think it was going to go any better this time than it had in 1967? The first day the band convened at his house to start rehearsing the vocals in earnest, the enormity of the challenge ahead sent Brian reeling into a panic attack. Bolting from the rehearsal in his living room (precisely at the moment the band was singing the line, *"Aloha nui means good-bye,"* which was either a joke on his part or an amusing coincidence), Brian jumped into his car and drove himself to the emergency room at St. John's Hospital, informing the doctors he was freaking out. "He totally lost his grip," Melinda recalls. The puzzled doctors called back to the Wilson home, sending Melinda and David and Eva Leaf screaming down the hill to see what was going on. Brian already seemed pretty calm by the time they got there, and the moment Melinda suggested they all go out for dinner at Ivy by the Shore in Santa Monica, Brian leaped off of his gurney and put on his shoes, completely healed.

And yet Brian's *Smile* anxiety continued to hover over him in the next few weeks. At times he'd be present and focused, riding the currents of the musical epic he was, at long last, bringing home. A moment later he'd squint and cock his head, his shoulders suddenly stooped beneath the weight of the years. Then he'd be lost inside himself for a while, wandering the familiar maze of hope, love, and fear until something else—usually the overwhelming sound of his music being played so well and so lovingly by his band—would bring him out again. His eyes would snap back into focus, and then Brian would be back. As the tour grew closer, they set up on a soundstage in their stage formation; Brian would sit at his keyboard, front and center, snapping his fingers and grooving along to the music. Then they were in London at the Royal Festival Hall, with just hours to go. Once again, Brian seemed to collapse into himself, sitting alone on an easy chair, waiting to be sucked into the vortex. When Paul McCartney came backstage to wish him good luck, Brian grabbed his hand and didn't want to let go. Then it was time to go out and play the opening set, and that slid by easily enough. Another break, and then the lights went down for the debut of *Smile*.

Brian walked out onto the dark stage and took his place behind the keyboard. Sitting in the blackness for those moments, gliding into the first a cappella chord of "Our Prayer," his heart fluttered in his chest. "I was so worried it wouldn't go over," he says. "It was so scary. I think fear and excitement, that's something that goes together. It's good scary." Then "Prayer" was over, and as they sang the little doo-wop verse, the light began to rise. Then the snare drum announced "Heroes and Villains" like a starter's pistol. And when Brian launched into the tale of the man who'd been taken for lost and gone and unknown for a long, long time, the entire hall burst into shimmering, incandescent light.

CHAPTER 18

In the spring of 2004, recording engineer Mark Linett is standing near the control panel of Your Place or Mine studios, talking about the ongoing recording sessions for *Smile*. It seems strange, after all these years, to be discussing *Smile* in the present tense. Stranger still that the mythical work is being completed in a recording studio located in the midst of suburban Glendale, California, in a studio space converted from Linett's own basement. Just outside his front door, neighborhood kids ride their bikes, and a couple of them jump skateboards over the curb. Upstairs, his cleaning lady scrubs down the kitchen counters. Linett, meanwhile, spins an early mix of the new "Cabin Essence" instrumental track. "It's still missing the 'doing-doings,'" he says as the first verse plays.

Linett is clearly a *Smile* buff with years of passion behind him. His work with Brian and the Beach Boys in the last fifteen years or so has turned him into a made man, of sorts. Now he has Carl's handwritten lyrics to "Surf's Up" (used during the 1971 vocal sessions) framed on his wall. He has the original tubes-and-dials control panel for Western's number two studio in the corner. And when he recognizes the passion in another fan's eye, he can walk to a filing cabinet and pull out something he knows is going to blow your mind. It is a dark metal container about the size of a small pizza box, only thicker, and he lays it gently in my hands. "You're gonna want to hold that," he says. "Those are master tapes from the original *Smile* sessions."

I look down at the yellowed index card taped to the top, which reads "Beach-boys: 'Tones'; 'Wind Chimes.'" I feel the weight of it in my palms while the wheels in my brain spin, trying to factor this moment into the years *Smile* has lived in my mind. It's wonderful to hold something so historical and mysterious. But at the same time, I also realize that something important is changing for me. In all these years of thinking about, mourning the loss of, returning obsessively to the fragments from, and pondering the overarching meaning of the legacy of *Smile,* I'd never really thought of it as something that could exist in the physical sphere I inhabit. But now I'm holding a part of it in my hands, standing on the very spot where Brian is breathing life into the finished recording. And how am I supposed to feel about that?

———

When the final note of *Smile* vibrated to a stop on February 20, 2004, the Royal Festival Hall erupted into a wild ovation that went on for ten full minutes before Brian could even call Van Dyke to the stage for a bow. The acclaim didn't end on that first night. Reviews of the *Smile* shows were ecstatic, to say the least. "Ground-breaking complexity and sophistication . . . [the premiere] of *Smile* made it seem like the grandest of American symphonies, and Wilson the natural heir to Charles Ives," wrote the critic in London's *The Guardian* the next morning. "What we do know now is that Wilson and Parks created a glorious piece of music whose grand ambition is outstripped only by its inherent beauty and cumulative power," Randy Lewis wrote in the *Los Angeles Times* a few days later.

The same electricity fired the next five nights in London, then followed the group through their brief tour of England and Europe. Back in the United States in the springtime, the group set to work recording a studio version of the now-completed *Smile*. And though Brian was credited as its producer and arranger, he tended to avoid the all-important mixing sessions, either because he figured his work on the project was done or because he still couldn't imagine hearing those sounds in the sanctified surroundings of a recording studio. "It was taxing for all of us because we knew what was being taken on," says Mark Linett. Still, they took it step by step, following the sonic blueprint Brian had laid down in the fall of 1966 in hopes of recapturing the original work's mystery, even as they transformed it into the sleek patterns of 1s and 0s that define digital recording. "Brian would come in, make comments, take stuff home, then make more comments," Linett continues. "The third time he came in, I gave him a CD and I said: 'Hey, there it is. *Smile*, ready to play on your CD player.' I swear you could see something change in him. And he's been different ever since."

A few weeks before Linett handed Brian that CD and a few months after the London debut, Brian sat in a delicatessen in a mall near his home in Beverly Hills. His latest solo album, *Gettin' In over My Head,* built largely from songs he'd been fiddling with on and off for as long as twenty years, was about to come out. The record featured guest shots from some of his most famous admirers—Paul McCartney, Elton John, Eric Clapton—but Brian was most excited to talk about *Smile*. "I was worried it wouldn't go over," he said, recalling opening night in London. "But I got a ten-minute standing ovation. Ten minutes! I mean, I got bored after a while. I said, 'Okay, that's enough!' but they wouldn't shut up. It's almost scary."

What was scary?

"That I couldn't believe they could like it so much."

Wasn't that exciting, too?

"Being afraid is like bordering on excitement," he said, pausing to think for a moment. "It's good scary."

But *Smile* used to summon the bad kind of scary, right?

"Yeah, I had a negative attitude about it."

What changed?

"I don't know. I just got hungry to get better."

As if to emphasize this point, Brian reaches for the barbecue beef sandwich he's been gnawing on between questions and takes a big bite. "This is really good," he said.

Intriguingly, some of Brian's most fervent fans and *Smile* admirers didn't share his appetite. As much as they had mourned its loss for so very long, the prospect of having a completely finished, officially released *Smile* proved unsettling. For now that Brian had taken the famously unfinished album back into his hands, he had simultaneously plucked it from theirs. Having a finished *Smile,* after all this time, changed everything about its accepted place in the cosmology of modern cultural history. In its unfinished, half-imaginary state, *Smile* had been both nothing and everything: a parable about corporate greed; a warning about the dangers of the drug culture; a modern retelling of the legend of Icarus. Or maybe it was just a record most people hadn't heard, but you had, with a depth of understanding no one else had ever achieved. Hence the endless and endlessly heated arguments about What Brian Had Really Meant, and Why It Ended, and so on. "Some of *Smile*'s majesty is its mystery," Jeff Turrentine wrote on the online magazine Slate.com. "To return to this now-mythic collection of songs is to gild the rarest, wildest lily in pop music."

Other critics and fans pursued the same line of reasoning, their musings and writings posing the same series of questions: What if the myth of *Smile* was actually better than the real thing? What if everything the world had come to believe about what had been lost in Brian's collapse turned out to be, well, *wrong*? This prospect seemed particularly likely considering the cruelty of the years that had come between. To compare the troubled, but unfathomably brilliant Brian of 1966—the man who had just created *Pet Sounds* and "Good Vibrations"—with the troubled, unfathomably damaged Brian of 2004—the man who made a point of declaring, "I don't think I have another *Pet Sounds* in me"—was sobering. How could this faded, emotionally hobbled middle-aged man pretend to finish the work of his razor-sharp younger self?

Nevertheless, anticipation built through the summer of 2004, spurring a wave of media attention that grew to a crescendo with *Smile*'s release in mid-September. The top-selling album on Amazon.com for two solid weeks, the album, formally titled *Brian Wilson Presents "Smile"* debuted at number thirteen on the *Billboard* album charts. The five-star review in *Rolling Stone,* written by the notoriously sharp-tongued Robert Christgau, set the tone for the avalanche of notices and features that would come: "This seemed like a terrible idea. Instead, it's a triumph . . . Wilson's voice has deepened and coarsened irreparably . . . but he can convey commitment and belief—belief that his young, bonkers self composed a work that captured possibilities now nearly lost to history. *Smile* proves that those possibilities are still worth pursuing."

Acclaim for the finished *Smile,* along with international sales that pushed it to platinum status and beyond, carried Brian through the winter. In March 2005 he traveled to Austin, Texas, with Van Dyke and David Leaf to discuss *Smile* as part of a panel discussion at the South by Southwest music convention. Brian did interviews the day before, shuttling around town in a limousine. Sitting in on a radio studio show, he listened to the new "Heroes and Villains" and sang along with the first verse. "I *love* this song!" he said to no one in particular. The disc jockey, Jody Denberg, interviewed Brian gently, interspersing questions about *Smile* with tracks from the album. When "Surf's Up" ended, Denberg paused for a moment of silence before saying, simply: "That's what love sounds like. Brian Wilson. 'Surf's Up.' From the album *Smile*." When he prefaced a question about the 1966 sessions by mentioning the Beach Boys, Brian interrupted him. "No, not with the Beach Boys. With Van Dyke Parks. The Beach Boys didn't sing on any of those tracks." Denberg, who knew better, stammered for a moment, then changed the subject.

The next morning Brian was in a less buoyant mood. Sitting in his suite atop the Four Seasons hotel, he seemed antsy and uncomfortable, looking back and seeing only the anguish that had shadowed him for so long. "The other Beach Boys didn't like *Smile;* they didn't want to do it," he said with a shrug. "But my new band is so much better. They play better and they sing better, too. I have a much better time with them, anyway."

This was something Brian had said before and would say again many times during the next few months. It was bracing to see that the version of "Good Vibrations" he'd chosen to use in the new "Smile" substituted the roughed-out lyrics Tony Asher had written early in the winter of 1966 for the Mike Love version that had been released a few months later. And it's easy to imagine that Brian's motivations for all this Beach Boy bashing had less to do with the musical support they had once provided than the emotional kind they hadn't. The triumph he'd finally achieved with *Smile* was both affirming and, on a bad day, devastating. What if he'd had the support to finish the record in 1967? What could he have gone on to achieve in 1968? These are the kinds of questions that are impossible to answer, particularly given the demons that had haunted him even during his most successful years. Nevertheless they spoke to him, and he talked back. Other ears were listening, too, and they would soon be speaking to him, as well.

———

A couple of months after Brian's visit to Austin, Mike Love sat in his suite atop the massive Mandalay Bay casino, its windows overlooking the fringe of Las Vegas's industrial grid and the dusty, undeveloped expanse beyond. He and the group that carries the Beach Boys license had played their usual set of oldies to a large, enthusiastic crowd on, in, and around the resort's artificial lagoon the previous night, and they would do the same thing that night. Mike drank from a jug of apple juice, regarding his guest suspiciously even as he cracked jokes and told his story.

"I think Van Dyke is really talented, brilliant, and fun. He's got a sense of humor. I ask[ed] Van Dyke Parks, 'What the hell does "Over and over the crow cries, uncover the cornfield" mean?' And he said, 'I haven't a clue, Mike!'" He laughed. "I don't know if he was saying that just because I was there in his face. But I always liked lyrics that are boy-girl, or made sense, or connected to the mind of people."

Did he ever wonder, in light of *Sgt. Pepper* and the subsequent rise of all things psychedelic just at the point when *Smile* was supposed to be released, if his resistance to Van Dyke's abstract verse might have been a mistake?

"Nuh-uh. Not at all. Never. I didn't fuck up. By not getting into the acid culture? I don't think I was a fuck-up. I mean, I can write abstract poetry. Yeah, I did 166 lines of iambic septameter. Yeah, that's me. But I'm talking about a three-minute pop single here."

At sixty-four, Mike is a stout middle-aged man who walks with a bit of a limp, but he puts on an energetic show with his group—they play the first thirteen songs of their set virtually nonstop. And years of meditating have kept him limber enough to twist his long legs into a half-yogi position as he continued, often contradicting stories and recollections that have long since been written, rewritten, and carved into the stone of accepted history.

"I had nothing to do with shelving *Smile*. It was Brian's paranoid schizophrenia . . . He became paranoid and a recluse for the most part. And who says I didn't like the words? Just because I said I didn't know what they meant didn't mean I didn't *like* them." He untwisted, then retwisted his legs. "I have zero against Van Dyke Parks. That's why I said, 'What the fuck does that mean?' It's not meant to be an insult. He didn't get insulted. He just said, 'I haven't a clue!' And it wasn't like I was *against* his lyrics. But people don't know the way I think. And they don't give a fuck about the way I think, either. But that's okay. I'm a big boy, and I can take that. I was just asking: *What did it mean?*"

Mike's cell phone rang, and when he picked it up, his features loosened and his voice softened. It was his youngest daughter, a grade-schooler, calling from home in Lake Tahoe. A moment of confusion—she was pretending to be someone else at first—ended quickly, and he got up from his chair and walked into the suite's open kitchen area, whispering gently to her about what she had been doing with her mom, what they had planned for the rest of the day, how long it would be until he got home to see her again. After a few minutes he hung up and sat back down again, wrapping his legs beneath him as his blue eyes sharpened and his face hardened for battle. "Where were we?"

Back where they have been for so long, waltzing obsessively with the hurt, anger, and unending hostility that has surrounded the Beach Boys since before they had even imagined they might be the Beach Boys. Perhaps it would have been different if their own parents had displayed the unconditional love Mike had just lavished upon his distant, happily chattering daughter. Nevertheless the Beach Boys survived, even thrived, transforming their own pain into music that captured something of the world around them. Just don't tell this to Bruce Johnston, the other quasi-real Beach Boy in Mike's current group, who responded via e-mail with a chuckle. "I can tell that you are far deeper into the Beach Boys thing than I will ever be in 100 lifetimes!" he wrote. "It's only *business* to me."

And not a pleasant business, either. First Bruce resisted an interview for this book because he said he was worried about getting sued. He changed his mind, briefly, but then changed it again when he got tired of Brian's barbed comments about the Beach Boys. "I spent years showing full support for Brian, but now that's all changed because of his current point of view," he wrote in another e-mail.

Brian and Carl could barely speak to one another in the last decade or two of Carl's life. Mike and his brothers, Stan and Stephen, are currently estranged. Stephen's tenure as the group's manager—which coincided with their most financially successful years in the mid- and late seventies—ended with him getting fired, rehired, and then fired again. Worried that the band would try to stiff him on his percentage of the CBS contract (an established pattern for the group, according to several sources), Stephen used his signatory power in the final days of his tenure to take the money for himself from the group's accounts. For this misdeed his brother and cousins had Stephen convicted of embezzlement.

Beach Boys–related litigation goes on endlessly. All of the original members of the group, except for Dennis, have sued at least one other member of the band, with Brian being everyone's favorite target, due perhaps to the perpetual flow of money from his songwriting royalties. No wonder there are three separate groups traveling the world singing three separate renditions of "Good Vibrations." "There's something pretty special about the [vocal] blend the Beach Boys have,"

Mike said. "But Carl's dead and Brian doesn't sing like that anymore. I'm not invited to sing with Brian, and Al and the rest of us are on the outs."

And it doesn't end with the Beach Boys, either. Brian, as guileless and sweet as he seems, has an amazing capacity to be the eye of a perpetually swirling tornado of rage, hurt feelings, and litigation. His late '90s partnership with Joe Thomas ended in a hail of lawsuits. The decision to use Tony Asher's original lyrics to "Good Vibrations" on the new *Smile* not only served as a public slap to Mike but also resulted in a bruising conflict between Melinda and Asher, who had never signed a publishing contract for his percentage of the song. Negotiations with original *Smile* artist Frank Holmes broke down too, so painfully that by the time Brian's tour hit San Francisco in the fall of 2004, the artist and part-time art teacher saw the show through his occasional job as an usher at the San Francisco Opera House.

Back in his hotel room, Mike said he hadn't heard the new *Smile*. He had no interest in it, really. Though now that the record has become an international hit, he had grown quite interested in the copyright laws that might arguably have restricted Brian from copying his original arrangements so closely. "I mean, we paid for [*Smile*]. We paid for the development of it. We sang on it; we developed those tracks and then Brian shelved it." Mike shifted toward legalese, explaining the concept of corporate opportunity, declaring that after spending years honing *Smile*'s legend, the Beach Boys deserved a chance to profit from its release. "I would have thought it would have been more honorable to put it together as the Beach Boys. That's what they chose *not* to do; they decided they could live without the Beach Boys, even though it was a Beach Boys project."

Except that Mike has to know this isn't true. Other than the previously recorded "Good Vibrations," *Smile* was entirely the work of Brian and Van Dyke. As Mike admitted in the same conversation, he and the rest of the group served almost entirely as session singers. "I was a singer in the production. I was not asked to participate in hardly anything, other than to sing in the parts." And even if the sessions were paid for out of the Beach Boys' recording advance from Capitol Records, Brian was at that point such a dominant figure in the group— he wrote, arranged, and/or produced virtually every note they sang, only occasionally with Mike's lyrical help, and often with himself as lead singer—the other guys didn't hesitate to refer to him as their all-knowing leader. "Brian *is* the Beach Boys," Dennis observed once. "We're his messengers."

But Dennis is dead. Mike is alive, and after all of these years being the Beach Boys' most public face, he seems determined to claim the group's legacy for his own. Brian's critical and commercial success with *Smile,* contradicting decades of Mike's own assertions that such abstract music would only alienate record buyers, seemed to strike him as a personal affront. Being all but dismissed from "Good Vibrations" (Mike's credit remained, albeit as the third collaborator) and publicly ridiculed in Brian's many statements comparing the Beach Boys so unfavorably to his new group only made him angrier. And even if his theory about corporate opportunity didn't bear fruit, Mike and his lawyers did manage to turn up a promotional CD that Brian's management had allowed the British newspaper *The Mail on Sunday* to give away as part of their *Smile* coverage. It was a solo work, compiling Brian's live renditions of his own Beach Boys songs with more recent solo songs. Unfortunately, the CD's cover used the words "Beach Boys" prominently, along with a couple of 1960s-era photographs of Brian with the band. Therein lay, according to the lawsuit Mike filed in October, "millions of dollars in illicit profits," "unfair competition, and infringing uses" stemming from a promotion that, as the complaint went on, "shamelessly appropriated Mike Love's songs, likeness, and the Beach Boys trademark."

Mike and his spokesmen continued to insist that he held no ill will toward his cousin, that he really blamed the handlers—meaning Melinda—who made all of his decisions and told him what to do. But such talk only sought to belittle Brian all the more, making a public point of his supposed helplessness. What seemed most clear was that Brian had something Mike wanted. He'd ventured back into the horizon and struck gold. And for reasons that had as much to do with the visions that had pulled their ancestors across the frontier as everything that had happened between them, Mike really felt that he was owed a share.

———————

Everyone else makes do with *Smile.* And for the several thousand people who have come to the Hollywood Bowl on September 4, 2005, it's more than enough. It's just after 9:00 p.m. now; the honeyed, late-summer sun has long since fallen toward the ocean, leaving a darkness that now seems rich with the promise of a warm, eucalyptus-scented night. Brian Wilson has come home, back to the same hills he used to look down upon when he was writing the music he's about to play. The stage is dark as Brian, his band, and half a dozen members of the

Stockholm Strings and Horns find their places and take their final breaths before launching the final performance of the *Smile* tour's title piece. They begin with the shimmering, wordless arcs of "Our Prayer," their voices falling through the blackness like shafts of light through the jeweled windows of a cathedral.

The snatch of the Crows' old doo-wop hit "Gee" ignites the rollicking "Heroes and Villains." Then the music hurtles forward, a riot of instruments and voices, sometimes clashing, sometimes weaving together, all of it capturing the clamor of the boomtown, the promise and danger of the frontier. When the action pauses, a darker reflection about this new society emerges: *"Bicycle rider, just see what you done/To the church of the American Indian . . ."* This meditation leads back to Plymouth Rock, to ponder the mysteries of the new land and the pilgrims' progress from the granite shores of New England to the verdant beaches of Hawaii. The newcomers bring their hopes, but also the limits of the old world: its economic imperatives, its military might. The music lopes through the verses, then snaps taut for the *". . . just see what you done done . . ."* choruses.

Then we're back on the frontier again, chugging westward past farms and fields, rolling hills and mountainsides where the stars touch the land and God's breath hangs thick in the air. But now comes a rumble in the distance, the roar of machinery—the industrialized future gnashing its teeth. Just above the fields, a Chinese worker laying the rails pauses, his eye drawn skyward by the cry of hungry birds wheeling through the air. *". . . Over and over, the crow cries, uncover the cornfield/Over and over, the thresher and hover the wheatfield . . ."*

After the rumbling, twirling end of "Cabin Essence," there is a brief pause before the start of "Wonderful"—the harpsichord, pizzicato strings, soaring background vocals, and muted trumpet jewel-like beneath Brian's voice, straining against the constraints of age as he ascends the scale to describe the resilience of innocence, even in the face of the nonbelievers. The music grows more pensive—taking in the circular pattern of life, growth, and death—as the perspective jumps from parent to child and back again, all the while pivoting off of a line Van Dyke borrowed from William Wordsworth's "My Heart Leaps Up When I Behold," *"Child is the father of the man."* Quiet wonder builds into a celebration, horns and bells joining a jangling keyboard into a Sousa-like figure that gives way again to the stuttering tempo of the "father of the man" chant and then the reassurance of the father: *"Easy, my child—It's just enough to believe . . ."*

The music shifts again, settling into the hushed grandeur of "Surf's Up," its jewelry-rattling percussion, tautly plucked strings, and fretting trumpet lines setting the stage for the self-deceptions of high society and the crumbling of a decadent civilization. But from the ashes, hope emerges anew: *"Surf's up! Aboard a tidal wave/Come about hard and join the young, and often, spring you gave,"* Brian sings, paying tribute to his own youthful vision even as he prepares to dive into the wild mysteries beyond the horizon. *"I heard the word, wonderful thing/A children's song . . ."*

The third movement begins in a town square, where an old-fashioned brass band oom-pa-pas through an instrumental version of the "Heroes and Villains" cantina section, while the fresh morning air stirs thoughts of love and old-fashioned health advice that is so obvious it seems positively comic. *"I wanna chow down my favorite vegetable/I love you most of all . . ."*

So there is escape. An exotic mix of marimbas, strings, slide whistle, and flutes sends the music over the horizon to the Pacific isles. *"A shanty town—a shanty in Waikiki/And juxtapose a man with a mystery . . ."* Pirates appear, luring us even further into the unknown. But never beyond the view of Plymouth Rock, and the restless impulse that peeks through the chorus's call for that old piece of granite to keep rock, rock, rolling on over.

The marimbas come back for a whispered idyll with wind chimes—the chiming, fluttering decorations catching the eye, but not quite distracting the mind from the sadness that never quite vanishes with the breeze. *"Now and then, a tear rolls down my cheek . . ."* A new variation of the "Heroes and Villains" theme erupts at full blast, the trombones sliding in and out of a bluesy seventh chord, upping the temperature until a rush of sirens and slide whistles heralds the full-throated roar of a fire, a wall of flame, smoke and torment played in tones of scream, distortion, and sonic destruction. This is the music Brian once thought had been powerful enough to ignite a series of fires across the city of Los Angeles in the spring of 1967. It terrified him so much that he didn't listen to it again for nearly forty years. Brian faced up to his terror in his way. As the embers of "Fire" die away, he sings a mournful phrase composed by Van Dyke to reflect the musician's own journey from 1966 to 2004: *"Is it hot as hell in here, or is it me?"* A little of both, perhaps, as the eerie chorus of wailing spirits implies. But he keeps moving westward—*"There's still a promise we must keep . . ."*—all the way back to Hawaii, beyond the sea, where the cool blue waters wash us right back into the tumbling light of "Our Prayer," falling into the sonic prism that sends them exploding out into the air again in the form of "Good Vibrations."

And now *Smile* has come full circle, to its point of departure in the summer of 1966, up somewhere beyond the physical realm, up in the air above Brian's piano, where a lifetime of hope, horror, joy, sorrow, and regret inspired the sonic waves that are just now vibrating in the leaves of the eucalyptus trees surrounding the Hollywood Bowl. Brian is hunkered down at his keyboard, his body nearly still, the expression on his face all but unreadable. He may be the only person in the Hollywood Bowl who isn't up on his feet, dancing to the music. But Brian is focused on singing his part. He sits behind his keyboard, his eyes half closed but his face alive with feeling as his music fills the night around him. *"Good, good, good, good vibrations,"* he sings. *"Good, good, good, good vibrations."*

BIBLIOGRAPHY

Alterman, Eric. *It Ain't No Sin to Be Glad You're Alive: The Promise of Bruce Springsteen*. New York: Little, Brown and Company, 1999.

Badman, Keith. *The Beach Boys: The Definitive Diary of America's Greatest Band on Stage and in the Studio*. San Francisco: Backbeat Books, 2004.

Crunden, Robert M. *A Brief History of American Culture*. New York: North Castle Books, 1996.

Cullen, Jim. *The Art of Democracy: A Concise History of Popular Culture in the United States*. New York: Monthly Review Press, 1996.

———. *Born in the U.S.A.: Bruce Springsteen and the American Tradition*. New York: HarperCollins, 1997.

Didion, Joan. *Slouching Towards Bethlehem*. New York: Farrar, Straus & Giroux, 1969.

———. *The White Album*. New York: Simon & Schuster, 1979.

Doe, Andrew G., and John Tobler. *The Complete Guide to the Music of the Beach Boys*. London: Omnibus Press, 1997.

Emerson, Ken. *Doo-Dah! Stephen Foster and the Rise of American Popular Culture*. Cambridge, Massachusetts: Da Capo Press, 1998.

Gaines, Steven. *Heroes & Villains: The True Story of the Beach Boys*. New York: New American Library, 1986.

Granata, Charles L. *Wouldn't It Be Nice: Brian Wilson and the Making of the Beach Boys' Pet Sounds*. Atlanta: A Cappella Books, 2003.

Leaf, David. *The Beach Boys and the California Myth*. New York: Grosset and Dunlap, 1978.

Marcus, Greil. *Mystery Train: Images of America in Rock 'n' Roll Music*. New York: Dutton, 1975.

Miles, Barry. *Paul McCartney: Many Years from Now.* New York: Henry Holt, 1997.

Milward, John. *The Beach Boys Silver Anniversary.* Garden City, New York: Doubleday Dolphin, 1985.

Preiss, Byron. *The Beach Boys.* New York: Ballantine, 1979.

Priore, Dominic, et al. *Look! Listen! Vibrate! Smile!* San Francisco: Last Gasp, 1995.

Ravitch, Diane, ed. *The American Reader: Words That Moved a Nation.* New York: HarperCollins, 1990.

Starr, Kevin. *Inventing the Dream: California through the Progressive Era.* New York: Oxford University Press, 1985.

Steinbeck, John. *The Grapes of Wrath.* New York: Penguin edition, 2002.

Twain, Mark. *The Adventures of Huckleberry Finn.* New York: Penguin edition, 1985.

Ver Steeg, Clarence L. *The Formative Years: 1607–1763.* New York: Hill & Wang, 1964.

White, Timothy. *The Nearest Faraway Place: Brian Wilson, the Beach Boys, and the Southern California Experience.* New York: Henry Holt & Co., 1994.

Williams, Paul. *Brian Wilson & the Beach Boys: How Deep Is the Ocean?* London: Omnibus Press, 1997.

———. *Outlaw Blues: A Book of Rock Music.* E.P. Dutton, 1969.

Wilson, Brian, and Todd Gold. *Wouldn't It Be Nice: My Own Story.* New York: HarperCollins, 1991.

Wise, Nick, ed. *The Beach Boys: In Their Own Words.* London: Omnibus Press, 1994.

CREDITS

"Don't Worry Baby"
Written by: Roger Christian and Brian Wilson.
© 1964 Careers-BMG Music Publishing (BMI) /
Irving Music, Inc. Copyright Renewed. All
rights for the US administered by Careers-
BMG Music Publishing (BMI). All rights
outside the USA controlled by Irving Music,
Inc. Used by Permission.

"Got to Know the Woman"
Written by: Greg Jakobson and Dennis
Wilson. © 1970, 2000 (renewed) Careers-
BMG Music Publishing (BMI) / Daywin
Music, Inc. (BMI) / Brother Publishing
Company (BMI). All rights for the US
administered by Careers-BMG Music
Publishing (BMI). All rights for Brother
Publishing Company administered by Wixen
Music Publishing. All Rights Reserved. Used
by Permission.

"Little Deuce Coupe"
Music by Brian Wilson, Words by Roger
Christian. © 1963 Careers-BMG Music
Publishing (BMI) / Irving Music Publishing.
Copyright Renewed. International Copyright
Secured. All Rights Reserved. All rights for
the US administered by Careers-BMG Music
Publishing (BMI). Used by Permission.

"Shut Down"
Words by Roger Christian, Music by Brian
Wilson. © 1963 Irving Music, Inc. Copyright
Renewed and Assigned to Irving Music, Inc.
and Careers-BMG Music Publishing (BMI)
for the USA. All Rights Reserved. Used by
Permission.

"Surf's Up" written by Van Dyke Parks and
Brian Wilson
© 1971, 1999 (renewed) Safe & Sane Music
(ASCAP). Administered by BUG / BriMel
Music (BMI)

"Do You Like Worms" written by Van Dyke
Parks and Brian Wilson
© 2006 Safe & Sane Music (ASCAP).
Administered by BUG / Brother Publishing
Company (BMI)

"Roll Plymouth Rock" written by Van Dyke
Parks and Brian Wilson
© 2004 Safe & Sane Music (ASCAP) and
BriMel Music. Administered by BUG /
BriMel Music. All Rights Reserved. Used by
Permission.

"Do You Like Worms/Roll Plymouth Rock"
by Brian Wilson and Van Dyke Parks.
© 1967, 1995 (renewed) Brother Publishing
Company (BMI). Administered by Wixen
Music Publishing. All Rights Reserved. Used
by Permission.

"Sail On, Sailor" written by Van Dyke Parks,
Brian Wilson, Raymond Kennedy, Tandyn
Almer and John Rieley III
© 1973 Safe & Sane Music (ASCAP) / Brother
Publishing Company (BMI). Administered by
BUG / Wixen Music Publishing (BMI). All
Rights Reserved. Used by Permission.

"Child Is The Father Of The Man" written by
Van Dyke Parks and Brian Wilson
© 2004 Safe & Sane Music (ASCAP) and
BriMel Music. Administered by BUG /
BriMel Music. All Rights Reserved. Used by
Permission.

"On A Holiday" written by Van Dyke Parks
and Brian Wilson
© 2004 Safe & Sane Music (ASCAP) and
BriMel Music. Administered by BUG /
BriMel Music. All Rights Reserved. Used by
Permission.

"In Blue Hawaii" written by Van Dyke Parks
and Brian Wilson
© 2004 Safe & Sane Music (ASCAP) and
BriMel Music. Administered by BUG /
BriMel Music. All Rights Reserved. Used by
Permission.

"All This Is That" by Al Jardine, C. Wilson,
M. Love
© 1972, 2000 (renewed) Wilojarston Music
(ASCAP). Administered by Wixen Music
Publishing. All Rights Reserved. Used by
Permission.

"I'm Bugged at My Ol' Man"
Words and Music by Brian Wilson. Copyright
© 1968 Irving Music, Inc. Copyright Renewed.
All Rights Reserved. Used by Permission.

"In My Room"
Words and Music by Brian Wilson and Gary
Usher. Copyright © 1964 Irving Music, Inc.
Copyright Renewed. All Rights Reserved. Used
by Permission.

"In the Back of My Mind"
Words and Music by Brian Wilson and Mike
Love. Copyright © 1965 Irving Music, Inc.
Copyright Renewed. All Rights Reserved. Used
by Permission.

"Kiss Me Baby"
Words and Music by Brian Wilson and Mike
Love. Copyright © 1965 Irving Music, Inc.
Copyright Renewed. All Rights Reserved. Used
by Permission.

"Let Him Run Wild"
Words and Music by Brian Wilson and Mike
Love. Copyright © 1965 Irving Music, Inc.
Copyright Renewed. All Rights Reserved. Used
by Permission.

"Little Bird"
Words and Music by Dennis Wilson and Steve
Kalinich. Copyright © 1968 Irving Music, Inc.
Copyright Renewed. All Rights Reserved. Used
by Permission.

"The Little Girl I Once Knew"
Words and Music by Brian Wilson. Copyright
© 1965 Irving Music, Inc. Copyright Renewed.
All Rights Reserved. Used by Permission.

"Our Car Club"
Words and Music by Brian Wilson and
Mike Love. © 1963 (Renewed 1991) Screen
Gems-EMI Music, Inc. All Rights Reserved.
International Copyright Secured. Used by
Permission.

"Passing By"
Words and Music by Brian Wilson. Copyright
© 1968 Irving Music, Inc. Copyright Renewed.
All Rights Reserved. Used by Permission.

"Please Let Me Wonder"
Words and Music by Brian Wilson and Mike
Love. Copyright © 1965 Irving Music, Inc.
Copyright Renewed. All Rights Reserved. Used
by Permission.

"She Knows Me Too Well"
Words and Music by Brian Wilson and Mike
Love. Copyright © 1964 Irving Music, Inc.
Copyright Renewed. All Rights Reserved. Used
by Permission.

"Surfers Rule"
Words and Music by Brian Wilson and Mike
Love. Copyright © 1963 Irving Music, Inc.
Copyright Renewed. All Rights Reserved. Used
by Permission.

"Time to Get Alone"
Words and Music by Brian Wilson. Copyright
© 1968 Irving Music, Inc. Copyright Renewed.
All Rights Reserved. Used by Permission.

"Vegetables"
Words and Music by Brian Wilson and Van
Dyke Parks. Copyright © 1967 Irving Music,
Inc. Copyright Renewed. All Rights Reserved.
Used by Permission.

"The Warmth of the Sun"
Words and Music by Brian Wilson and Mike
Love. Copyright © 1964 Irving Music, Inc.
Copyright Renewed. All Rights Reserved. Used
by Permission.

"Wendy"
Words and Music by Brian Wilson and Mike
Love. Copyright © 1964 Irving Music, Inc.
Copyright Renewed. All Rights Reserved. Used
by Permission.

"When I Grow Up (To Be a Man)"
Words and Music by Brian Wilson and Mike
Love. Copyright © 1964 Irving Music, Inc.
Copyright Renewed. All Rights Reserved. Used
by Permission.

"Wind Chimes"
Words and Music by Brian Wilson and Van
Dyke Parks. Copyright © 1967 Irving Music,
Inc. Copyright Renewed. All Rights Reserved.
Used by Permission.

"With Me Tonight"
Words and Music by Brian Wilson. Copyright
© 1967 Irving Music, Inc. Copyright Renewed.
All Rights Reserved. Used by Permission.

"Wouldn't It Be Nice"
Words and Music by Brian Wilson, Tony
Asher and Mike Love. Copyright © 1966
Irving Music, Inc. Copyright Renewed. All
Rights Reserved. Used by Permission.

"You're So Good to Me"
Words and Music by Brian Wilson and Mike
Love. Copyright © 1965 Irving Music, Inc.
Copyright Renewed. All Rights Reserved. Used
by Permission.

"High Coin" written by Van Dyke Parks
Copyright © 1964, Black Hawk Music. All
Rights Reserved. Used by Permission.

"Marketplace" written by Brian Wilson and
Andy Paley. Copyright © 1987, Twilite Tunes.
All Rights Reserved. Used by Permission.

"It's Not Easy Being Me" written by Brian
Wilson and Andy Paley. Copyright © 1987,
Twilite Tunes. All Rights Reserved. Used by
Permission.

"Gettin' In Over My Head" written by Brian
Wilson and Andy Paley. Copyright © 2004,
Twilite Tunes / BriMel Music. All Rights
Reserved. Used by Permission.

"Student Demonstration Time"
Words and Music by Jerry Leiber and Mike
Stoller. © 1954 (Renewed) Jerry Leiber Music
and Mike Stoller Music. All Rights Reserved.

"Caroline, No"
Words and Music by Brian Wilson and Tony
Asher. Copyright © 1966 Irving Music, Inc.
Copyright Renewed. All Rights Reserved. Used
by Permission.

"Wonderful"
Words and Music by Brian Wilson and Van
Dyke Parks. Copyright © 1967 Irving Music,
Inc. Copyright Renewed. All Rights Reserved.
Used by Permission.

"In My Car"
Written by Brian Wilson. © 1989 Beach Bum
Music (on behalf of Beach Bum Music and
GLVD Publishing). All Rights Reserved. Used
by Permission.

"Love and Mercy"
Written by Brian Wilson. © 1988 Beach Bum
Music (on behalf of Beach Bum Music and
GLVD Publishing). All Rights Reserved. Used
by Permission.

"Walkin' the Line"
Written by Brian Wilson. © 1988 Beach Bum
Music (on behalf of Beach Bum Music and
GLVD Publishing). All Rights Reserved. Used
by Permission.

"Baby, Let Your Hair Grow Long"
Written by Brian Wilson. © 1988 Beach Bum
Music (on behalf of Beach Bum Music and
GLVD Publishing). All Rights Reserved. Used
by Permission.

"Smart Girls"
Written by Brian Wilson. © 1991 Beach Bum
Music (on behalf of Beach Bum Music and
GLVD Publishing). All Rights Reserved. Used
by Permission.

"Brian"
Written by Brian Wilson. © 1991 Beach Bum
Music (on behalf of Beach Bum Music and
GLVD Publishing). All Rights Reserved. Used
by Permission.

"Sloop John B"
Written by Brian Wilson. © 1966 New
Executive Music. All Rights Reserved. Used by
Permission.

"I'm So Lonely"
Written by Brian Wilson. © 1985 Beach
Bum Music. All Rights Reserved. Used by
Permission.

"Melt Away"
Written by Brian Wilson. © 1988 Beach Bum
Music (on behalf of Beach Bum Music and
GLVD Publishing). All Rights Reserved. Used
by Permission.

"Surfin' "
Written by Brian Wilson and Mike Love.
© 1961 Guild Music Company (BMI).
Administered by Original Sound
Entertainment

"Surfin' Safari"
Written by Brian Wilson and Mike Love.
© 1962 Guild Music Company (BMI).
Administered by Original Sound
Entertainment

"Surfer Girl"
Written by Brian Wilson. © 1962 Guild Music
Company (BMI). Administered by Original
Sound Entertainment

DISCLAIMER: Every effort has been made to contact other copyright holders; the editor would
be pleased to hear from any other copyright holders not acknowledged.

INDEX

Beach Boys *(cont'd)*
  Caesar's Palace show (1987), 251–52
  Carnegie Hall concert (1971), 155
  Central Park concert (1977), 218
  Chaplin and, 174–75, 191, 194
  Cocktail and, 266
  comeback of (1971), 164, 167, 191–92
  declining years of, 136–37, 143
  double-tracking vocals and, 41
  drug use and, 134
  Dylan and, 95–97
  Fataar and, 174–75, 191, 194
  fifteenth anniversary of (1976), 208
  filler tracks for albums of, 75
  at Fillmore East, 156–57
  Fourth of July concert (1983), 246–47
  Grateful Dead and, 156–58
  Grillo and, 100
  Guercio and, 194–95
  "Help Me, Rhonda" recording session
      (1965), 53–59
  Hendrix and, 123
  image of, 37, 61–63
  John (Elton) and, 196
  at Knebworth Festival (England), 236
  label contracts
    Candix, 31, 34
    Capitol Records, 34–35, 38, 66, 145, 148,
      192
    CBS Records, 217, 220, 222, 235
    Reprise, 149–52, 162
    Warner Brothers, 179, 194, 199, 220,
      224, 226
  Landy (Eugene) and, dislike of, 214–15,
      254, 267
  lawsuit against Capitol Records by, 145
  Leaf (Earl) and, 62–63
  Levine and, 248
  Marks and, 2, 37, 287
  minor league baseball show (1987), 250–51
  Monterey Pop Festival and, 122, 154
  monument to, ceremony for, 1–3
  Netherlands trip, 179
  original name of, 31
  personnel shakeups (1971) and, 174
  photo shoot of, 107–9
  political issues in music of, 159
  popularity of, 35, 42, 48, 96
  Radio City Music Hall concert, 230
  in Reagan era, 234, 245

  Rieley and, 155, 158–60, 182, 185
  Rock 'n' Roll Hall of Fame and, 252–53
  St. Paul, Minnesota, concert (1981), 238
  Sam Houston Coliseum concert, 59
  Seattle Center Coliseum concert (1976), 203
  Seattle concert (1980), 236
  Smile recording sessions (1966) and, 115–17,
      309
  Special Olympics party and, 246
  start of, 28–31
  Sunkist deal and, 250
  surf culture and, 36–37
  Taylor (Derek) and, 88, 100–101, 105,
      109–10, 120–21
  theater tour (1993), 280
  twenty-fifth anniversary of (1987), 250, 252
  Universal Amphitheater concert, 231
  Vail and, 48, 50
  Vosse's exit from, 119
  wealth of, 63–64
  Wembley Stadium concert, 196
  Wenner's article about, 136
  women in songs of, 69–70
Beach Boys, The (1985 album), 248–49, 254
Beach Boys and the California Myth, The
      (biography), 275, 286
Beach Boys Concert (1964 album), 62
Beach Boys in Concert (1973 album), 124, 131,
      175, 184, 191–92
Beach Boys Family and Friends (musical
      group), 299
Beach Boys Love You, The (album), 213–15,
      222–23, 290
Beach Boys Medley (album), 240
Beach Boys Party! (album), 66–67
Beach Boys Today (1965 album), 63, 72–73
"Beaks of Eagles, The," 183
Beatles
  Beach Boys and, 50–51
  Capitol Records contract and, 50
  Maharishi and, 134–35
  popularity of, 50, 61, 85
  Rock 'n' Roll Hall of Fame and, 252
  "Sgt. Pepper's Lonely Hearts Club Band"
      and, 122, 137, 313
  White Album, The, of, 129, 137
  Wilson (Brian) and, 75, 136–37
"Beatrice of Baltimore," 173
Beautiful Dreamer (documentary), 65, 70
Becher, Curt, 198, 230

Johnston, Bruce *(cont'd)*
  Imagination album and, 294
  Love (Mike) and, 298
  Sandler and, 176

Kalinich, Stephen (Steve), 132, 169–70, 195,
    197, 207
Kaye, Carol, 104
Kaye, Chuck, 102–3
"Keep an Eye on Summer," 292
"Keepin' the Summer Alive," 235
Keepin' the Summer Alive (1980 album), 234–37
Kennedy, Ray, 184
Kingston Trio (musical group), 23, 25, 46, 79
"Kiss Me, Baby," 73
Knebworth Festival (England), 236
"Kokomo," 266–67, 292
"Kona Coast," 225–26
Korthof, Steve, 101, 226–27

LaBiancas (married couple), 143–44
"Lady Lynda," 229
L.A.: Light Album (album), 229–30
Lamm, Karen, 204, 220–21
Landy, Eugene
  background of, 200–201
  Beach Boys' dislike of, 214–15, 254, 267
  book by, 201
  Campo on, 212
  charges against, 262–63, 269, 272
  clients of, 200
  Felton's story about Brian Wilson and, 211
  girlfriend of, live-in, 257, 265
  "Life's Suite" and, 260–61
  Love (Stan) and, 269–70
  Love (Steve) and, 215
  recording process of Beach Boys and, 260–61
  Wilson (Audree) and, 269
  Wilson (Brian) and, 114–15, 199–201,
    211–12, 214–15, 243–44, 254–64,
    269–70, 272–73
  Wilson (Marilyn) and, 199–201
  Wilson (Melinda) and, 271
Late Night with David Letterman (TV show),
    266
Law, Johnny, 92–93
"Lay Down Burden," 287, 292
Leaf, David
  Anderle (David) and, 99
  Asher and, 76

documentary of, 65, 70
Love (Mike) and, 285–86
Reum and, 272
Schwartz and, 65
wife of, 300, 306
Wilson (Brian) and, 70, 75, 110, 262,
    275–76, 280, 306, 311
Wilson (Marilyn Rovell) and, 84
Leaf, Earl, 62–63
Leaf, Eva, 300, 306
"Leavin' This Town," 183
Ledbetter, Melinda. *See* Wilson, Melinda
    Ledbetter
"Lei'd in Hawaii," 124
Lennon, John, 66, 88, 106, 172, 236, 290
Lent, Keith, 15, 23–24
"Let Him Run Wild," 73–74
"Let It Shine," 265
"Let's Go Away for Awhile," 297
"Let's Go to Heaven in My Car," 259
"Let's Put Our Hearts Together," 214
"Let the Wind Blow," 131
"Let Us Go On This Way," 213
Lieber, Jerry, 157, 159, 259
"Life Is for the Living," 216
"Life's Suite," 260–61
"Like a Rolling Stone," 95–96, 193
Linett, Mark, 269, 271–72, 283, 308–10
"Little Bird," 132
"Little Children," 265
"Little Deuce Coupe," 40, 42–43, 47–48
"Little Girl I Once Knew, The," 66
Live/Dead (Grateful Dead album), 148
"Lonely Boy," 170
"Long Promised Road," 159
"Lookin' at Tomorrow," 159
Lott, Elliott, 268, 287
Love, Emily Wilson (Glee), 20–21, 25–26
Love, Margie, 20
Love, Maureen, 20, 26
Love, Michael (Mike)
  A&M lawsuit and, 278
  age of, in 1963, 46
  Beach Boys and
    arguments among band members, 219
    "Belles of Paris," 225
    "Big Sur," 183
    Caesar's Palace show, 251–52
    Carl and the Passions album, 174–75
    "Don't Back Down," 51

Wilson, Brian Douglas. *See also* Wilson,
 Marilyn Rovell; Wilson, Melinda
 Ledbetter
A&M lawsuit of, 278
age of, in 1963, 46
Almer and, 173
Anderle (David) and, 119
anxiety attacks of, 54–55, 306
Asher and, 12, 76–79, 81–84, 91
astrologer and, 121
autobiography of, 269–70, 272–73
Bacharach and, 141
baseball and, 13–14
Beach Boys and
 in 1962, 33–35
 in 1977, 216
 1984 tour, 249
 Beach Boys Love You, The album, 222–23
 Beach Boys Party! album, 66–67
 "Bull Session with the Big Daddy" and, 63
 credit for, 277–78
 exit from tour and, first, 59
 Friends album, 132–33
 "Good Vibrations" and, 66, 89–92,
  94–97, 108, 319
 monument ceremony, 2–4
 M.U.I. Album, 225
 new music for, 61–62, 114–17
 new name for, 147
 at Opera House in Seattle, 168
 Pet Sounds album, 79–86, 89–90, 277
 removal of, from creative duties, 127–28,
  223–24
 Reprise contract, 150–51
 St. Paul, Minnesota, concert, 238
 Saturday Night Live show, 210–11
 Seattle Center Coliseum concert (1976),
  205
 Smile album, 104–6, 108–9, 120,
  123–24, 127, 148–49
 Smiley Smile album and, 123–24, 128–29
 Spring album, 176–79
 start of, 28–31
 Still Cruisin' album, 268
 Surfer Girl album, 42–43
 20/20 recording sessions, 148
 at Whisky a Go-Go Club in Los Angeles,
  168
 Wild Honey album, 131–32
Beatles and, 75, 136–37

biographies of, 75, 275
Bowles (Judy) and, 40
brothers and
 Carl, 12, 130, 222, 228, 268–69,
  287–88, 314
 Dennis, 12, 19, 222, 227, 239
Cale's article on, 276–77
Callahan (now Fernandez) and, 17–18
child abuse of, 11–12
childhood years of, 1, 10–14
Christian (Roger) and, 39–40
church and, 18
college years of, 27
comeback of, 167–68, 202, 206–10, 216–17
cosmetic surgery of, 257
country music project of, 285
daughters of
 adopted, 290
 Carnie, 140, 166, 179, 181, 196–97, 224,
  281, 287, 299
 Wendy, 179, 181, 197, 281, 299
defamation suit against, 278
demons of, 87–88
depression of, 112, 128, 160–61, 169, 226–27
Desper and, 128–29, 139–41, 147–48,
  150–51, 160, 163, 176, 178, 232
detachment from world by, 72, 160–61,
  171–72, 196–98, 227
at discussion panel in Austin, Texas, 311–12
divorce of, 226
drug use of, 65, 81, 91, 100, 113–14, 128,
  139, 224, 242–43
eating habits of, 100, 196–97, 227
eccentricities of, 102–3, 139–40, 172–73
Equinox Records and, 198
falsetto voice of, 19
family heritage of, 4–5
at fan convention (1990), 271
fans of, 276
father and, 4, 7, 12, 19–90, 54–56, 74, 149,
  167, 255–56
favorite albums of, 290
fear as motivation and, 58
Florida trip of, 228–29
Foster (Stephen) and, 70
Giant record label and, 292
health store job of, 165–66
hearing loss of, 12
high school years of, 14–25
home of, first, 71